Jivya Soma Mashe

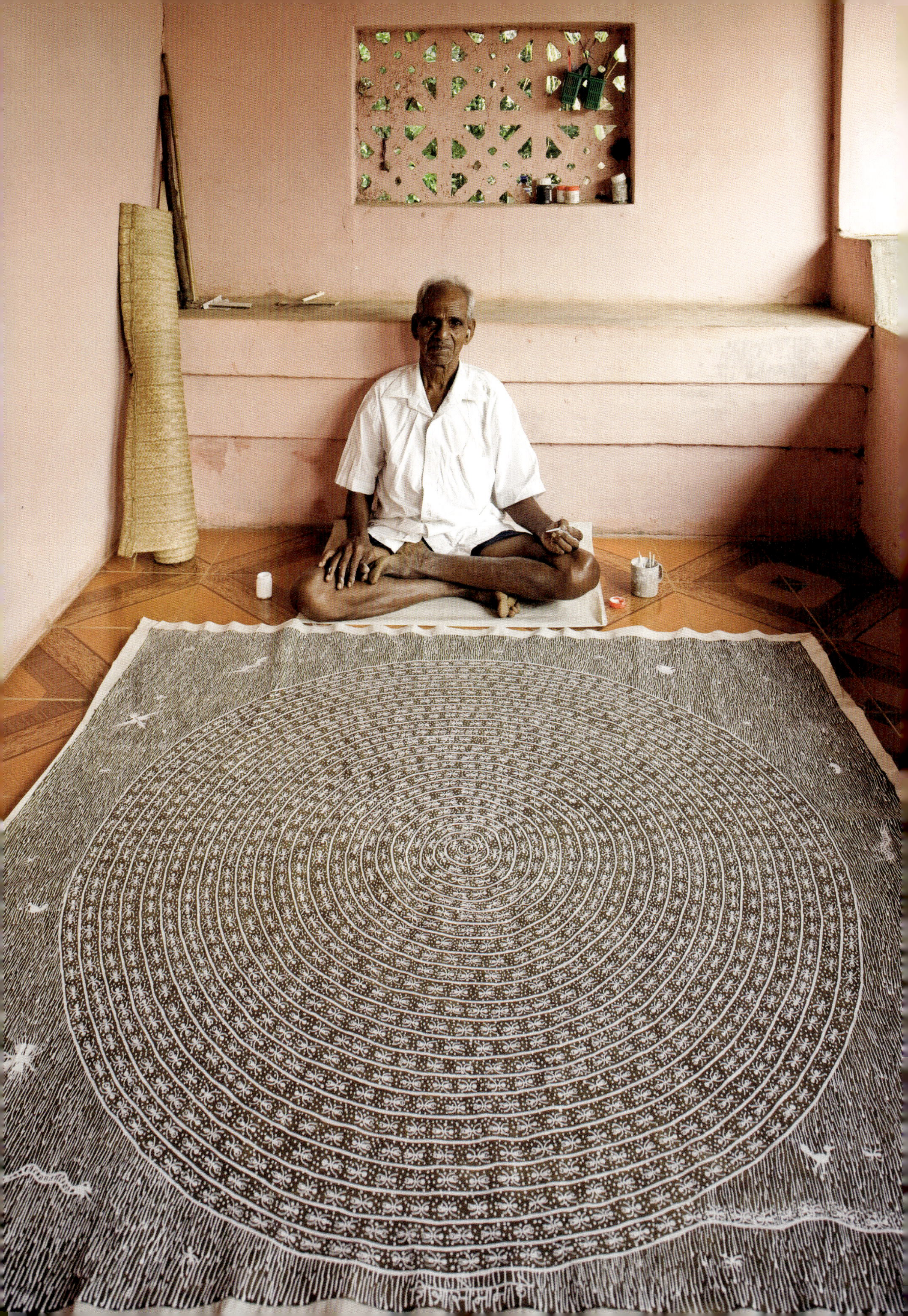

Jivya Soma Mashe

HERVÉ PERDRIOLLE

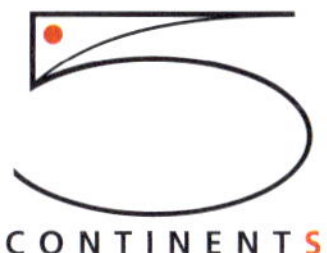

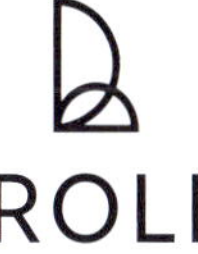

Page 2
Jivya Soma Mashe, Ganjad (Maharashtra, India).
Photo by Antonio Martinelli, 2009.

CONTENTS SOMMAIRE

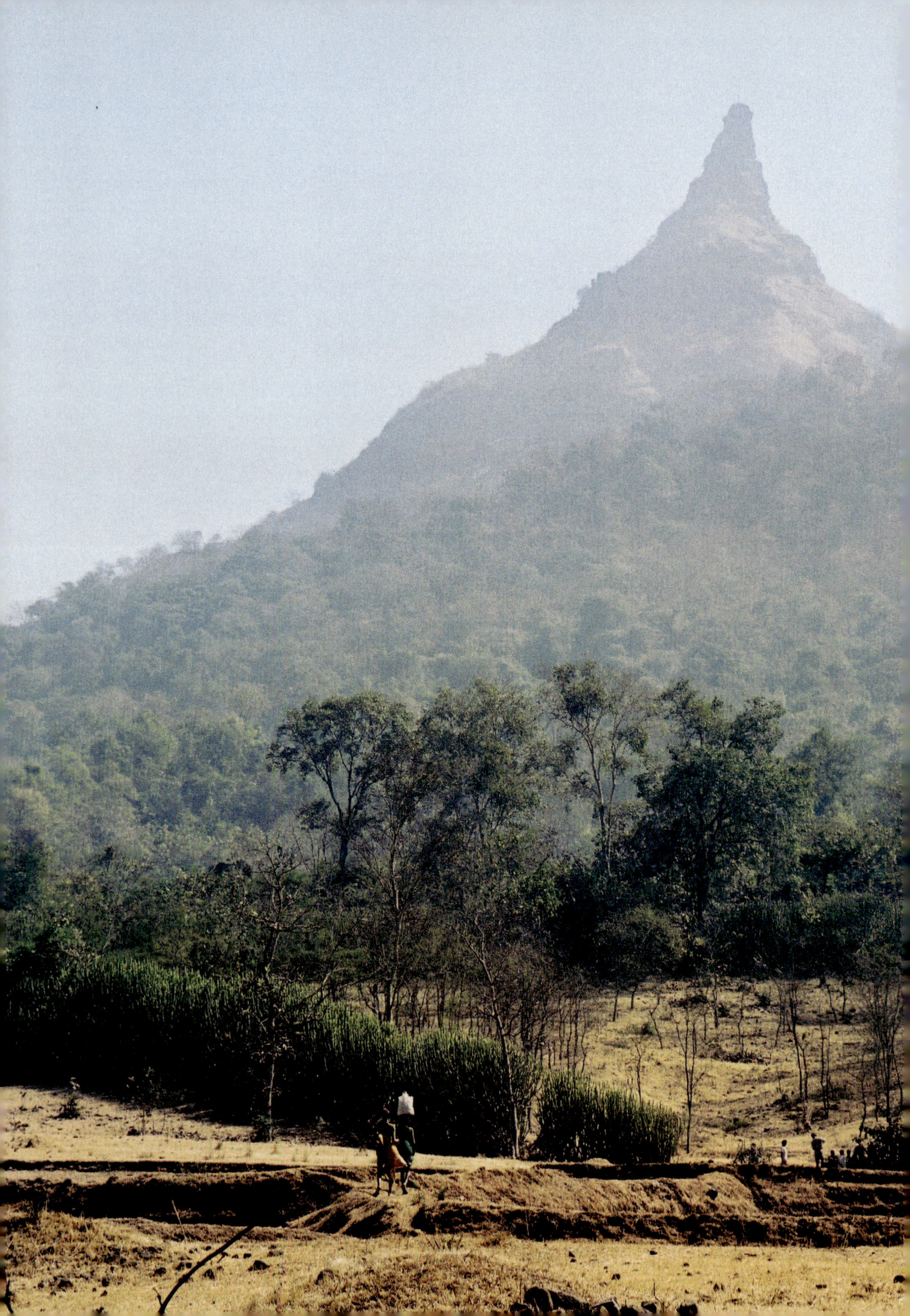

ADIVASI, INDIGENOUS PEOPLES OF INDIA

ADIVASIS, PEUPLES ABORIGÈNES DE L'INDE

Indians call members of the tribal communities *adivasi*, which literally means 'first inhabitants'. The fundamentally animist origins of the *adivasi* cultures predate all those that commonly spring to mind when one thinks of India. Spread right across the subcontinent, *adivasi* represent ten percent of the Indian population and form several hundreds of communities, all of which have their own dialect, customs, and belief systems. However, very little is known of their art, particularly in the West. Over the last two thousand years, an abundance of Buddhist, Jain, Hindu, and Muslim sacred arts has almost completely overshadowed Indian tribal art.

One of the rare testimonies that has come down to us is the art of the Naga. With its sculptures, finery, and architecture, the art of this formerly head-hunting tribe, who were converted to Christianity in the 1950s, rivalled the most beautiful works of African and Oceanian tribal art. The few other testimonies come from the exceptional work of ethnologists, such as Verrier Elwin during the 1930s, who studied the Gond tribe in the state of Madhya Pradesh in Central India. Sadly, few ancient works have been preserved, and it is rare that we are able to admire them.

Fortunately, thanks to the Indian government and the punctilious assistance given by enlightened art lovers, tribal art in India has not completely ceased. In the 1970s, aware of the gradual loss of this artistic heritage, the Indian government took active steps to assist these different ethnic communities. In an attempt to preserve these traditionally ephemeral ritual arts, government representatives encouraged artists to use other media, such as paper and canvas. Easy to transport and exhibit, the new media also allowed these ancestral art forms to become known beyond their geographical limits. Displayed and sold

View of the sacred mountain from the lands
of Jivya Soma Mashe, Ganjad (Maharashtra, India).
Photo by Hervé Perdriolle.

Les Indiens appellent les individus issus de communautés tribales les « Adivasis », ce qui signifie littéralement les « premiers habitants ». De fait, les origines des cultures adivasis, fondamentalement animistes, sont antérieures à toutes celles qui nous viennent communément à l'esprit lorsque l'on évoque l'Inde. Les Adivasis représentent 10 % de la population indienne et composent plusieurs centaines de communautés ayant toutes leurs propres dialectes, coutumes et systèmes de croyance. Les Adivasis sont répartis sur tout le territoire de ce vaste sous-continent. Pourtant, particulièrement en Occident, de l'art tribal indien nous ne connaissons presque rien. Durant plus de deux mille ans, le foisonnement des arts sacrés bouddhistes, jaïns, hindous ou encore musulmans a presque totalement occulté l'art tribal de ce sous-continent.

L'un des rares témoignages qui nous soient parvenus est celui de l'art des Naga. L'art de cette tribu, jadis coupeurs de têtes et christianisée dans les années 1950, avec ses sculptures, ses parures ou son architecture, a rivalisé avec les plus belles pièces de l'art tribal d'Afrique et d'Océanie. Les quelques autres témoignages nous viennent du travail exceptionnel d'ethnologues dont celui, dans les années 1930, de Verrier Elwin à propos de la tribu des Gond dans l'État du Madhya Pradesh, au cœur de l'Inde. Malheureusement peu de pièces anciennes ont été conservées et il est rare d'avoir l'occasion de les admirer.

Fort heureusement, grâce au gouvernement indien et à l'aide ponctuelle d'amateurs éclairés, l'art tribal de l'Inde ne s'est pas complètement éteint. Dans les années 1970, le gouvernement indien, conscient de la disparition progressive de ce patrimoine artistique, est venu en aide à l'ensemble de ces diverses communautés ethniques. Afin de pouvoir conserver une trace durable de ces arts rituels pour la plupart traditionnellement éphémères, les émissaires du gouvernement ont introduit auprès des artistes d'autres supports tels que le papier et la toile. Faciles à transporter et à exposer, ces nouveaux supports ont permis également de faire connaître ces formes d'art ancestral hors de leurs frontières géographiques. Exposés et vendus dans les magasins

in government shops, the paintings and drawings also brought additional income to communities that were often very poor. Chiefly aimed at the tourist market, this artistic production drew the attention of specialists and discerning amateurs to a few particular artists. It was during the early 1970s that most of those who would subsequently become the leading representatives of contemporary Indian tribal art were discovered, including Jivya Soma Mashe, Jangarh Singh Shyam, and Bhuri Bai, to name only three.

d'État, les peintures et dessins avaient aussi pour finalité d'apporter un complément de revenu à des communautés le plus souvent très démunies. Parmi cette production artistique essentiellement destinée à une clientèle de touristes, quelques personnalités particulièrement singulières retinrent l'attention de spécialistes ou d'amateurs éclairés. Ainsi furent découverts, dès le début des années 1970, la plupart de celles ou de ceux qui allaient devenir les représentants majeurs de l'art tribal indien contemporain, parmi lesquels Jivya Soma Mashe, Jangarh Singh Shyam ou encore Bhuri Bai, pour n'en citer que quelques-uns.

THE WARLI TRIBE
LA TRIBU WARLI

Settled in the Thane district, about 150 kilometres north of Mumbai, the Warli tribe today numbers more than 600,000. Having their own belief system, life, and customs, they have no connection with Hinduism. The Warlis speak their own unwritten dialect, a blend of words originating in Sanskrit, Marathi, and Gujarati. The word Warli is derived from *warla*, meaning a plot of land or field. In his book *The Painted World of the Warlis*, Yashodhara Dalmia notes that the Warlis are the continuation of a tradition that originated between 3000 and 2500 BCE. Their wall paintings have affinities with those made between 10000 and 5000 BCE in the rock shelters of Bhimbetka, in Madhya Pradesh. The extremely rudimentary iconography of their wall paintings is based on a very basic graphic vocabulary: circles, triangles, and squares. The circle and the triangle were born from the observation of nature; the circle from the observation of the moon and the sun, and the triangle from that of mountains, particularly the sacred mountain with its sharp, pointed summit, or trees with their peaks reaching towards the sky. Only the square does not seem to have been derived from their observation of nature, and thus appears to be a human invention that indicates a sacred enclosure or piece of land. Every ritual painting has at its centre the motif of the square, the *chauk* (or *chaukat*), within which resides Palagatha, the mother goddess and symbol of fertility. It should be noted that male divinities are almost non-existent among the Warlis, and are more often than not spirits in human form. The central motif of these ritual paintings

Située dans le Thane District, à approximativement 150 km au nord de Mumbai, la tribu warli compte encore aujourd'hui plus de 600 000 membres. Les Warlis n'ont rien à voir avec l'hindouisme. Ils ont leur propre mode de croyance, de vie et de coutumes. Les Warlis parlent un dialecte qui ne s'écrit pas. Il est un mélange de mots issus du sanskrit, du marathi et du gujarati. Le mot warli viendrait du mot « warla » qui désigne une parcelle de terrain, un champ. Yashodhara Dalmia, dans son livre intitulé *The Painted World of the Warlis*, note que les Warlis seraient le prolongement d'une tradition dont les origines se situent entre 2500 et 3000 avant J.-C. Leurs peintures murales s'apparentent à celles faites entre 5000 et 10000 avant J.-C. dans les grottes de Bhimbetka, dans l'État du Madhya Pradesh, au cœur de l'Inde. L'iconographie extrêmement rudimentaire de leurs peintures murales est construite autour d'un vocabulaire graphique des plus basiques : le rond, le triangle et le carré. Le rond et le triangle sont nés de l'observation de la nature : le rond de l'observation de la lune et du soleil et le triangle de celle des montagnes, et plus particulièrement de la montagne sacrée au sommet acéré, aigu, ou des arbres aux cimes pointées vers le ciel. Seul le carré ne semble pas né de l'observation de la nature et apparaît alors comme une création de l'homme afin de délimiter l'enclos sacré, la parcelle de terrain. Aussi, le motif central de chaque peinture rituelle est celui du carré, le « cauk » (ou caukat), au centre duquel l'on trouve Palagatha, la déesse mère, symbole de fécondité et de fertilité. Il est important de noter que les divinités masculines sont quasiment inexistantes chez les Warlis et qu'elles s'apparentent, le plus souvent, à des esprits ayant pris

is surrounded by scenes of hunting, fishing, and agriculture, festivities and dancing, as well as figures representing trees and animals. Humans, and many animals too, are represented by two triangles that meet at their tip, the upper triangle representing the torso, the lower triangle the pelvis. The uncertain balance between these triangles symbolises the balance of the universe and between the human couple. The articulation between the tips of the triangles also has the practical and playfully capacity of easily imbuing bodies by simply tilting one triangle relative to the other, which would otherwise be absent from Warli art. This elemental pictography is depicted using an equally rudimentary technique. Ritual paintings are generally created inside huts, which usually have no internal partitions. A symbolic separation divides the space between the human occupants and their livestock. The walls are made of a mixture of branches, earth, and cow dung. Their colour is that of terracotta. It is this red ochre colour that provides the background for the motifs in Warli wall paintings. The Warlis only use one colour, white, which is obtained by mixing rice paste and water. To this they add gum to act as a binder. The colour is applied using a bamboo stick whose end has been chewed to give it the flexibility of a brush. These mural paintings are only created on rare occasions, such as weddings and harvests.This lack of regular artistic practice explains the undeveloped style of Warli ritual paintings. Until the late 1960s, the tribe's pictorial art was the exclusive preserve of women (*see photographs pages* 18-19).

forme humaine. Autour du motif central de ces peintures rituelles, viennent principalement des scènes de chasse, de pêche et de culture, de fête et de danse, des figures représentant arbres et animaux. Les corps des êtres humains, comme ceux de nombreux animaux, sont représentés à l'aide de deux triangles inversés qui se rejoignent en leur pointe respective, le triangle supérieur figure le torse, le triangle inférieur le bassin. L'équilibre précaire de ces triangles symbolise l'équilibre de l'univers, du couple. Cet équilibre a aussi l'aspect pratique et ludique de pouvoir aisément animer les corps en inclinant simplement un triangle par rapport à l'autre. Équilibre sans lequel rythme et vie seraient absents de leur art. Cette pictographie réduite à l'essentiel est réalisée à l'aide de moyens picturaux eux aussi rudimentaires. Les peintures rituelles sont créés de manière générale à l'intérieur des huttes. Celles-ci ne possèdent ordinairement pas de cloisons intérieures. Une séparation symbolique répartit l'espace entre les humains et le bétail. Les murs sont faits d'un mélange de branchages, de terre et de bouse de vache. Leur couleur est celle de la terre cuite. C'est cet ocre rouge qui va servir de fond à la peinture murale. Pour peindre, les Warlis n'utilisent qu'une seule couleur, le blanc. La couleur blanche est obtenue à partir d'un mélange de pâte de riz, d'eau et de gomme qui sert de liant. Cette peinture sera appliquée à l'aide d'un bâtonnet de bambou préalablement mâchonné en son extrémité afin de lui donner une souplesse semblable à celle d'un pinceau. Ces peintures murales ne sont réalisées qu'en de rares occasions, celles des mariages et des récoltes. Cette absence de pratique artistique régulière explique le style extrêmement brut des peintures rituelles warli. Jusqu'à la fin des années 1960, l'art pictural de cette tribu était le fait exclusif des femmes (*voir photos pages* 18-19).

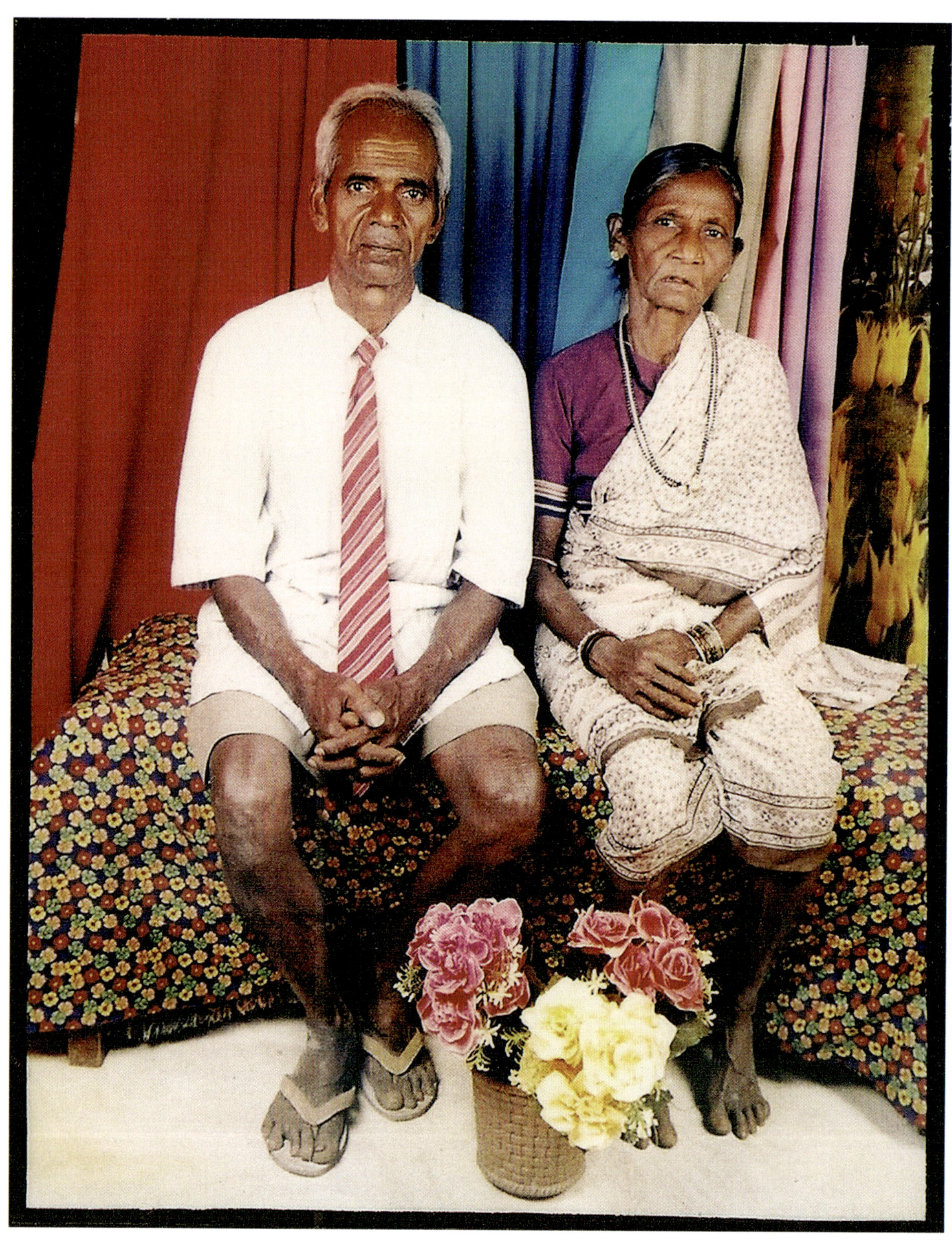

Jivya Soma Mashe and his wife, Pavani.
Studio portrait in Ganjad (Maharashtra, India), circa 2000.

JIVYA SOMA MASHE, THE LEGENDARY ARTIST OF THE WARLI TRIBE
JIVYA SOMA MASHE, LE LÉGENDAIRE ARTISTE DE LA TRIBU WARLI

During the 1970s, Warli ancestral ritual art underwent a radical change: a man, Jivya Soma Mashe, took up painting, not just on ritual occasions, but every day. His talent was very quickly noticed across India and he received, from the country's most important politicians – both Nehru and Gandhi – India's highest artistic awards, followed by international recognition when his work was included in leading exhibitions, including *Magiciens de la terre* in Paris in 1989.

Jivya Soma Mashe had an exceptional life. Abandoned by his family when still very young, he retreated inside himself,withdrawing in complete silence. His only means of expression was through drawings he made on the ground – an unusual behaviour that brought him a particular status in his community. The first government envoys, sent out to protect and promote Warli art, were astonished by Jivya Soma Mashe's talent. It was conjectured that his heightened sensitivity and unusually powerful imagination were a legacy of his early introspective period. Paper and canvas freed him from the constraints of working on the rough surface of walls, and he has metamorphosed the abrupt aspect of the ephemeral paintings into a free and deeply sensitive style.

Walking is omnipresent, both within the Warli landscape, with its countless tracks marking the ground like the remnants of an unfinished sedentarisation, and in the paintings of Jivya Soma Mashe. In his painting, walking takes the form of tracks, usually represented by a single line. One or more lines, which traverse and structure the composition, invite us to follow his characters, his 'walkers', who are always on the move.

When looking closely at the paintings of Jivya Soma Mashe, what stands out the most is the 'movement', the quality of the details, their lightness, and yet also the precision of the strokes. There is no hesitation in Jivya Soma Mashe's execution. He goes directly and unambiguously to the essence of the matter in both the design and composition, applying the simplicity of the obvious, the naive, and the natural. This is borne out

Cet art rituel ancestral allait, au cours des années 1970, subir un changement radical. Un homme, Jivya Soma Mashe, se mit à peindre, non pas à la seule occasion des rituels, mais quotidiennement. Son talent fut très vite remarqué au niveau national, et il reçut directement de la main des plus hauts responsables politiques de l'Inde – tels Nehru ou encore Indira Gandhi – les plus importantes récompenses artistiques indiennes, puis au niveau international, participant à des expositions remarquées, dont *Magiciens de la terre* en 1989 à Paris.

L'histoire de Jivya Soma Mashe est singulière. Abandonné par sa famille dès son plus jeune âge, il s'enferme dans un mutisme total. Sa seule façon de s'exprimer alors est de tracer des dessins à même le sol. Cette attitude étrange lui vaut rapidement un statut particulier au sein de sa communauté. Les premiers émissaires du gouvernement, en charge de conserver et de promouvoir l'art des Warlis, sont vite étonnés par les qualités artistiques de cet homme. De cette période de repli sur lui-même, Jivya Soma Mashe semble avoir conservé un imaginaire et surtout une sensibilité hors du commun. Le travail sur des supports comme le papier et la toile lui ont permis de s'affranchir des contraintes de la surface irrégulière du mur. Jivya Soma Mashe a métamorphosé l'aspect abrupt des peintures éphémères en un style libre et franc d'où émane une sensibilité propre.

La marche est omniprésente, tant dans les paysages warli, avec ses innombrables pistes marquant le sol comme les vestiges d'une sédentarisation inachevée, que dans les peintures de Jivya Soma Mashe. Dans ses peintures, la marche s'inscrit également sous la forme de pistes, représentées le plus souvent par une simple ligne. Une ou plusieurs lignes, qui parcourent et structurent la toile, nous invitent à suivre ses personnages toujours en mouvement, ses « marcheurs ».

En regardant attentivement les peintures de Jivya Soma Mashe, ce qui frappe le plus c'est le « mouvement », la qualité du détail, la légèreté et, dans un même temps, la précision du trait. L'hésitation n'existe pas dans l'œuvre de Jivya Soma Mashe.

by every detail of his paintings. Lines and dots abound and vibrate on the canvas, combining to form skilful compositions that together intensify the general resonance. The details and overall composition both contribute to a sense of energy and movement. Recurring themes, from daily tribal life and Warli legends, are also a pretext for celebrating movement.

Jivya Soma Mashe summed up the deep feeling that animates the Warli soul, saying, 'There are human beings, birds, animals, insects, and so on. Day and night there's movement. Life is movement'.

This book chiefly presents a selection of paintings by Jivya Soma Mashe that I was fortunate enough to collect between 1998 and 2016. Most have since joined such outstanding collections as those belonging to the Fondation Cartier pour l'art contemporain and Agnès B. The book's emphasis on visual presentation is to bring out the quality of the details in these paintings, through which Jivya Soma Mashe conveyed his perception of movement and life.

L'artiste va à l'essentiel, tant dans le dessin que dans la composition. Directement, sans ambages, avec la simplicité de l'évidence, de l'ingénu, du naturel. Chaque détail de ses peintures en est le témoignage. Le trait, la ligne et les points foisonnent, fourmillent sur la toile, vibrent et s'agencent au gré de compositions habiles qui, elles-mêmes, renforcent la vibration de l'ensemble. Le détail et la composition générale de l'œuvre sont, l'un et l'autre, au service du mouvement. Les thèmes récurrents de son œuvre, l'activité quotidienne des siens et les légendes warli, sont eux aussi le prétexte à un éloge constant du mouvement.

« Il y a les êtres humains, les oiseaux, les animaux, les insectes, etc. Jour et nuit il y a du mouvement. La vie est mouvement. » Par ces propos, Jivya Soma Mashe, décrit le sentiment profond qui anime l'âme warli.

Ce livre présente majoritairement une sélection des peintures de Jivya Soma Mashe que j'ai eu la chance de rassembler entre 1998 et 2016. La plupart d'entre elles ont rejoint de belles collections comme celles de la Fondation Cartier pour l'art contemporain et d'Agnès B. Le parti pris visuel de cet ouvrage a été de mettre en valeur la qualité des détails de ces peintures par lesquels Jivya Soma Mashe retranscrit sa perception du mouvement, de la vie.

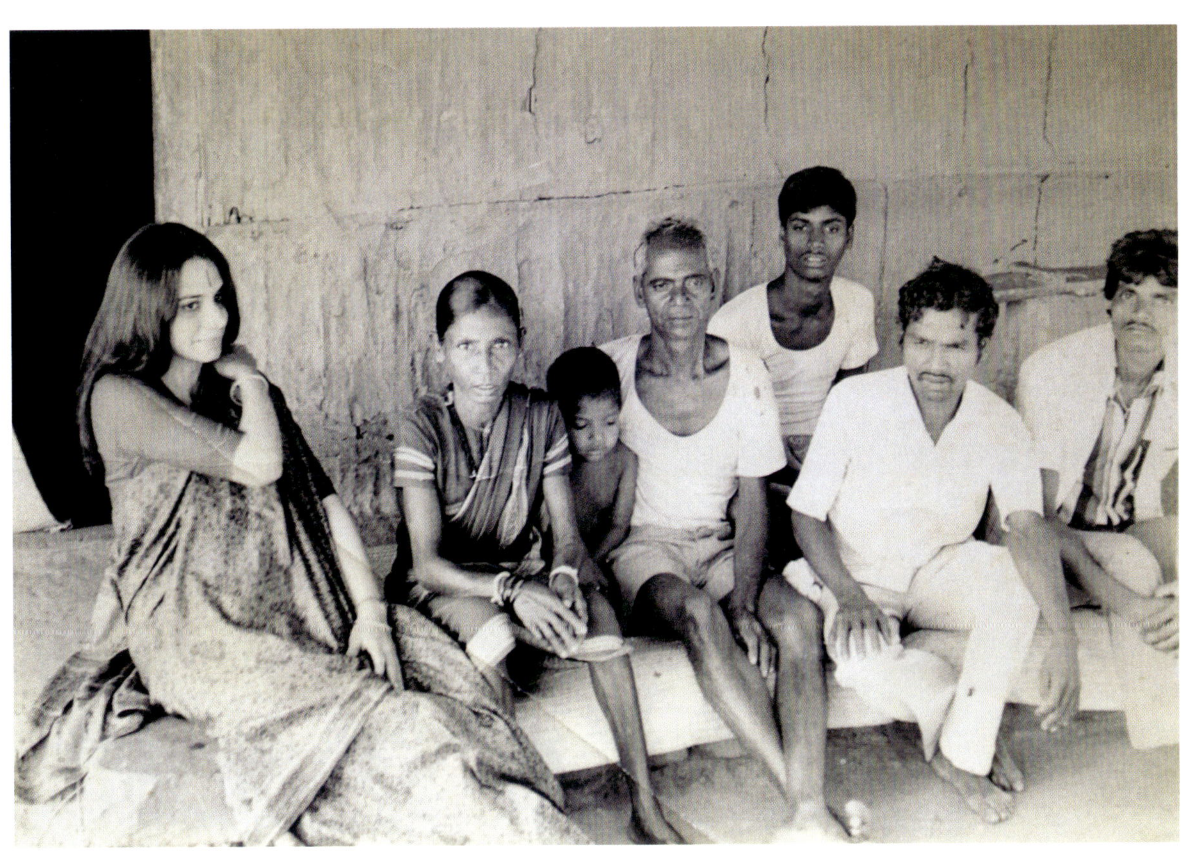

Yashodhara Dalmia, Pavani and Jivya Soma Mashe, Balu and Sadashiv Mashe, Ganjad (Maharashtra, India), circa 1980. Photographer unknown.

Pages 14–15
Jivya and Pavani Soma Mashe, Ganjad (Maharashtra, India), circa 2000. Photographer unknown.

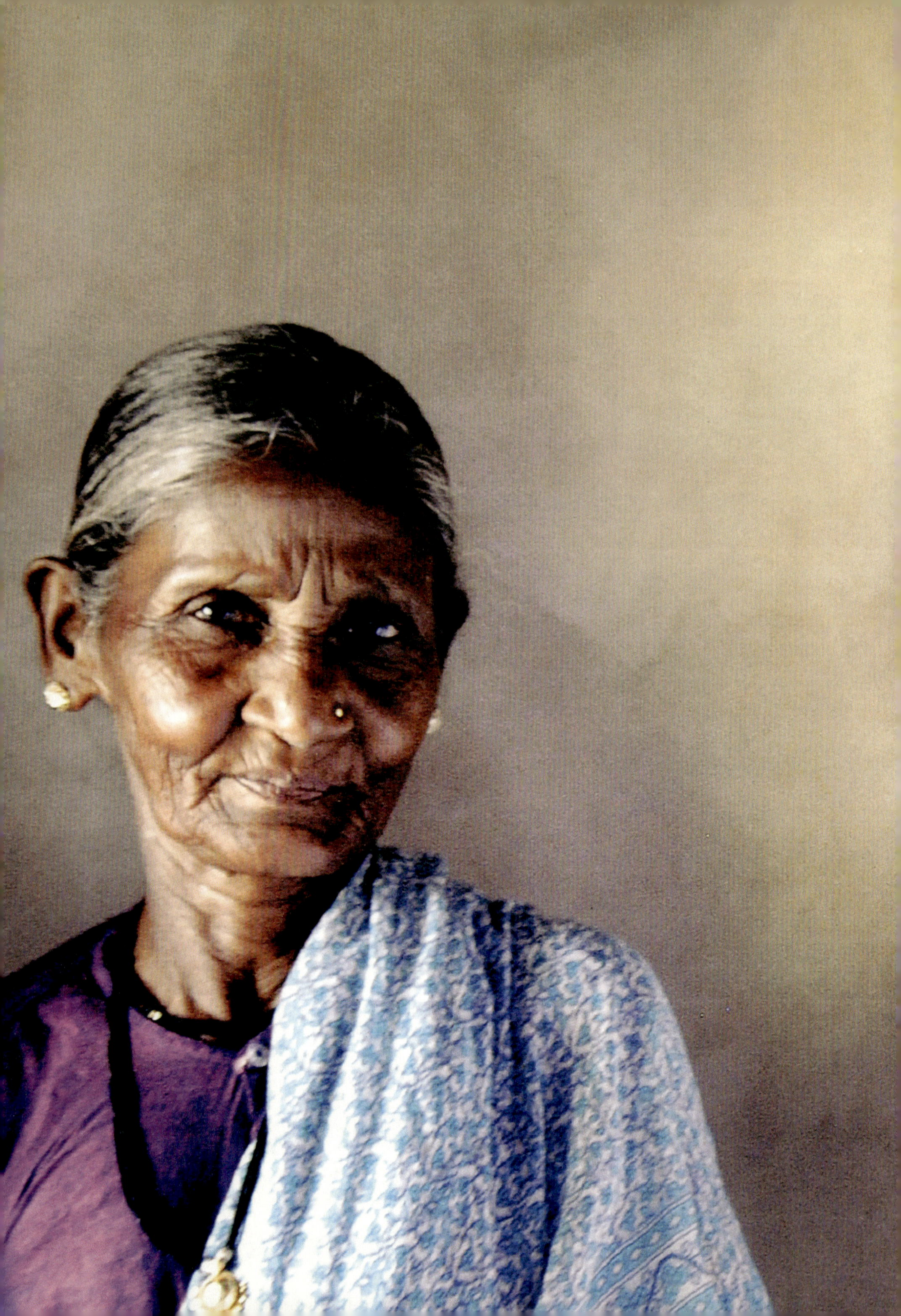

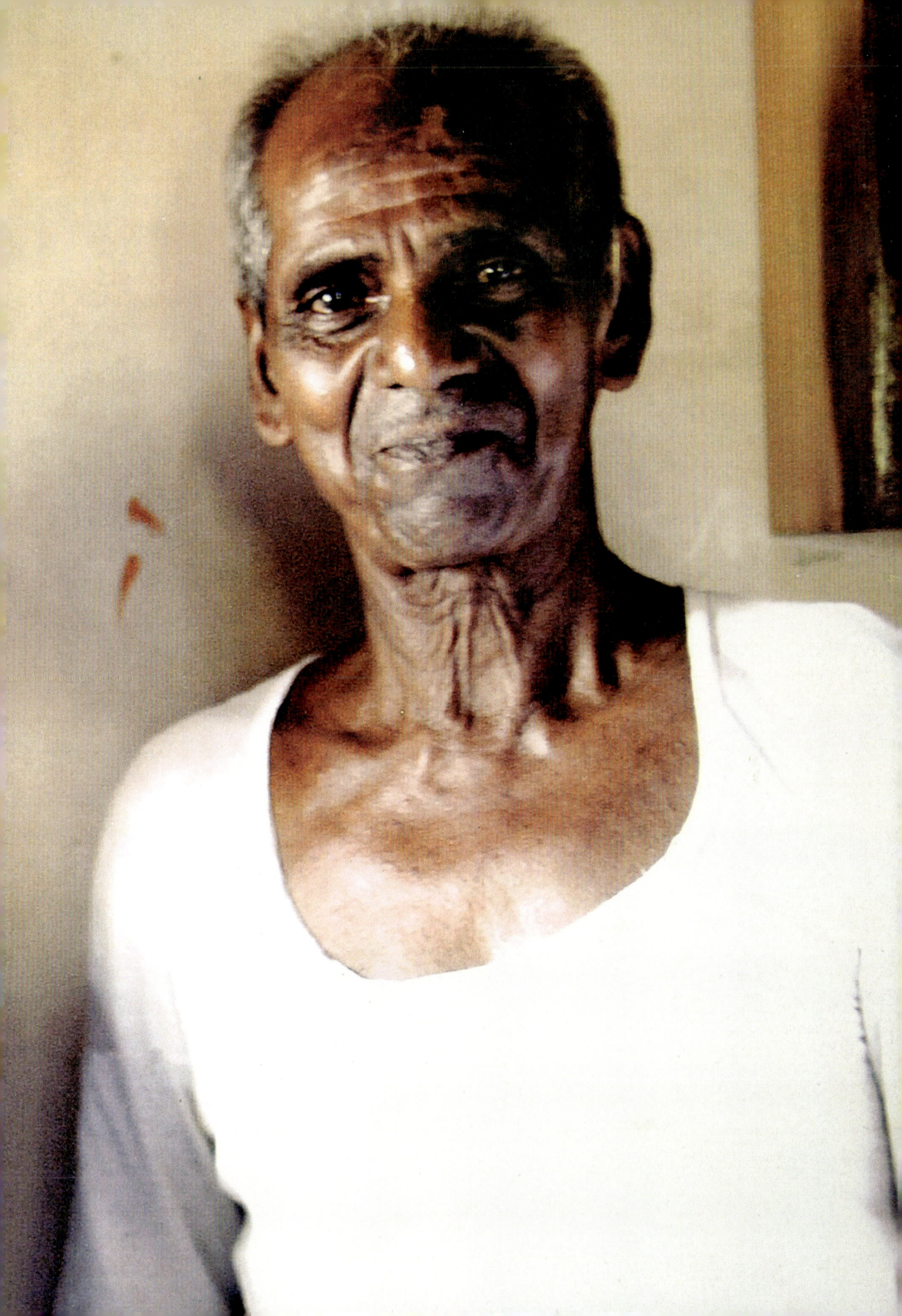

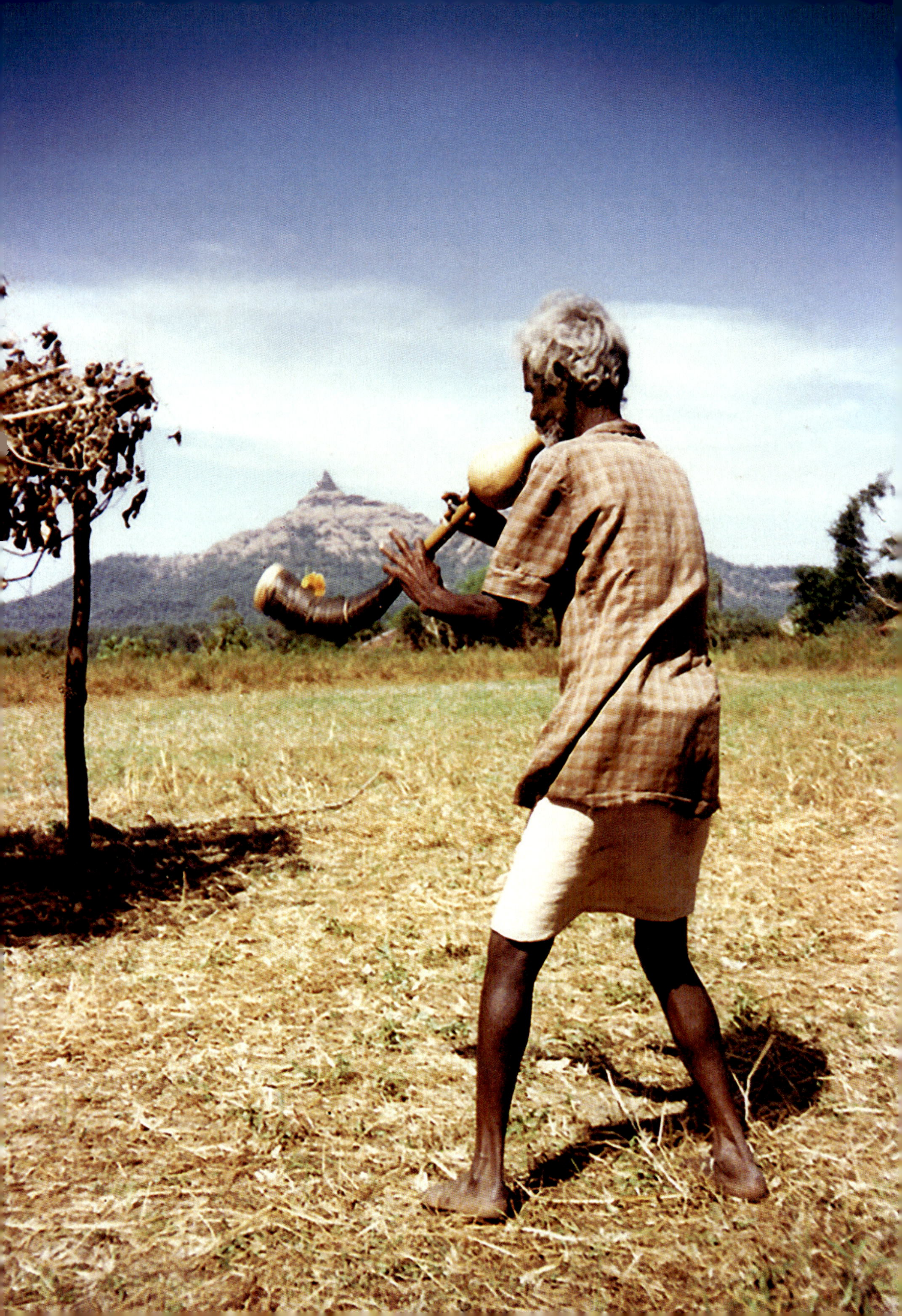

THE PAINTED WORLD OF THE WARLIS

by Yashodhara Dalmia

The art of the Warlis takes place within a ritual context for a specific purpose. What is the result of removing this art from its context, introducing it on paper and making it available to an urban audience both in India and abroad? In this chapter some of the consequences of this will be examined by looking at the work of Jivya Soma Mashe, the most well known of the Warli artists, as it developed over a crucial period of his life, a little after he was 'discovered'.

The first artists to be 'discovered', however, were some old Warli women who were asked to translate to paper what they made on the hut wall. The results were an array of wondorous trees, looming magnificently towards the sky. We witnessed some of these wonderful tree paintings at an exhibition held at an art gallery in Bombay in 1975. Other paintings at the same exhibition were made by a middle-aged tribal man, Jivya Soma Mashe. Jivya's paintings on paper won acclaim as early as 1974 in India and very soon began to be exhibited internationally. Soon after, many visitors and film-makers began streaming into his hut to witness and record Warli art. His work, however, can in no way be equated with Warli art, which exists at a specific place for a specific purpose. If anything, he is the only successful example of a person who has been able to make a break with his tradition and yet carry it forward.

Jivya's early work consisted of an energetic description of human activity as if it had been awaiting a long release.

The groups of men break out into their daily work on the field. The space of the painting gets divided into rectangles where different stages of field activity take place simultaneously. Thus, men can be seen digging the earth, sowing the seeds, and ploughing all at the same time. The trees in this painting have *pipal* leaves, and men replace the monkeys of the

Tarpa player (a traditional Warli wind instrument)
in front of the sacred mountain, circa 1990.
Photo by Remigius de Souza.

L'art des Warlis prend place dans un contexte rituel et un propos spécifiques. Quel est le résultat de la sortie de cet art de son contexte, de son introduction sur papier et de sa mise à disposition d'un public urbain en Inde et à l'étranger ? Dans ce texte, nous examinerons certaines des conséquences de cette situation en examinant l'œuvre de Jivya Soma Mashe, le plus connu des artistes warli, telle qu'elle s'est développée au cours d'une période cruciale de sa vie, peu après sa « découverte ».

Les premiers artistes à être « découverts » furent cependant des femmes warli âgées à qui on demanda de traduire sur papier ce qu'elles avaient fait sur le mur de la hutte. Le résultat fut une série d'arbres merveilleux, se dressant magnifiquement vers le ciel. Nous avons pu admirer certaines de ces magnifiques peintures d'arbres lors d'une exposition organisée dans une galerie à Bombay en 1975. D'autres peintures de la même exposition furent réalisées par un homme d'âge moyen, Jivya Soma Mashe. Les peintures sur papier de Jivya ont été acclamées dès 1974 en Inde et ont très vite commencé à être exposées à l'échelle internationale. Peu après, de nombreux visiteurs et cinéastes ont commencé à affluer dans sa hutte pour observer et enregistrer l'art warli. Son travail, cependant, ne peut en aucun cas être comparé à l'art warli, qui existe dans un lieu spécifique pour un but spécifique. Il est en fait le seul exemple réussi d'une personne qui a été capable de rompre avec sa tradition tout en la faisant avancer.

Les premières œuvres de Jivya consistaient en une description énergique de l'activité humaine présentée comme si elle attendait une longue libération.

Les groupes d'hommes se lancent dans leur travail quotidien dans les champs. L'espace du tableau est divisé en rectangles où se déroulent simultanément différentes étapes de l'activité des champs. Ainsi, on peut voir des hommes creuser la terre, semer les graines et labourer dans le même espace-temps. Les arbres de ce tableau ont des feuilles de *pipal* et les hommes remplacent les feuilles par des singes dans l'arbre aux singes. Dans un autre tableau remarquable, on peut voir des hommes

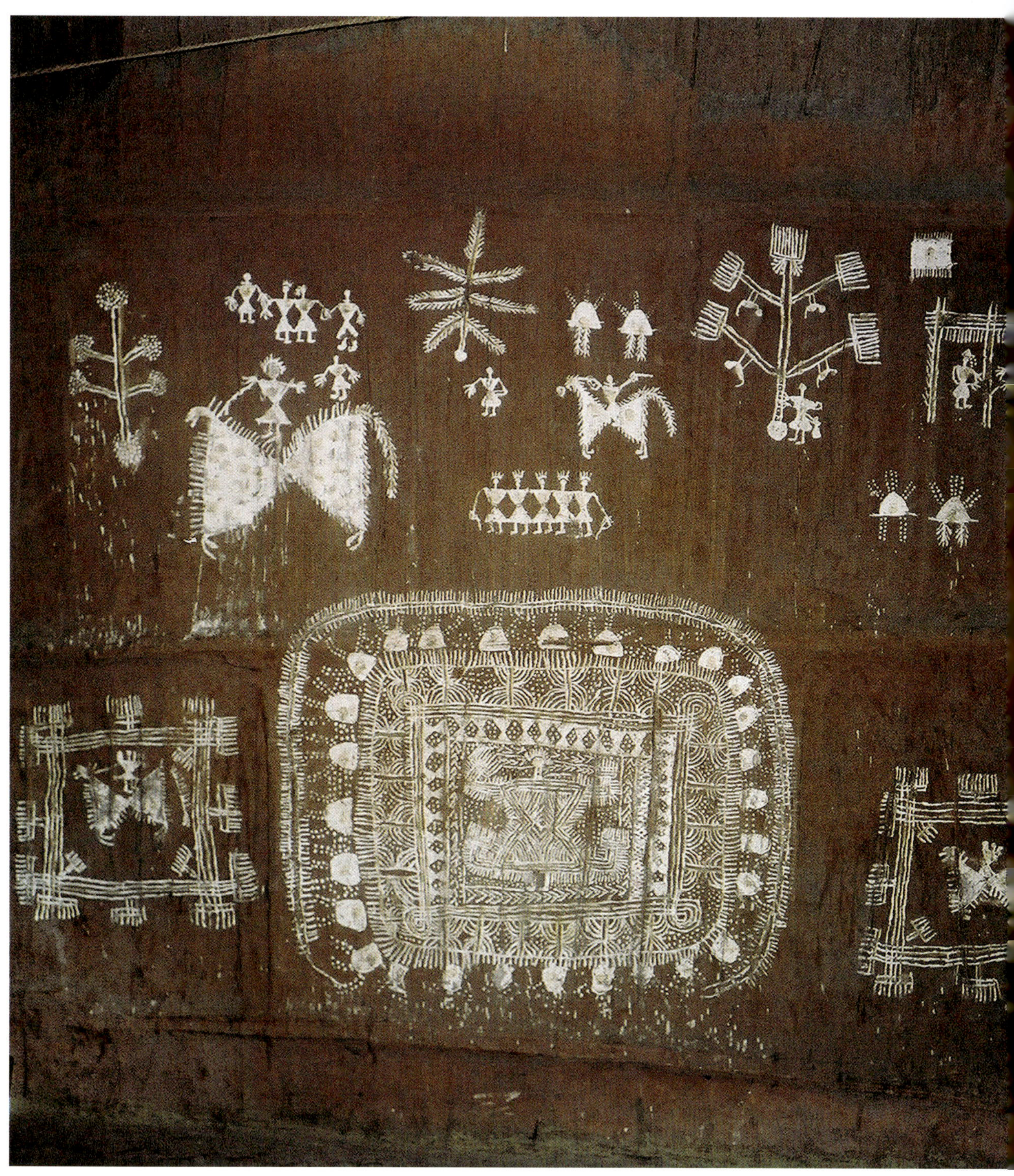

Photograph by Hervé Perdriolle, 1997, of a ritual painting created for a wedding on the wall of a Warli house, alongside double-page images from Yashodhara Dalmia's book *The Painted World of the Warlis*, Lalit Kala Akademi, New Delhi, India, 1988.

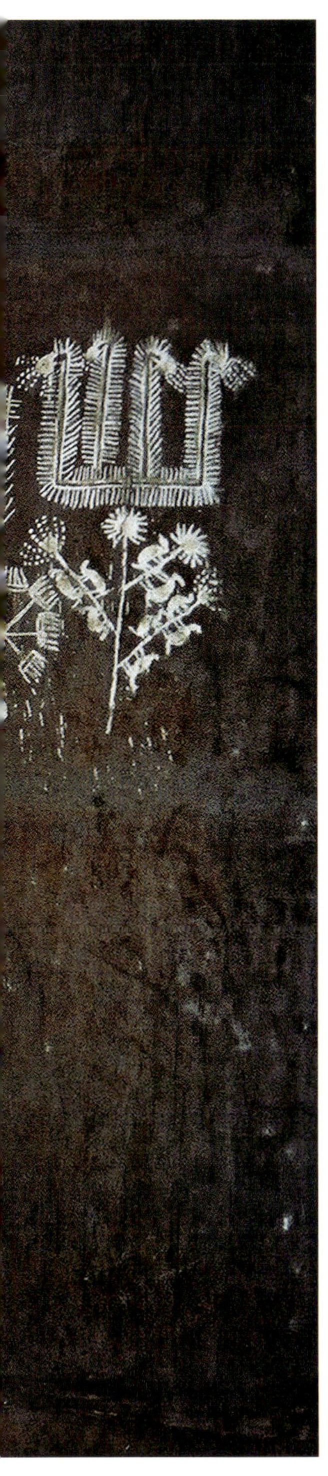

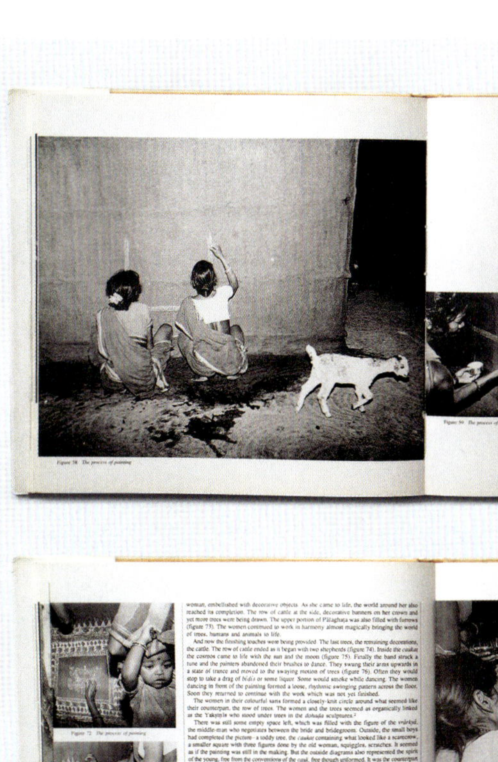

Figure 58 The process of painting

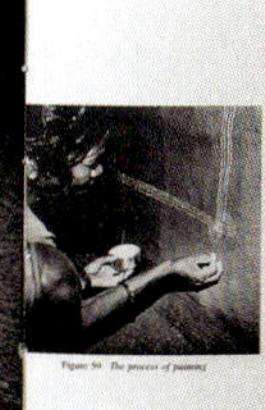

Figure 59 The process of painting

The Process of Painting

"Life itself-the different ways in which the difficult problems of human association have been solved-represents the ultimate and chief of the arts of Asia"

A.K. COOMARSWAMY

The process of painting, during the wedding, is as important as the completed picture itself. This is evident in the careful preparations that are made for the painting, as well as the actual making of it, which is a slow, well orchestrated movement towards completion. At each stage in painting, the series of events that take place simultaneously seem to have been planned in a deliberate manner. And yet they seem totally spontaneous. The order in the process as it emerges, step by step, according to convention, leads to the progressive development of the painting. At the same time, the young women who are painting, reach a state of fulfilment culminating in drinking and dancing. It seems as if the gradual attainment of a 'brimming over' state, not only in themselves but as a symbol of the whole community, seems to be the unconscious aim of the artists who make the picture.

Only a *suvāsinī*, or a woman whose husband is alive, can make the main portion of the painting consisting of the *caukaṭ* and the mother goddess, Pālaghaṭa. Strangely enough, the *suvāsinī's* who are to paint, beg pardon from the gods for being 'impure' because they have had sexual relations with their men.[1] They also ask for forgiveness for the impurity of the soil, cowdung, water, flour and other painting objects which might contain insects. After this they set about to paint.

On the day before the wedding we watched two *suvāsinī's* at Sāmbar's hut in Dambipada prepare the rice-paste with which the painting would be made. Of the two artists, one was a young woman and the other a middle-aged peasant woman with a careworn face. Both had the busy, harried look of women who had several functions to perform like working on their fields, looking after their children, cooking food.

They crouched around the rice-hole, sifting the flour by shaking it in a winnowing fan and allowing the husk to fall on the floor. The finer portion was collected in a wicker basket. Small amounts of this were mixed with water in a *vāṭī* (metal cup). After this thin, reed-like sticks, about three inches long, were broken off the *baharu* tree which they used as pens.

127

Figure 72 The process of painting

Figure 73 The process of painting

woman, embellished with decorative objects. As she came to life, the world around her also reached its completion. The row of cattle at the side, decorative banners on her crown and yet more trees were being drawn. The upper portion of Pālaghaṭa was also filled with furrows (figure 73). The women continued to work in harmony almost magically bringing the world of trees, humans and animals to life.

And now the finishing touches were being provided. The last trees, the remaining decorations, the cattle. The row of cattle ended as it began with two shepherds (figure 74). Inside the *caukaṭ* the cosmos came to life with the sun and the moon (figure 75). Finally the band struck a tune and the painters abandoned their brushes to dance. They swung their arms upwards in a state of trance and moved to the swaying motion of trees (figure 76). Often they would stop to take a drag of *bidis* or some liquor. Some would smoke while dancing. The women dancing in front of the painting formed a loose, rhythmic swinging pattern across the floor. Soon they returned to continue with the work which was not yet finished.

The women in their colourful saris formed a closely-knit circle around what seemed like their counterpart, the row of trees. The women and the trees seemed as organically linked as the Yakṣiṇīs who stood under trees in the *dohada* sculptures.[2]

There was still some empty space left, which was filled with the figure of the *vrārkyā*, the middle-man who negotiates between the bride and bridegroom. Outside, the small boys had completed the picture - a toddy tree, the *caukaṭ* containing what looked like a scarecrow, a smaller square with three figures done by the old woman, squiggles, scratches. It seemed as if the painting was still in the making. But the outside diagrams also represented the spirit of the young, free from the conventions of the *cauk*, free though unformed. It was the counterpart to the strictly regulated painting inside.

Soon after, the *dhavleris* or wedding priestesses entered carrying lamps. Sitting in a row adjacent to the painting, they began singing. The *suvāsinī's* drew a *cauk* with white flour, around the rice-hole, in front of the *dhavleris* (figure 78). This *cauk* was similar to the *deva cauk* in the painting. On this *cauk* was placed a board, over which rice was heaped. Led by the *suvāsinī's*, the grooms, covered by a white cloth began to circumambulate the *cauk* on the floor.

The real ceremony of invocation, however, would begin only in the night (*deva cadhavane*). During this time the painting would be covered entirely with white cloth and on either side of it the two grooms would sit, cloaked in white. The *dhāk bhagats* would sing songs of the god Hirvā (see chapter on marriage). And only when they had reached a state of possession along with the grooms, of the Tiger God, would the painting be uncovered. Now it would be animated with life.

We see that the main artists of the painting are the *suvāsinīs* or women whose husbands are alive and this fact indicated that they performed a fertile function - that of painting. Just as the touch of beautiful women in the *dohada* sculptures, could fulfil the pregnancy longing of the tree and make it bear fruit, the touch of the fertile woman could bring the painting to life and make it similarly fertile.

It was interesting that the act of painting itself was always seen as 'writing' (*cauk lihane*) for it was the primary means of expression for the artists. The visual forms and sometimes non-forms were the only means that the artists had for mirroring their own well of experience.

2. The word *dohada* means pregnancy longing and the tree is represented as feeling like a woman, such a longing, nor can its flowers open until it is satisfied. See Coomaraswamy, 1971, p. 35.

136

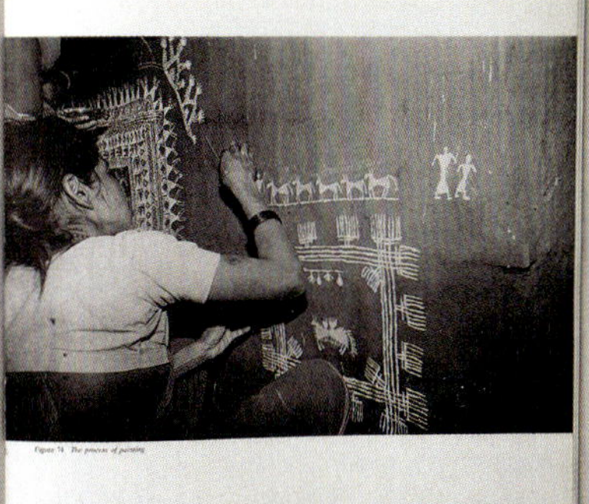

Figure 74 The process of painting

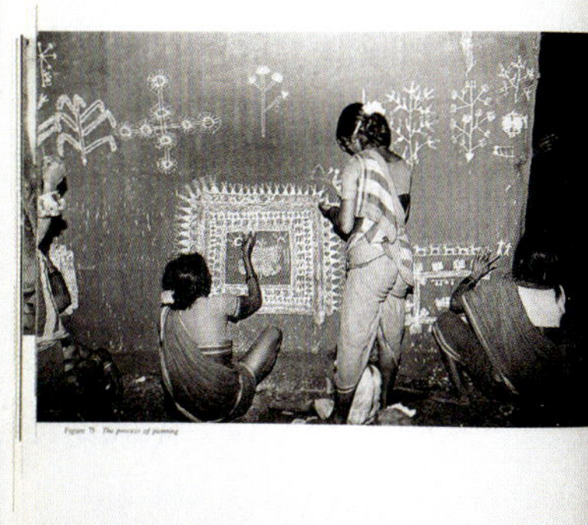

Figure 75 The process of painting

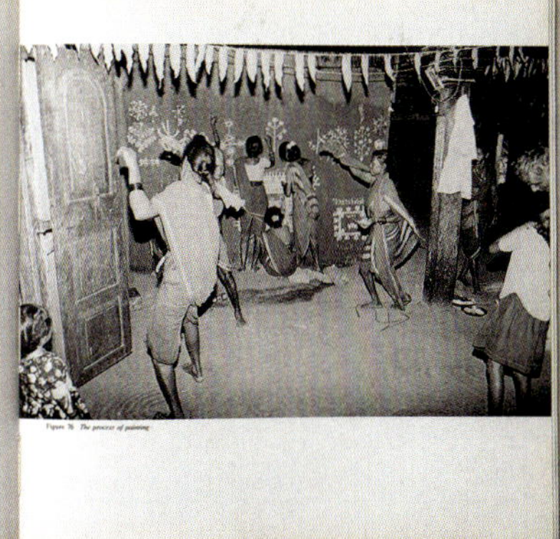

Figure 76 The process of painting

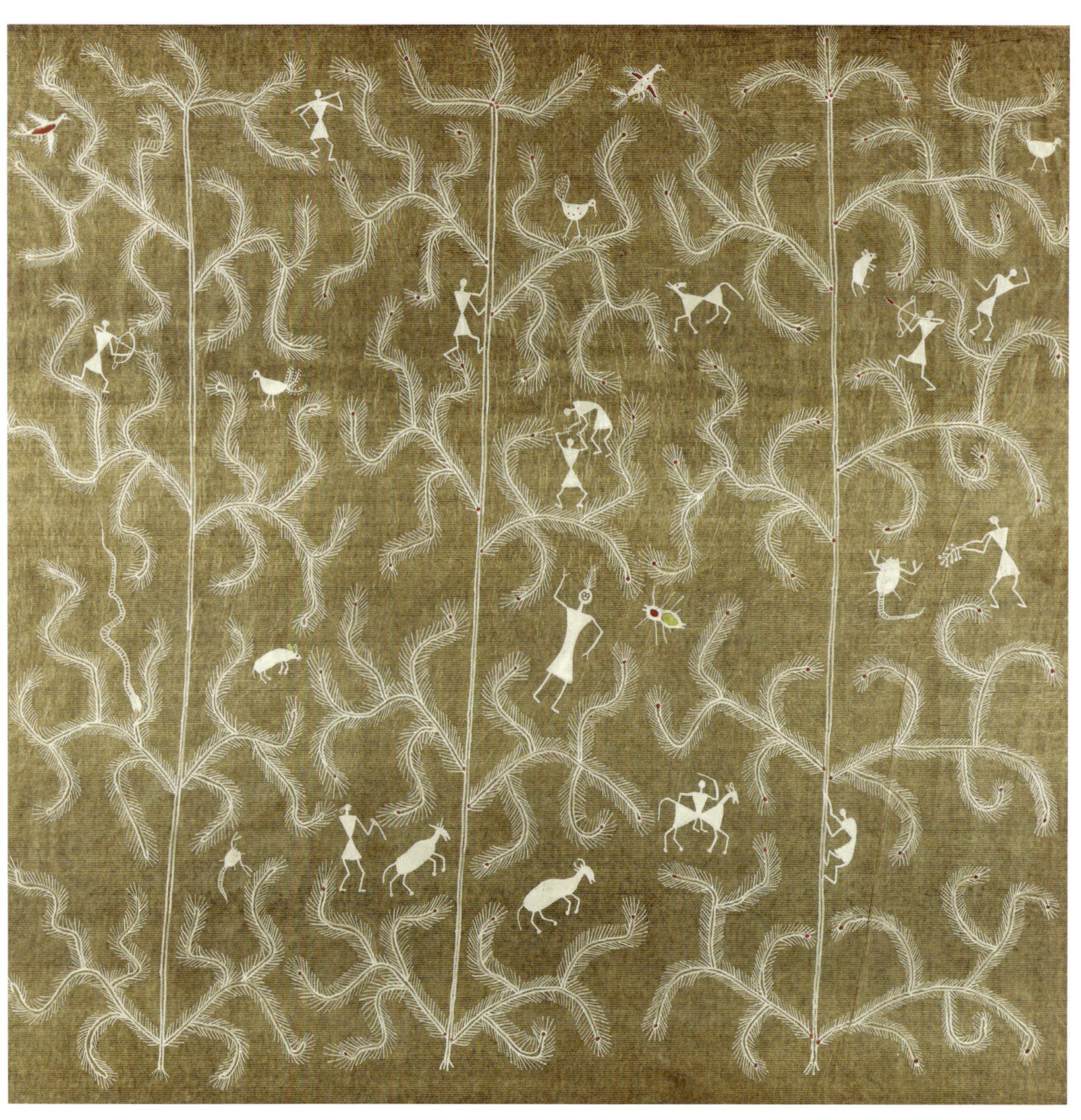

Jivya Soma Mashe, *Untitled*, circa 1970,
acrylic on tarred craft paper,
120 × 120 cm; 47.24 × 47.24 in.
Collection of Lina and David Lebard.
Photo by Annik Wetter.

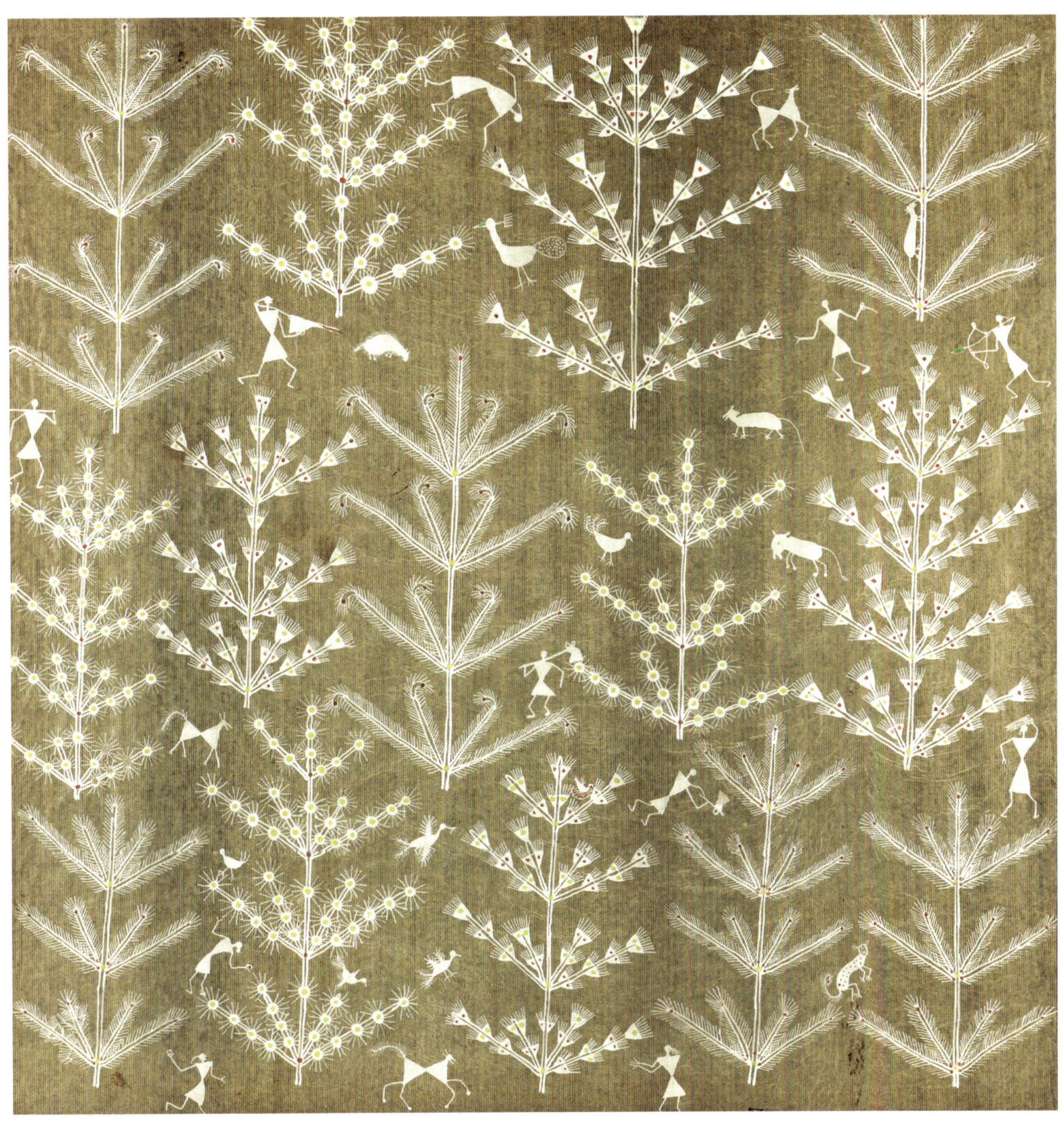

Jivya Soma Mashe, *Untitled*, circa 1970,
acrylic on tarred craft paper,
120 × 120 cm; 47.24 × 47.24 in.
Collection of Elsa Lepeu Cauro.
Photo by Annik Wetter.

Jivya Soma Mashe, *Untitled*, circa 1970,
acrylic on tarred craft paper,
101 × 108 cm; 39.73 × 42.51 in.
Collection of Maximiliano Modesti.
Photo by Vansh Deep Agarwal.

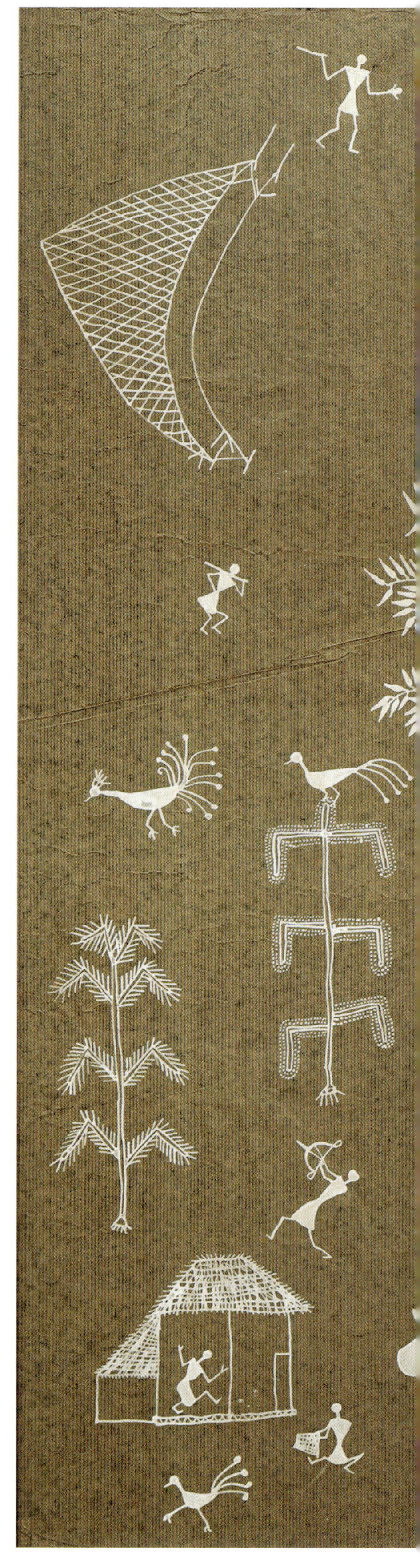

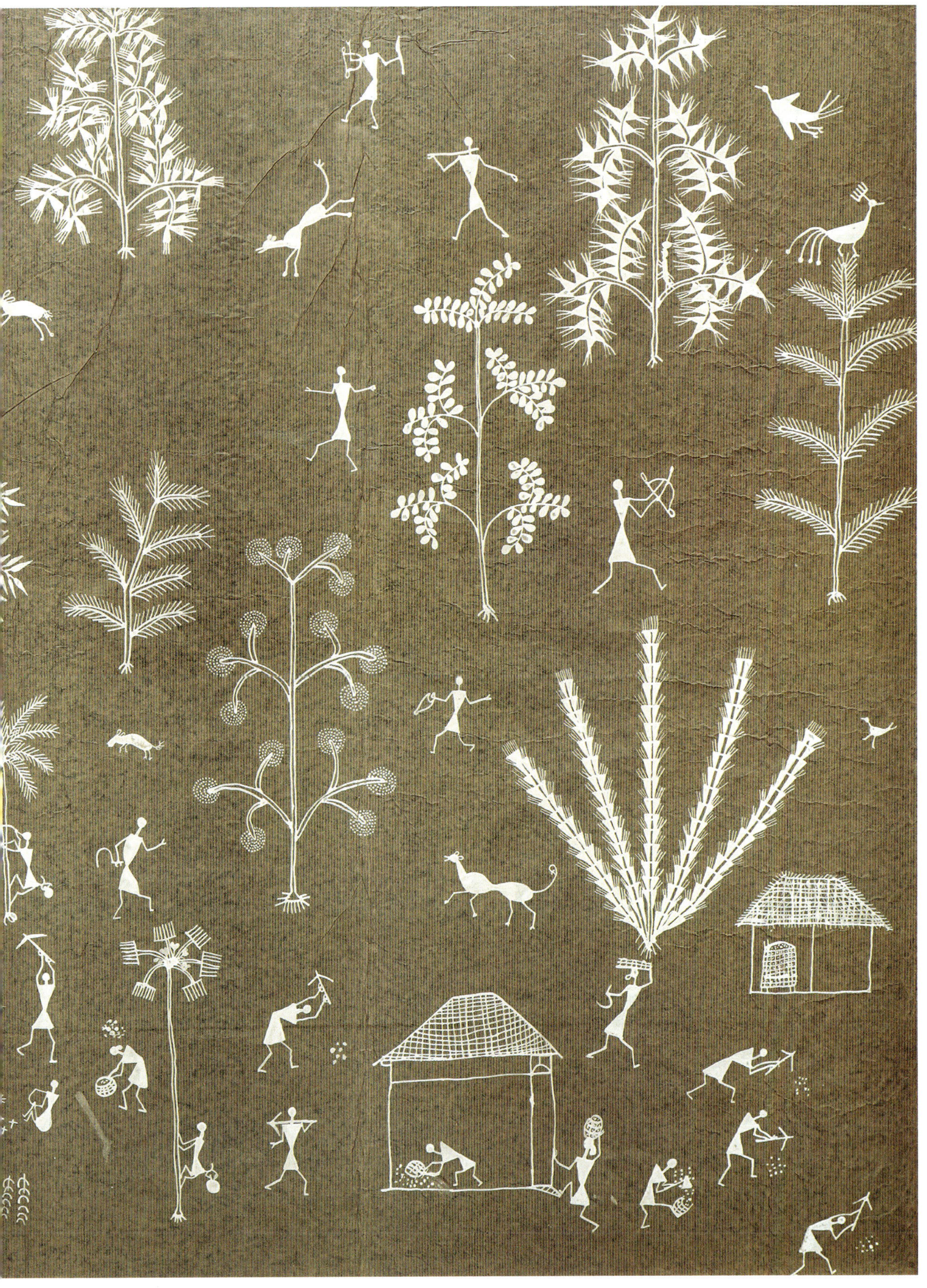

monkey tree. In another remarkable painting, men can be seen harvesting the field. They stand in a row, each at a different stage of activity but united in an underlying rhythm. If they give the impression of floating it is because they are again wallowing up from the boundless depths. That is why simultaneous, synchronised activity is still possible.

We see then that in his first series of paintings Jivya is concerned with a description of activity which is entirely human and has little to do with gods. It is as if all the pent-up frustrations of placing miniscule men against the soaring trees finds a burst of release in entirely secular paintings. Jivya considerably increases the vocabulary of human activity in these paintings, where men are engaged in work actually related to their lives and not hidden within the specified form of the *caukat*.

On a hill grow thin strokes of paddy. Many, many field animals can be seen lazing their way through these. The rat burrows a hole, the snake crawls, the scorpion and other tiny animals are visible. Below dance a circle of ants. Above stands a deer in solitary splendour. This web of events acts as a background to the tale of the Tiger God. The tiger emerges growling from behind the rocks, scaring away the grass-cutter. On the other side he emerges, harmless, innocuous, the god of the people! Different varieties of trees silhouette the hill. Through these crawl men and women, toiling. Right on top, flying above everything is the magician (the spirit – recognisable by his long hair).

If Jivya now began to observe reality with a microscopic precision, he did not deprive it of its magical life. His main concern was with the minute strands which make up the whole. A fishing net is spread over the length of the entire canvas. On top stands a tiny fisherman holding a net. Small river animals can be seen trapped within its mesh. Nothing surpasses the intricacy with which Jivya has woven this net with its finely interlocked loops. No two loops are alike, each one separate, unique, and yet organically connected with the whole. The tone is neutral, calm, without frenzy.

Was Jivya's work likely to become commercialised? At this stage he seemed poised between different tendencies – on the edge of the precipice as it were. His best works revealed a desire to isolate and explore facts of everyday life. He was moving back and forth not only over external reality but over himself. A new, altogether exciting sense of awareness was evident in these works. And he could enhance this with an innate

moissonner les champs. Ils se tiennent en rang, chacun à un stade d'activité différent, mais unis dans un rythme sous-jacent. S'ils donnent l'impression de flotter, c'est parce qu'ils s'activent à nouveau dans un espace, en l'absence totale de perspective, sans limite. C'est pourquoi une activité simultanée et synchronisée y est toujours possible.

Nous voyons alors que dans sa première série de peintures, Jivya s'intéresse à la description d'une activité qui est entièrement humaine et qui n'a pas grand-chose à voir avec les dieux. C'est comme si toutes les frustrations accumulées en plaçant des hommes minuscules contre des arbres vertigineux trouvaient un éclat de soulagement dans des peintures entièrement profanes. Jivya augmente considérablement le vocabulaire de l'activité humaine dans ces peintures où les hommes sont engagés dans un travail réellement lié à leur vie et non caché dans la forme spécifiée du *caukat* (peinture rituelle de mariage).

Sur une colline poussent de fines bandes de rizières. On peut y voir de très nombreux animaux des champs se faufiler entre elles. Le rat creuse un trou, le serpent rampe, le scorpion et d'autres petits animaux sont visibles. Au-dessous danse un cercle de fourmis. Au-dessus se tient un cerf dans sa splendeur solitaire. Cette série d'événements sert de toile de fond à l'histoire du Dieu Tigre. Le tigre surgit de derrière les rochers en grognant, effrayant le coupeur d'herbe. De l'autre côté, il émerge, falot, inoffensif, le dieu du peuple ! Différentes variétés d'arbres silhouettent la colline. À travers eux rampent, déambulent, des hommes et des femmes qui travaillent. Tout en haut, volant au-dessus de tout, il y a le magicien (l'esprit – on le reconnaît à sa longue chevelure).

Si Jivya commence alors à observer la réalité avec une précision microscopique, il ne la dépouille pas de sa vie magique. Dans le troisième tableau, il se préoccupe surtout des minuscules fils qui composent l'ensemble. Un filet de pêche est tendu sur toute la longueur de la toile. Au-dessus se tient un minuscule pêcheur tenant un filet. On peut voir de petits animaux de rivière piégés dans ses mailles. Rien ne surpasse la subtilité avec laquelle Jivya a tissé ce filet aux boucles finement imbriquées. Il n'y a pas deux boucles semblables, chacune est séparée, unique et pourtant organiquement reliée à l'ensemble. Le ton est neutre, calme, sans frénésie.

L'œuvre de Jivya était-elle susceptible d'être commercialisée ? À ce stade, le peintre semblait en équilibre entre différentes

sense of design. But the decorative element could become too formal, losing its vitality, and then he appeared to have moved over to the other side. It seemed as if his forms would never unfreeze again.

One reason for this duality was the pressure being placed on him from the outside world. A little before our visit, a group of designers from the National Institute of Design, Ahmedabad, had visited him. In the course of their experiments, Jivya was encouraged to use colours like blue, yellow, and green in his work. The group left placing an order for fifteen paintings. What sort of paintings would these be? Would they be disfigured by colour, which the Warlis have not used without any significance in the past? When asked to paint in sheer number it was likely that Jivya would resort to painting mechanically, as he would think of them as commodities. On the other hand, he would not be able to resist such a lucrative offer which would bring him a sizeable amount of money. This was but one example of the continuous demand being made on Jivya, by the government, by private and international agencies, to produce work.

But to what extent would he be able to sustain this position? Or would he succumb to external pressures? This could only depend on Jivya's own ability to not only accept contradictions but to comprehend them and thus work towards a synthesis.

'For a man to begin practising, what for centuries has been a woman's art form is surprisingly unorthodox. No ordinary man could have attempted this, without fearing the loss of status among his fellow men. But then Jivya Soma Mashe is not an ordinary man', wrote Ulli Beier from the Institute of Papua New Guinea Studies in 1977.

Excerpts from the book by Yashodara Dalmia,
Lalit Kala Akademi, New Delhi, India, First Edition, 1988

tendances, au bord du précipice en quelque sorte. Ses meilleures œuvres révélaient un désir d'isoler et d'explorer les faits de la vie quotidienne. Il allait et venait non seulement sur la réalité extérieure mais sur lui-même. Un nouveau sens de la conscience, tout à fait excitant, était évident dans ces œuvres. Et il pouvait l'améliorer avec un sens inné du design. Mais l'élément décoratif pouvait aussi devenir trop formel, perdre sa vitalité.

L'une des raisons de cette dualité était la pression exercée sur lui par le monde extérieur. Peu avant notre visite, un groupe de designers de l'Institut national de design d'Ahmedabad lui avait rendu visite. Au cours de leurs expériences, Jivya avait été encouragé à utiliser des couleurs comme le bleu, le jaune et le vert dans son travail. Le groupe est parti en passant commande de 15 tableaux. De quel genre de tableaux s'agirait-il ? Seraient-ils défigurés par la couleur, que les Warlis n'ont pas utilisée sans raison dans le passé ? Si on lui demandait de peindre en grand nombre, il était probable que Jivya se contenterait de peindre mécaniquement, car il considérerait ses peintures comme des marchandises. D'un autre côté, il ne pourrait pas résister à une offre aussi lucrative qui lui rapporterait une somme d'argent considérable. Ce n'était qu'un exemple de la demande continue faite à Jivya par le gouvernement et les agences privées et internationales pour produire des œuvres.

Mais dans quelle mesure serait-il capable de maintenir cette position ? Ou succomberait-il aux pressions extérieures ? Cela ne pouvait dépendre que de la capacité de Jivya à non seulement accepter les contradictions mais à les comprendre et ainsi à travailler à une synthèse.

« Pour un homme, commencer à pratiquer ce qui a été pendant des siècles une forme d'art réservée aux femmes est étonnamment peu orthodoxe. Aucun homme ordinaire n'aurait pu tenter cela sans craindre de perdre son statut parmi ses semblables. Mais Jivya Soma Mashe n'est pas un homme ordinaire », écrivait Ulli Beier de l'Institut d'études de Papouasie–Nouvelle-Guinée en 1977.

Extraits du livre de Yashodara Dalmia,
Lalit Kala Akademi, New Delhi, India, 1re Édition, 1988

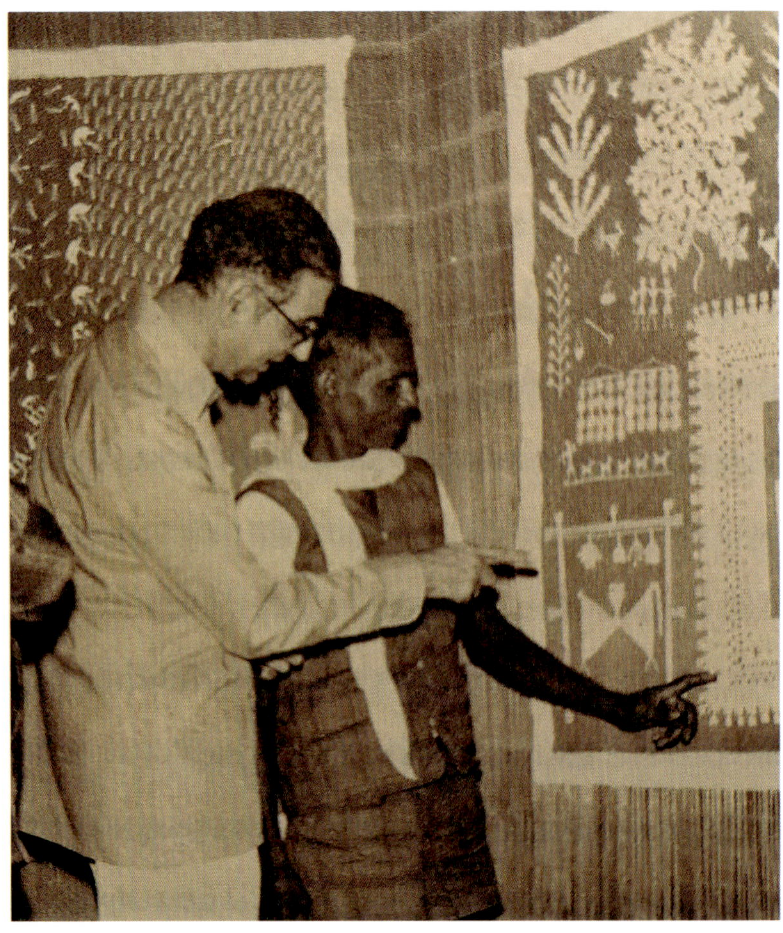

Kekoo Gandhy (1920–2012) opened his first gallery – the Gallery Chemould – in 1963 in Bombay, as a space on the first floor of the Jehangir Art Gallery. Today, it is run by his daughter Shireen in a splendid new space close by. Kekoo Gandhy's passion for Indian modern and contemporary art led him to exhibit many artists who have since won international recognition. In parallel, his interest in Indian popular and tribal art encouraged him to promote these forms and to organise the first exhibition of the work of Jivya Soma Mashe in his gallery in 1975. Ten years later, the gallery published the book *The Warlis: Tribal Paintings and Legends*.

Kekoo Gandhy (1920-2012) a ouvert sa première galerie en 1963 à Bombay, la Gallery Chemould, un espace situé au premier étage de la Jehangir Art Gallery. Aujourd'hui, c'est sa fille, Shireen, qui a repris le flambeau dans un nouvel et merveilleux espace non loin de là. La passion pour l'art moderne et contemporain indien de Kekoo Gandhy l'a amené à exposer nombre des artistes aujourd'hui reconnus internationalement. En parallèle, son intérêt pour l'art populaire et l'art tribal indien lui a permis de promouvoir ces formes d'art et d'organiser la première exposition de Jivya Soma Mashe dans sa galerie en 1975. En 1985, la galerie Chemould publie le livre *The Warlis: Tribal Paintings and Legends*.

Photographs of Kekoo Gandhy and Jivya Soma Mashe,
1970s and 2000s.
Courtesy Gallery Chemould.

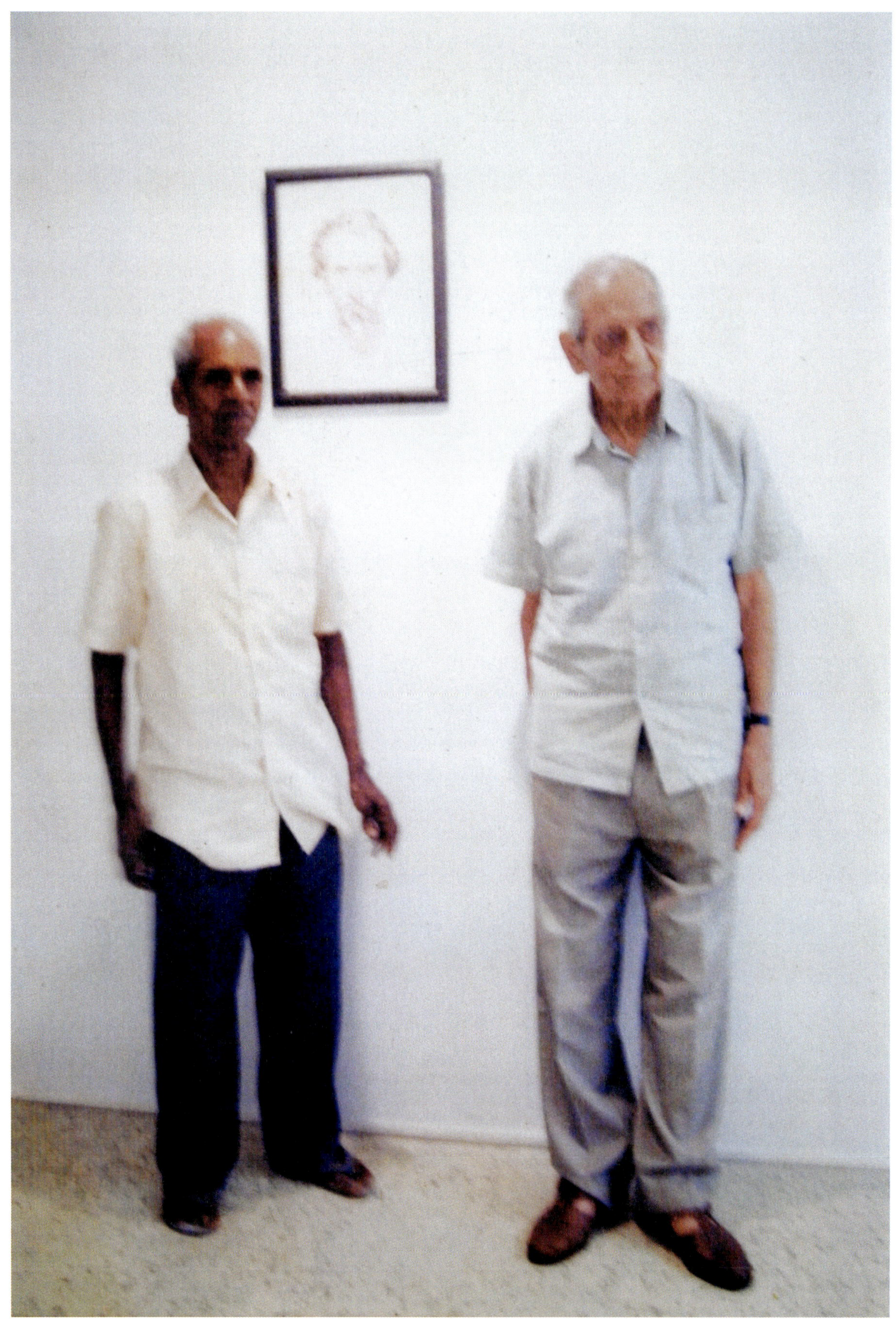

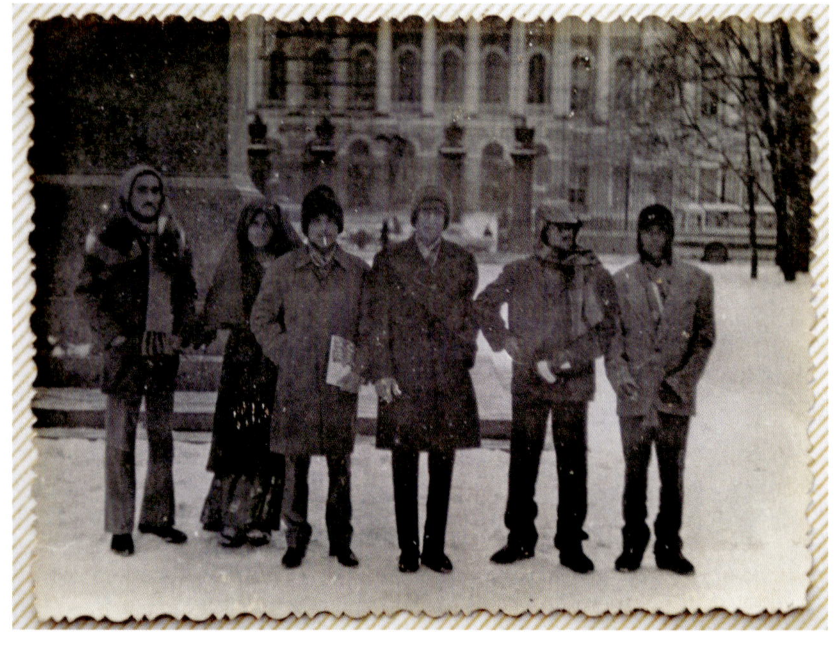

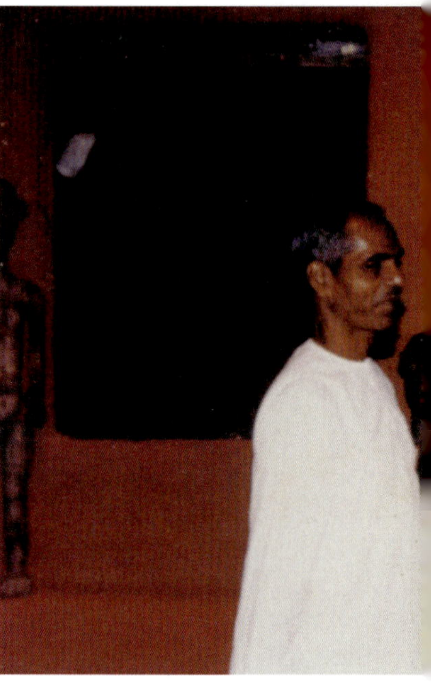

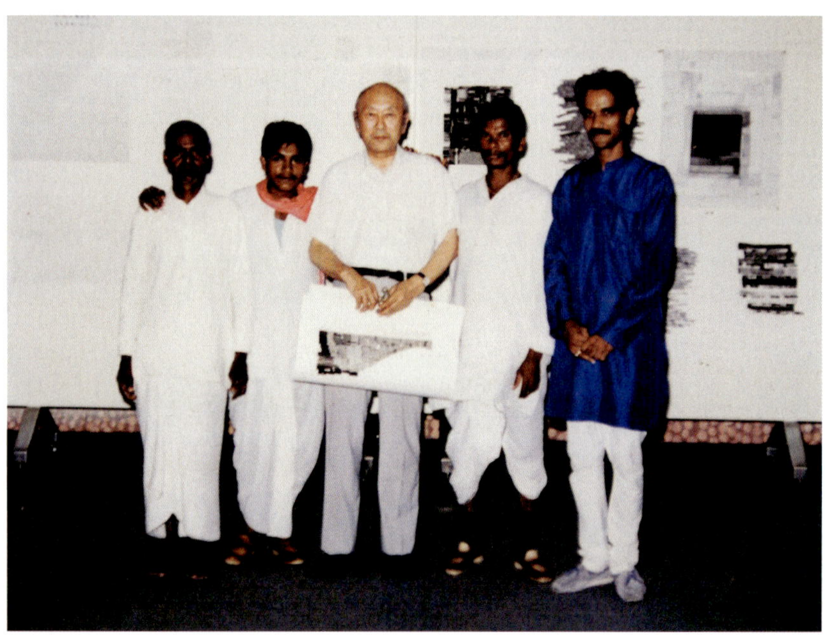

Jivya Soma Mashe 'around the world'.
From left to right: in the United States; with Pupul Jayakar in the Craft Museum in Delhi; in Italy; in Japan (on the left in the photo; to his left, Jangarh Singh Shyam with the red scarf and Akilesh on the far right with the blue *kurta*); with Sadashiv in Germany; and in Canada.

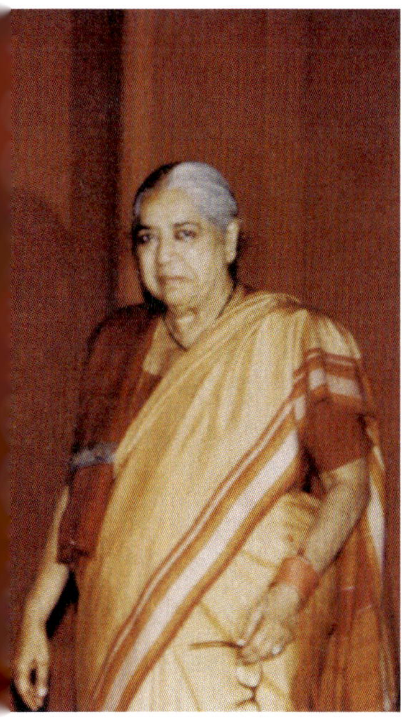
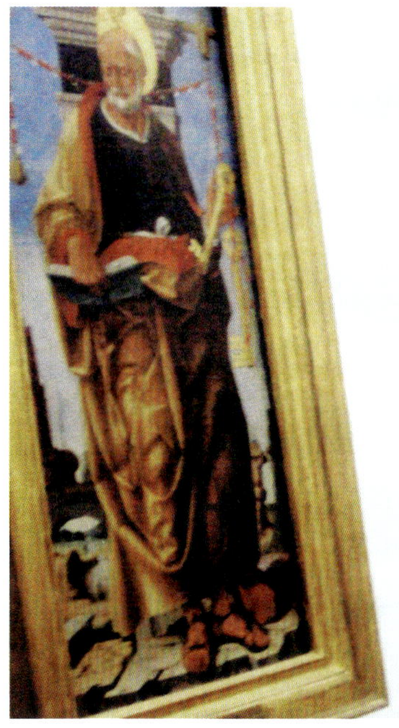
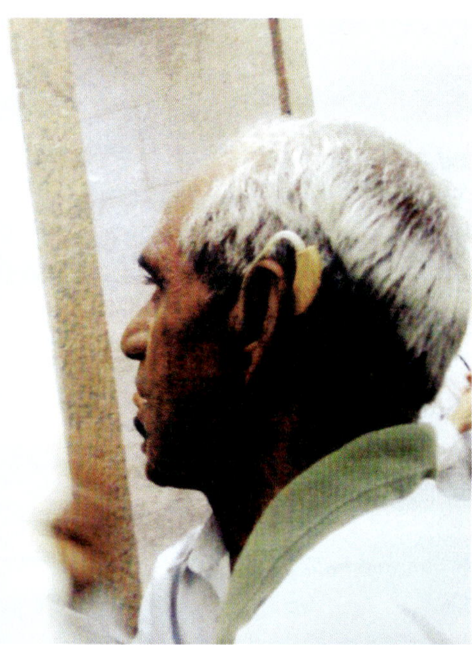
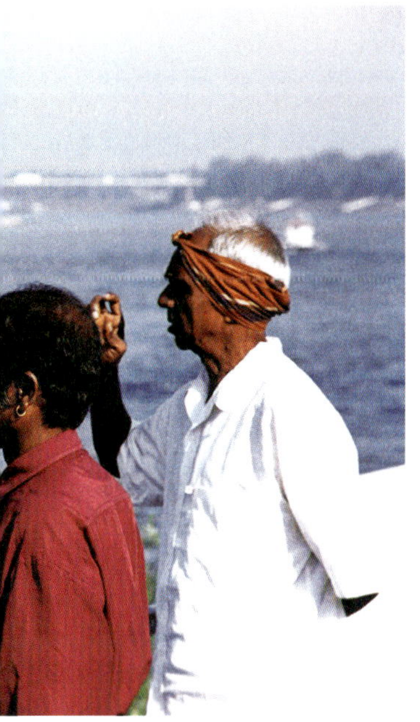
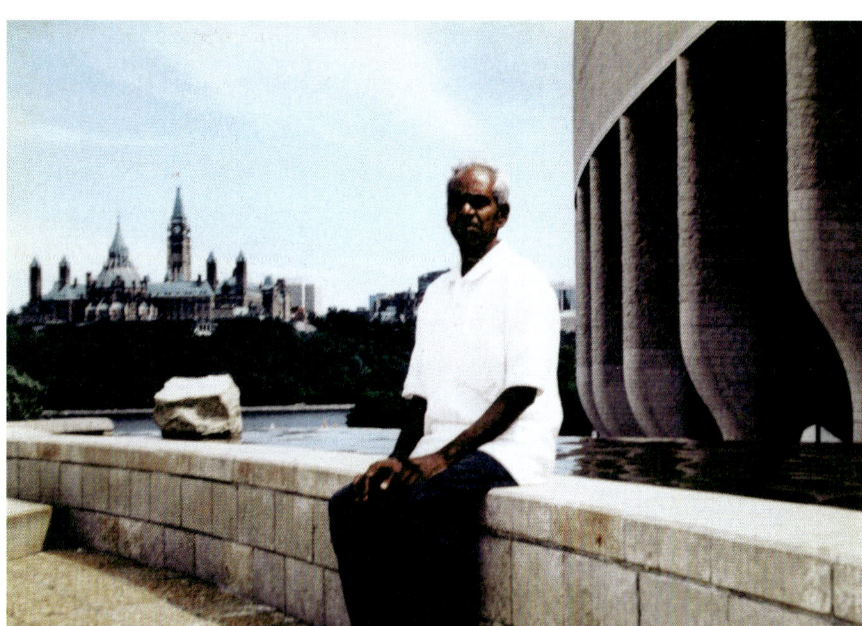

Pages 30–31
Jivya Soma Mashe and Indira Gandhi during the ceremony for his first national award in 1976.
Photo taken by Hervé Perdriolle, under the awning of Jivya Soma Mashe's house, Ganjad (Maharashtra, India), 2011.

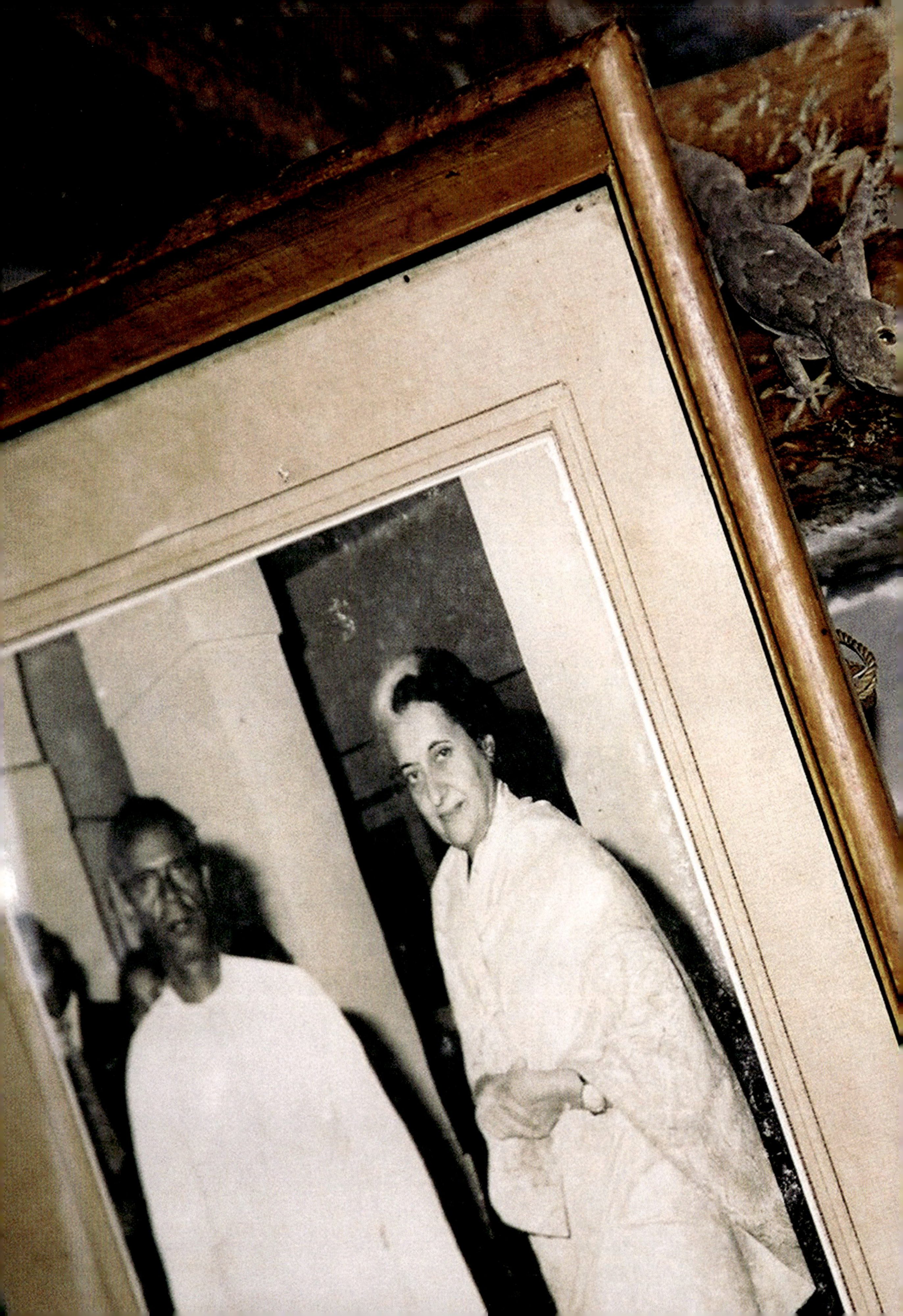

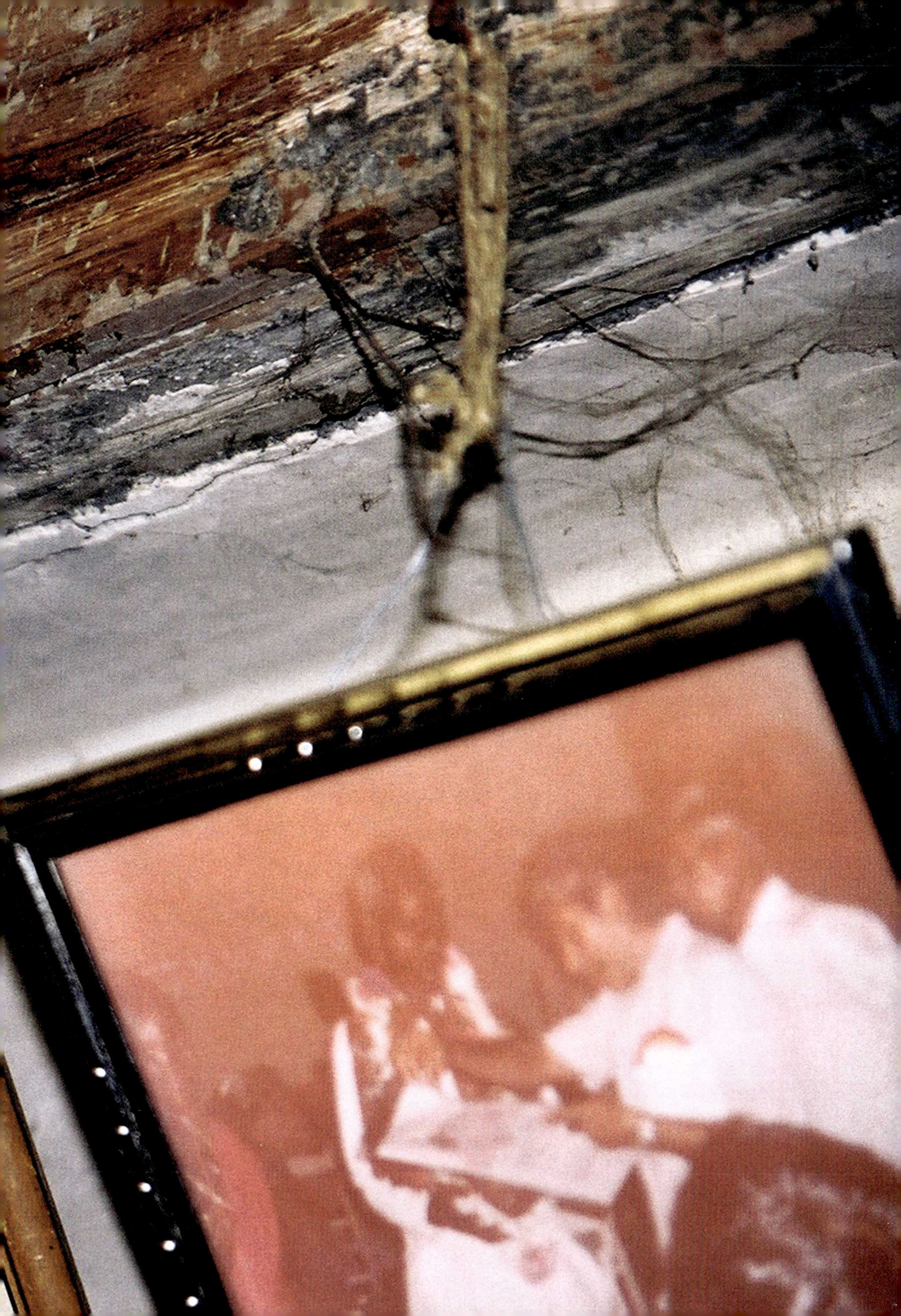

A MEETING WITH JIVYA SOMA MASHE
RENCONTRE AVEC JIVYA SOMA MASHE

My first exploratory trip regarding Indian tribal and popular art took me to the Warli tribe in the Thane district (Maharashtra) in 1997. Yashodhara Dalmia's book *The Painted World of the Warlis*, which I read in Pondicherry, was one of the most recent and complete on the subject. During this trip, I benefited from a contact at the Alliance française in Mumbai. An exhibition on Warli painting had been set up there by Vishwas Kulkarni. Vishwas is the nephew of Bhaskar Kulkarni, one of the first emissaries sent out by Pupul Jayakar during the 1970s to meet with the various tribal communities, the Warlis in particular. Bhaskar's passion for this tribe and the time he devoted to it had given him the opportunity to learn the Warli dialect. Taking his nephew on his many trips, he had begun to teach Vishwas the dialect too. Consequently, Vishwas Kulkarni became an ideal intermediary with regard to this ethnic group. I first met him at the Alliance française in the company of a young Warli artist, Shantaram Chintya Tumbada. Together they showed me several small paintings and a poster that showed a painting on the end wall of a six-storey building. The effect it had was very powerful. I quickly glanced at the caption to know who had been so daring as to commission it. To my great surprise, I saw that this enormous fresco had been executed in 1995 for the Musée Tony Garnier in Lyon, the city where I was born! I had travelled halfway round the world to discover something I could have learned fifteen minutes from my birthplace.

The lands of the Warlis are between 150 and 200 kilometres from Mumbai, on the road that leads to Ahmedabad. But in 1996 the highway between the two cities had not been built, and it took us several hours to leave the megalopolis, then get on a two-lane – and sometimes three-lane – road with its apocalyptic traffic conditions: thousands of lorries, buses, and cars, occasionally spectacular accidents, which cranes lining the road took hours to clear. Eventually, we left the main road. The first painter I met on Warli territory was

Mon premier voyage à la découverte de l'art tribal et de l'art populaire indien en 1997 me conduisit à la rencontre de la tribu warli dans le Thane District (Maharashtra). Le livre de Yashodhara Dalmia, *The Painted World of the Warlis*, que j'avais pu consulter à Pondichéry, était l'un des plus récents et des plus complets. Pour ce premier voyage, je profitai d'un contact à l'Alliance française de Mumbai. Une exposition consacrée à la peinture warli y avait été organisée par Vishwas Kulkarni. Vishwas était le neveu de Bhaskar Kulkarni, l'un des premiers émissaires de Pupul Jayakar dans les années 1970 à la rencontre de diverses communautés tribales, et tout particulièrement celle des Warlis. Sa passion pour cette tribu et le temps qu'il lui avait consacré lui avaient donné la possibilité d'apprendre le dialecte warli. Emmenant son neveu dans ses nombreux déplacements, il l'avait initié à ce dialecte. Aussi, Vishwas Kulkarni était l'intermédiaire idéal. Je le rencontrai pour la première fois à l'Alliance française en compagnie d'un jeune artiste warli, Shantaram Chintya Tumbada. Ils me montrèrent quelques peintures de petit format et un poster où l'on pouvait voir une peinture sur le mur pignon d'un immeuble de six étages. L'effet était saisissant. Je regardai hâtivement la légende accompagnant ce mur afin de savoir qui avait eu l'audace d'une telle commande. À ma grande stupeur, je découvris que cette fresque avait été réalisée pour le musée urbain Tony Garnier à Lyon, ma ville natale, en 1995 ! J'avais fait le tour du monde pour découvrir ce qui se trouvait à quinze minutes de mon lieu de naissance.

Les terres warli sont situées à seulement entre 150 et 200 km de la mégapole, sur la route qui va de Mumbai à Ahmedabad. Mais en 1996, l'autoroute reliant les deux villes n'était pas encore construite, et il nous fallut plusieurs heures pour sortir de la ville, puis emprunter une route à deux voies, parfois trois, à la circulation apocalyptique, avec ses milliers de camions, de bus et de voitures, et ses accidents spectaculaires, où les grues qui jalonnaient la route mettaient des heures à dégager les véhicules accidentés. Nous quittâmes enfin la route principale. Le premier peintre que je rencontrai sur les terres

Ratna Raghia Dushalda. I later had the chance to buy a large and atypical painting from him (for the background of this painting, he had mixed a neutral acrylic base with ash from his fire). He and my guide were well acquainted and were happy to spend time together. We drank palm wine while the women prepared the meal. The time passed. I had come from Pondicherry (1300 km away) to discover Warli painting, and this first day was passing without me having had the opportunity to see more than a dozen paintings. I showed my impatience but it was either not noticed or not understood. So I took advantage of the time required to prepare the meal to visit the village, then it was time to leave. It was only on the way back, once again stuck in endless traffic jams and then affected by the bustle of Mumbai, that I began to regret my failure to appreciate those first moments, so calm and soothing, spent in the Warli lands.

Jivya Soma Mashe is the artist with whom I have spent most time in India. Between 1997 and 2017 we saw one another at least once a year. Some photographs, in particular those taken in an exhibition in Düsseldorf, show us in deep discussion. Yet he and I were speaking different languages: he only knew his dialect, and I have only French at my command and a rather poor English.

It was not easy to meet him. At first, my contacts had led me to understand that he was no longer alive, but, during discussions with other people who had travelled in the region, I was not convinced of the fact. I badgered my contacts and they finally agreed that he was still alive but no longer painted on account of his age. However, far from satisfied with this hearsay, I located his village and set out on my first journey.

Without an address or fax or phone number, and even less internet (it was 1997), it was impossible for me to announce my arrival in advance. I left Pondicherry for Thane district on a journey that would take me two days (from Pondicherry to Madras, to Mumbai, and then to Ganjad, the village closest

warli était Ratna Raghia Dushalda. J'aurai l'occasion plus tard de lui acheter une grande peinture atypique (pour le fond de cette peinture, il avait mélangé une base acrylique neutre avec les cendres de son feu). Mon guide et lui se connaissaient bien. Ils prirent le temps de partager ce moment. Nous bûmes de l'alcool de palme pendant que les femmes préparaient le repas. Le temps passait. Je venais de Pondichéry (à 1 300 km de là) pour découvrir la peinture warli et voilà que cette première journée se déroulait sans que j'aie eu la possibilité de voir plus d'une dizaine de peintures. Je manifestai mon impatience, sans qu'elle soit ni perçue ni comprise. Alors, je profitai de la préparation du repas pour visiter le village. Puis arriva le moment de repartir. C'est seulement sur la route du retour, pris à nouveau dans des embouteillages interminables puis par l'agitation de Mumbai, que je commençai à regretter ces premiers instants, si calmes et apaisants, passés sur les terres warli, que je n'avais pas su apprécier.

Jivya Soma Mashe est l'artiste avec lequel j'ai passé le plus de temps en Inde. De 1997 à 2017, nous nous voyions au moins une fois par an. Certaines photos, je pense notamment à celles prises lors d'une exposition à Düsseldorf, nous montrent en pleine discussion. Pourtant, lui et moi parlons des langues différentes : lui ne parlant que son dialecte ; moi, le français et ne disposant que d'un anglais précaire.

Il ne m'a pas été facile de le rencontrer. Les premiers temps, mes contacts m'avaient laissé entendre qu'il était décédé. Au fil des discussions avec d'autres personnes ayant voyagé dans cette région, je n'en demeurais pas convaincu. J'insistai auprès de mes interlocuteurs. On me dit alors qu'il était toujours parmi nous mais que, très âgé, il ne peignait plus. Loin de me satisfaire de ces ouï-dire, je localisai son village et entrepris un premier voyage.

Sans adresse précise ni fax ni téléphone, et encore moins d'internet (en 1997), il m'était impossible de prévenir de mon arrivée. Je partis de Pondichéry pour le Thane district : un voyage de deux jours, de Pondichéry à Madras, de Madras à Mumbai,

to his home). But he was not at home. I took advantage of the situation to admire the sacred mountain visible in the distance from his home (*see page* 6), then headed back.

A few months later, I set out to meet him once again, but we only spent a little time together before he said he had to leave me. As I patiently awaited his return, I was told he had gone to the river to wash his clothes, as the men of his village do, because he had an exhibition in Delhi at which he had to be present. In contrast, my third trip was to be successful.

My perseverance seemed to have been appreciated. Jivya Soma Mashe showed me a few paintings, all of which were already promised to other buyers. I placed my first order with him. The paintings were to be ready three months later. It was eight months before I was able to return and take possession of them, and, as it was impossible for me to inform him of the delay, I had to hope that my order had not ended up in the hands of one of the many people who had travelled from the four corners of the world to meet him. My paintings were still there, carefully rolled up and placed out of sight on one of the few pieces of furniture in his house. This was the expression of a trust that never altered from the time of our first meeting.

When in India, I always make sure that I have a driver who speaks Marathi, the language of Jivya's home state of Maharashtra. Jivya's sons, Sadashiv and Balu, who speak Warli and Marathi, were our translators. However, I always had the impression that I spent a lot of time talking directly with Jivya. When we met, we would exchange words in his house or walking on his land. We travelled together to Germany for an exhibition that I organised with him and Richard Long. I also had the pleasure of receiving him in my home in Paris. And on each occasion, often without a translator, we continued our discussions.

What I am in search of through his art, as through that of other artists I work with, is to divest myself of superfluous knowledge. I'm in favour of cultural degrowth. I've always believed that there is little or nothing to say. These exchanges I had with Jivya Soma Mashe remind me of the theatre of Samuel Beckett, or the idea I have of it: they are like a *mise en abîme* of dialogue. Like his painting, a simple paean to movement, our discussions also remind me of the cinema of Jacques Tati, in which gestures and attitudes often replace

de Mumbai à Ganjad, le village le plus proche de sa maison. Il n'était pas là. Je profitai du voyage pour admirer la montagne sacrée qui se dresse au loin, en face de sa maison *(voir p. 6)* et fis demi-tour.

Quelques mois plus tard, je repartis à sa rencontre. Je ne le vis que très peu de temps avant qu'il ne s'éloigne. On m'expliqua, alors que j'attendais patiemment son retour, qu'il était parti à la rivière laver son linge comme le font les hommes de sa tribu, car il devait se rendre à Delhi pour une exposition. Mon troisième voyage fut le bon.

Ma persévérance semblait avoir été appréciée. Jivya Soma Mashe me montra quelques peintures, toutes déjà réservées. Je lui passai ma première commande. Les toiles devaient être prêtes trois mois plus tard. Je ne pus retourner en prendre possession qu'au bout de huit mois, espérant, puisqu'il était impossible de le prévenir de mon retard, que ma commande n'avait pas fini entre les mains d'un des nombreux voyageurs venant des quatre coins du monde pour le rencontrer. Mes peintures étaient toujours là, soigneusement roulées et posées à l'abri des regards en haut d'un des rares meubles de sa maison. C'était là la marque d'une confiance qui ne s'est jamais altérée depuis notre première rencontre.

Je fais toujours en sorte d'avoir un chauffeur parlant le marathi, langue de l'État du Maharashtra où habite Jivya. Les fils de Jivya, Sadashiv et Balu, qui parlent le warli et le marathi, nous servent de traducteurs. Cependant, j'ai toujours eu l'impression d'avoir passé beaucoup de temps à parler directement avec Jivya. Lors de nos rencontres, nous échangeons des paroles, dans sa maison, en nous promenant sur ses terres. Nous avons voyagé ensemble en Allemagne à l'occasion d'une exposition que j'ai organisée avec lui et Richard Long. J'ai eu le plaisir de le recevoir aussi chez moi à Paris. Et dans toutes ces occasions, bien souvent sans traducteur, nous avons continué nos conversations.

Ce que je recherche à travers son art, comme à travers celui d'autres artistes avec lesquels je travaille, c'est de me défaire de connaissances superflues. Je suis en faveur de la décroissance culturelle. J'ai toujours considéré qu'il n'y a rien à dire ou si peu. Ces échanges avec Jivya Soma Mashe, ces dialogues, me font penser au théâtre de Beckett, à l'idée que je m'en fais, le connaissant peu : une mise en abîme du dialogue. Nos discussions me font également penser, tout comme sa peinture, simple éloge du mouvement, au cinéma de Tati, bien souvent sans paroles, les gestes et les attitudes se substituant au dia-

dialogue, or of Godard, which eludes meaning and instead abstracts it to achieve a state of grace, that of the present moment. Jivya Soma Mashe's acclamation of life and movement in his work is also a eulogy to the present moment. We shared this need for solitude and shared silence.

Not having precise instructions on how I wanted my paintings on canvas, for my first commission Jivya Soma Mashe produced them on a terracotta-coloured background, like the paintings on the walls of Warli houses, and used a brush with white acrylic to paint the motifs. Like almost all Warli artists, Jivya often preferred painting on canvas, if only to meet an ever-increasing demand for his works. The result pleased both his commissioners and his buyers. The clarity of the contrast between the background and the motifs, and the clean definition of the brushstrokes, were universally more appreciated than the results achieved by the traditional bamboo stick, with its somewhat random, imprecise marks. The widespread use of the terracotta background colour was also no doubt due to the possibility of using it in all seasons, something that was not the case with the juice of cow dung: in the dry season, cow dung juice is a dark brown, which is not just attractive but also effective with regard to the contrast obtained with motifs painted white; however, from the rainy season onward, which produces lush vegetation, this juice turns a bland and unattractive greenish colour.

Previously, notably for his exhibitions in the 1970s of paintings on paper, Jivya Soma Mashe coated the paper with a background colour made from cow dung juice. Up until that time, a purification ceremony had been performed on mud walls before any ritual painting was made. These backgrounds, applied by hand, left traces of the broad sweeping motions made by the artist's arm. These movements of great visual effectiveness can still be seen each morning on the earth floors in Warli houses, made during the daily practice of purifying and washing the floors.

For the next works on canvas I commissioned, I asked Jivya Soma Mashe to create these cow dung juice backgrounds on the blank canvas. They contributed considerably to the final result of each painting, allowing the painted scenes to create a vibrating effect through their layering over broad circular movements. I also asked Jivya not to work with a brush but to use the traditional bamboo stick instead.

I wanted him to do only medium and large paintings for me.

logue, ou encore au cinéma de Godard qui déjoue le sens pour l'abstraire et arriver à un état de grâce, celui de l'instant présent. L'éloge de la vie et du mouvement dans l'œuvre de Jivya Soma Mashe est aussi celui du temps présent. Nous avions en commun ce besoin de solitude et de silence partagé.

Pour ma première commande de peintures sur toile, sans instructions précises, Jivya Soma Mashe les avait réalisées avec un fond couleur *terracotta*, comme les murs des maisons, et à l'aide d'un pinceau à l'acrylique blanche pour les sujets peints. Ce parti pris pour les peintures sur toile était devenu alors souvent le sien, comme celui de la quasi-totalité des artistes warli, simplement pour répondre à une demande de plus en plus forte. Le résultat plaisait à ses commanditaires et acheteurs. L'efficacité du contraste extrêmement lisible entre le fond et les sujets, l'aspect propre et appliqué du trait au pinceau, étaient globalement plus appréciés que l'utilisation du traditionnel bâtonnet de bambou en guise de pinceau et son tracé aléatoire et peu précis. La généralisation de la couleur *terracotta* répondait aussi sans doute à la possibilité de l'utiliser en toutes saisons, ce qui n'était pas forcément le cas pour le jus de bouse de vache. De fait, dans les saisons sèches, le jus de bouche de vache obtenu était d'un brun sombre, particulièrement séduisant et efficace dans le contraste obtenu avec les sujets peints en blanc, et, à partir de la saison des pluies suivie d'une végétation florissante, ce jus devenait verdâtre, une couleur fade et peu attrayante.

Précédemment, notamment pour ses expositions dans les années 1970 de peintures réalisées sur papier, Jivya Soma Mashe enduisait ses feuilles de papier d'un fond réalisé à l'aide d'un jus de bouse de vache. Un rituel de purification qui était jusqu'alors utilisé sur les murs en torchis avant la réalisation de toute peinture rituelle. Ces fonds réalisés à l'aide de ce jus directement à la main laissaient la trace des larges mouvements circulaires du bras. Un geste circulaire ample d'une grande efficacité visuelle que l'on peut encore apercevoir chaque matin au sol en terre des maisons warli, pratique quotidienne pour purifier et laver les sols.

Pour mes prochaines œuvres sur toiles, je demandai à Jivya Soma Mashe de réaliser directement sur la toile vierge ces fonds en jus de bouse de vache. L'apport des fonds ainsi obtenus était considérable dans le résultat final de chaque peinture, permettant aux scènes peintes d'offrir un effet de vibration grâce à leurs superpositions aux amples mouvements circulaires. Je demandai à Jivya également de ne plus utiliser le pinceau mais le traditionnel bâtonnet de bambou.

Considering that this art form used to be exclusively mural-based, I thought he would be more at ease with these sizes and that his imagination would be more creative.

After several visits to him, I noticed that he sometimes asked for help from his friends and family. As this must be the custom for commercial commissions, I asked him to work on my paintings by himself.

I rarely made requests for a specific theme, except for an occasional demand for the themes of the fishing net and ant spiral, two subjects at which Jivya excelled. The collectors I worked with were as fond of these two themes as I was. Jivya painted some thirty pictures of fishing nets in the course of his life, all of them intimately different. To see several of them together is a wonderful experience, as I had the chance to do when I exhibited three of them in the same room at the Manoir de Martigny in 2018, the year Jivya Soma Mashe died (*see pages* 208–209).

This book unites forty or so of Mashe's paintings, most of which were created for me between 1997 and 2016. Today, they have for the most part found their way into high quality collections, including those of the Fondation Cartier, Agnès B, the Florence and Daniel Guerlain Collection, the Pierre-Alexis and Sophie Dumas Collection, and Société Générale.

Jivya stopped painting Palagatha, the mother goddess, in works of a secular nature, leaving this figure in ritual paintings alone. When he painted *chauks*, the square, the enclosed space, he no longer placed Palagatha at its centre but Gauri and Mahadev, the foundational couple of the Warli cosmogony, or sometimes a simple representation of a bride and groom on a horse.

Jivya Soma Mashe broadened his representations of human activities in the Warli lands and began to paint images of his tribe's tales and legends, which have been passed down orally from generation to generation. Such stories have existed in all latitudes for as long as collective memory has existed, edifying tales that teach lessons of human conduct, parables, as in the fables of La Fontaine, and fabliaux, as if to illustrate such lessons. The titles of Jivya's works found in this book that have been taken from tales include *The Wandering Tribes*, *The Man Who Didn't Want to Work*, and *The Hermit's Daughter*. Nursery rhymes also convey an awareness of ecology and the timeless interdependence between man and nature.

Je souhaitais qu'il réalise pour moi uniquement des peintures de moyen et grand format. Considérant que cet art était autrefois exclusivement mural, j'imaginais qu'il serait plus à l'aise sur ce type de formats et que son imaginaire pourrait mieux s'y déployer.

Ayant observé après quelques visites qu'il se faisait parfois aider par ses proches, comme cela devait être l'usage pour des commandes commerciales, je lui demandai qu'il intervienne seul pour chaque œuvre qu'il réaliserait à mon intention.

Mes requêtes n'incluaient pratiquement jamais de thème spécifique, excepté une demande sporadiquement ravivée pour le filet de pêche et la spirale de fourmis, deux sujets dans lesquels Jivya Soma Mashe excellait. Les collectionneurs avec lesquels je travaillais aimaient tout autant que moi ces deux thèmes. Jivya a peut-être réalisé au cours de sa vie une trentaine de filets de pêche, tous intimement différents. Voir plusieurs d'entre eux rassemblés serait merveilleux, ce que j'eus la possibilité d'entrevoir lorsque j'en exposai trois dans une même pièce, au Manoir de Martigny, en 2018, l'année de la disparition de Jivya Soma Mashe (*voir pages* 208-209).

Ce livre rassemble une quarantaine de peintures que Jivya Soma Mashe a réalisées, majoritairement à mon attention, entre 1997 et 2016, peintures qui ont aujourd'hui pour la plupart rejoint de belles collections, dont en France celles de la Fondation Cartier, d'Agnès B, de la collection de Florence et Daniel Guerlain, de Pierre-Alexis et Sophie Dumas, ou encore de la Société Générale.

Dans ses peintures profanes, Jivya Soma Mashe a cessé de représenter Palagatha, la déesse mère, laissant cette représentation aux seuls usages des peintures rituelles. Lorsqu'il peint encore des *cauks*, le carré, l'espace clos, ce n'est plus Palagatha que l'on y voit en son centre mais Gauri et Mahadev, le couple initial fondateur de la cosmogonie warli, ou parfois la simple représentation des mariés sur un cheval.

Jivya élargit ses représentations des activités humaines observées sur les terres warli aux contes et légendes de sa tribu transmis jusqu'alors oralement de génération en génération. Des contes et légendes semblables à ceux et à celles qui existent sous toutes les latitudes depuis aussi longtemps que la mémoire collective nous permet de nous en souvenir. Des légendes comme des récits édifiants à travers lesquels apparaissent des leçons de conduite. Des paraboles, comme dans les fables de La Fontaine, des fabliaux comme pour illustrer un

The primary focus of this book is on details of many of these paintings, because it is through them that Jivya Soma Mashe's work can be properly appreciated, as well as the degree to which it stands apart from the commercial production that still too often typifies Warli painting in the eyes of the general public.

enseignement. *Les tribus errantes*, *L'homme qui ne voulait pas travailler*, *La fille de l'ermite*, sont parmi les titres des contes que l'on retrouve dans ce livre. Ces comptines expriment aussi une conscience de l'écologie, comme la manifestation d'une interdépendance immémoriale entre l'homme et la nature.

Le parti pris de ce livre a été de privilégier les détails de nombre de ces peintures, car c'est réellement à l'aune de ces détails que s'apprécie l'œuvre de Jivya Soma Mashe et qu'elle se démarque pleinement d'une simple production commerciale qui caractérise encore trop souvent la peinture warli aux yeux du grand public.

The early collectors of Jivya Soma Mashe's works were essentially collectors of contemporary art whose curiosity had been piqued by the exhibition *Magiciens de la terre*. One of them surprised me by his personal approach to Warli painting. An expert in sixteenth- and seventeenth-century Flemish paintings at Sotheby's, he was especially fascinated by the very special attention given in this tribal painting to scenes of daily rural life, a subject that was little addressed in art history.

The painting opposite shows the different phases in the cultivation of rice, from sowing to harvest.

Parmi mes premiers collectionneurs des œuvres de Jivya Soma Mashe, essentiellement des collectionneurs d'art contemporain à la curiosité aiguisée par l'exposition *Magiciens de la terre*, l'un d'entre eux m'a surpris par son approche personnelle de la peinture warli. Expert en peinture flamande des XVIe et XVIIe siècles auprès de Sotheby's, il était surtout séduit par le fait de retrouver dans cette peinture tribale une attention toute particulière apportée aux scènes quotidiennes de la vie rurale, un sujet peu abordé dans l'histoire de l'art.

La toile ci-contre rassemble, à travers les scènes peintes, les diverses étapes de la culture du riz, de la semence à la récolte.

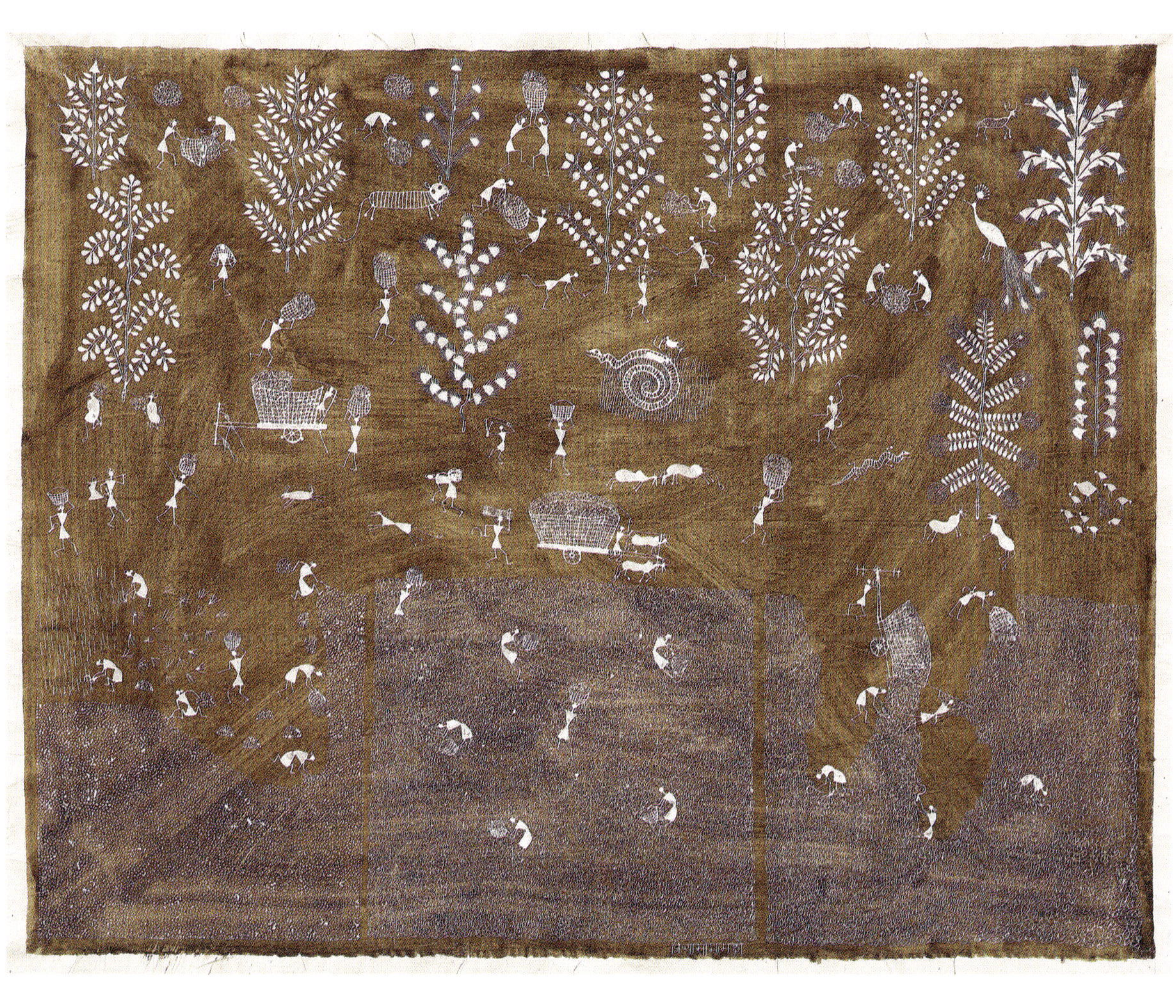

Jivya Soma Mashe, *Rice Season*, 1997,
acrylic and cow dung on canvas,
100 × 125 cm; 39.37 × 49.21 in. (*details on pages* 40–43)
Collection of Fidelity, London.
Photo by Christian Baraja.

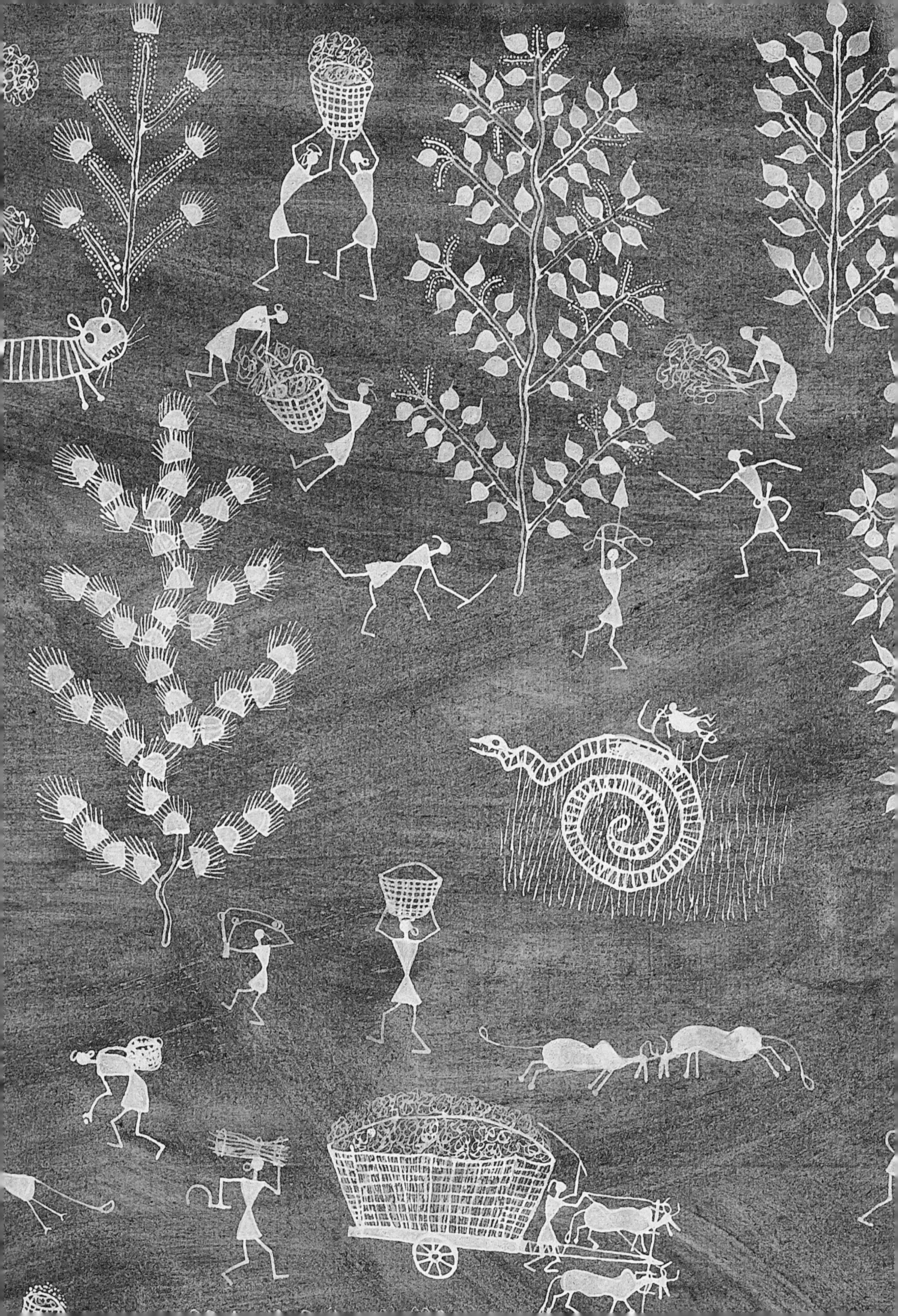

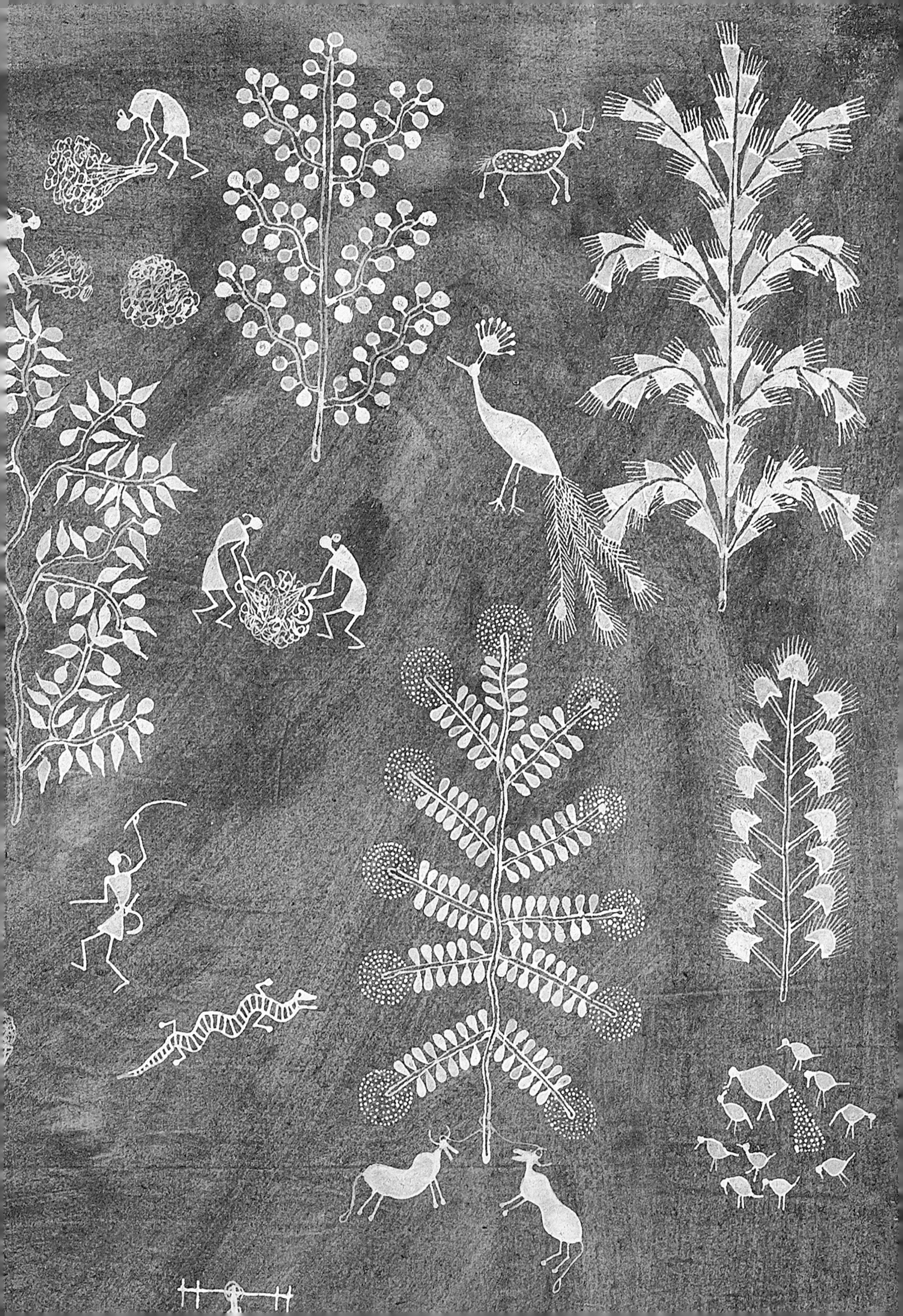

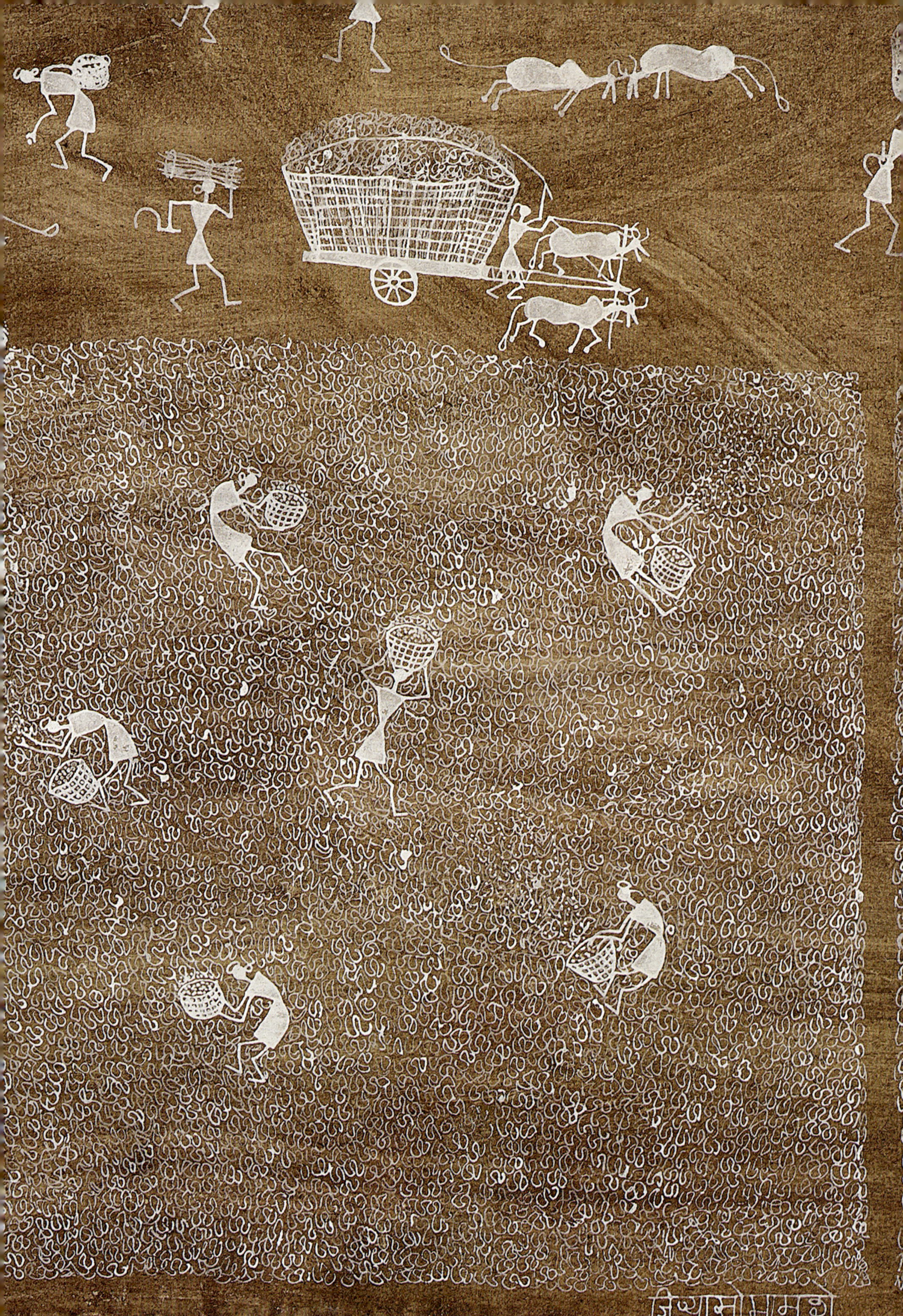
जिव्या सोमा मशे

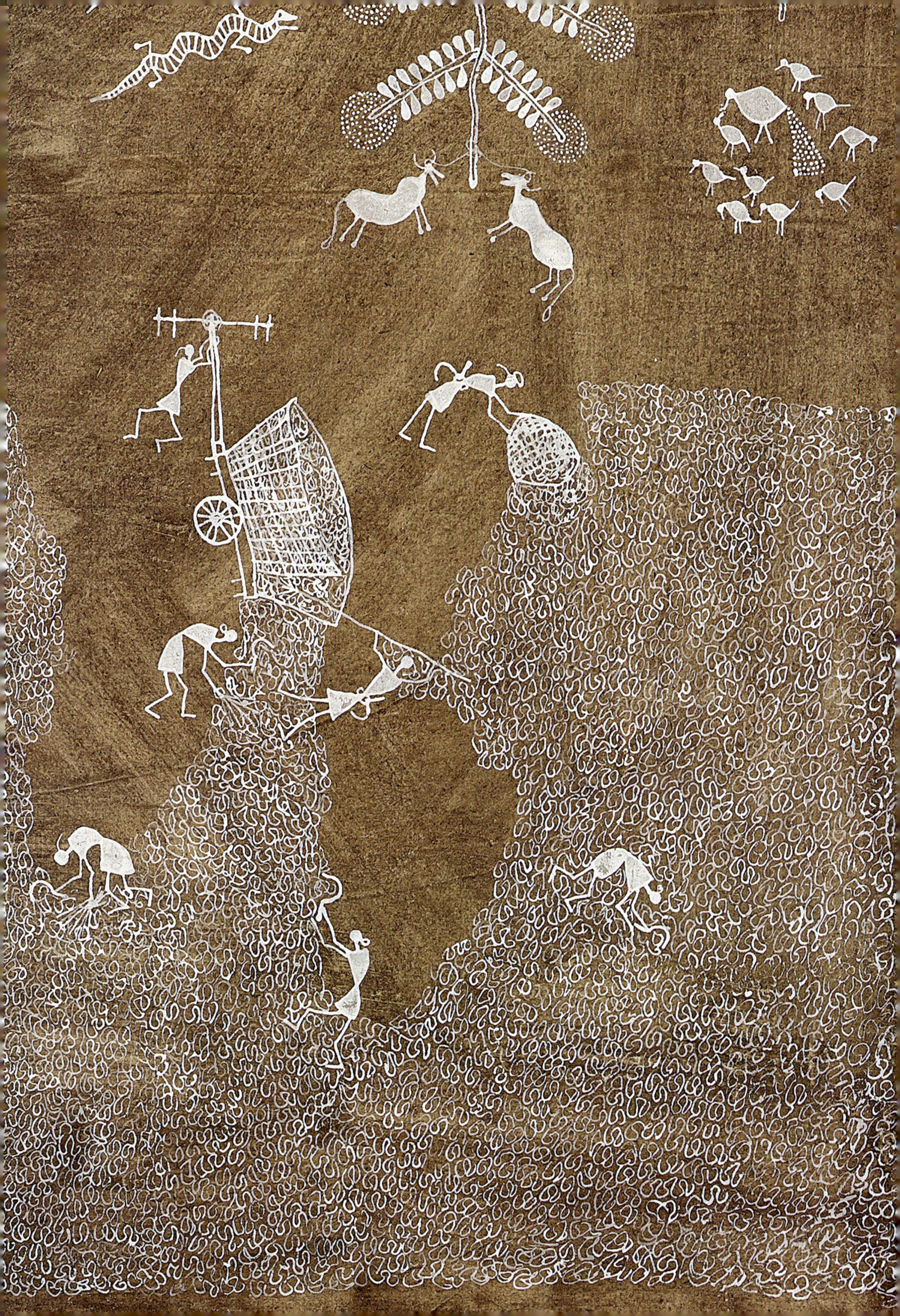

JIVYA SOMA MASHE, PAINTER AND FARMER

JIVYA SOMA MASHE, PEINTRE ET PAYSAN

Yashodhara Dalmia's text, published in 1988, foreshadowed what would happen to Warli painting in the following decades. It became divided between a broad and increasingly uncritical demand from an audience mainly interested in exotic paintings and a few rare discerning enthusiasts keen to understand this artistic evolution on durable mediums (paper and canvas) while striving to preserve its essence.

Interest in Indian folk and tribal arts steadily grew in the subcontinent, bolstered by the greater presence of these forms of expression in India's state emporiums in all the country's major cities. This enthusiasm encouraged a trend that initially directed public interest toward Madhubani (or Mithila) painting, the art of the Gond and Bhil tribes, and later toward the Warlis. One trend replaced another, only to return at a later moment to an earlier one.

Warli art is as well-known in India as the paintings of Australian Aboriginal artists are in Europe and the United States. Some fashion designers draw on Warli pictography for use in their own creations. It was also a direct source of inspiration for all the signage used at the 2008 Commonwealth Youth Games in Pune. Coca-Cola used Warli pictorial style as the basis for its national advertising campaign during the Diwali festival in 2010 (TV adverts, hoardings, press campaigns, and posters), and Warli art was featured on a five-rupee postage stamp issued in 2012, printed in a run of 1,100,000.

This success has allowed hundreds of Warli families to boost their often meagre and unpredictable agricultural income by selling small paintings purely for commercial reasons.

Among these families, a few members of the Warli tribe have, like Jivya Soma Mashe, stood out for their pictorial style and attracted the attention of museums and collectors in India and abroad. Since 2010, Warli women, who had withdrawn from this ancestral practice that had originally been their own, have returned to painting on canvas and paper. Given the extent to which the contemporary market for tribal art has expanded since 2000, the questions Yashodhara Dalmia had posed in the

Le texte de Yashodhara Dalmia publié en 1988 préfigurait bien ce qu'il allait advenir dans les décennies suivantes de la peinture warli, partagée par une large et de plus en plus forte demande peu exigeante d'un public principalement intéressé par des peintures exotiques et par quelques rares amateurs éclairés soucieux d'appréhender cette évolution picturale sur des supports durables (papier et toile) tout en tâchant d'en préserver l'essence.

L'intérêt pour les arts populaires et tribaux indiens dans le sous-continent allait grandissant, renforcé par une présence accrue de ces formes d'expression dans les emporiums d'État de toutes les grandes villes. Cet engouement avait un effet de mode portant l'intérêt du public d'abord vers le Madhubani painting (ou Mithila painting), la peinture des tribus gond et bhil, puis vers celle de la tribu warli. Une mode chassant l'autre pour revenir alternativement à l'une de ces premières tendances.

On peut dire que l'art des Warlis est aussi connu en Inde que la peinture des peintres aborigènes d'Australie en Europe et aux États-Unis. Certains couturiers s'inspirent de la pictographie warli pour leurs propres créations. Pictographie qui a été aussi la source d'inspiration directe pour toute la signalétique des Jeux du Young Commonwealth en 2008 à Pune. Coca-Cola a fait sa campagne nationale pour la fête de la Diwali 2010 en empruntant leur style pictural (spots télévisés, billboard, campagne presse et affichage). L'art des Warlis a fait l'objet de l'émission en 2012 d'un timbre-poste de 5 roupies indiennes édité à 1 100 000 exemplaires.

Ce succès a permis à des centaines de familles warli de compléter leurs revenus agricoles, souvent maigres et aléatoires, par la vente de petites peintures à de seules et salvatrices fins commerciales. Parmi ces centaines de familles, quelques autres membres de la tribu warli, à l'instar de Jivya Soma Mashe, se sont distingués par leur style pictural et ont attiré l'attention de musées et de collectionneurs en Inde et à l'étranger. Depuis les années 2010, il est à noter que les femmes warli, qui s'étaient éloignées de cette pratique artistique ancestrale qui initialement était la leur, font leur retour à la peinture sur toile et papier. Les questionnements de Yashodhara Dalmia dans les années 1980

1980s about Jivya Soma Mashe's ability to remain principled and to cope with the growing commercial demand can now be extended to any artist. The demand today for the work of celebrated artists, regardless of their cultural origin, is so strong that it is legitimate to wonder about their ability to withstand the recurring pressure for their most popular works. The leap into the unknown that a tribal artist may have been obliged to take when confronted with the contemporary art world has also evolved over the past few decades. From *Magiciens de la terre* in 1989 at the Centre Pompidou to the *Stranieri Ovunque – Foreigners Everywhere* exhibition at the 2024 Venice Biennale, the contemporary art world has progressively opened its doors to all minorities that were previously little represented or almost entirely excluded. The combination of the internet, mobile phones, and easier travel have facilitated access to and the circulation of artworks, whatever their cultural or geographical origins.

The global village has grown larger and increasingly become a reality in which works by contemporary artists from ancestral communities with worldviews based on animism and the fellowship of all living beings are now infused with an undeniable contemporaneity. Their art, rooted in some of the most ancient traditions still practised today, address issues current in today's world: otherness (from the Low Latin word *alteritas*, meaning difference) and climate change. Our relationship with art is changing. What might previously have been considered a simple search for exoticism has become a source of inspiration and food for thought. *Partage d'exotismes*, the name of an exhibition curated by Jean-Hubert Martin for the Lyon Biennale in 2000, is illustrative of this change of direction. The art of Jivya Soma Mashe belongs to this new landscape. His integrity, discussed by Yashodhara Dalmia, stems from the simple fact that all his life he was both a painter and a farmer. By narrowing the gap between working on his paintings and working in the fields, he remained close to his subject and his identity.

sur la capacité de Jivya Soma Mashe à rester intègre et à pouvoir faire face à une demande commerciale accrue peuvent s'étendre depuis les années 2000 à tout artiste, tant le marché de l'art contemporain s'est développé. La demande aujourd'hui est tellement impressionnante pour un artiste apprécié, courtisé, quelles que soient ses origines culturelles, que l'on peut aussi s'interroger sur sa capacité à ne pas céder à une demande récurrente pour ses œuvres les plus appréciées. Le saut dans l'inconnu qui pouvait être celui d'un artiste d'origine tribale confronté au monde de l'art contemporain a lui aussi changé ces dernières décennies. Des *Magiciens de la terre* en 1989 au Centre Pompidou à l'exposition *Stranieri Ovunque – Foreigners Everywhere* à la Biennale de Venise en 2024, le monde de l'art contemporain a ouvert progressivement ses portes à toutes les minorités jusque-là peu représentées ou quasiment exclues. Internet, la téléphonie mobile et les facilités de déplacement favorisent l'accès et la circulation des œuvres, quelles que soient leurs origines culturelles et géographiques.

Le village global s'étend et devient de plus en plus une réalité où les propositions des artistes contemporains issus de communautés ancestrales liées à l'animisme, à la communauté des êtres vivants, apparaissent dès lors dans une contemporanéité d'évidence. Leur art, dérivant de pratiques artistiques parmi les plus anciennes encore pratiquées de nos jours, dialogue avec nos problématiques actuelles, l'altérité (bas latin *alteritas*, différence) et l'urgence climatique. Notre rapport à l'art change. Ce qui pouvait être perçu jusqu'alors comme une simple recherche d'exotisme devient source de réflexion et d'inspiration. *Partage d'exotismes*, titre d'une exposition organisée par Jean-Hubert Martin pour la Biennale de Lyon 2000, illustre ce changement de cap. L'œuvre de Jivya Soma Mashe s'inscrit dans ce nouveau paysage. Son intégrité évoquée par Yashodhara Dalmia tient également au simple fait qu'il a été toute sa vie peintre et paysan. En réduisant la séparation entre le travail artistique et le travail aux champs, il a su rester au plus près de son sujet, de son identité.

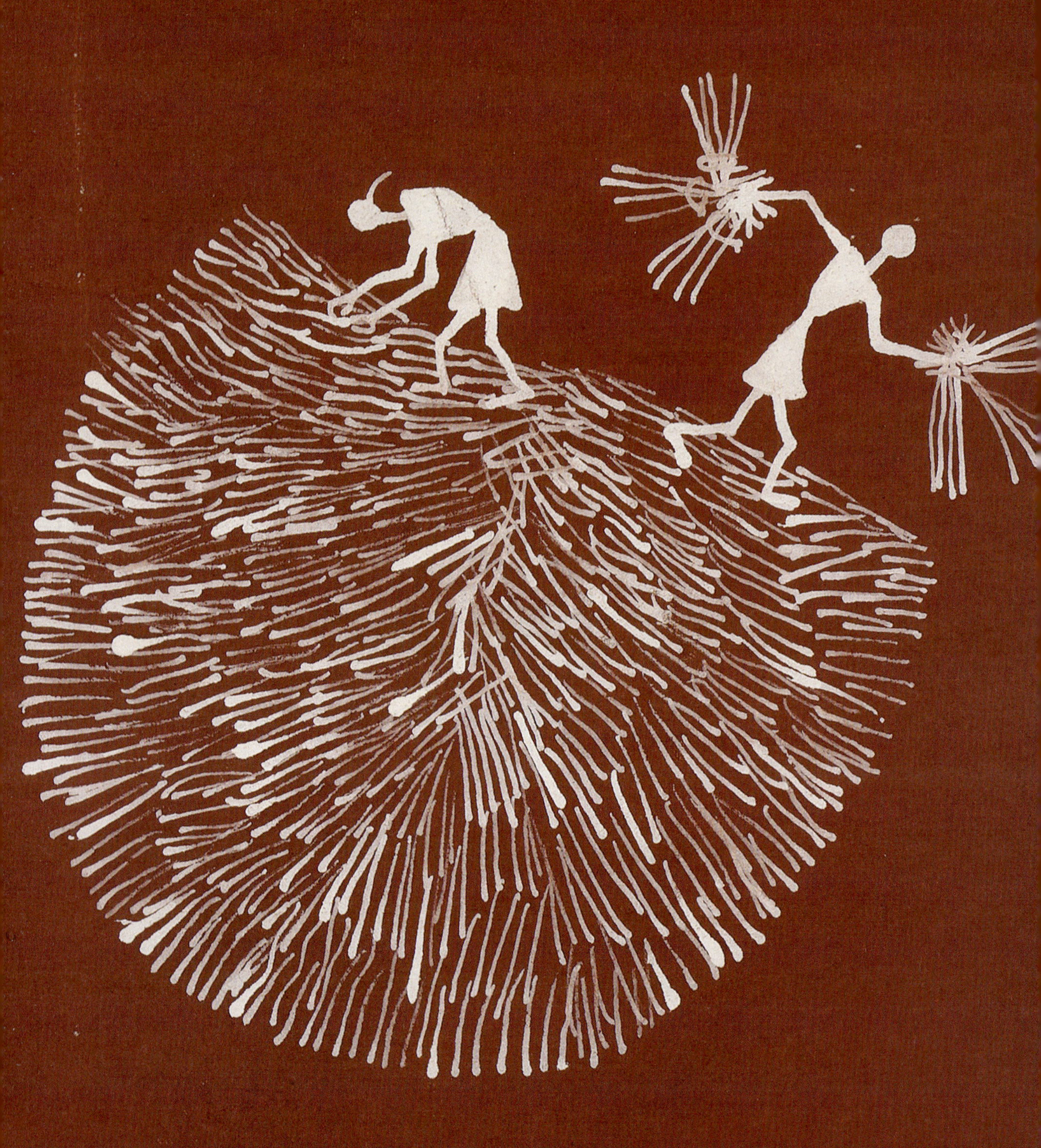

For this painting, Jivya Soma Mashe used white acrylic for the motifs and a neutral acrylic base mixed with pigment similar to the terracotta colour of Warli house walls for the background. Rather than a paintbrush, the artist used a bamboo stick chewed at the end so that it resembled the hairs of a brush. The inevitably imprecise result means the lines of the painting are irregular. The overall appearance is not dissimilar to rock art. The subject of the painting is the bailing of rice straw at the time of the rice harvest. The figures in movement suggest the early days of moving pictures, when the speed of eighteen images per second made it possible to interpret the many individual intermittent images as a single moving image. The decomposition of movement in the painting also has affinities with the chronophotography of Étienne-Jules Marey and Eadweard Muybridge, in which the many stages of the movements of a figure or animal were shown on a single photograph.

Pour cette peinture, Jivya Soma Mashe utilise pour les sujets peints de l'acrylique blanche et pour le fond de la toile une base acrylique neutre mélangée avec un pigment coloré semblable à la couleur *terracotta* des murs des maisons warli. En lieu et place de pinceau, Jivya peint avec un bâtonnet de bambou mâchonné afin de l'assouplir comme les poils d'un pinceau. L'aspect toujours irrégulier qui en résulte confère à l'œuvre peinte un trait lui-même irrégulier. L'aspect général de cette petite peinture n'est pas sans évoquer l'art rupestre. Le sujet en est la description du travail lié à la récolte du riz, de la paille de riz, et plus précisément à la mise en balle de la paille de riz. Les personnages en mouvement peuvent évoquer le début du cinématographe. La technologie du cinématographe en ces temps-là réduite à 18 images par seconde laisse voir le mouvement interrompu en de multiples vues intermittentes. La décomposition du mouvement dans le tableau présente également des affinités avec la chronophotographie d'Étienne-Jules Marey et d'Eadweard Muybridge, dans laquelle les nombreuses étapes des mouvements d'une figure ou d'un animal étaient montrées sur une seule photographie.

Bailing Hay, 2001 (*detail*),
acrylic on canvas,
46 × 61 cm; 18.11 × 24.01 in.

Pages 48–49
Jivya Soma Mashe, *Bailing Hay*, 2001,
acrylic on canvas,
46 × 61 cm; 18.11 × 24.01 in.
Collection of Patrick Le Guen-Ténot.
Photo by Christian Baraja.

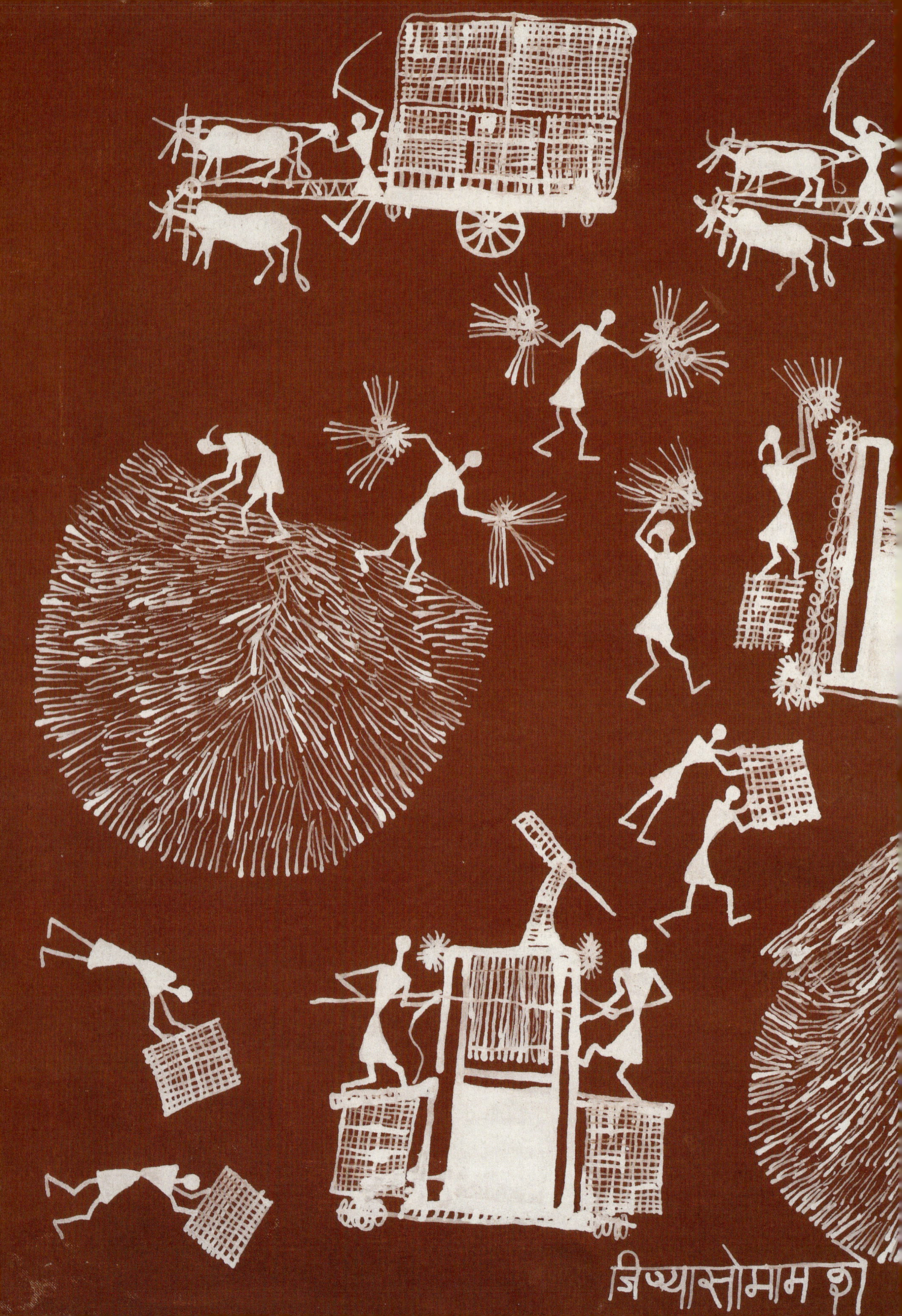
जिव्यासोमाम शे

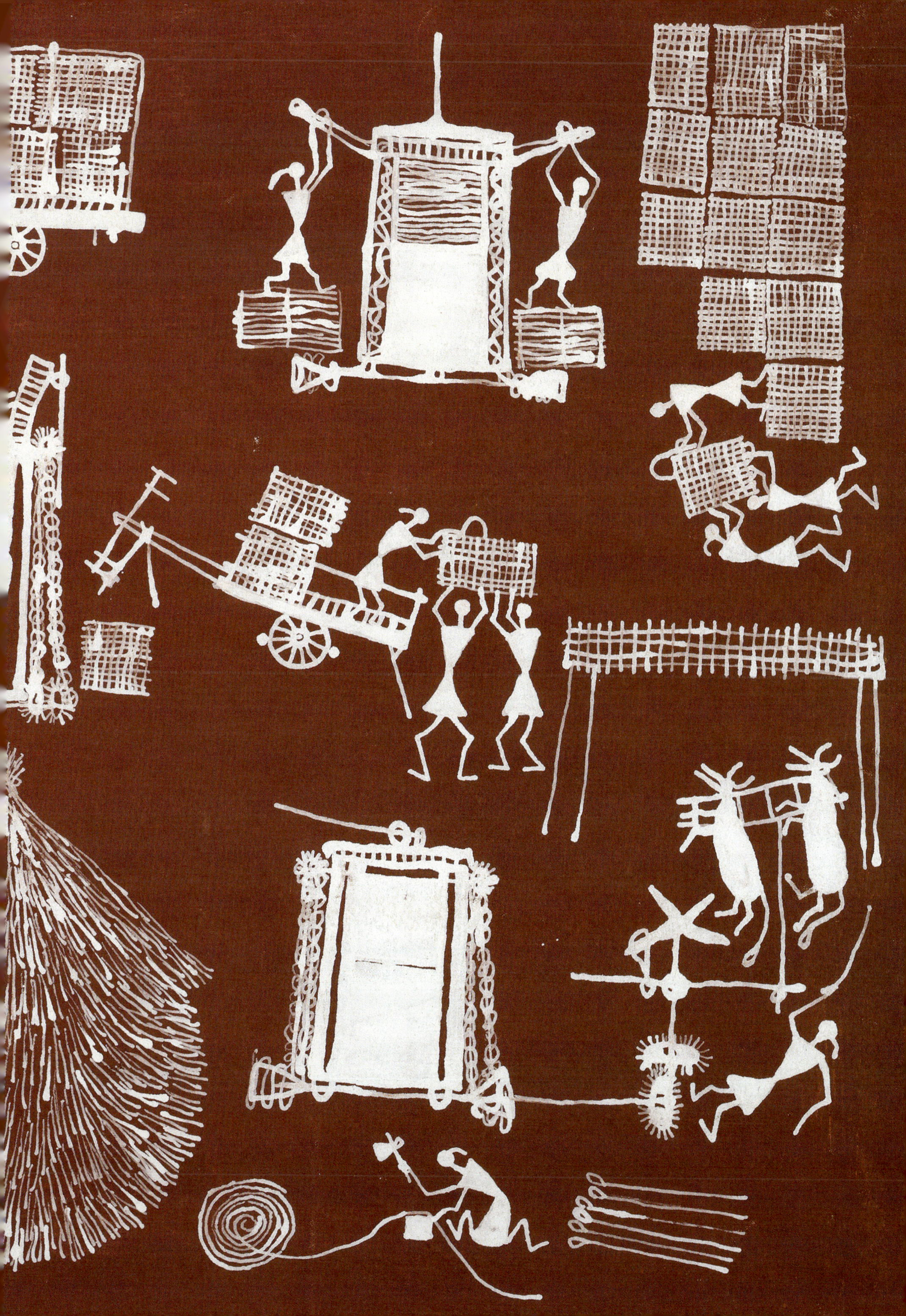

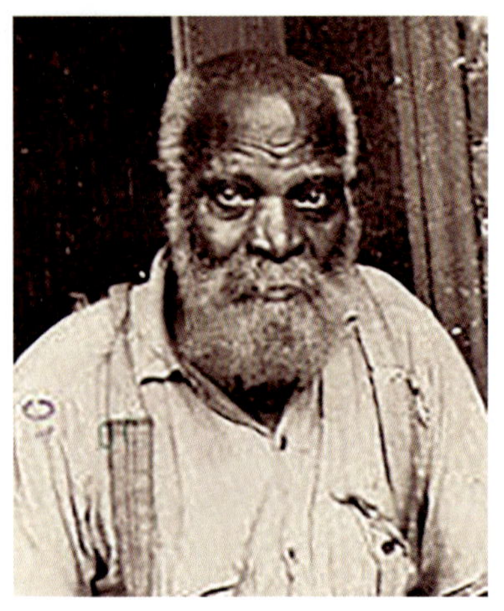
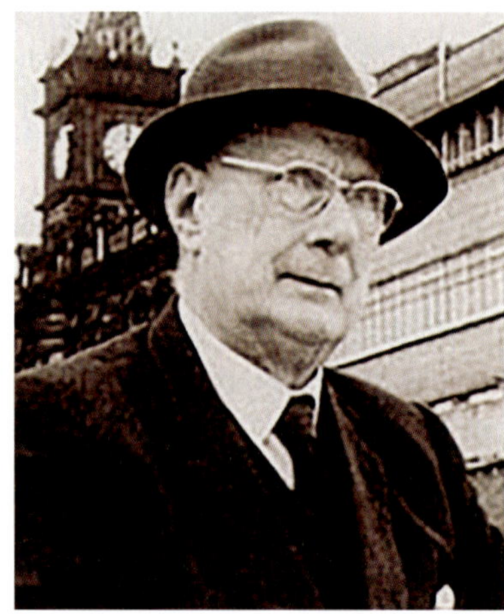
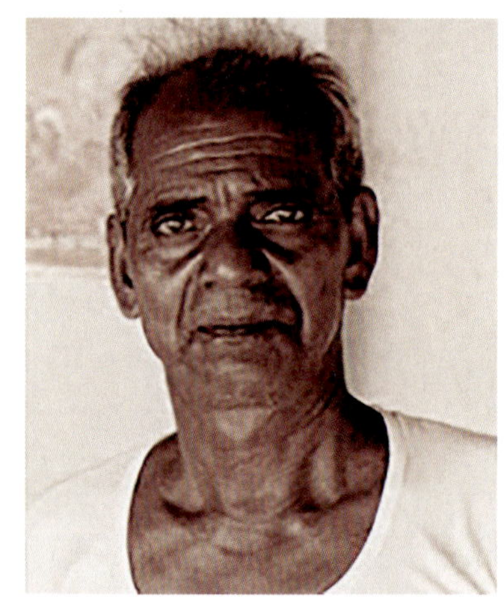

TRAYLOR, LOWRY, MASHE: THE INVISIBLE CONNECTION
TRAYLOR, LOWRY, MASHE : LA CONNEXION INVISIBLE

by Debu Barve
par Debu Barve

This is a story about three painters. Each of them belongs to a different timeline, nationality, and social background. But despite their varied origins, these three artists share an astonishing connection through their styles of creative expression. These three artists are American artist Bill Traylor (1854–1949), British artist L. S. Lowry (1887–1976), and Jivya Soma Mashe (1934–2018), an artist from India. Of these three, two are officially recognised as 'outsiders' (Traylor, Mashe) and one is not (Lowry), but his artistic philosophy is evidently more aligned with outsider art rather than the mainstream.
'Outsider art' is a term broadly used to categorise the art created outside the boundaries of official culture. Typically, those labelled as outsider artists have little or no contact with the mainstream art world or art institutions. Although the term 'outsider art' has been in use for many years, its meaning is constantly evolving. Earlier it was used mainly to categorise aboriginal and folk art; later it took the form of an important French art movement, Art Brut, which placed a larger emphasis on the rejection of established values within modernist art.

C'est l'histoire de trois peintres appartenant chacun à une époque différente, à une nationalité et à un milieu social différents. Mais si les origines de ces trois artistes sont diverses, une connexion étonnante se révèle dans leurs styles d'expression créative.
Ces trois artistes sont l'Américain Bill Traylor (1854-1949), le Britannique L.S. Lowry (1887-1976) et l'Indien Jivya Soma Mashe (1934-2018). Deux d'entre eux sont officiellement reconnus comme des *outsider artists*, Traylor et Mashe, alors que Lowry ne l'est pas. Mais sa philosophie artistique s'aligne manifestement plus sur l'*outsider art* que sur le courant dominant.
L'*outsider art* est un terme largement utilisé pour définir un art créé en dehors des canons de la culture officielle. En règle générale, les artistes qui le pratiquent n'ont que peu ou pas de contact avec le monde de l'art ou avec les institutions artistiques. Bien que le terme *outsider art* ait cours depuis longtemps, sa définition est en constante mutation. On l'utilisait principalement à l'origine pour caractériser l'art aborigène, l'art populaire, etc. Il est ensuite devenu le nom d'un important mouvement artistique français (Art Brut) s'appuyant sur le rejet des valeurs établies dans l'art moderniste.

William 'Bill' Traylor was a self-taught artist born into slavery on a plantation in Lowndes County, Alabama. He started drawing and painting late in life – when he was eighty-five – and made 1,500 drawings over the next three years. He drew scenes of life on the farm and people on the streets. His art was based on things that he had seen, heard, and experienced. He worked in primary colours and made use of simple compositions to create his bold and extremely original style. Later he met Charles Shannon, a painter, who helped him by supplying art material and also buying his drawings. Bill Traylor lived and died in obscurity, his work getting recognition only thirty years after his death.

Bill Traylor : William « Bill » Traylor est un artiste autodidacte né esclave dans une plantation du comté de Lowndes, en Alabama. Il commence à dessiner et à peindre très tard dans sa vie, à l'âge de 85 ans, et a réalisé 1 500 dessins au cours des trois années suivantes, représentant des scènes de vie à la ferme et dans la rue. Son art est fondé sur des choses qu'il a vues, entendues et vécues. Il travaille avec des couleurs primaires et utilise des compositions simples pour créer un style audacieux et extrêmement original. Il rencontre plus tard Charles Shannon, lui aussi peintre, qui lui fournit du matériel pour son art et lui achète ses dessins. Bill Traylor a vécu dans l'ombre jusqu'à sa mort, et son œuvre n'a été reconnue que 30 ans plus tard.

Laurence Stephen Lowry, popularly known as L. S. Lowry, would say: 'I am not an artist. I am a man who paints'. Lowry lived in Northern England and painted his famous industrial scenes. He had a distinctive style of painting and used a 'matchstick' style representation for human figures. He studied at the Salford School of Art until 1925. He lived most of his quiet and secluded life in Mottram in Longdendale, Cheshire, and was well recognised and honoured in his later years. Today the Lowry Centre at Salford Quays holds the world's largest collection of his works.

L. S. Lowry : « Je ne suis pas un artiste. Je suis un homme qui peint », a déclaré Laurence Stephen Lowry, plus connu sous le nom de L. S. Lowry. Lowry vivait dans le nord de l'Angleterre où il peignait ses célèbres scènes industrielles, dont le style de représentation des figures humaines, « les hommes-allumettes », est caractéristique. Après avoir étudié à la Salford School of Art jusqu'en 1925, il mène une vie tranquille et isolée à Mottram in Longdendale, dans le Cheshire, et sera reconnu et honoré à la fin de sa vie. Aujourd'hui, le « Lowry Centre », à Salford Quays, abrite la plus grande collection au monde de ses œuvres.

Jivya Soma Mashe is known for his renditions of Warli tribal art, from the Maharashtra state in India. To position him correctly, we can say that he is as important to Warli tribal art as Emily Kame Kngwarreye is to Australian indigenous art. Jivya Soma Mashe was a pioneer in transforming Warli art from a mere element of tribal ritual to a pure expression of art. Initially he painted on mud walls and later started using flexible painting surfaces like canvas. This transition helped him immensely in developing his unique painting style. But even in his new style, the subject matter is still related to Warli tribes, forests, birds and animals, and traditional patterns. The magic of his work is that it draws you into its unique world and makes you feel like you are a part of the activity inside the painting. His work is widely exhibited around the world and is well recognised. In 2011, he received the Padma Shri (the fourth highest civilian award by the Government of India) for his contribution to Warli painting.

Jivya Soma Mashe est connu pour ses interprétations de l'art tribal warli, provenant de l'État du Maharashtra en Inde. Pour le situer précisément, nous pouvons dire qu'il est aussi important en tant qu'artiste de l'art tribal warli que peut l'être Emily Kame Kngwarreye pour l'art indigène australien. Jivya a fait œuvre de pionnier en élevant l'art warli du statut de simple élément des rituels tribaux à celui d'expression artistique pure. Peignant au départ sur des murs en terre, il travaille ensuite sur des supports souples comme la toile. Cette transition a été décisive dans l'évolution de son style unique de peinture. Cependant, son nouveau style reste fidèle aux thèmes des tribus warli, aux forêts, aux oiseaux et aux animaux, ainsi qu'aux motifs traditionnels. La magie de son travail est telle qu'il attire le regardeur dans son monde unique et lui donne l'impression de faire partie de l'activité représentée sur la toile. Les œuvres de Jivya sont largement exposées dans le monde et jouissent d'une grande notoriété. En 2011, il a reçu le « Padma Shri» (la quatrième plus haute distinction civile décernée par le gouvernement indien) pour sa contribution à la peinture warli.

RICHARD LONG, JIVYA SOMA MASHE: AN ENCOUNTER IN INDIA

RICHARD LONG, JIVYA SOMA MASHE : UNE RENCONTRE EN INDE

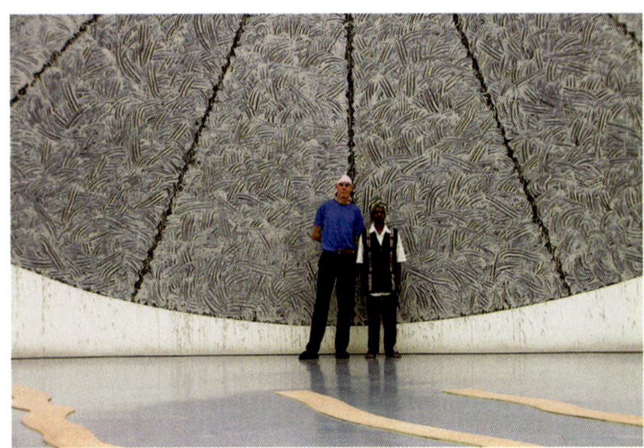

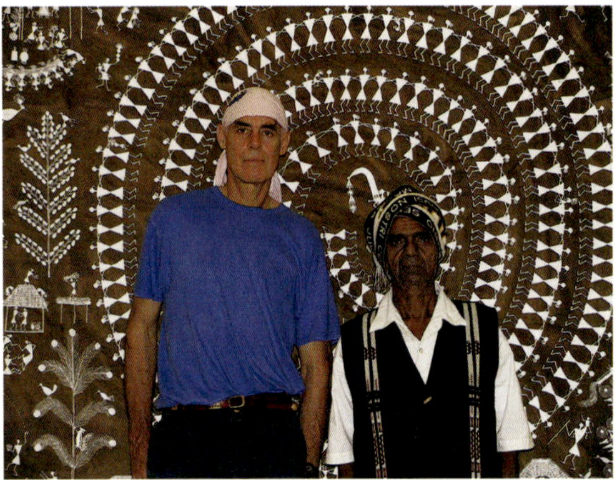

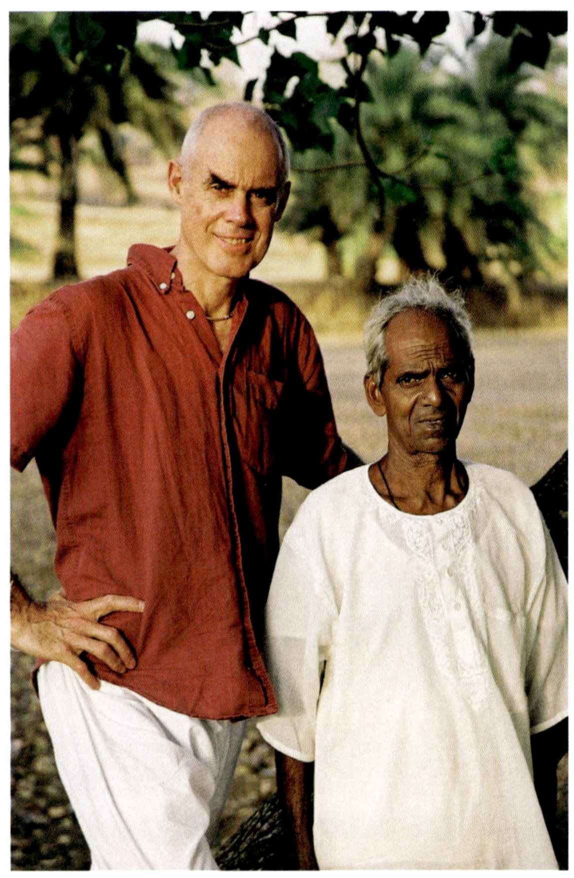

Richard Long and Jivya Soma Mashe in front of a work by Richard Long, Kunstpalast Museum, Düsseldorf, 2003. Photo by Isabel Kauenhoven.

Richard Long and Jivya Soma Mashe in front of a painting by Jivya Soma Mashe, Kunstpalast Museum, Düsseldorf, 2003. Photo by Isabel Kauenhoven.

Richard Long and Jivya Soma Mashe, Ganjad (Maharashtra, India), 2003. Photo by Hervé Perdriolle.

I had the idea for this meeting during my time in India from 1996 to 1999, on one of my many trips devoted to discovering and studying Warli tribal art. On each trip, I had the opportunity to walk for hours between villages. The raw beauty of the landscapes, and, even more so, their countless details caused by human intervention, subtly reminded me of land art, specifically the work of Richard Long, which has that same raw beauty.

In the way they lay out simple pieces of wood to dry in the sun, spread their rice harvest on the ground, or simply clean the floor of their mud hut each day, the Warli people remind us, through the gentle, graceful attentiveness they give to each of these actions, that their only deity is the mother goddess, the goddess of the earth and fertility: Palagatha. This worship, if it can be called that, continues to inspire them with a deep respect for nature. Each Warli painting, in particular those by Jivya Soma Mashe, seems to be a hymn of praise to the Earth, as is every work of land art.

And so the idea for this exhibition was born, or rather germinated, journey after journey, season after season. The idea, which at the outset was no more than a feeling, an indefinite perception as we wandered through the Warli landscape, took the form of a meeting between two artists, two men from very different cultures, but who above all belong to the same world, to the same Earth, and have the same regard for it.

I did not know Richard Long. I sent him the definitive book on Warli art, Yashodhara Dalmia's *The Painted World of the Warlis*. He wrote back that he had never visited India and that the idea interested him. All I had to do was to find someone to sponsor the journey. This, of course, was Jean-Hubert Martin, who accepted immediately. The physical meeting in India, to take place in late January and early February 2003, could be extended artistically in two exhibitions that would place the works by the two artists in dialogue, in the two museums where he was curator at the time: the Kunstpalast in Düsseldorf (13 September–3 November 2003) and the PAC-Padiglione d'Arte Contemporanea in Milan (24 June–19 September 2004).

L'idée de cette rencontre est née lorsque j'habitais en Inde de 1996 à 1999, au cours de mes nombreux voyages consacrés à la découverte et à l'étude de l'art de la tribu warli. Au cours de chacun de ces voyages, j'avais l'occasion de marcher de nombreuses heures, de village en village. Les paysages dans leur rudimentaire beauté, mais plus encore, de multiples détails dus à l'intervention des hommes dans la nature, m'évoquaient imperceptiblement le land art, et plus précisément l'œuvre de Richard Long, elle aussi dans sa rudimentaire beauté.

Dans leurs façons d'étaler à terre de simples morceaux de bois afin de les faire sécher au soleil, d'étendre au sol leur récolte de riz ou simplement encore, et parmi bien d'autres exemples, de nettoyer quotidiennement le sol de leurs huttes en terre battue, les Warlis rappellent, par l'attention recherchée, sensible, gracieuse, apportée à chacune de ces actions, que leur seule divinité est la déesse mère, déesse de la terre, de la fertilité : Palagatha. Ce culte, s'il en est, leur a inspiré, et leur inspire encore de nos jours, un profond respect pour la nature. Chaque peinture warli, et plus particulièrement celles de Jivya Soma Mashe, semblent être un éloge à la Terre tout comme semble l'être aussi toute œuvre issue du land art.

Ainsi est né, ou plutôt a germé, l'idée de cette exposition, voyage après voyage, saison après saison. L'idée, qui n'était au départ qu'un sentiment, qu'une perception indéfinie au hasard de marches dans le paysage warli, prit la forme de cette rencontre, celle de deux artistes, de deux hommes issus de cultures certes fort différentes, mais appartenant avant tout au même monde, à la même Terre, et ayant à son attention de semblables égards.

Je ne connaissais pas Richard Long. Je lui envoyai la bible sur l'art des Warlis, le livre *The Painted World of the Warlis* de Yashodhara Dalmia. Il me répondit qu'il n'était encore jamais allé en Inde et que ce projet l'intéressait. Il me restait à trouver un partenaire pour financer ce voyage. Ce fut tout naturellement Jean-Hubert Martin, qui accepta spontanément. Cette rencontre en Inde, fin janvier début février 2003, allait pouvoir se prolonger grâce à deux expositions faisant dialoguer les œuvres de Jivya Soma Mashe et de Richard Long dans les deux musées qu'il dirigeait alors, le Kunstpalast Museum (Düsseldorf, du 13 septembre au 3 novembre 2003) et le PAC-Padiglione d'Arte Contemporanea (Milan, du 24 juin au 19 septembre 2004).

TALES AND LEGENDS
CONTES ET LÉGENDES

The Warli legends are metaphors for how we treat our fellow beings, edifying tales that teach lessons of human conduct, parables, as in the fables of La Fontaine, and fabliaux, as if to illustrate such lessons. The titles of Mashe's works found in this book that have been taken from tales include *The Wandering Tribes*, *The Man Who Didn't Want to Work*, and *The Hermit's Daughter*. Nursery rhymes also convey an awareness of ecology and the timeless interdependence between man and nature. Naturally, these allegories are based on their animist culture, on their attribution of a soul or spirit to everything in their environment. These tales and legends have been passed down from generation to generation since the dawn of time, mainly by the women in the community.

The other themes in Warli paintings are their daily activities: farming, fishing, and hunting, as well as dances and ritual festivals.

Les légendes warli sont autant de métaphores permettant de transmettre les interactions des êtres humains entre eux. Des légendes comme des récits édifiants à travers lesquels apparaissent des leçons de conduite. Des paraboles, comme dans les fables de La Fontaine, des fabliaux comme pour illustrer un enseignement. *Les tribus errantes*, *L'homme qui ne voulait pas travailler*, *La fille de l'ermite*, sont parmi les titres des contes que l'on retrouve dans ce livre. Ces comptines expriment aussi une conscience de l'écologie, comme la manifestation d'une interdépendance immémoriale entre l'homme et la nature. Enfin, ces allégories nous évoquent leur culture animiste, cette façon d'attribuer à tout ce qui constitue leur environnement une âme, un esprit. Ces contes et légendes se transmettent depuis la nuit des temps de génération en génération, principalement par les femmes de la communauté.

Les autres thèmes des peintures warli décrivent leurs activités quotidiennes, les cultures, la pêche, la chasse, les danses et fêtes rituelles.

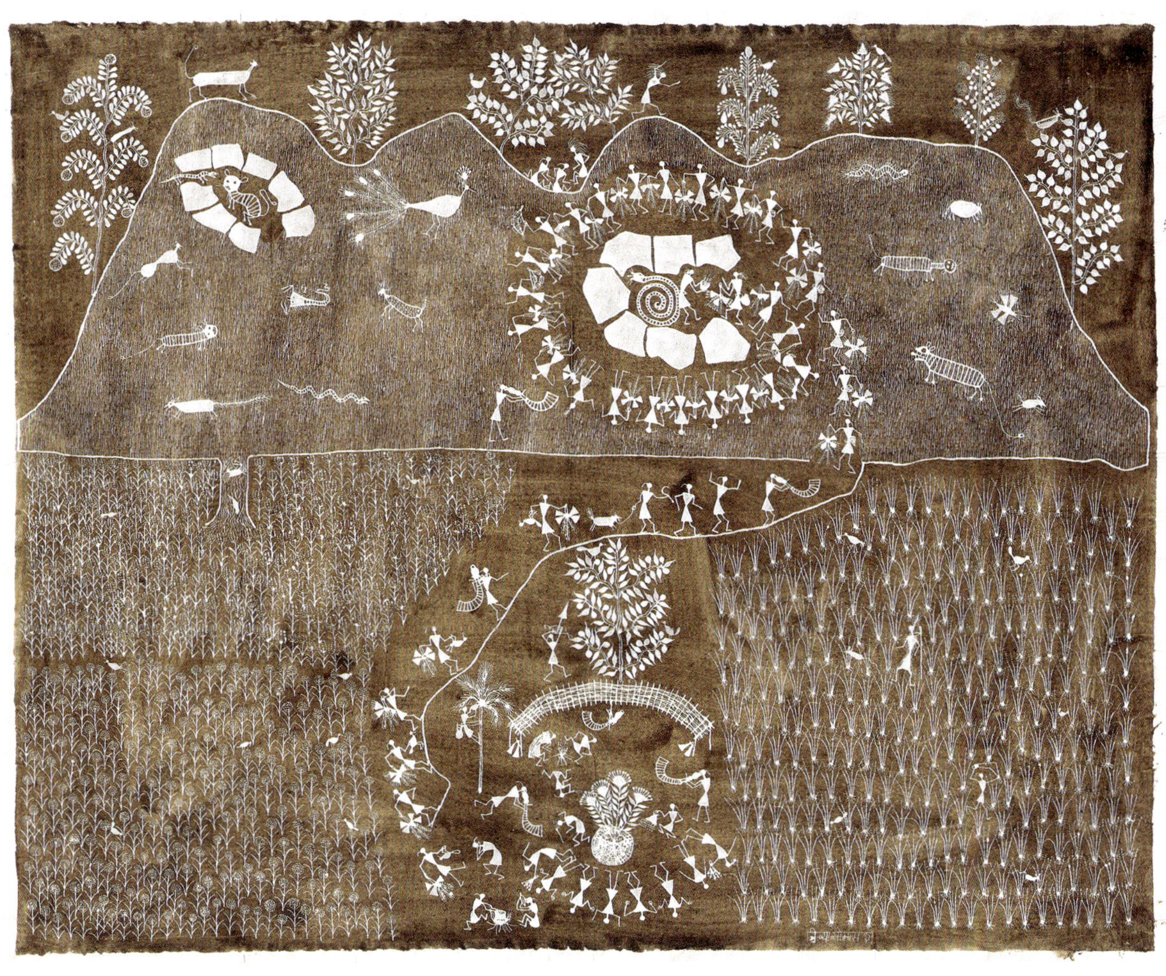

Jivya Soma Mashe, *Untitled*, 1997,
acrylic and cow dung on canvas,
100 × 125 cm; 39.37 × 49.21 in. (*details on pages* 56–59)
Collection of Hervé Perdriolle.
Photo by Christian Baraja.

Pages 60–63
Views of Jivya Soma Mashe's house, Ganjad
(Maharashtra, India), 2003.
Photos by Hervé Perdriolle.

Page 64
View of Jivya Soma Mashe's second house (now owned
by his son Balu), Ganjad (Maharashtra, India), 2011.

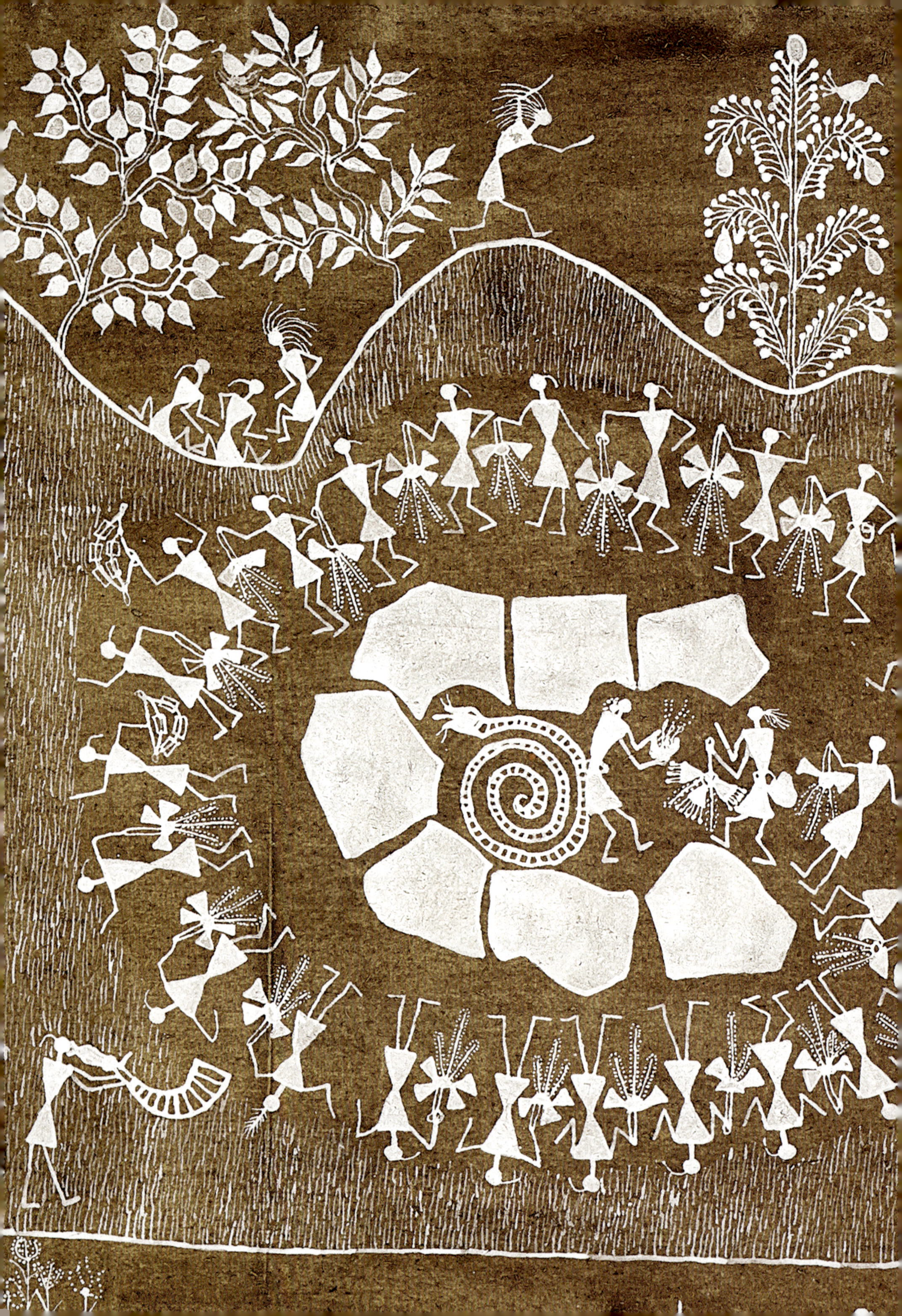

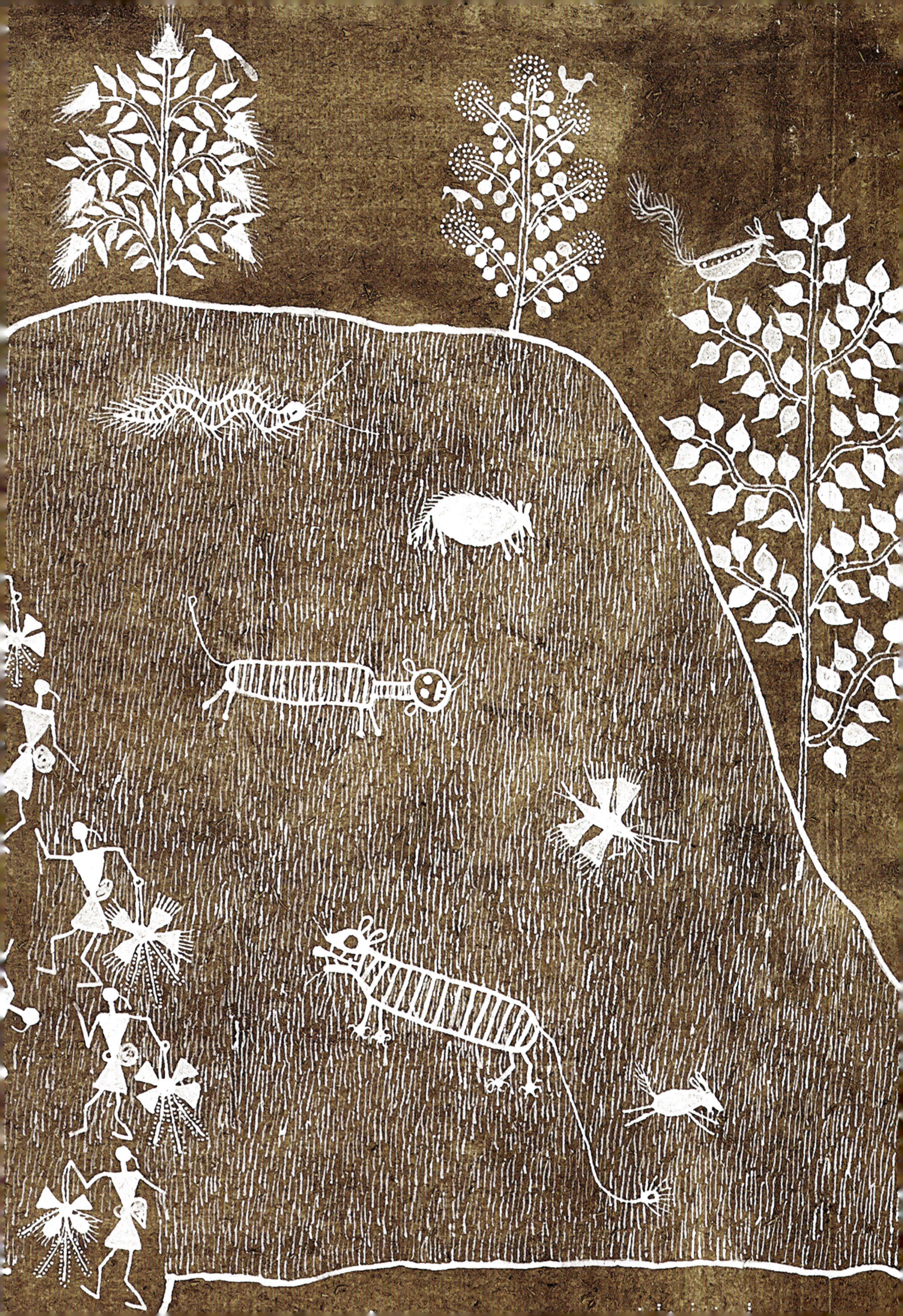

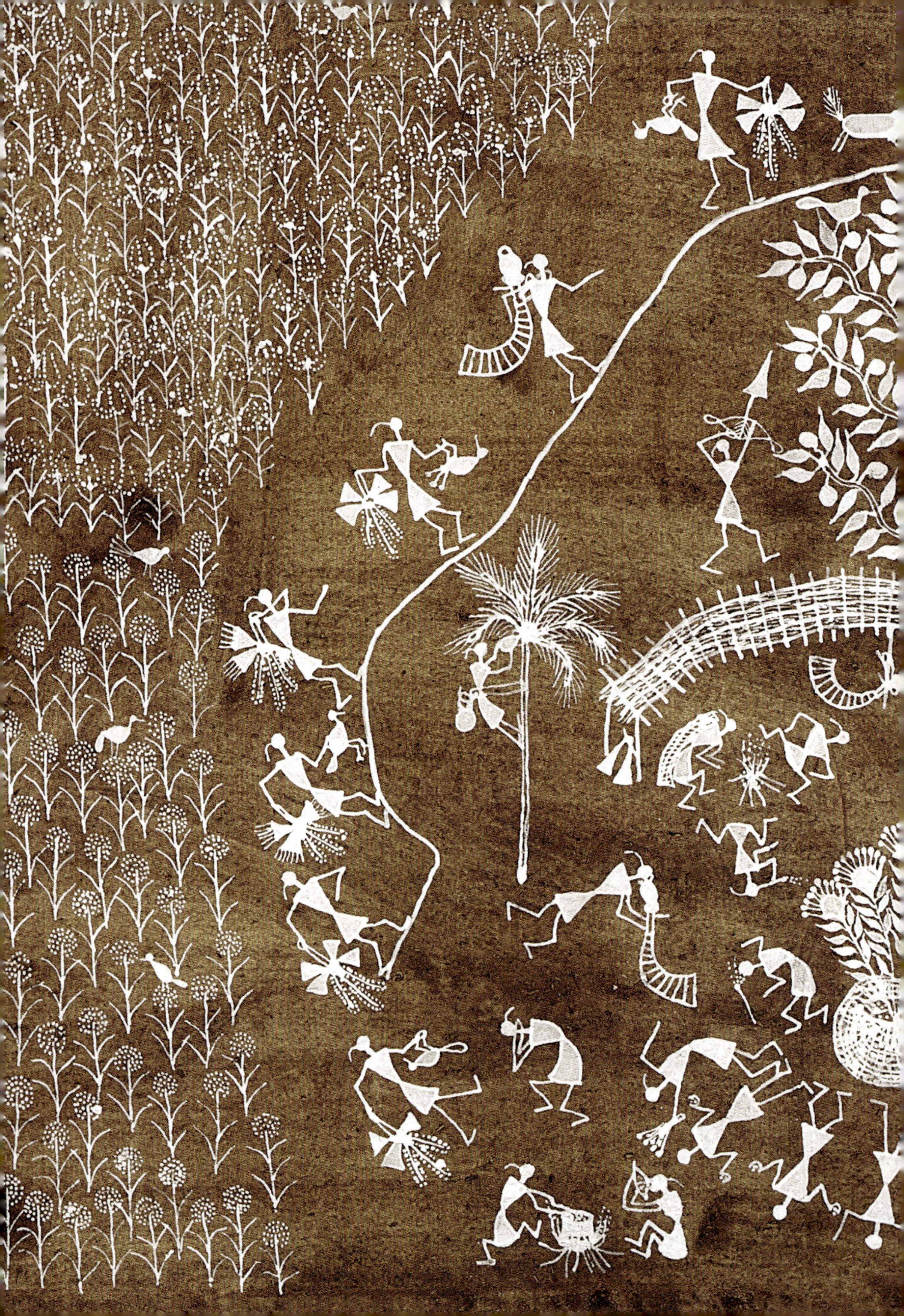

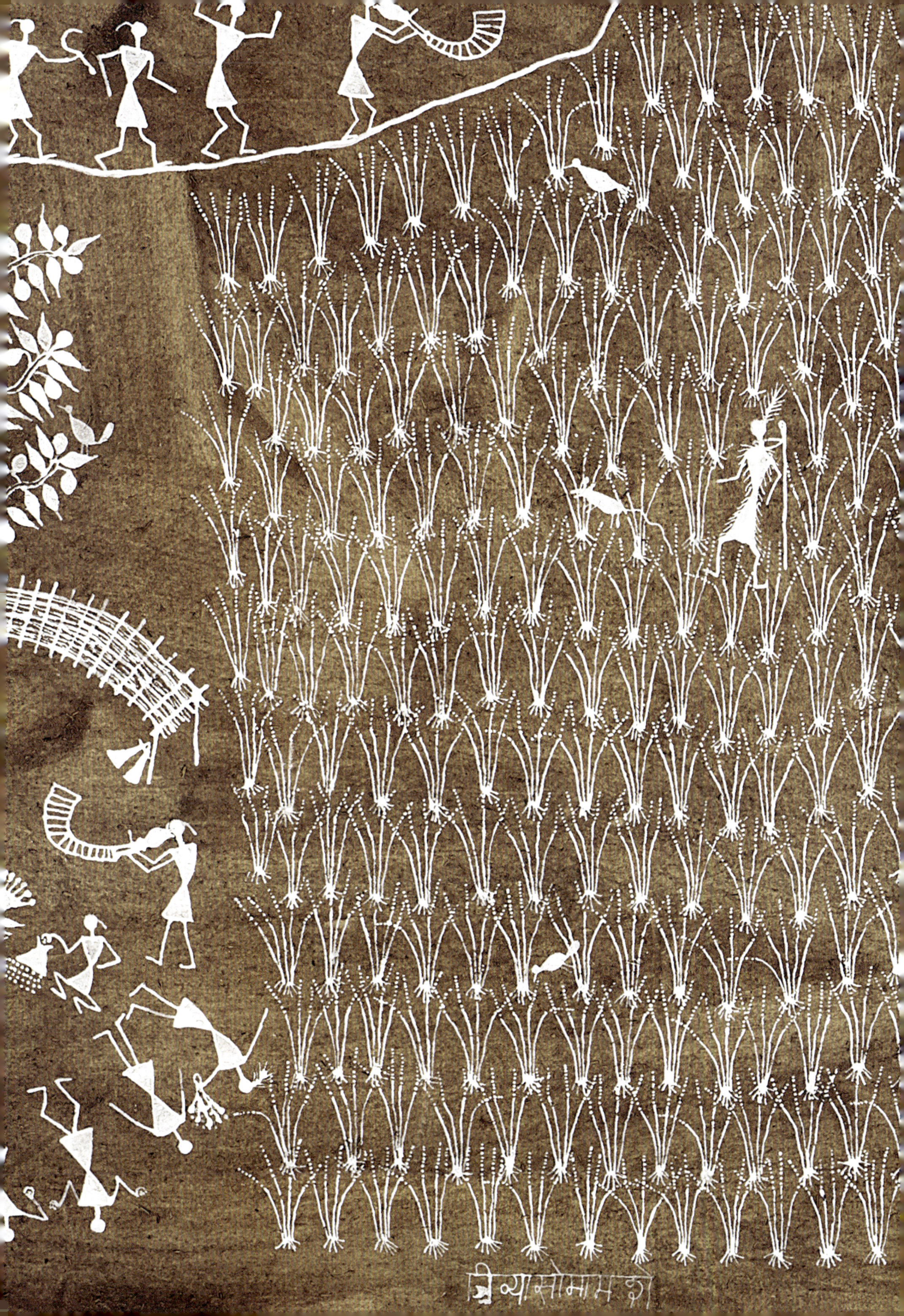

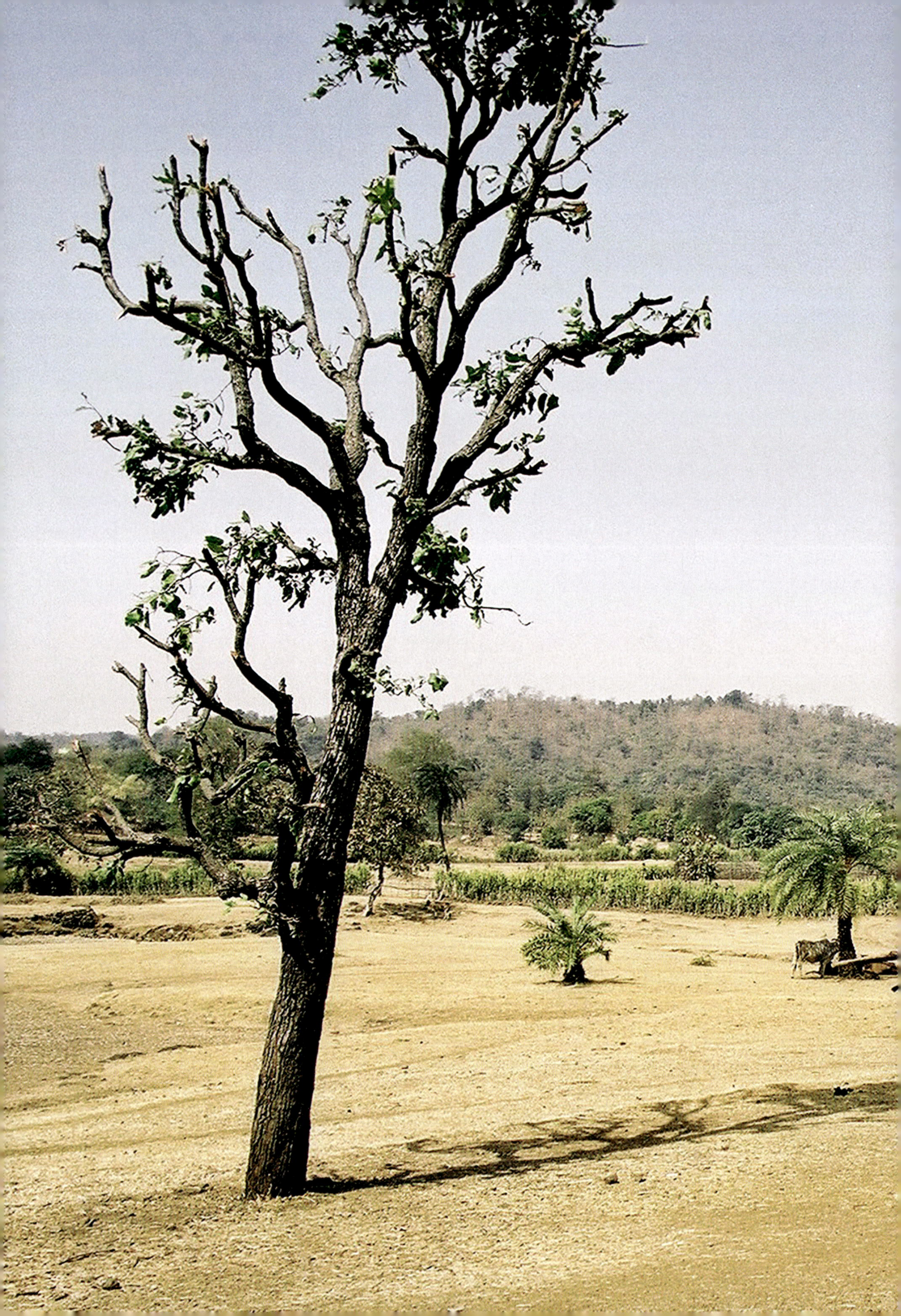

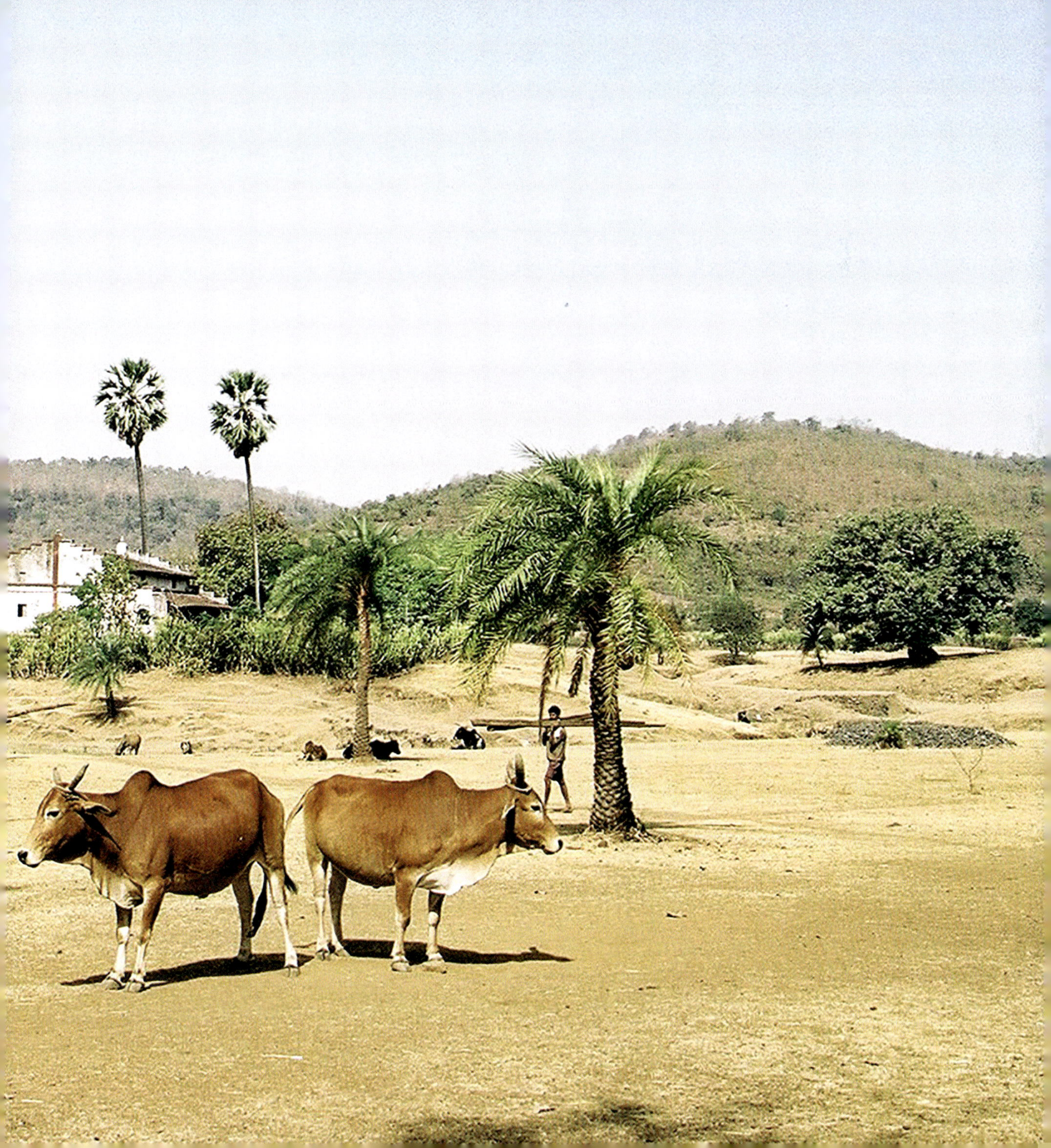

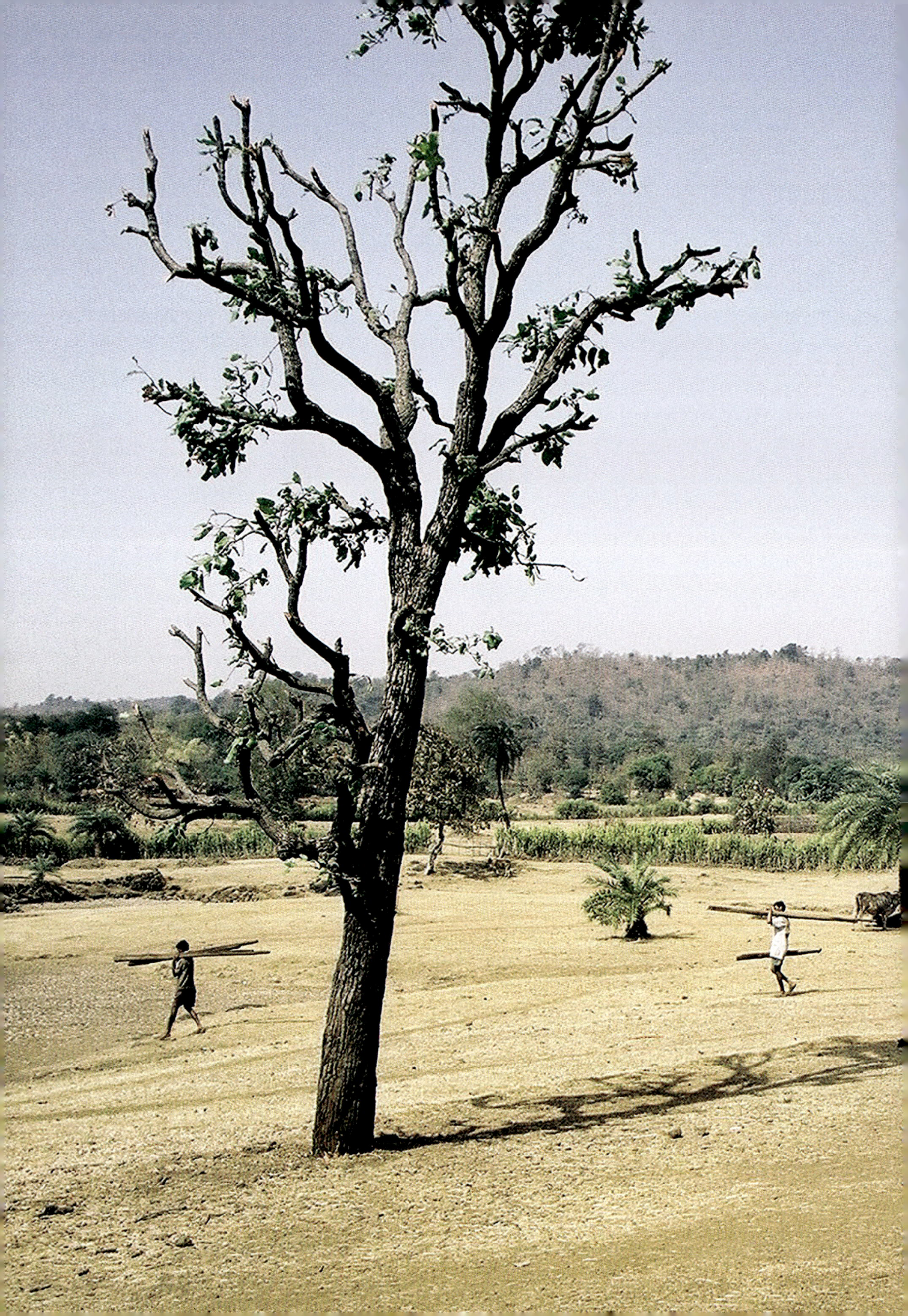

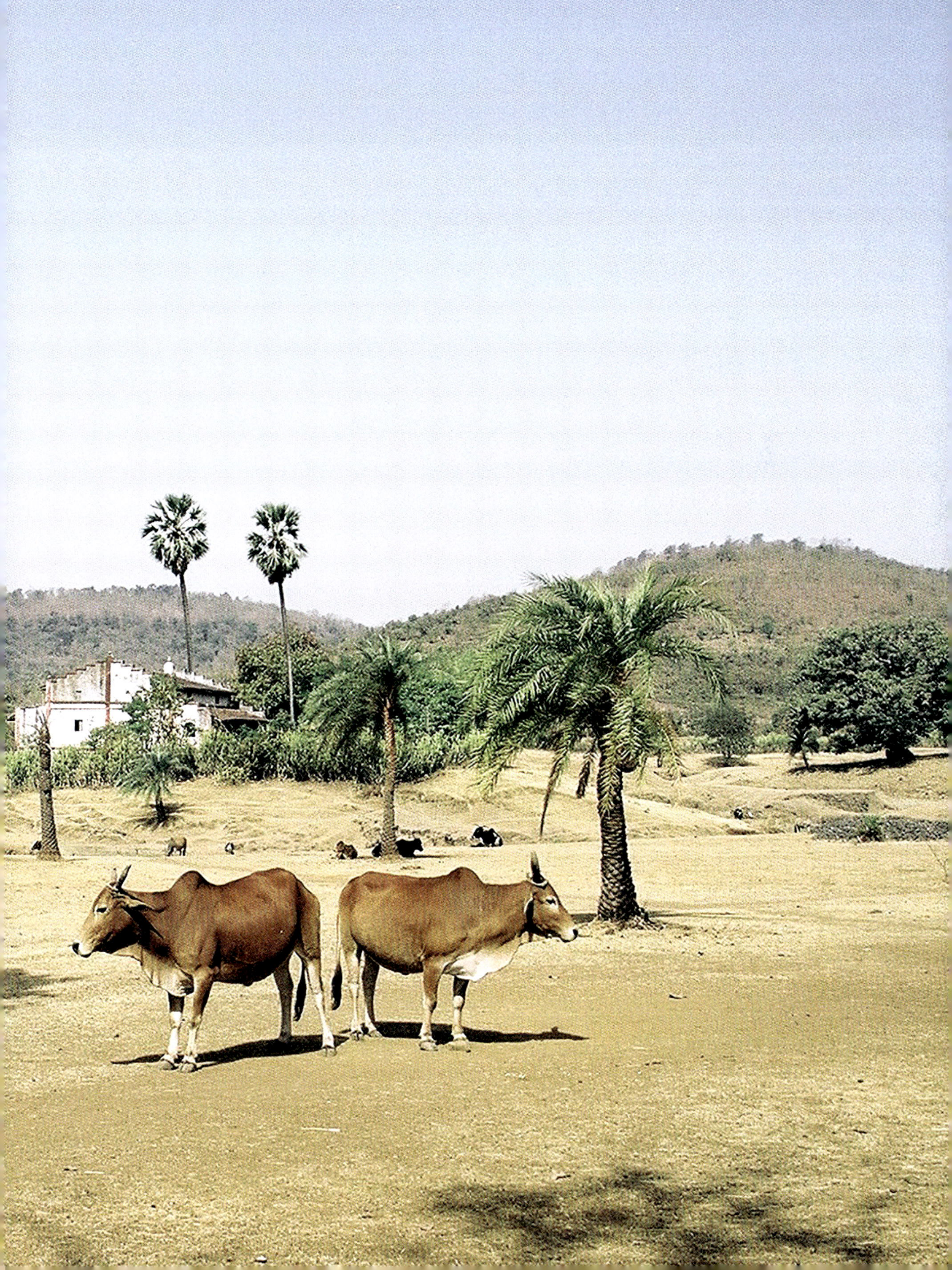

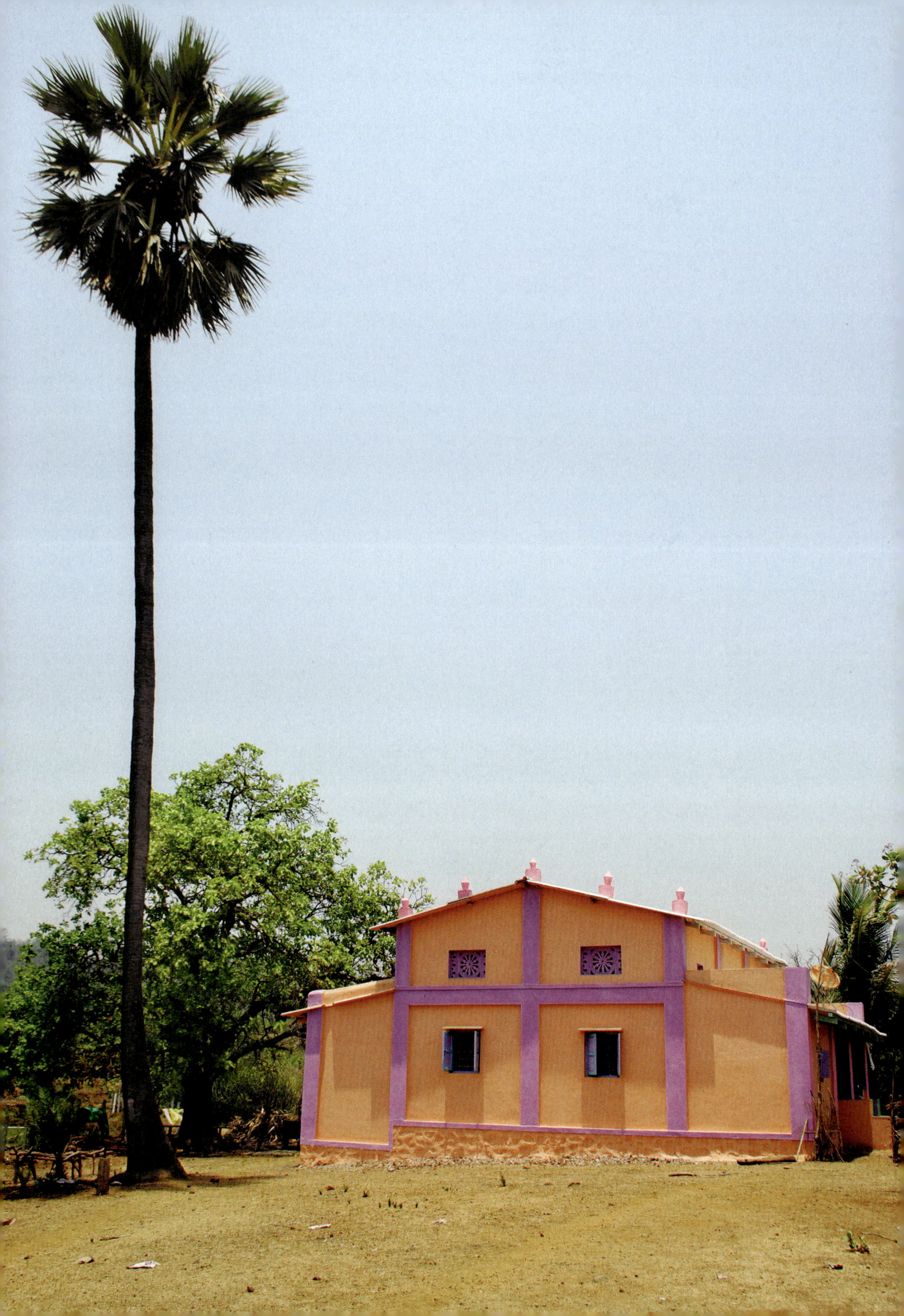

Two photographs taken in 2003 from the same viewpoint, about twenty seconds apart. In the background stands Jivya Soma Mashe's house. In the first, two men are carrying wood and two cows stare into space facing in opposite directions. In the second, one of the men has passed in front of the other but the two cows don't seem to have moved an inch – only the position of the tail of one of them indicates an almost imperceptible movement. When I look at the photos, I feel a notion of time that is different from that of us city dwellers in the modern world. For the Warlis, time seems to have a different consistency, it seems to stretch and unfurl in a different continuity. You have to know how to allow yourself to be absorbed by it, to enfold yourself in it. Not simply spending it as you might do on a pastime, but experiencing it, merging with it, becoming part of it. Be a part of the moment in order to perceive that other world, that other universe.

I love Jivya Soma Mashe's houses. At the time of my first visit, in 1996, there was only one house there, the first one in the photo. For that part of the country, it was a huge home built from masonry. It has an unusual design and, thanks to its stepped structure, it blends in with the landscape, disappearing progressively into the sky. Inside, there is an earthen floor and no ostentatious sign of wealth, just a television that is rarely turned on. In the early 2000s, Jivya had another house built for his children and family, an identical extension of his own: same size, same architecture. And the same pyramidal roof pointing towards the sky like the summit of the sacred mountain the two houses face. At the start of the 2010s, Jivya Soma Mashe had a third house built, this time in the centre of the village, where he would end his days. Again, the same volume and same architecture. He built on a plot of land that Indira Gandhi had promised him when he received his first national award in 1976. This promise had been forgotten but was revived in a discussion during Rajiv Gandhi's visit to the village in 2009. A promise kept over thirty years later.

The colours of Mashe's houses changed with almost every new visit, in keeping with the monsoons and resulting degradation. The colours are always bright, bold, and surprising, in contrast to the use of only two rudimentary colours in Warli paintings: white for the motifs and brown, or terracotta, for the background.

Deux prises de vues faites en 2003 de la même place et à quelques dizaines de secondes d'intervalle. Au fond, la maison de Jivya Soma Mashe. Deux hommes portent du bois. Deux vaches en position symétriquement inversée regardent l'horizon en ses points opposés. L'un des hommes a dépassé l'autre et parcouru quelques dizaines de mètres. Les deux vaches semblent n'avoir pas bougé d'un iota. Seul le balancement de la queue de l'une indique un imperceptible mouvement. En regardant ces deux photos, je ressens cette notion du temps si différente de la nôtre, celle des citadins, celle de notre monde moderne. Chez les Warlis, le temps semble avoir une autre consistance, il paraît s'étirer, se déployer en une autre permanence. Il faut savoir s'y immerger, s'y lover. Non pas simplement prendre le temps comme pour un passe-temps, mais le vivre, s'y confondre, en faire partie, s'y inscrire. Être de ce temps-là pour percevoir cet autre monde, cet autre univers.

J'aime les maisons de Jivya Soma Mashe. Lors de ma première visite, en 1996, il n'y avait là qu'une maison, la première sur l'image. Pour la région, c'était une vaste maison construite en dur. Son architecture était singulière et, grâce à son profil en escalier, s'intégrait au paysage, disparaissant progressivement dans le ciel. À l'intérieur de la maison, un sol en terre battue et aucun signe de richesse exubérant, juste un meuble télévision rarement allumée. Au début des années 2000, Jivya a fait construire pour l'un de ses enfants et sa famille, dans le prolongement de cette première maison, une seconde à l'identique. Même dimension, même architecture. Et toujours ce toit pyramidal pointé vers le ciel comme le sommet acéré de la montagne sacrée à laquelle ces deux maisons font face. Au début des années 2010, Jivya fera construire une troisième maison, cette fois-ci dans le centre du village, maison où il finira ses jours. Même volume, même architecture. Il l'a fait construire sur un terrain que lui avait promis Indira Gandhi lors de la remise de son premier National Award en 1976. Promesse oubliée et ravivée au cours d'une simple discussion lors de la visite en 2009 de Rajiv Gandhi dans le village de Jivya. Promesse tenue une trentaine d'années plus tard.

Quasiment à chaque nouvelle visite, au rythme des moussons et des dégradations qui en résultent, les couleurs des maisons de Jivya Soma Mashe changent. Toujours des couleurs vives, franches, étonnantes, en contraste avec l'utilisation, dans les peintures warli, de seulement deux couleurs rudimentaires, le blanc pour les sujets peints et le brun, ou la couleur *terracotta*, pour les fonds.

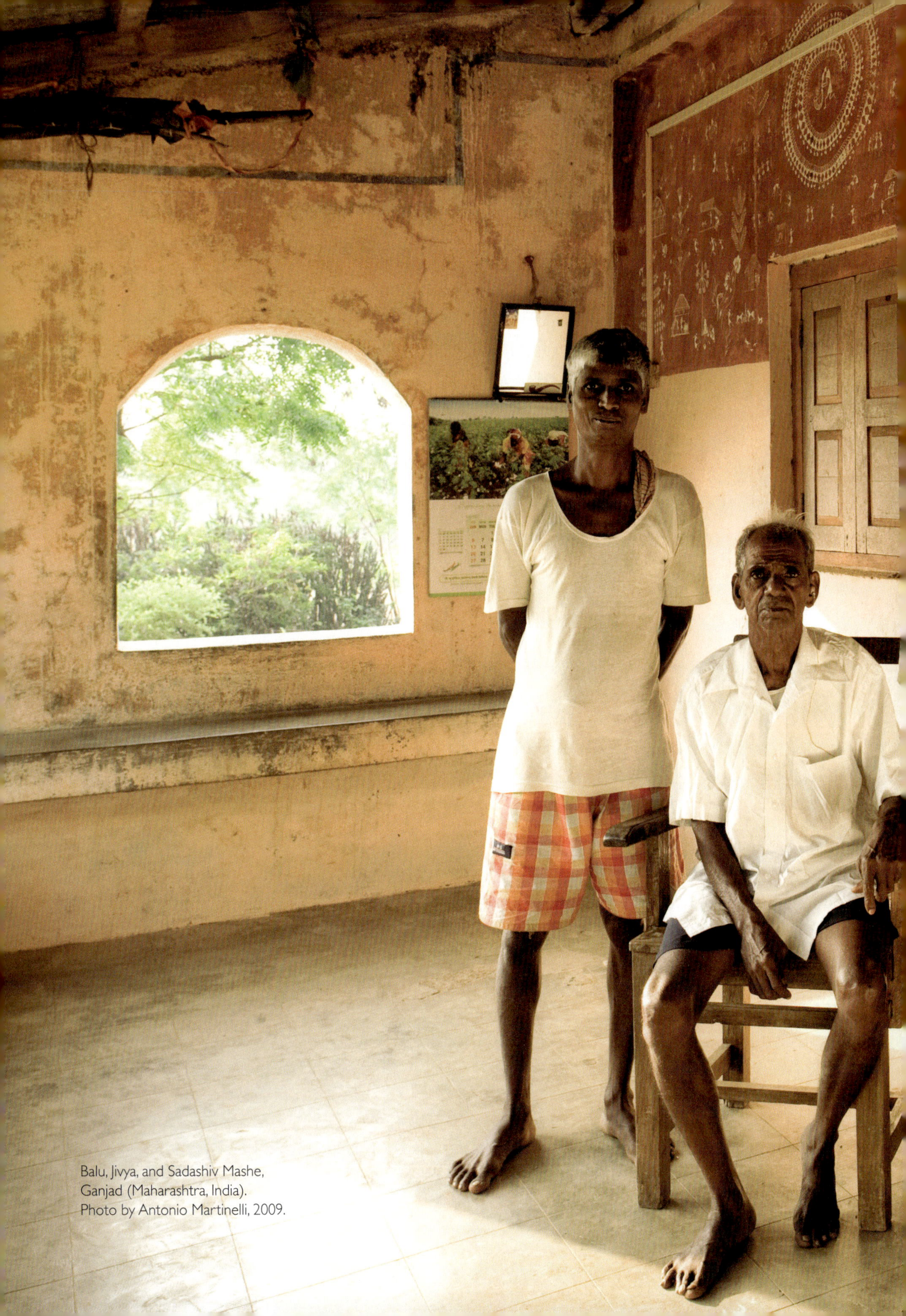

Balu, Jivya, and Sadashiv Mashe,
Ganjad (Maharashtra, India).
Photo by Antonio Martinelli, 2009.

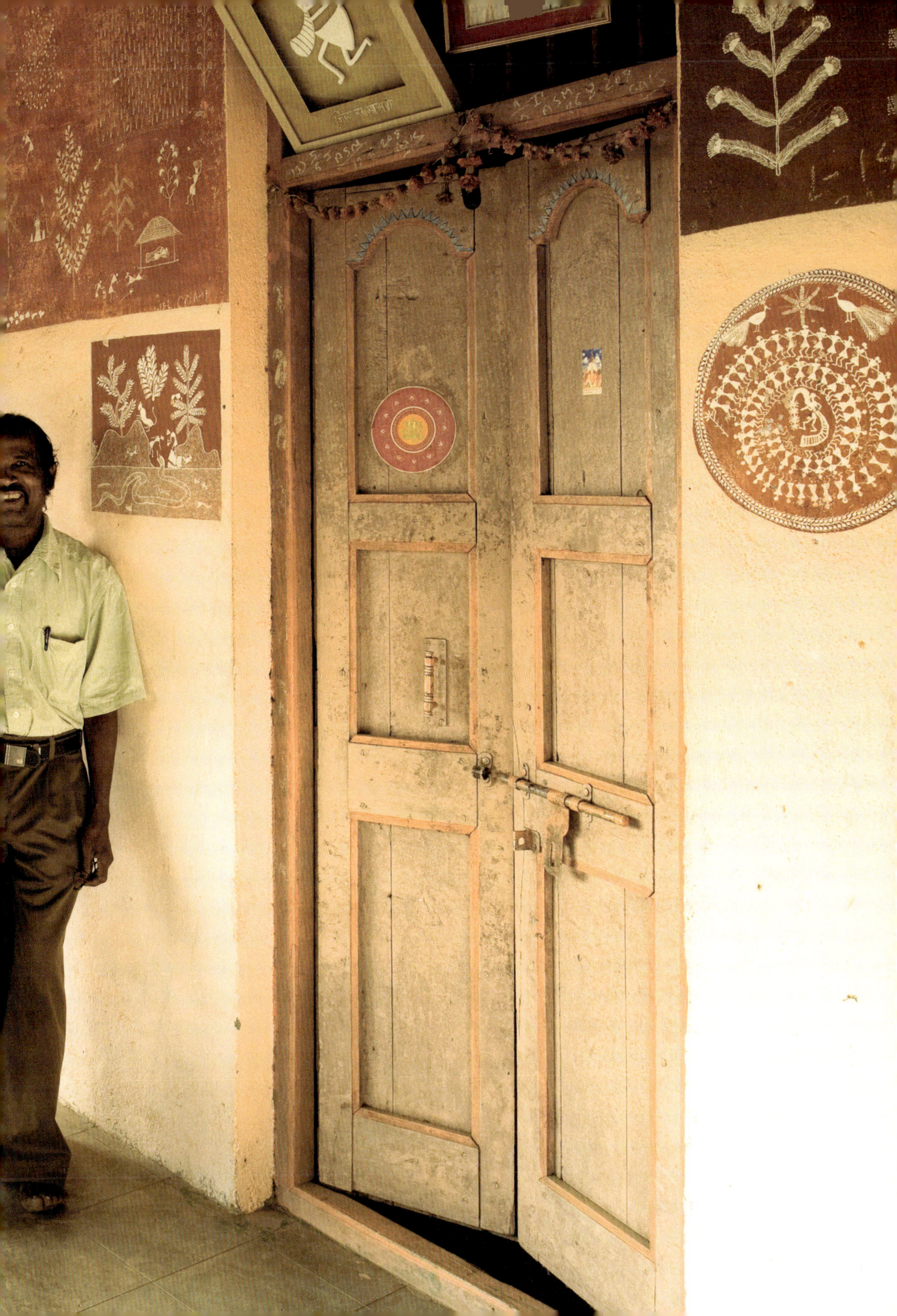

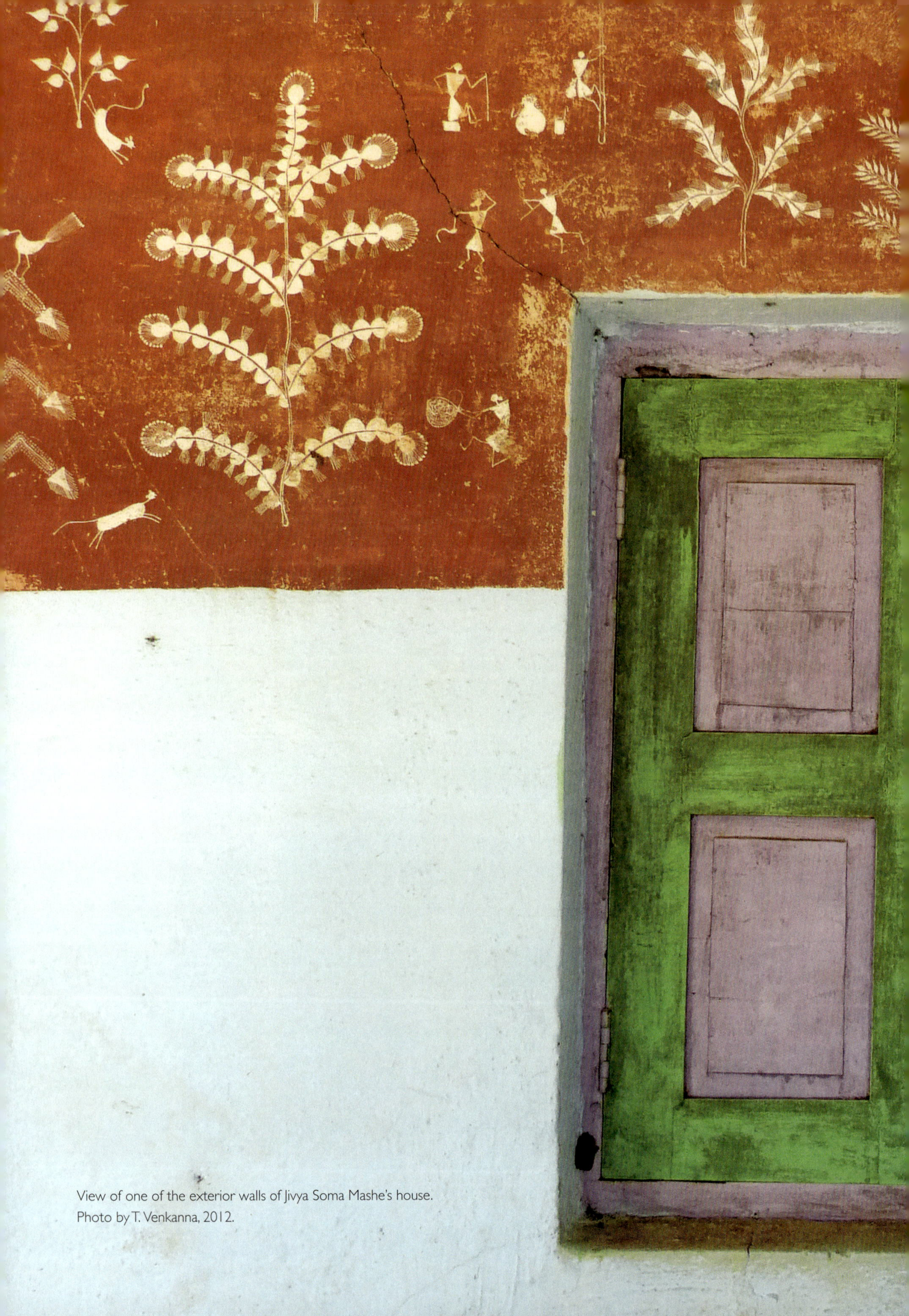

View of one of the exterior walls of Jivya Soma Mashe's house.
Photo by T. Venkanna, 2012.

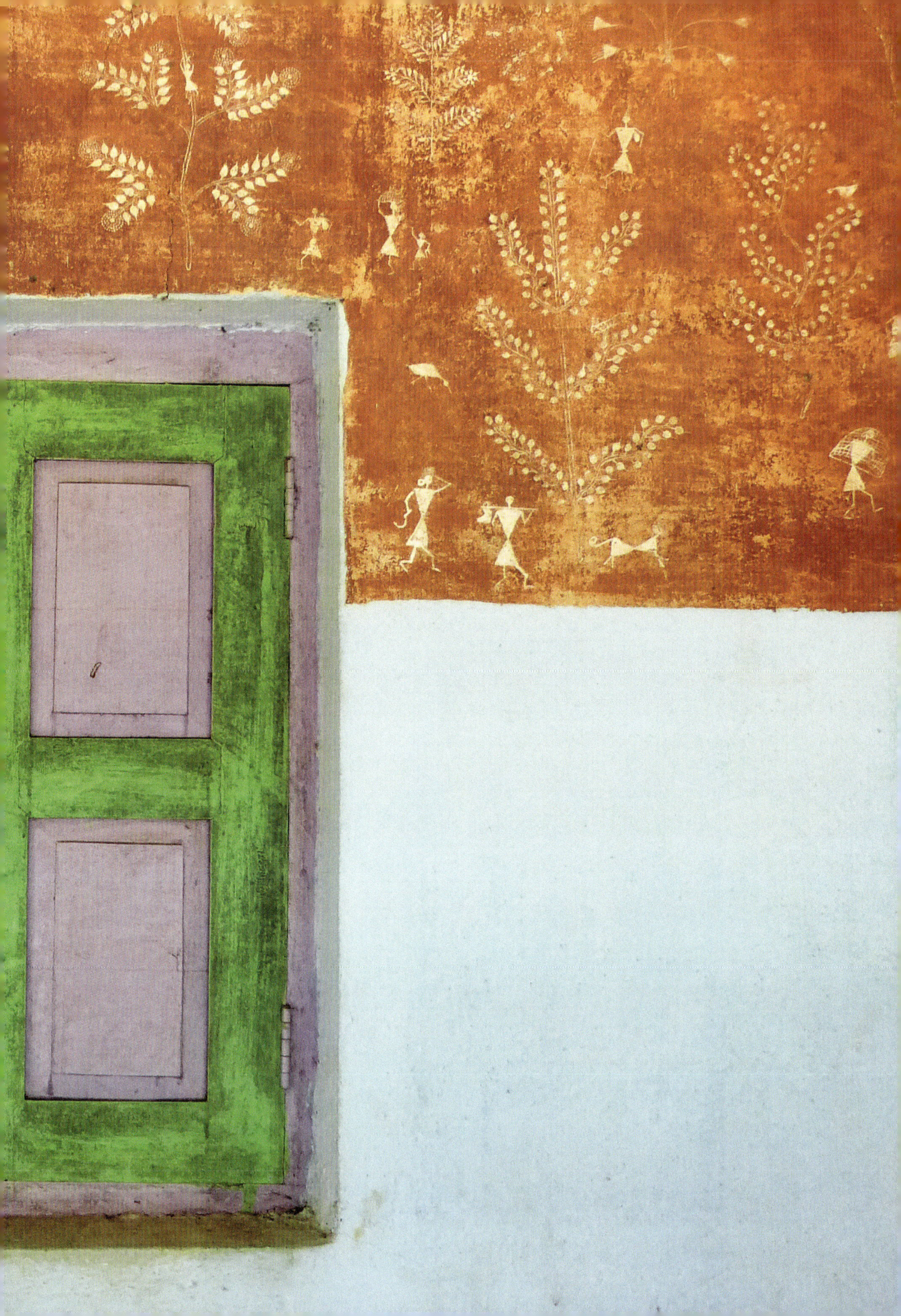

THE ORIGIN OF WARLI FAMILY NAMES
L'ORIGINE DES NOMS DE FAMILLE DE LA POPULATION WARLI

The Warlis recount the legend that their lands were flooded by an immense rainstorm that swept away their villages and dispersed their tribes. The people had to start again from scratch. The survivors were renamed on the places where they found themselves once the water receded.

The Waghat owe their name to the fact that their ancestor had found shelter in a tiger's den (*wagh*). The story of the Sabar was 'spiny', in that their forefather was found near a thorn bush (*sabar*). The ancestor of the Vangad managed to float on the waters surrounded by aubergines (*wangi*), while the precursors of the Handwa were found amid a pile of saucepans (*handas*). The forefathers of the Kurhade were found drifting while grasping onto an axe (*kurhad*). Fate determined that five (*pas*) of the ancestors of the Pasare survived, and those of the Govare with a herd of cattle. One of them reappeared after the catastrophe with a heap of leaves (*pala*) so his family name became Palkar. The Dongare began a new life on rocky ground (*dongar*), and the Bhavar were so named because the waves carried them to a honeycomb (*bhaura*). But the most beautiful story is that of the Thackerays, whose ancestor continued to sleep peacefully through the entire cataclysm, stretched out on his bed (*thaka*).

Les Warlis racontent qu'un immense déluge s'abattit sur leur contrée, emportant leurs villages et dispersant leurs tribus. La population dut repartir de zéro. Les rescapés furent rebaptisés d'après les lieux où ils furent retrouvés après le retrait des eaux. Les Waghat doivent leur nom au fait que leur ancêtre avait trouvé refuge dans le repaire d'un tigre (*wagh*). L'histoire des Sabar fut « épineuse » : leur aïeul fut retrouvé à proximité d'un buisson d'épines (*sabar*). L'ancêtre des Vangad réussit à surnager, entouré d'aubergines (*wangi*). Les ascendants des Handwas furent retrouvés au milieu de casseroles (*handas*). Ceux des Kurhades s'accrochèrent à une hache (*kurhad*) à la dérive. Le sort voulut que les ancêtres des Pasares en réchappent à cinq (*pas*) et ceux des Govares avec un troupeau de bovins. L'un d'entre eux réapparut, après la catastrophe, avec un monceau de feuilles (*pala*) si bien que son nom de famille devint Palkar. Les Dongares entamèrent une vie nouvelle sur un sol de pierres (*dongar*) et les Bhavars furent ainsi appelés car les flots les déposèrent auprès d'un rayon de miel (*bhaura*). Mais la plus belle histoire est celle des Thackerays dont l'ancêtre continua de dormir, pendant tout le cataclysme, d'un sommeil paisible, allongé sur sa couche (*thaka*).

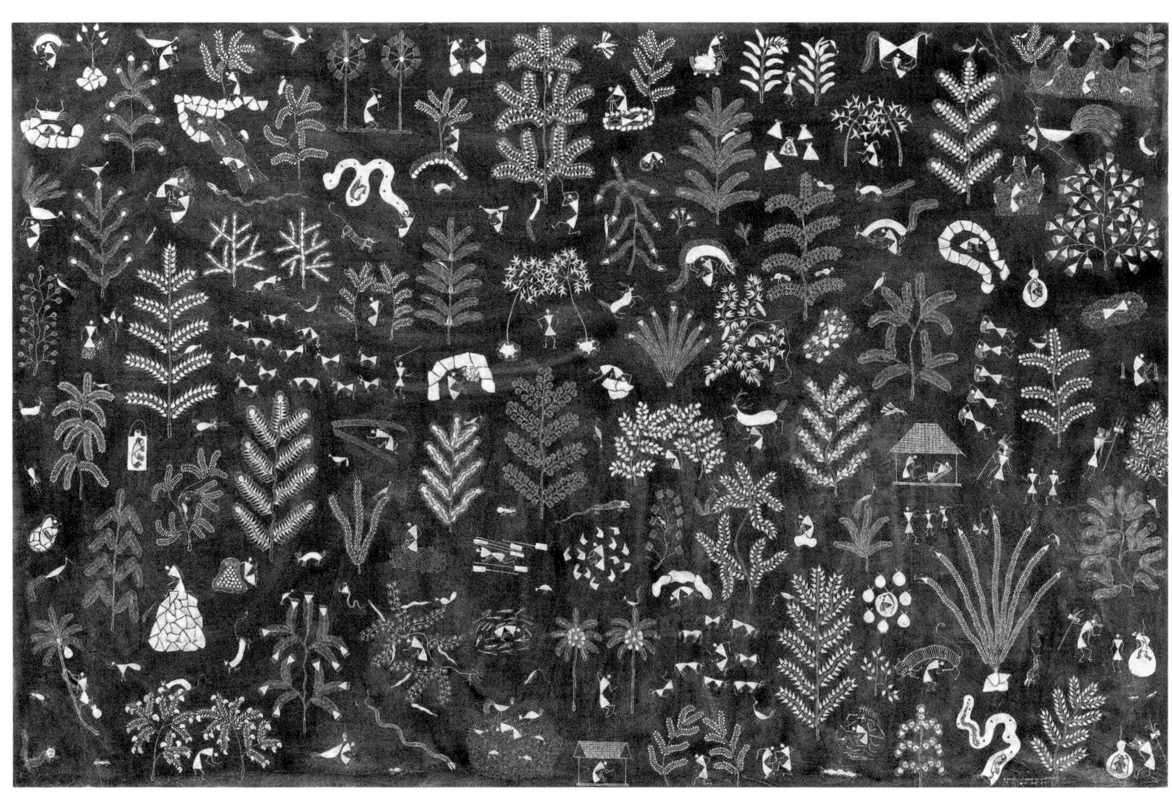

Jivya Soma Mashe, *How People Got Their Name*, 1999,
acrylic and cow dung on canvas,
138 × 230 cm; 54.33 × 90.55 in. (*details on pages* 72–81)
Fondation Cartier pour l'art contemporain Collection.
Photo by André Morin.

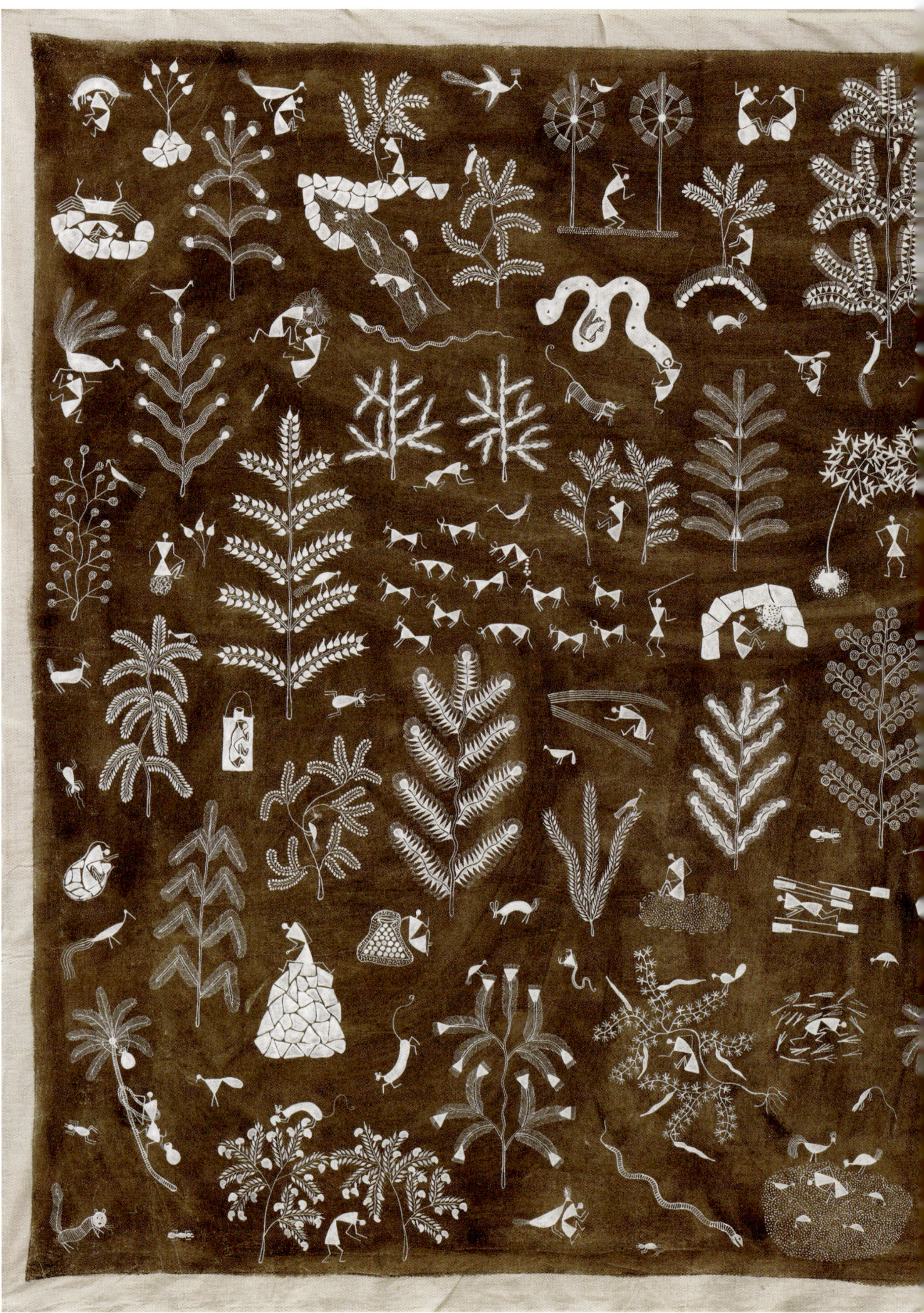

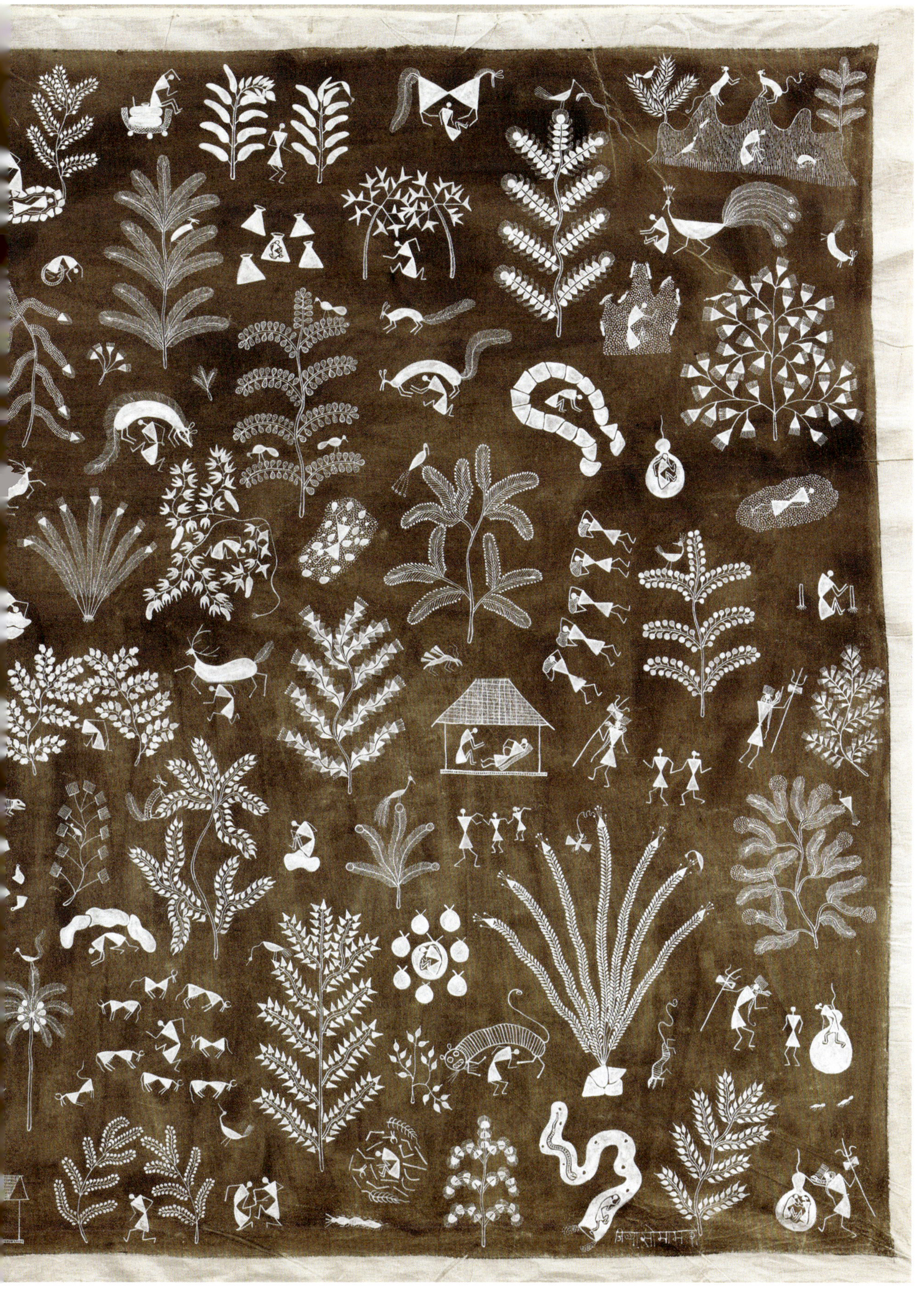

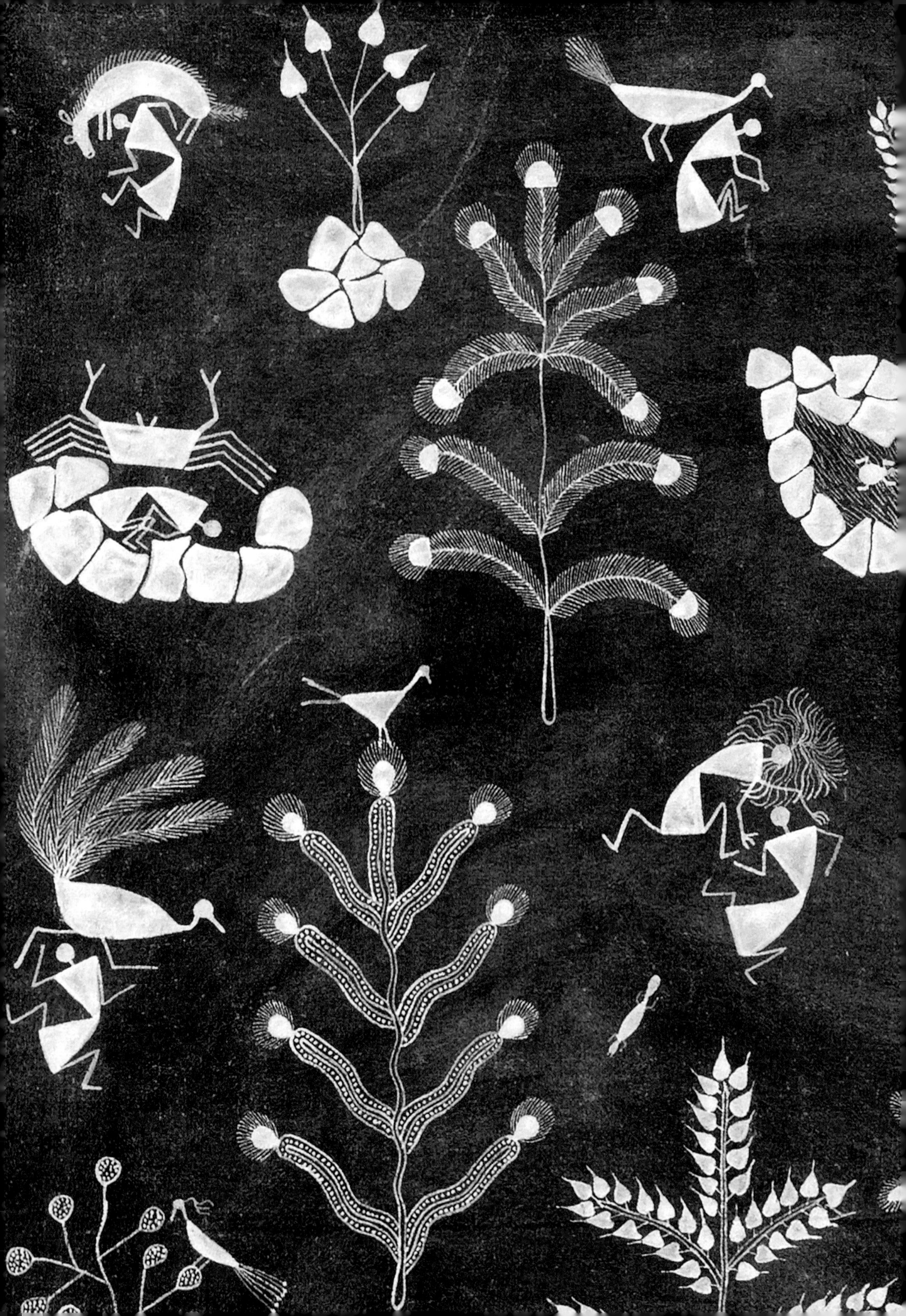

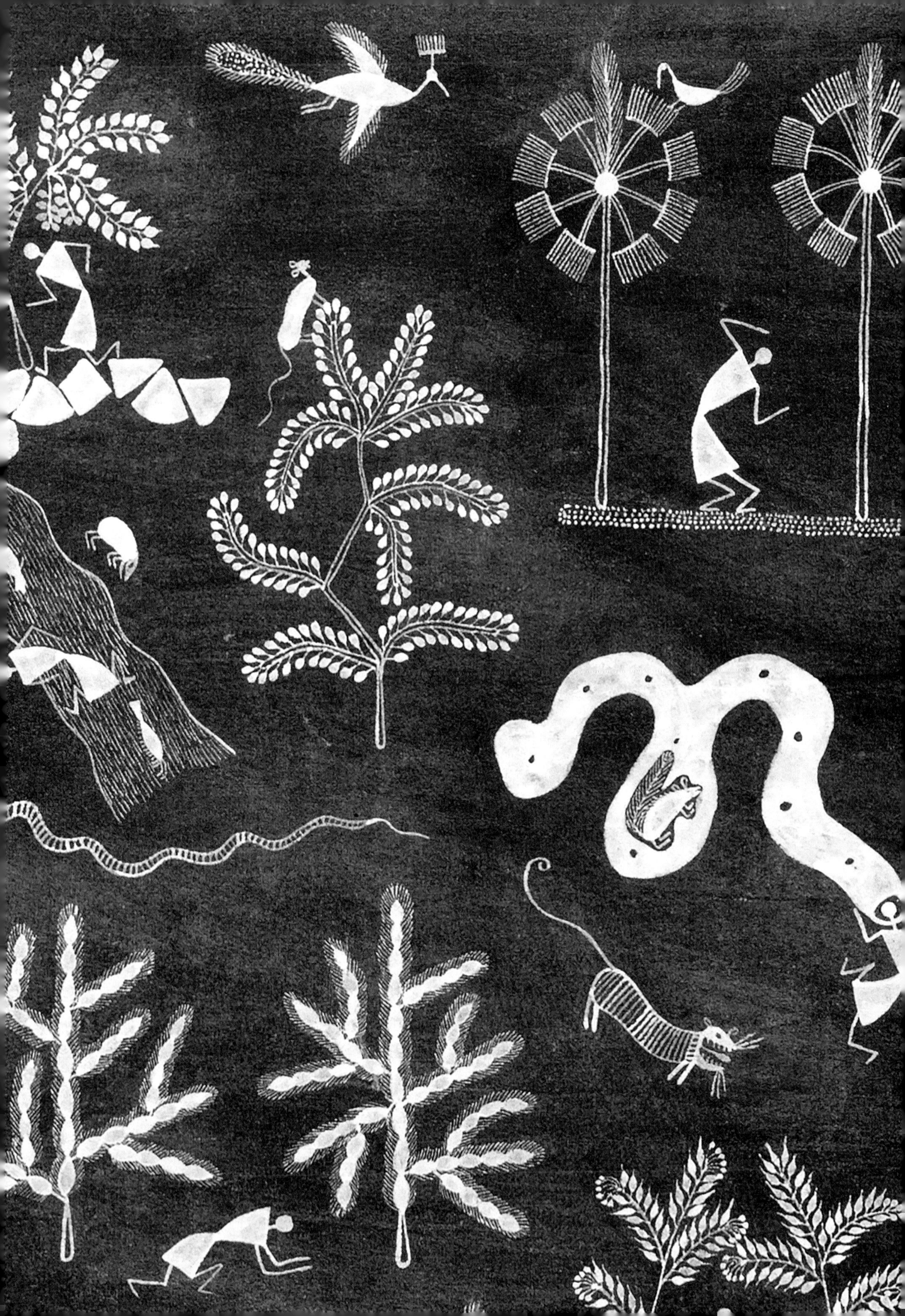

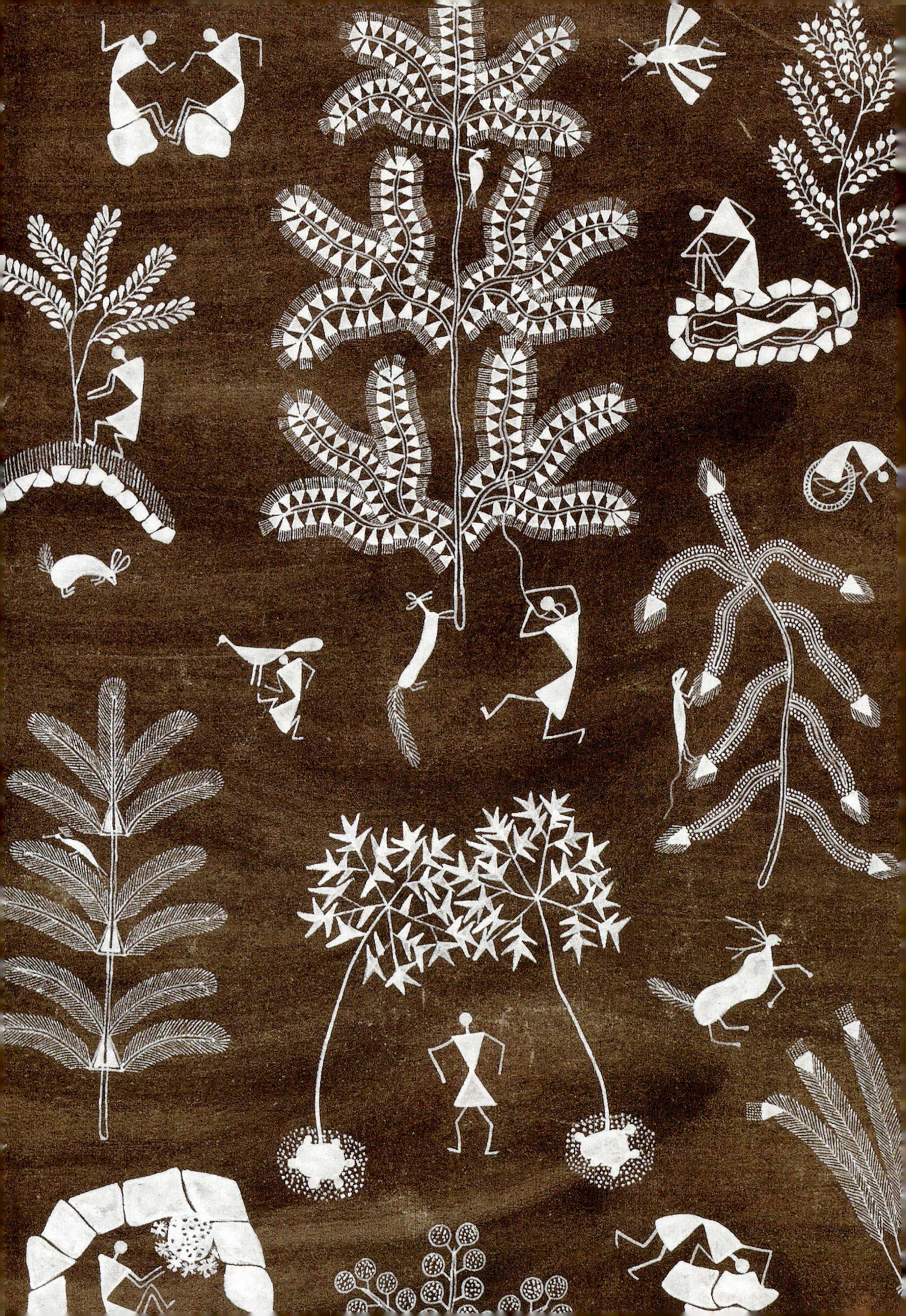

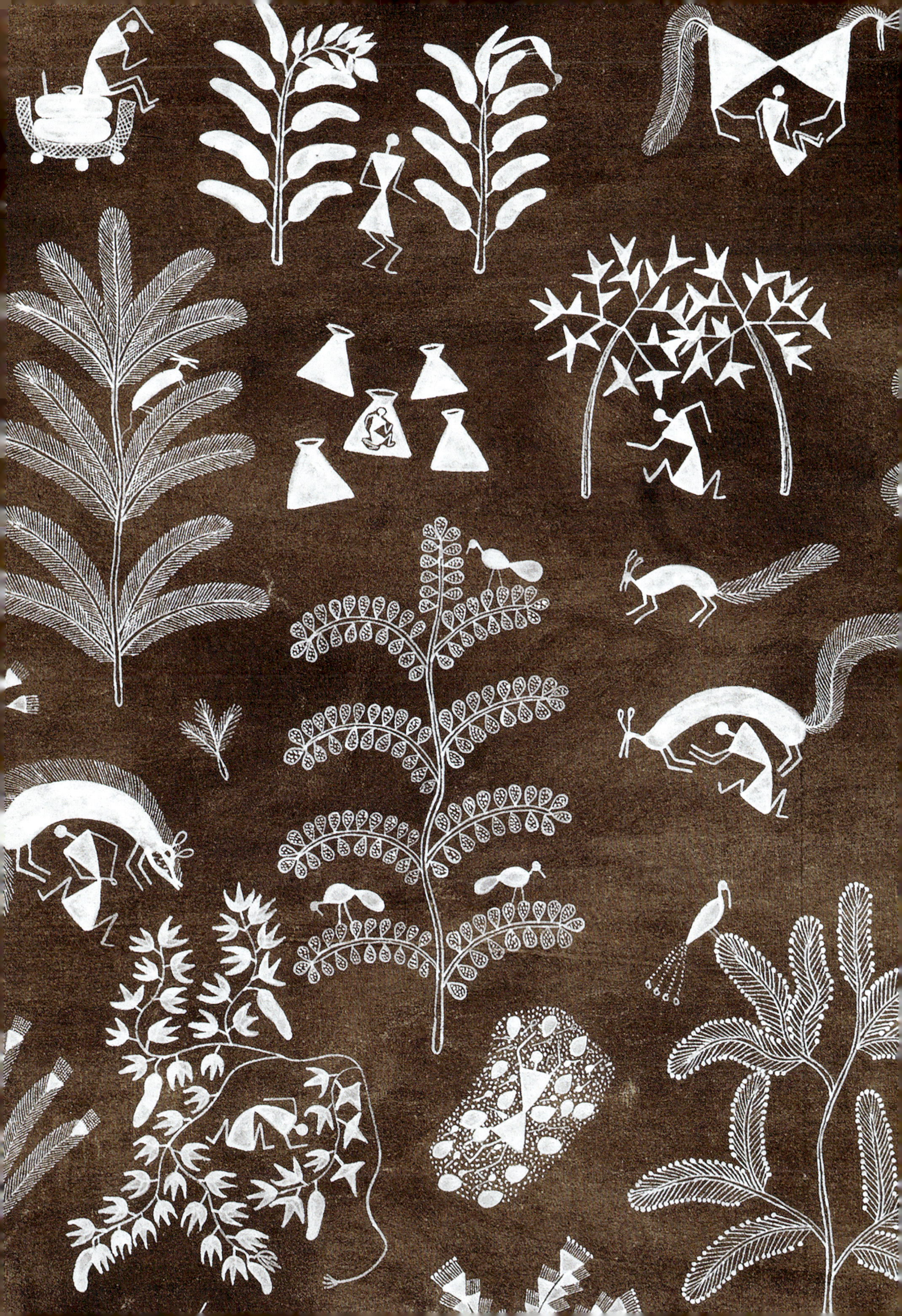

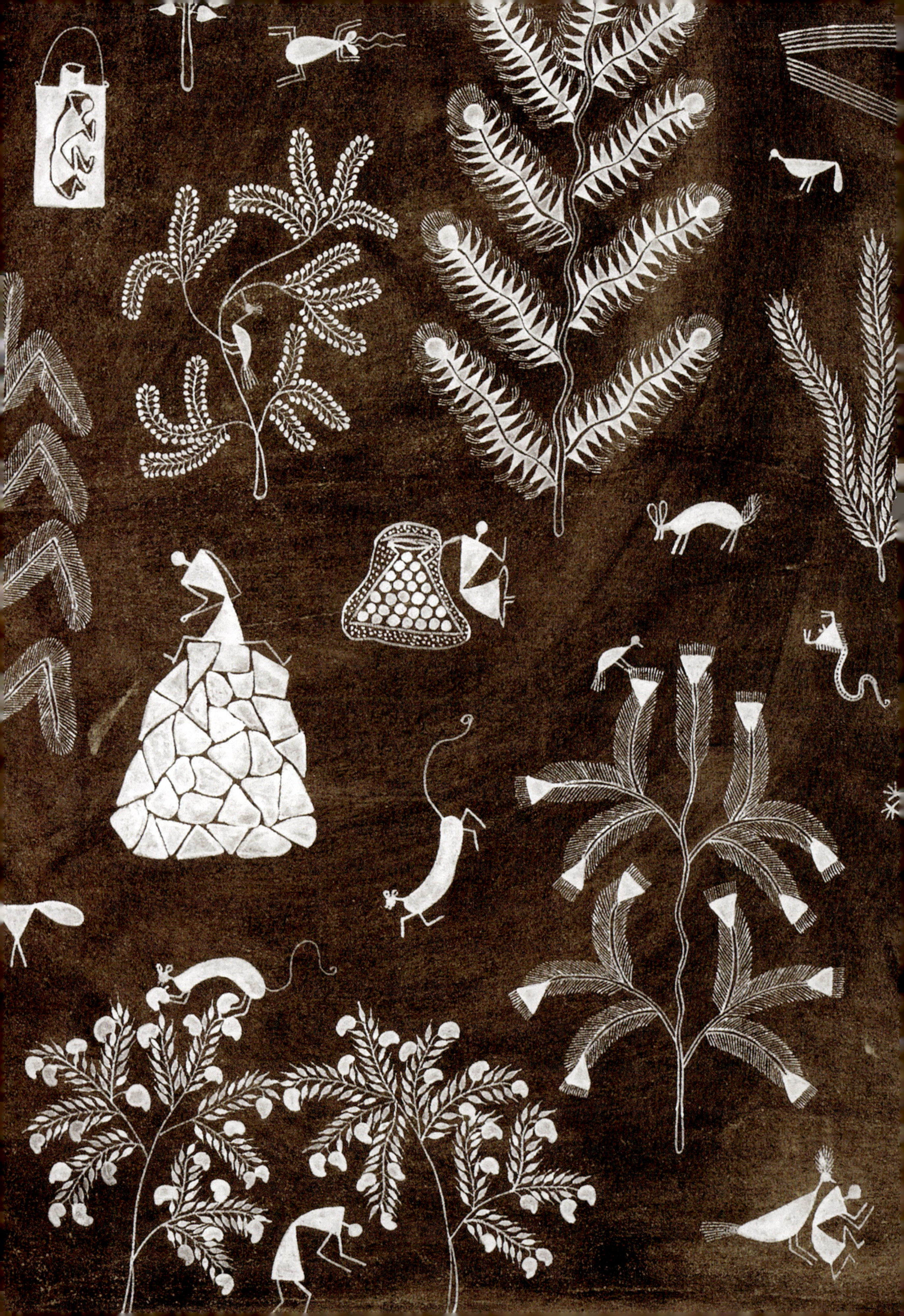

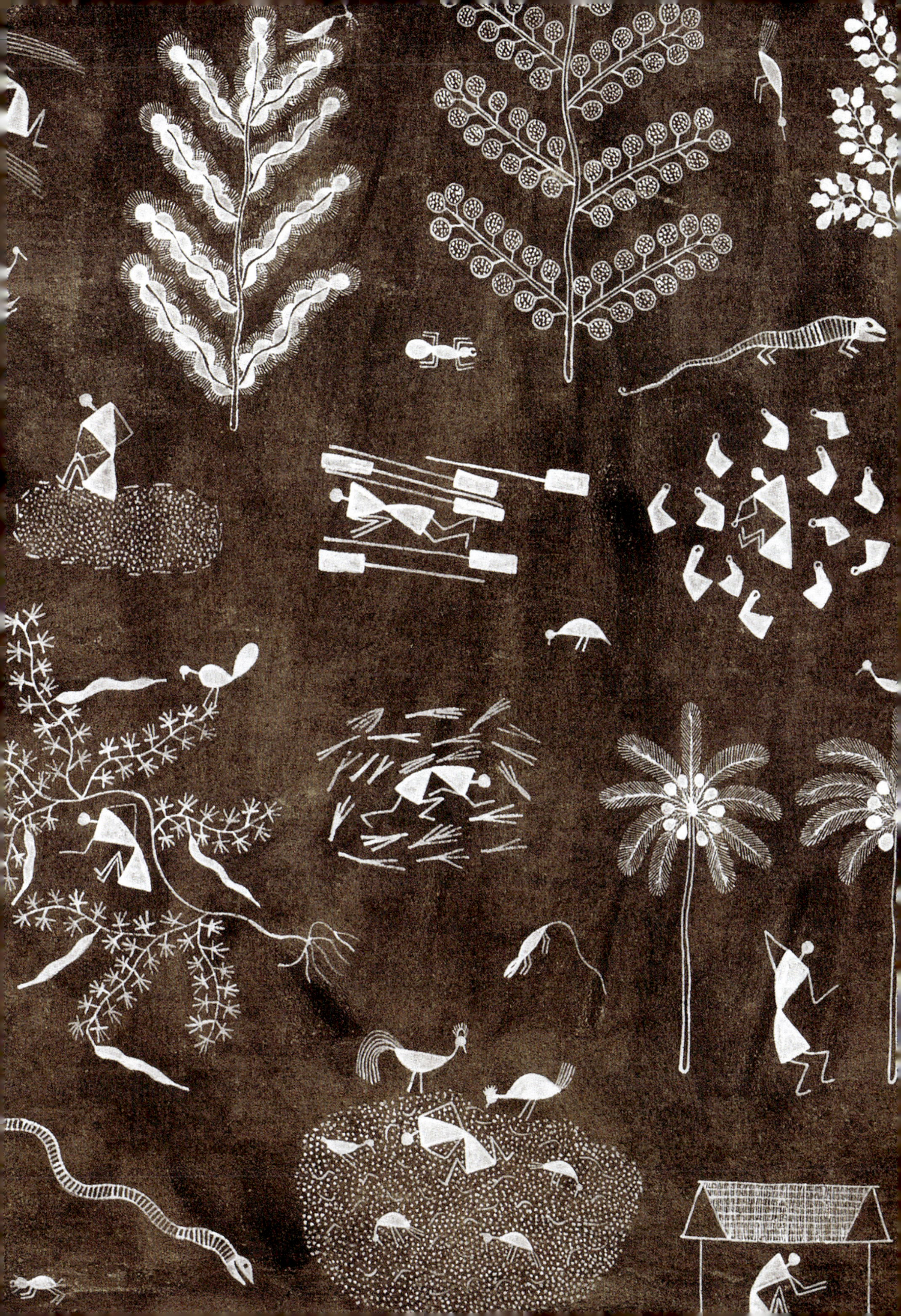

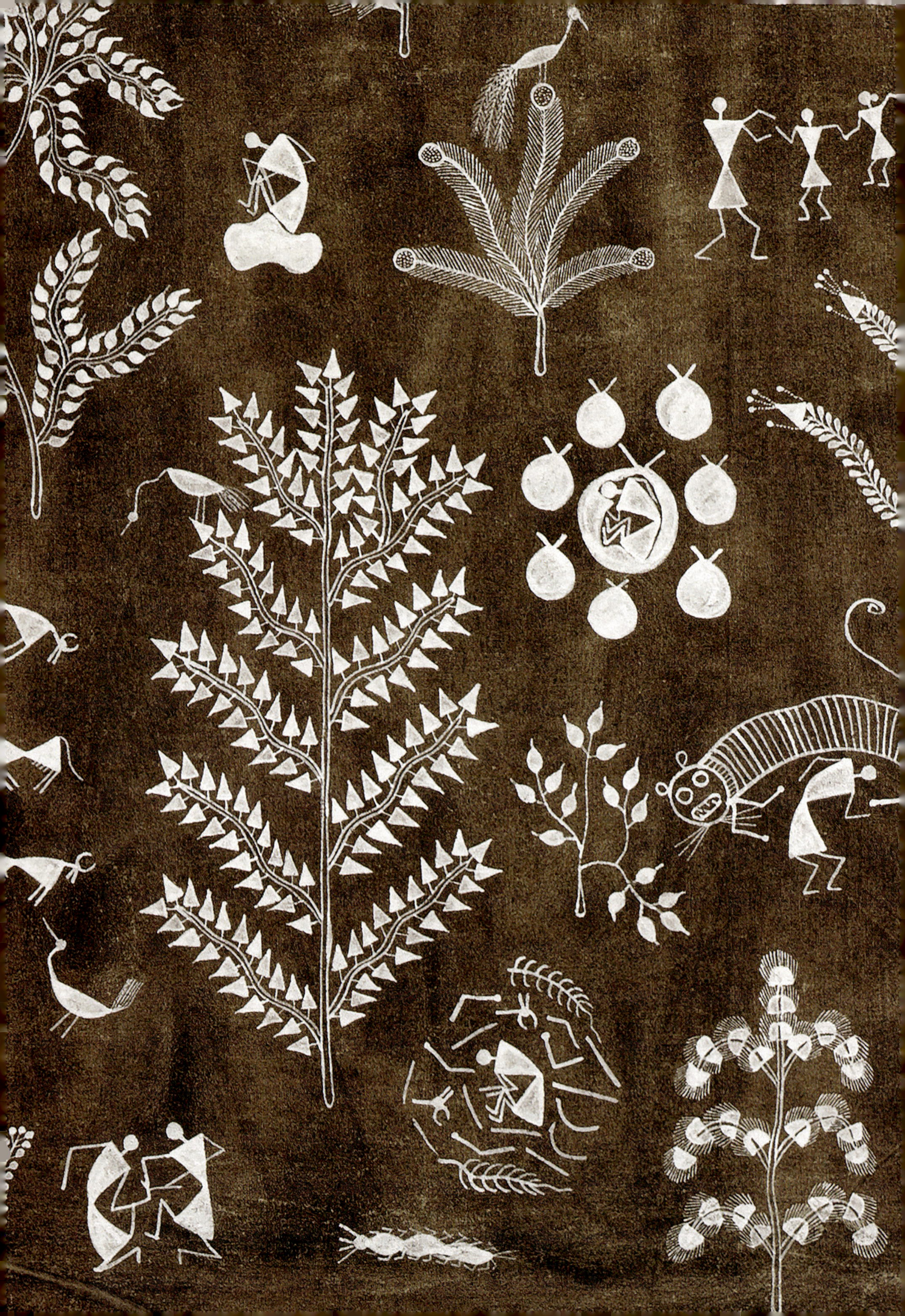

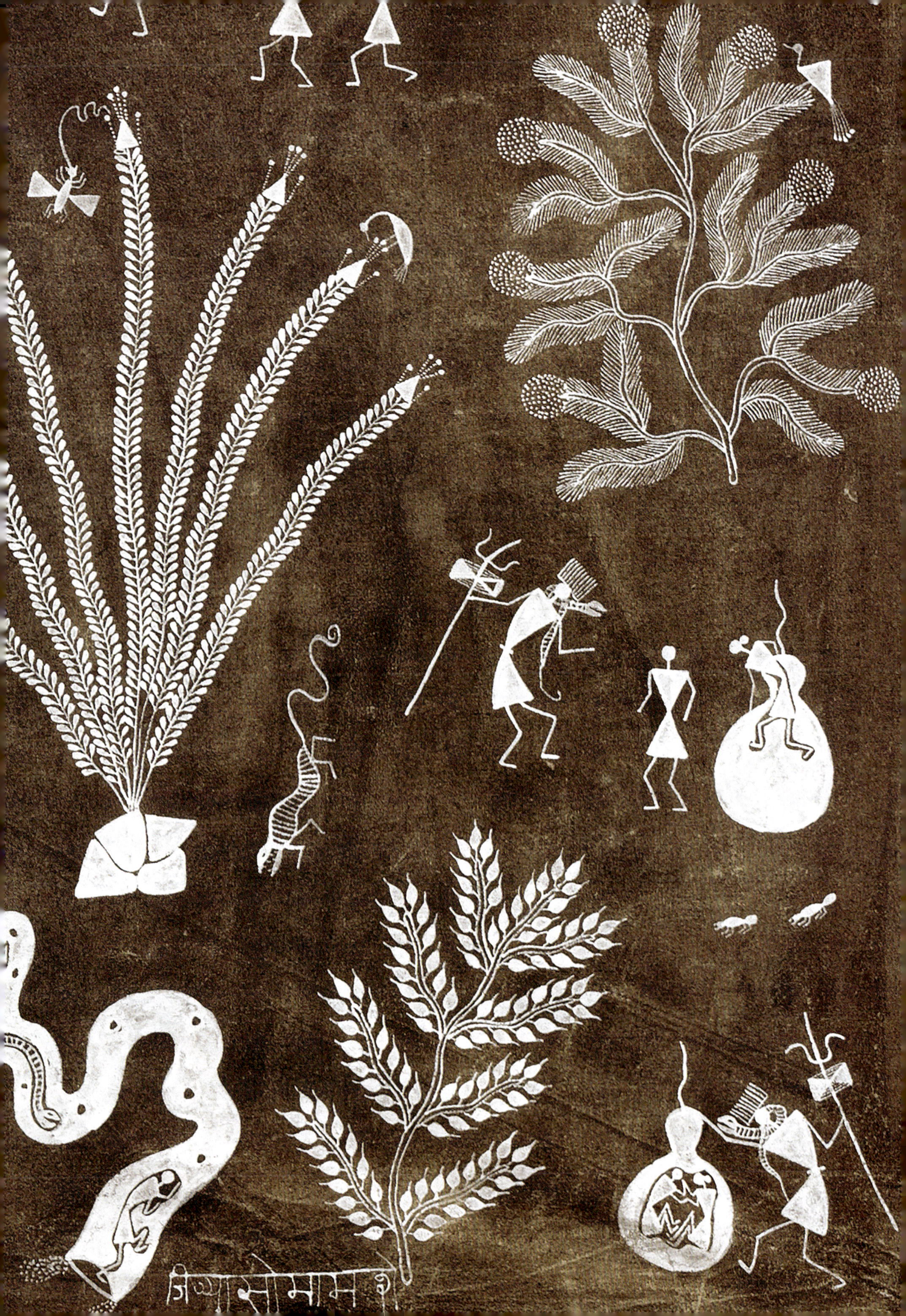
जिव्यासोमामशे

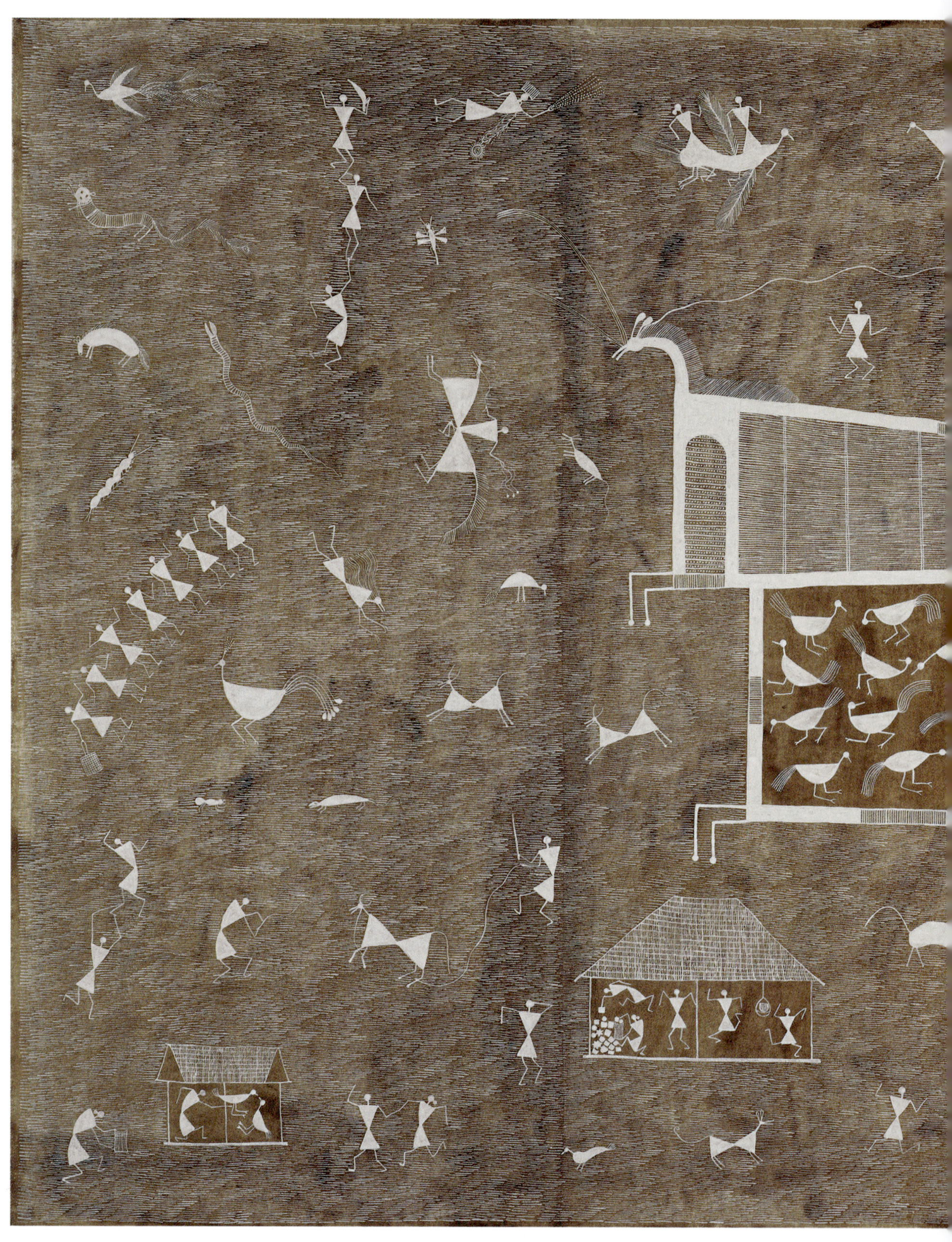

Jivya Soma Mashe, *Untitled*, 1999, acrylic and cow dung on canvas, 136 × 227 cm; 53.54 × 89.37 in. Collection of Pierre-Alexis and Sophie Dumas. Photo by Christian Baraja.

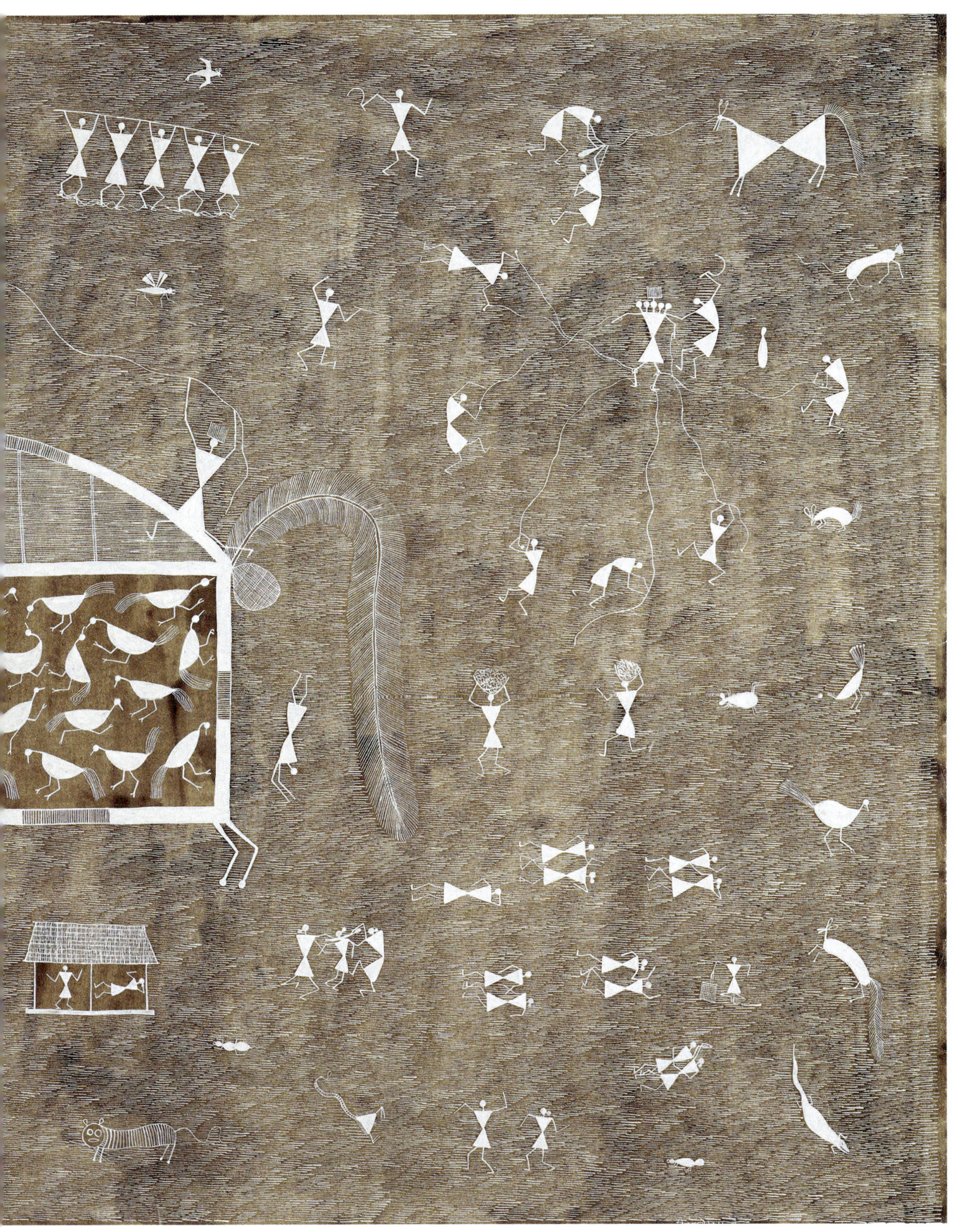

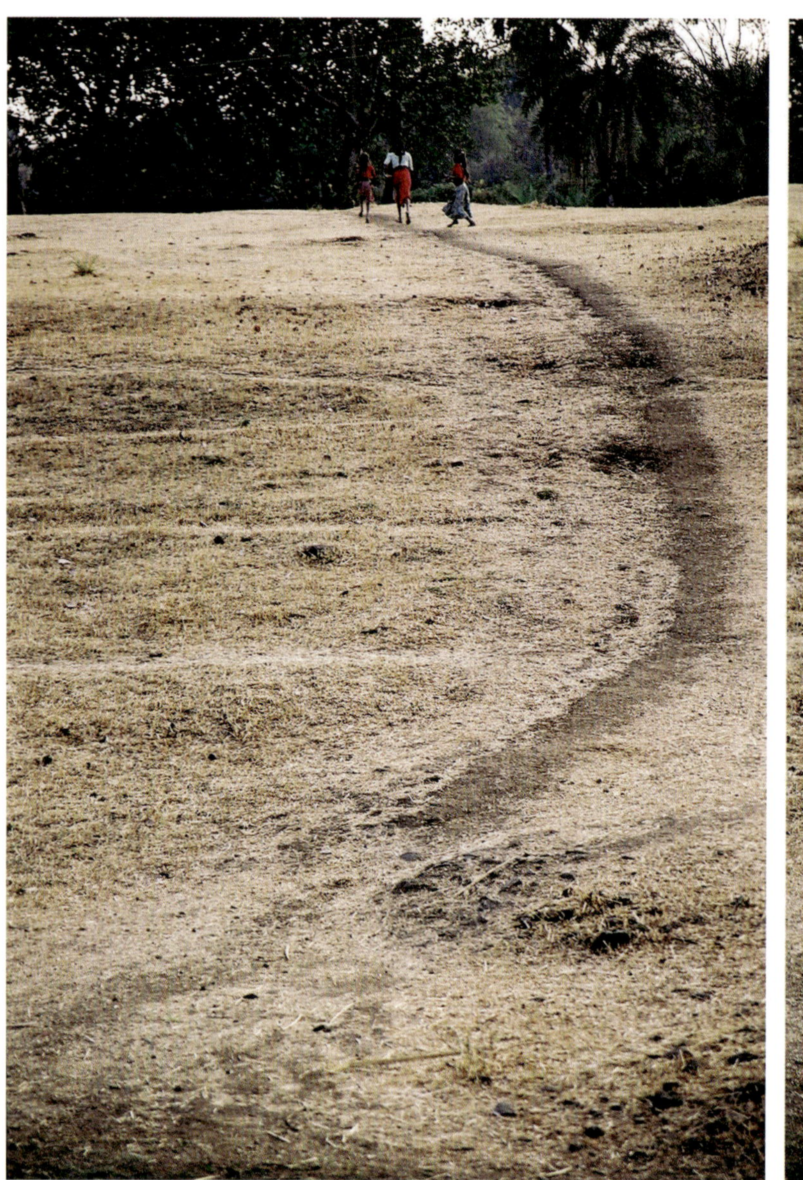

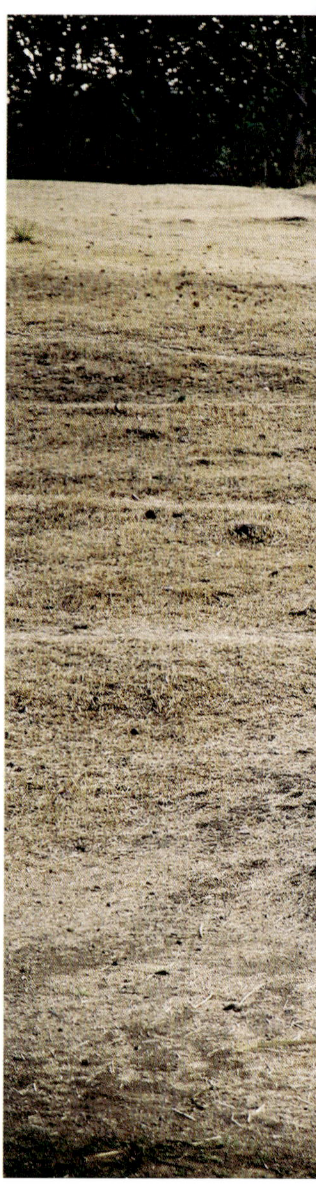

Walking is omnipresent in Warli landscapes, with countless trails marking the land like the remnants of incomplete sedentarisation, as well as in Jivya Soma Mashe's paintings. Walking is also represented as tracks, most often depicted as simple lines. One or more lines traverse and structure the canvas, inviting us to follow his characters, always in motion – his 'walkers'. (Photos by Hervé Perdriolle, Ganjad, 2012)

La marche est omniprésente tant dans les paysages warli, avec ces innombrables pistes marquant le sol comme les vestiges d'une sédentarisation inachevée, que dans les peintures de Jivya Soma Mashe. Dans ses peintures, la marche s'inscrit également sous la forme de pistes, représentées le plus souvent par une simple ligne. Une ou plusieurs lignes, qui parcourent et structurent la toile, nous invitent à suivre ses personnages toujours en mouvement, ses « marcheurs ». (Photographies de Hervé Perdriolle, Ganjad 2012)

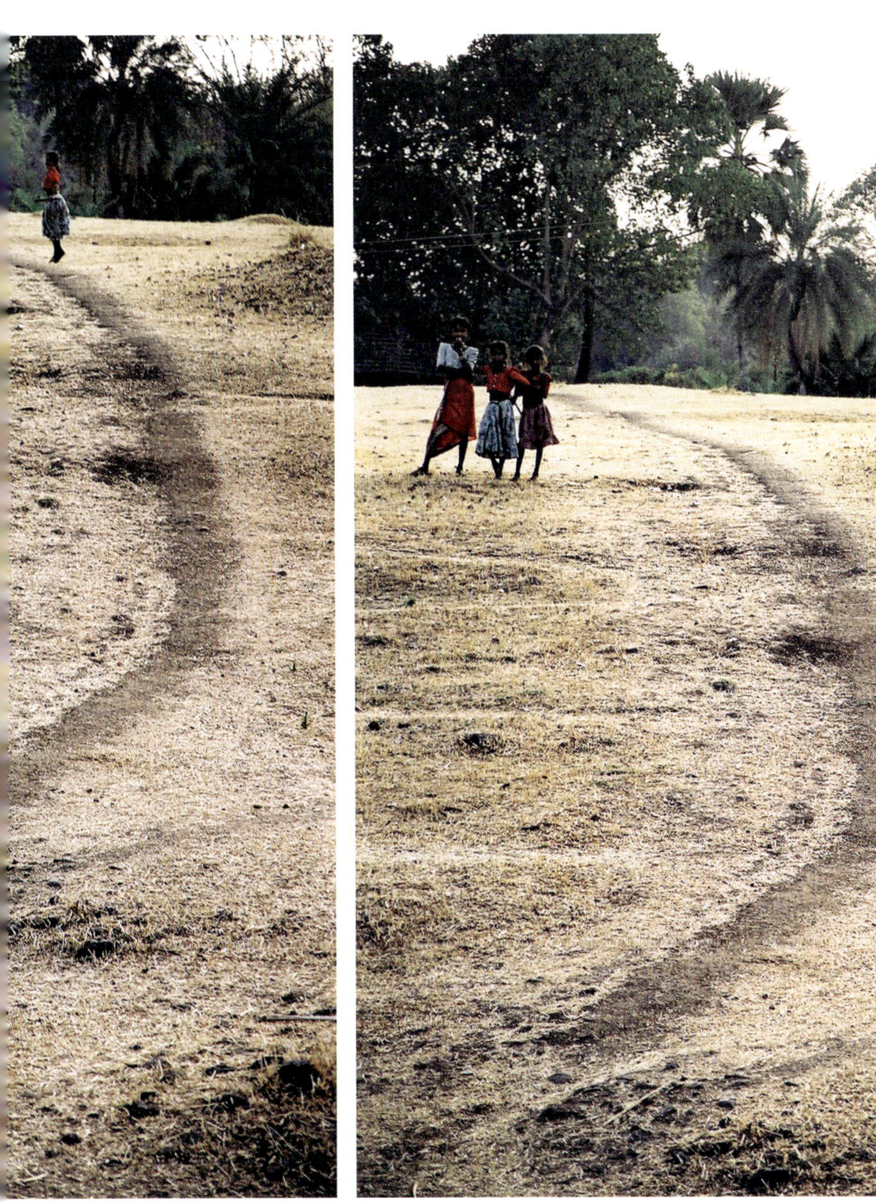

Pages 86–87
Jivya Soma Mashe, *Untitled*, 1998,
acrylic and cow dung on canvas,
138 × 200 cm; 54.33 × 78.74 in. (*details on pages* 88–95)
Collection of Hervé Perdriolle.
Photo by Christian Baraja.

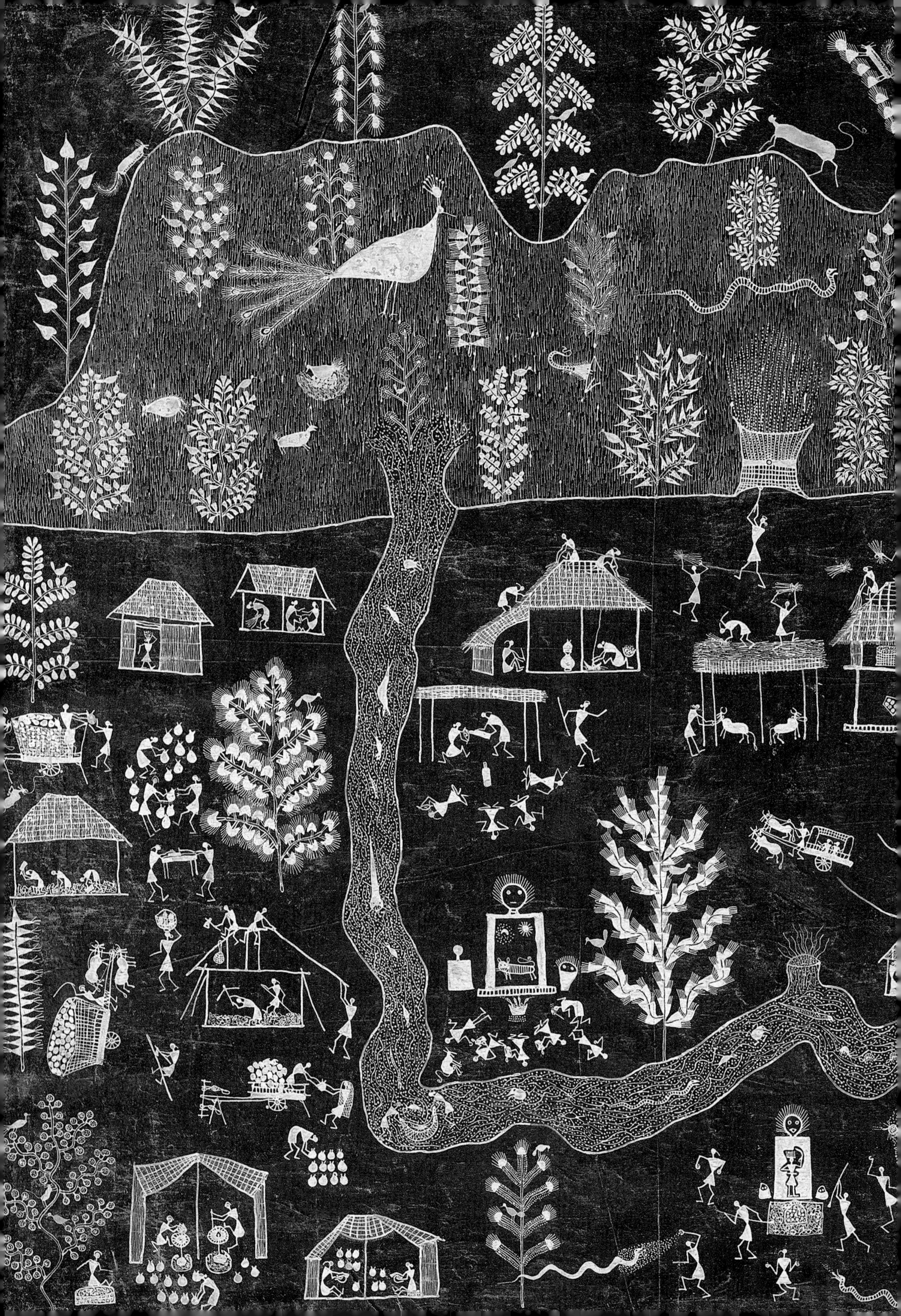

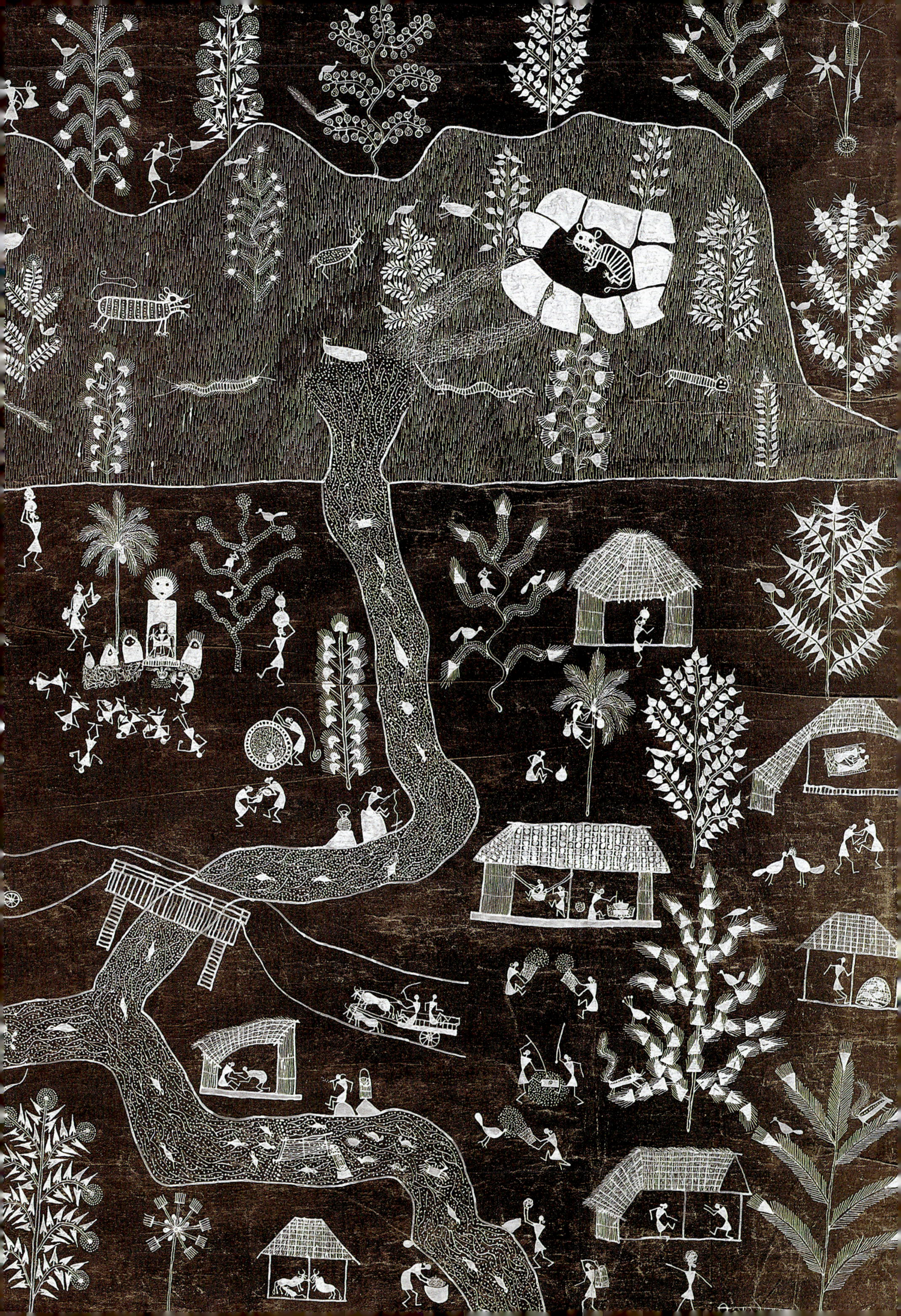

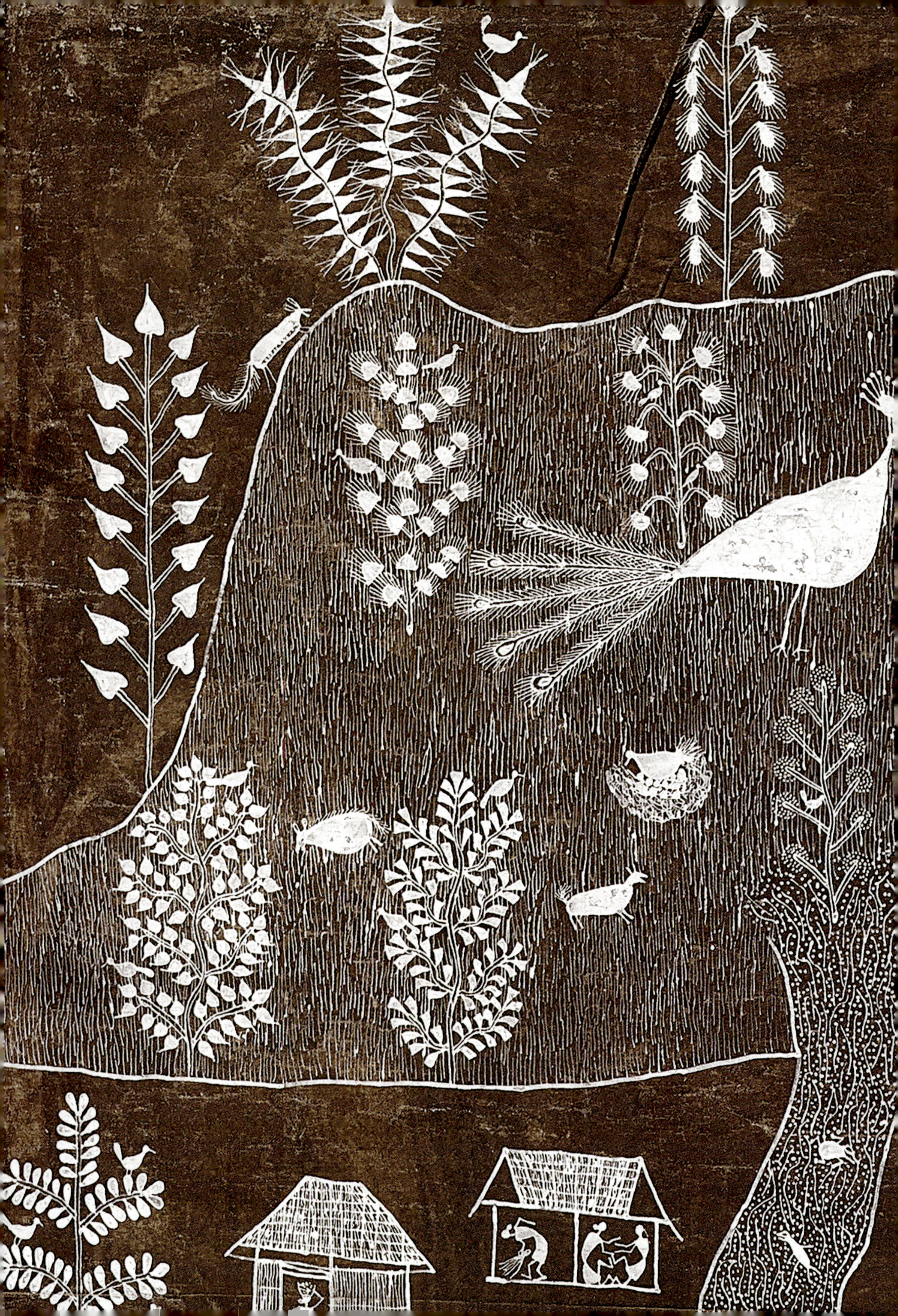

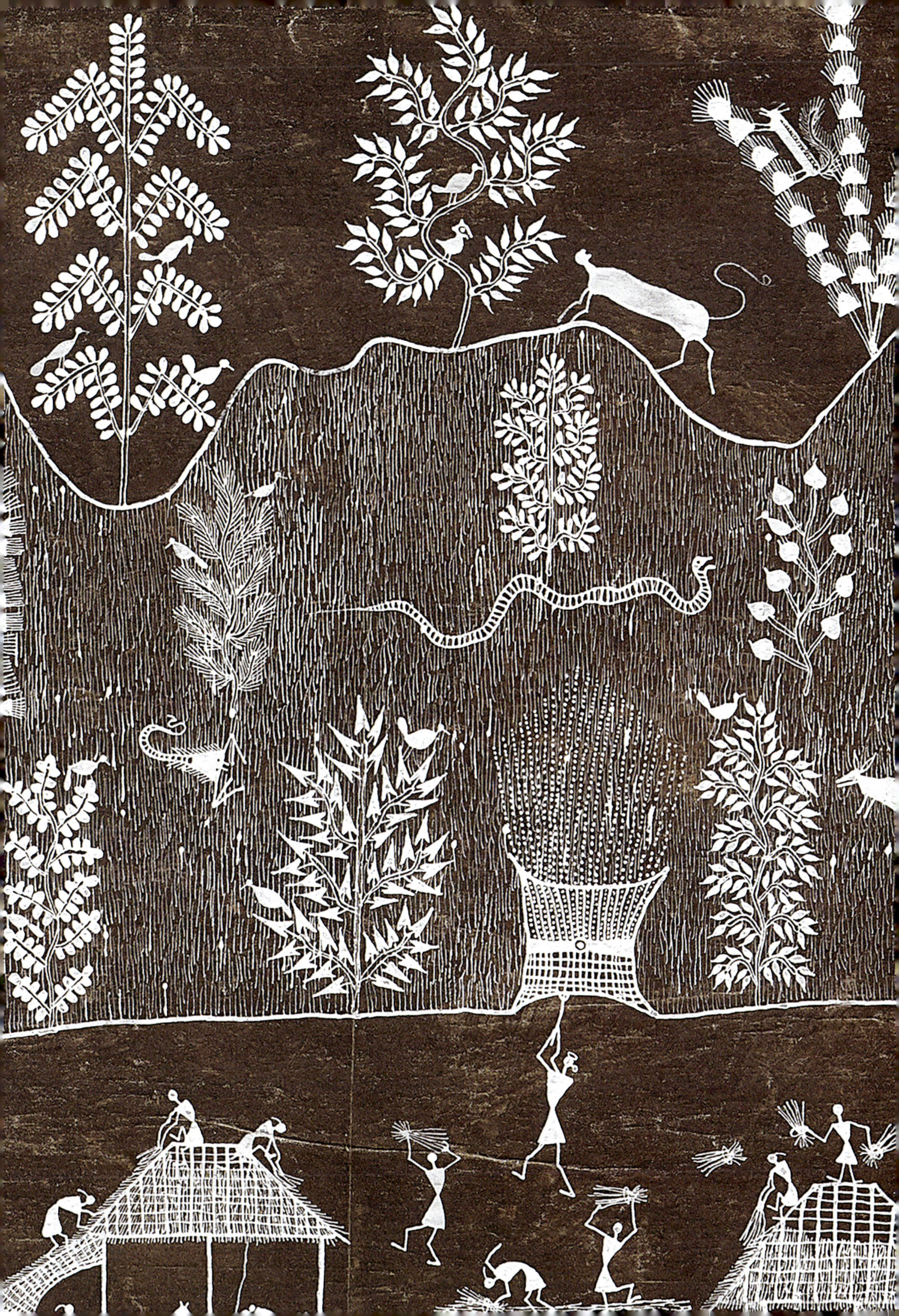

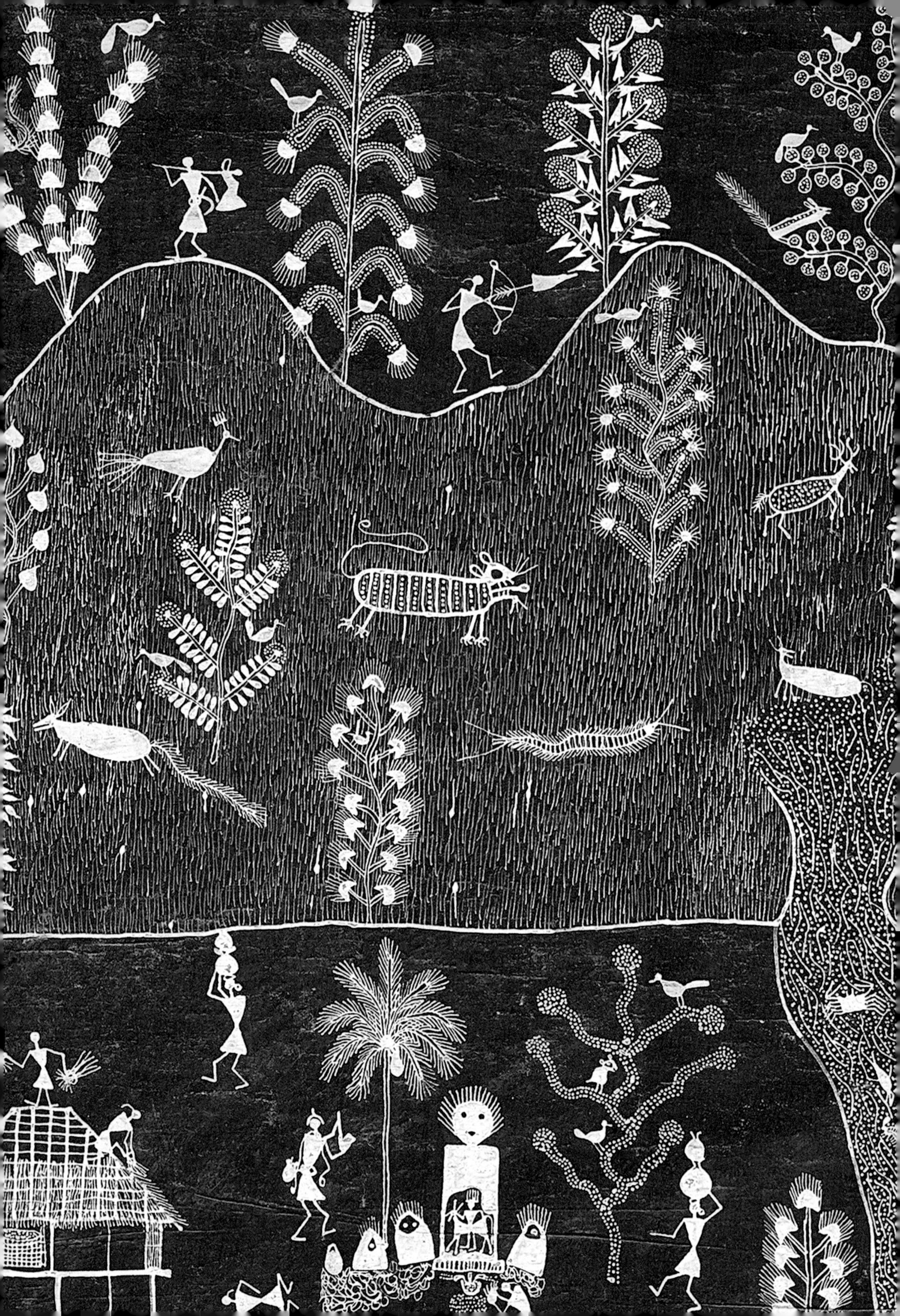

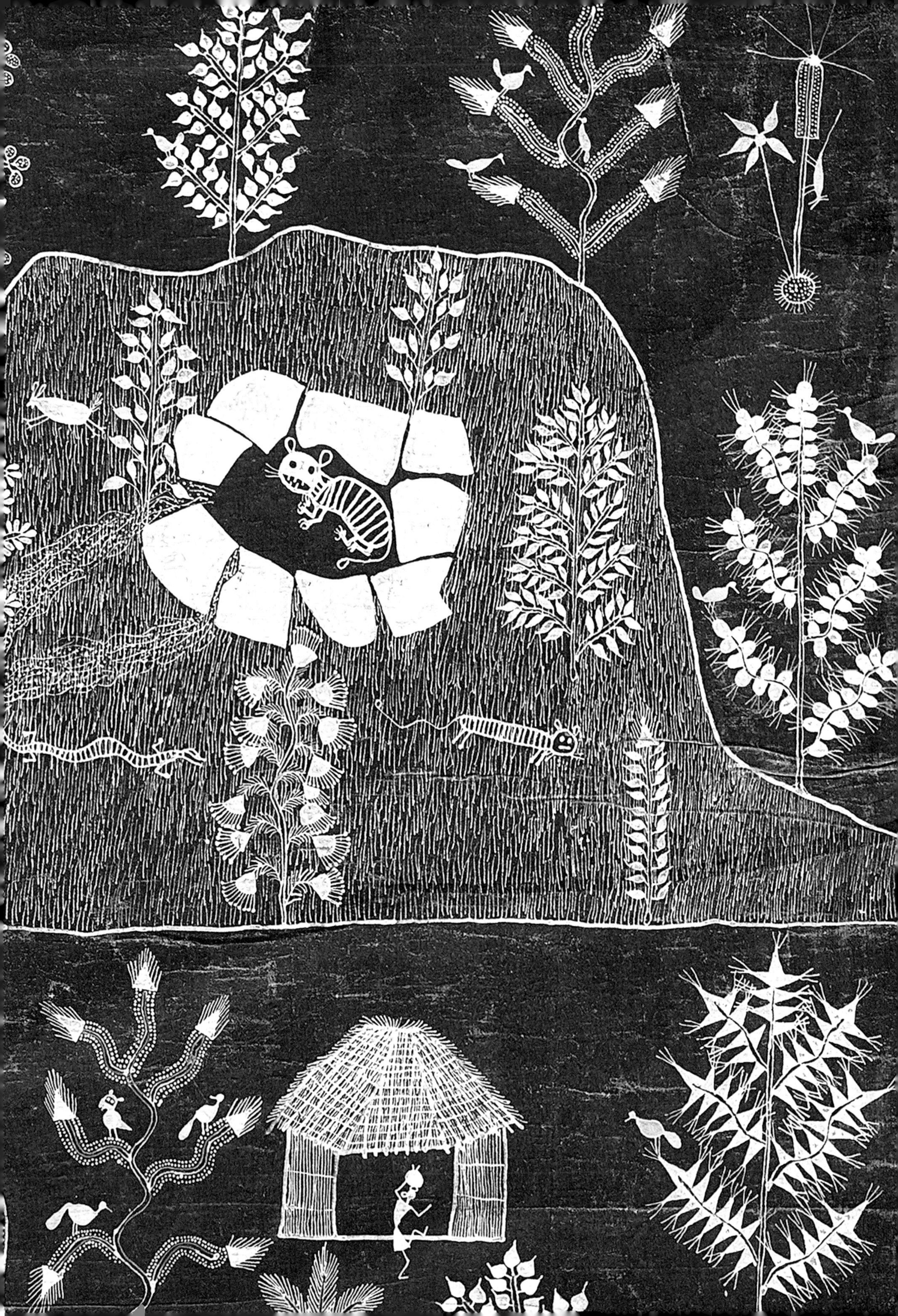

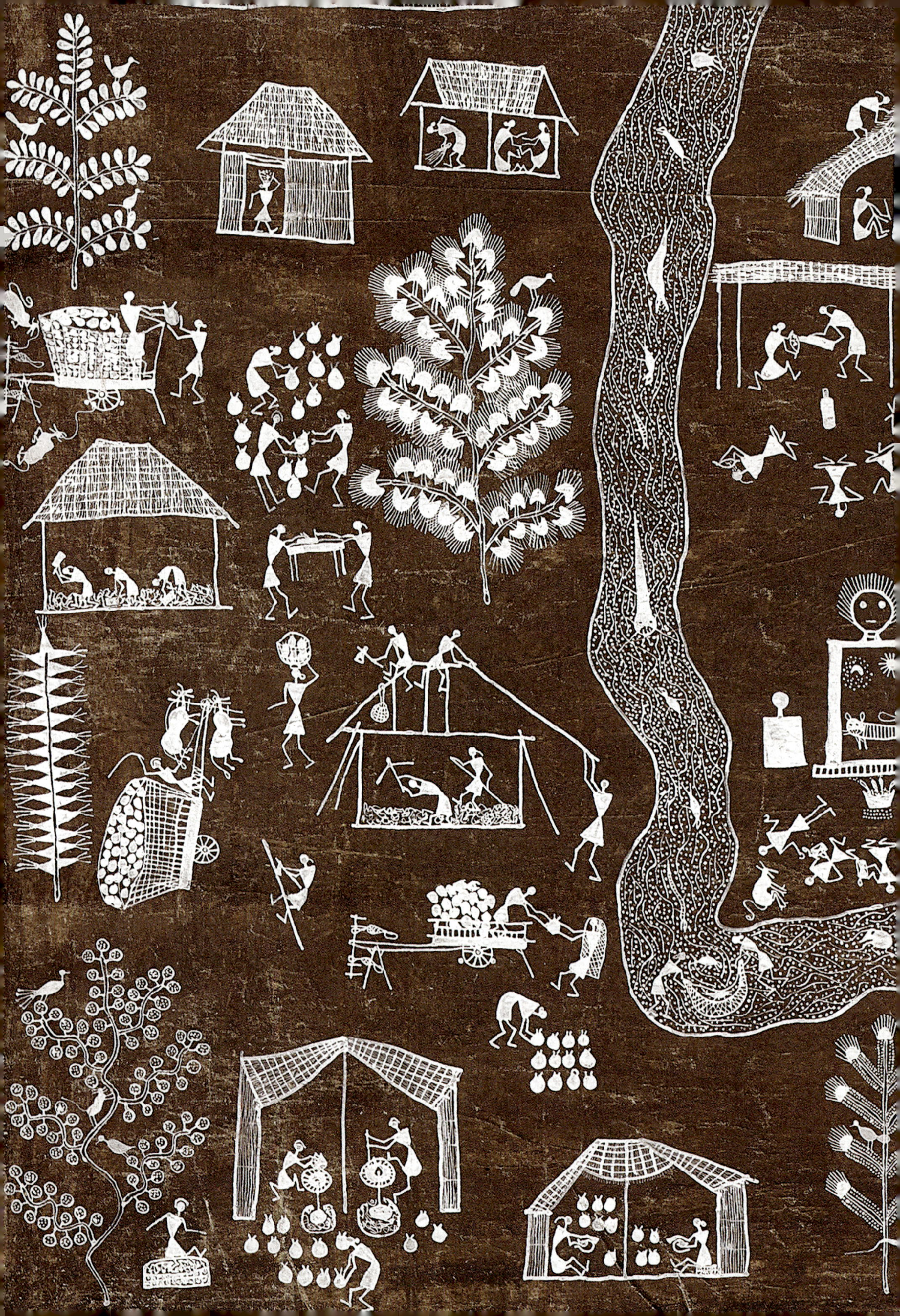

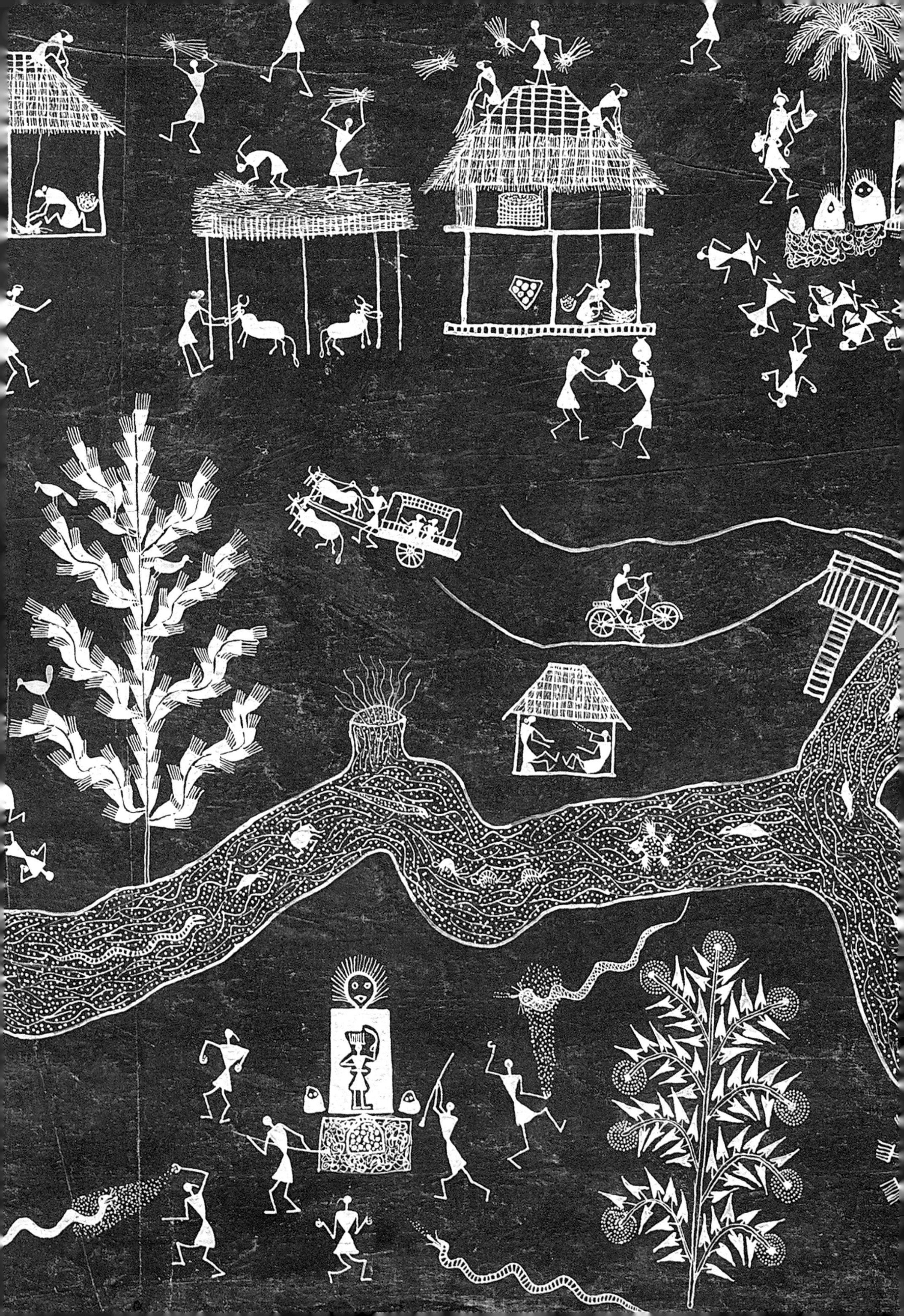

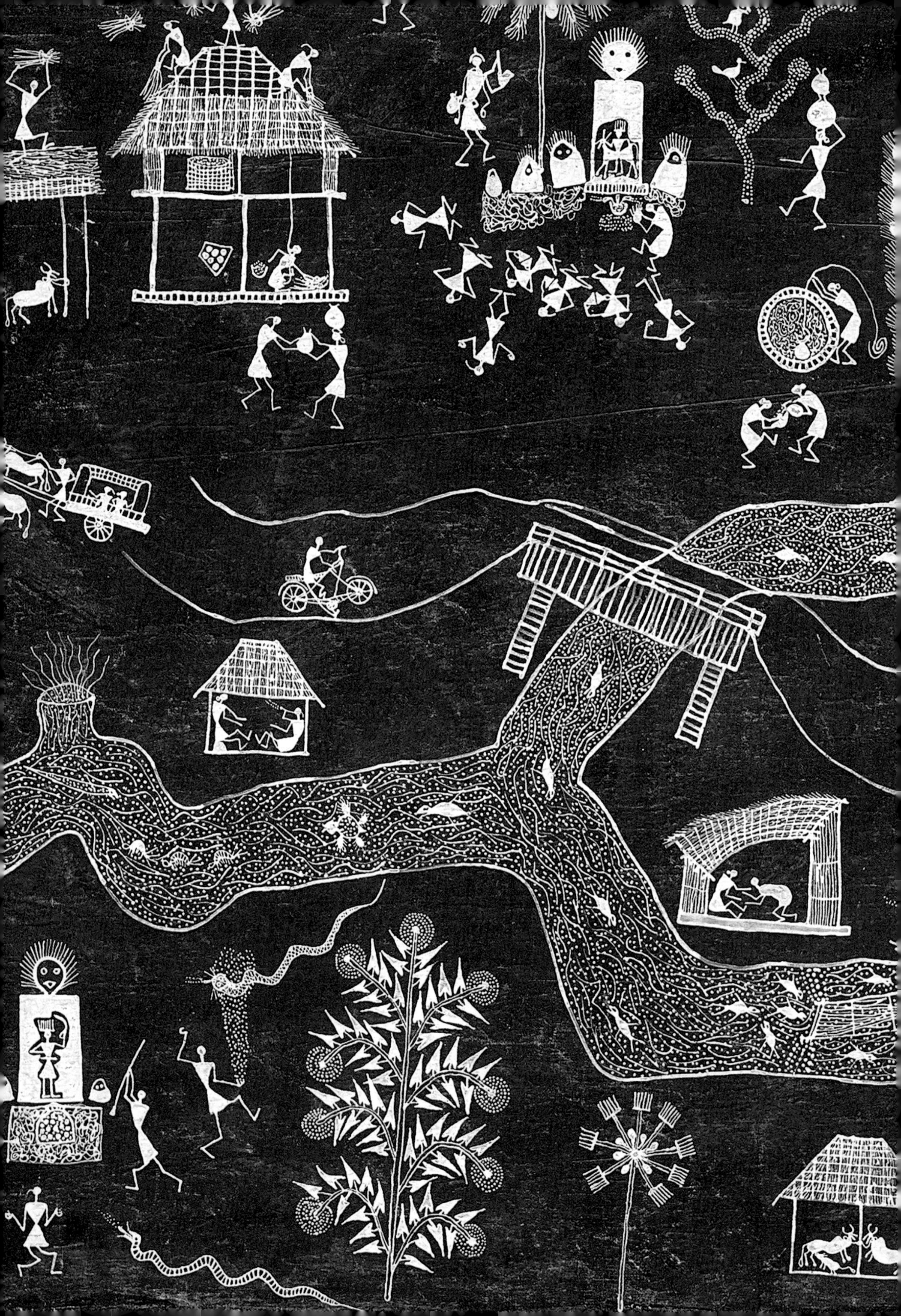

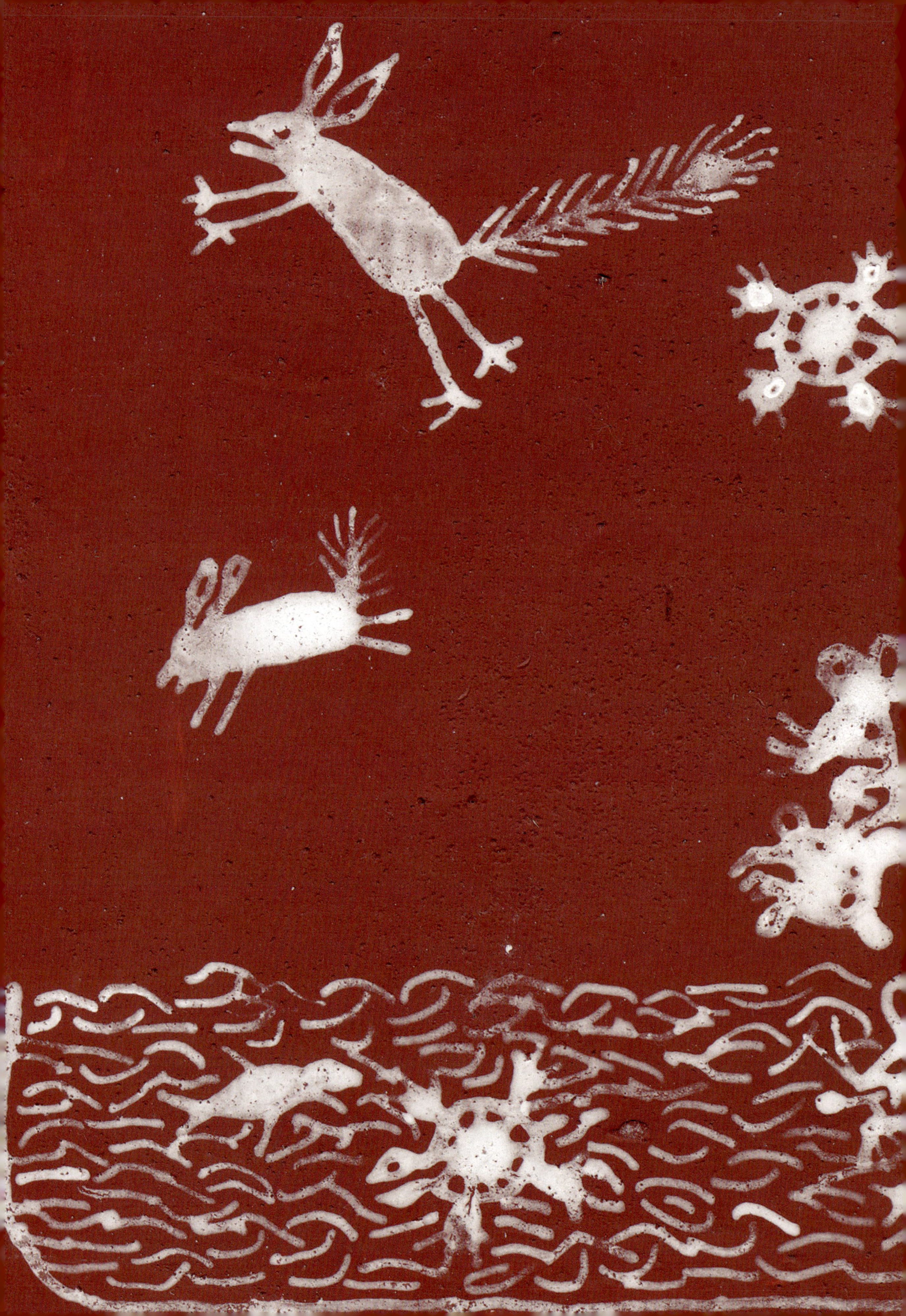

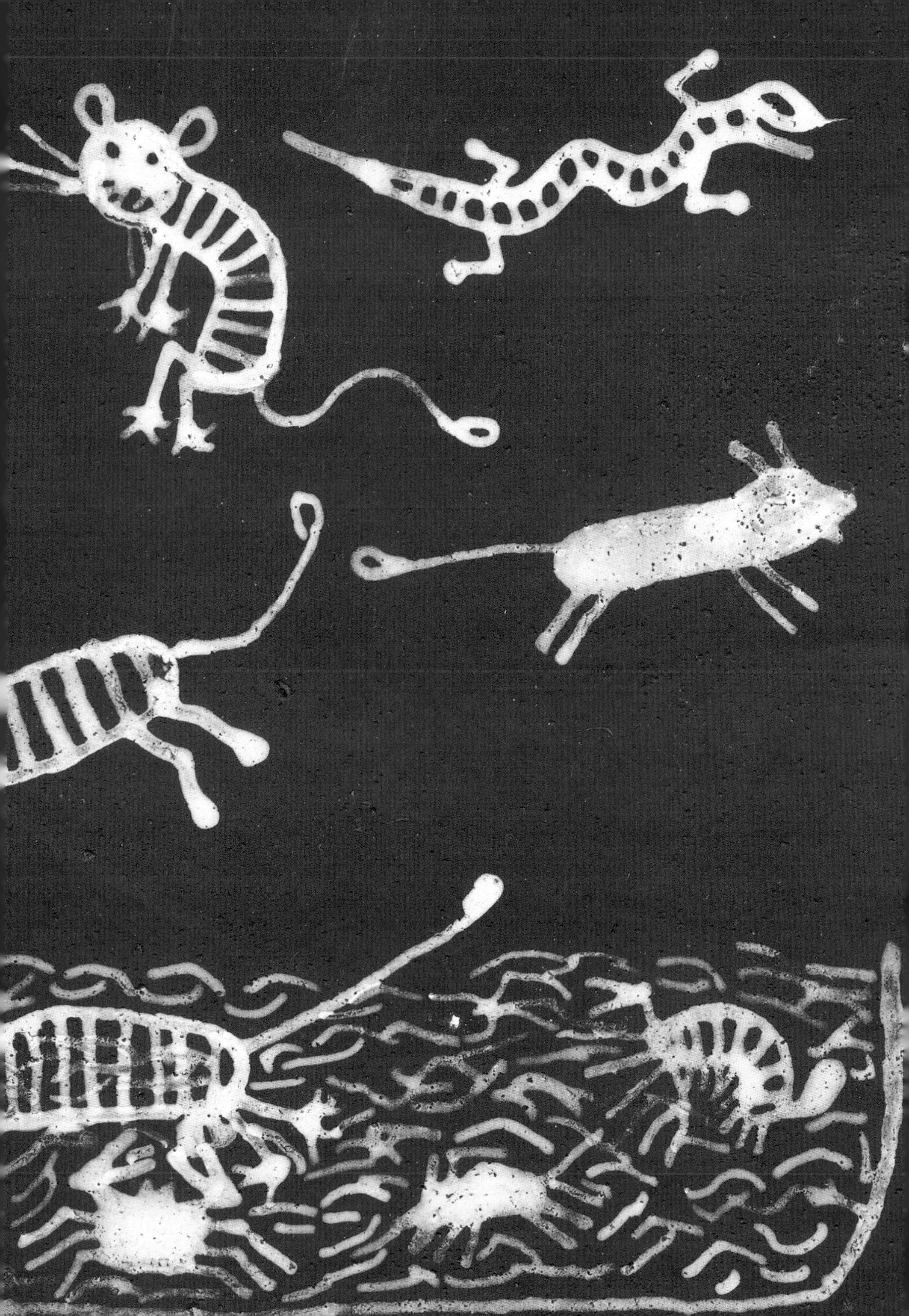

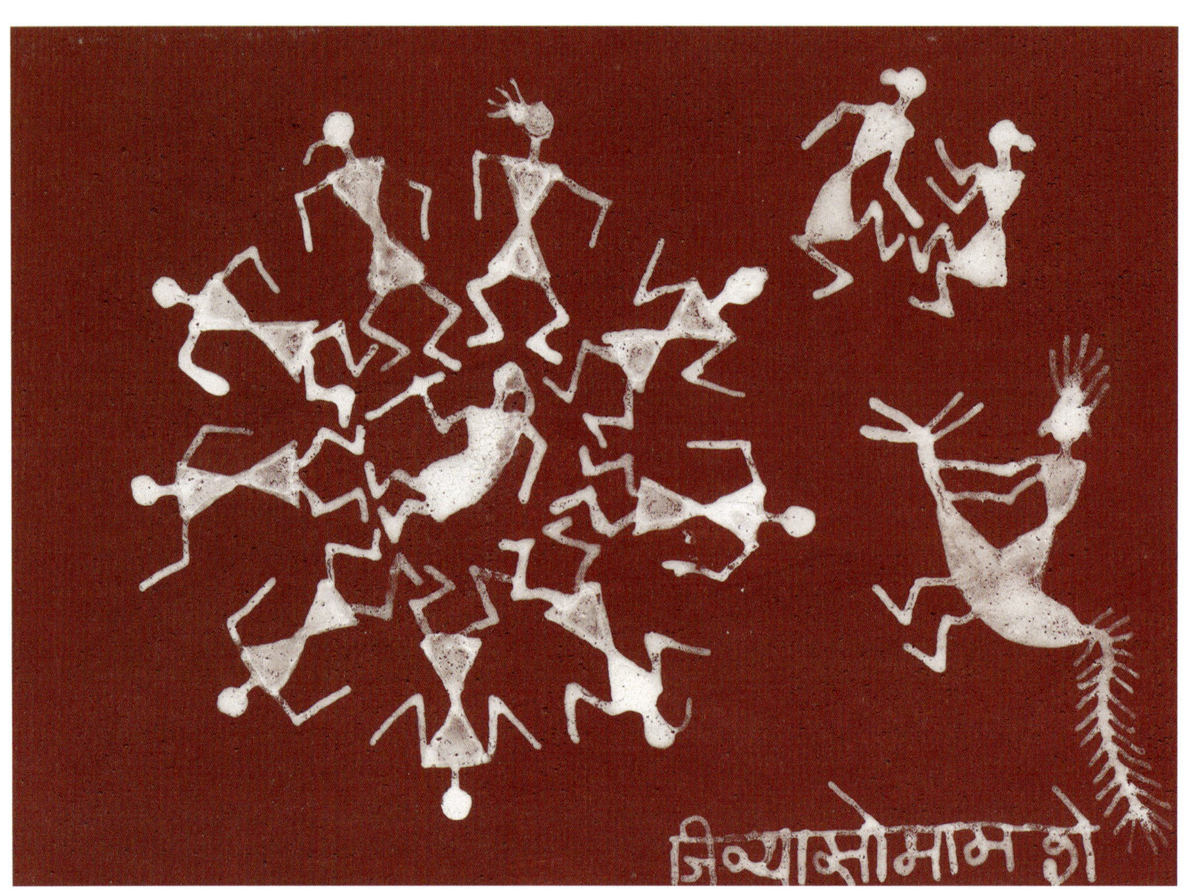

A short while after our first meetings, Jivya Soma Mashe offered me some superb small paintings that I still keep carefully. They are the only paintings I have of the ritual art form. The paper is coated with the natural terracotta colour mixed with a thick and irregular acrylic base that imbues the surface with the roughness of the walls in Warli huts. The white paint was obtained, as before, with rice paste diluted with water. Today, acrylic is used in place of the rice paste as this, once it has dried, disintegrates. What was acceptable in ephemeral works is not suited to permanent ones.

Jivya Soma Mashe m'avait offert, quelque temps après nos premières rencontres, de merveilleuses petites peintures que je garde auprès de moi avec une attention toute particulière. Elles sont le seul témoignage pictural en ma possession de ce que fut cette forme d'art rituel. Le papier est recouvert de pigment naturel couleur *terracotta* mélangé avec une base acrylique, épaisse et irrégulière, conférant à cette surface l'aspect rudimentaire des torchis recouvrant les murs des huttes warli. Le blanc, comme jadis, est obtenu à partir de pâte de riz diluée avec de l'eau. Aujourd'hui, l'acrylique a remplacé la pâte de riz car celle-ci, une fois sèche, s'effrite. Ce qui était valable pour des œuvres éphémères ne l'est plus pour des œuvres pérennes.

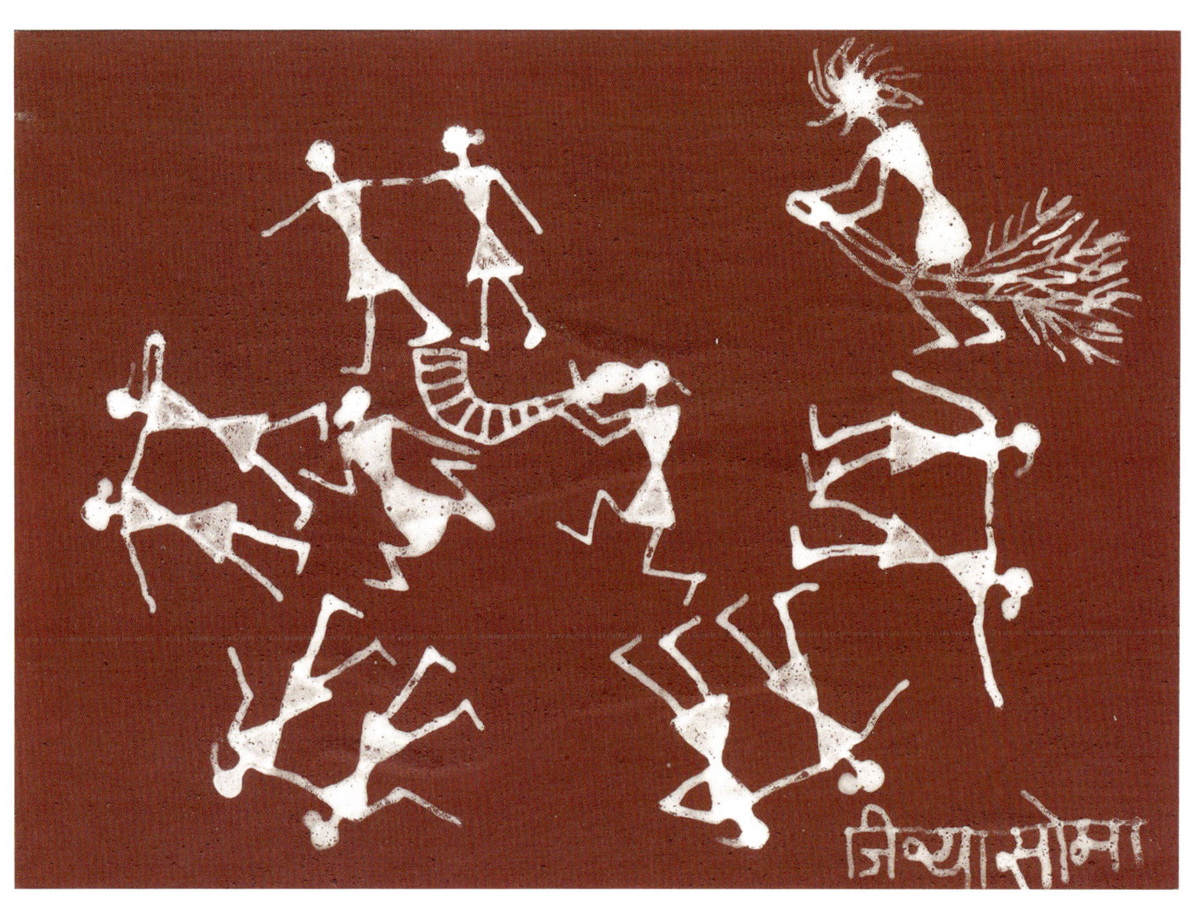

Pages 96–97, 98, 99, 100–101
Jivya Soma Mashe, *Untitled*, circa 1990,
rice paste and acrylic on paper,
12.8 × 18.1 cm; 5.03 × 7.1 in.

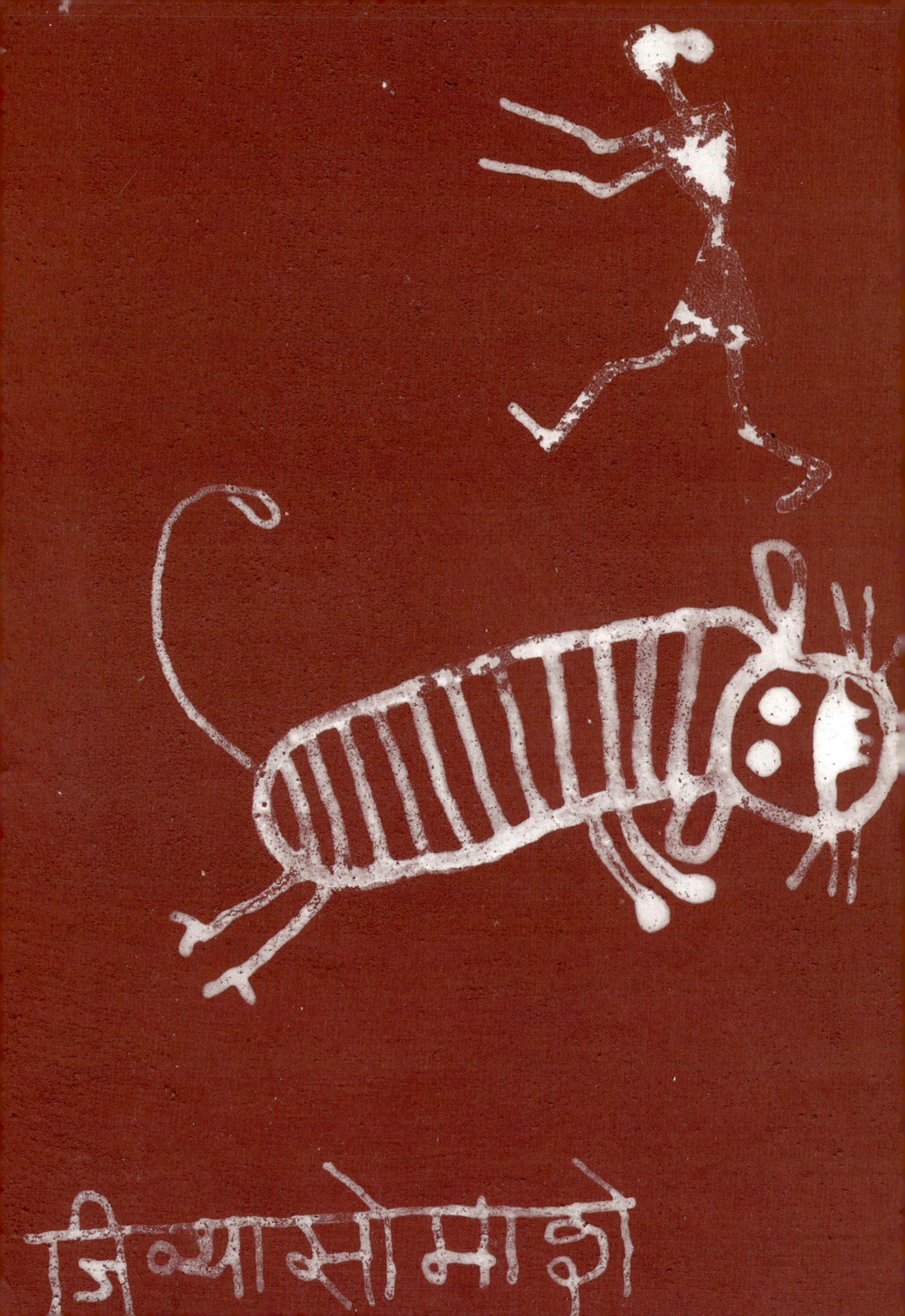

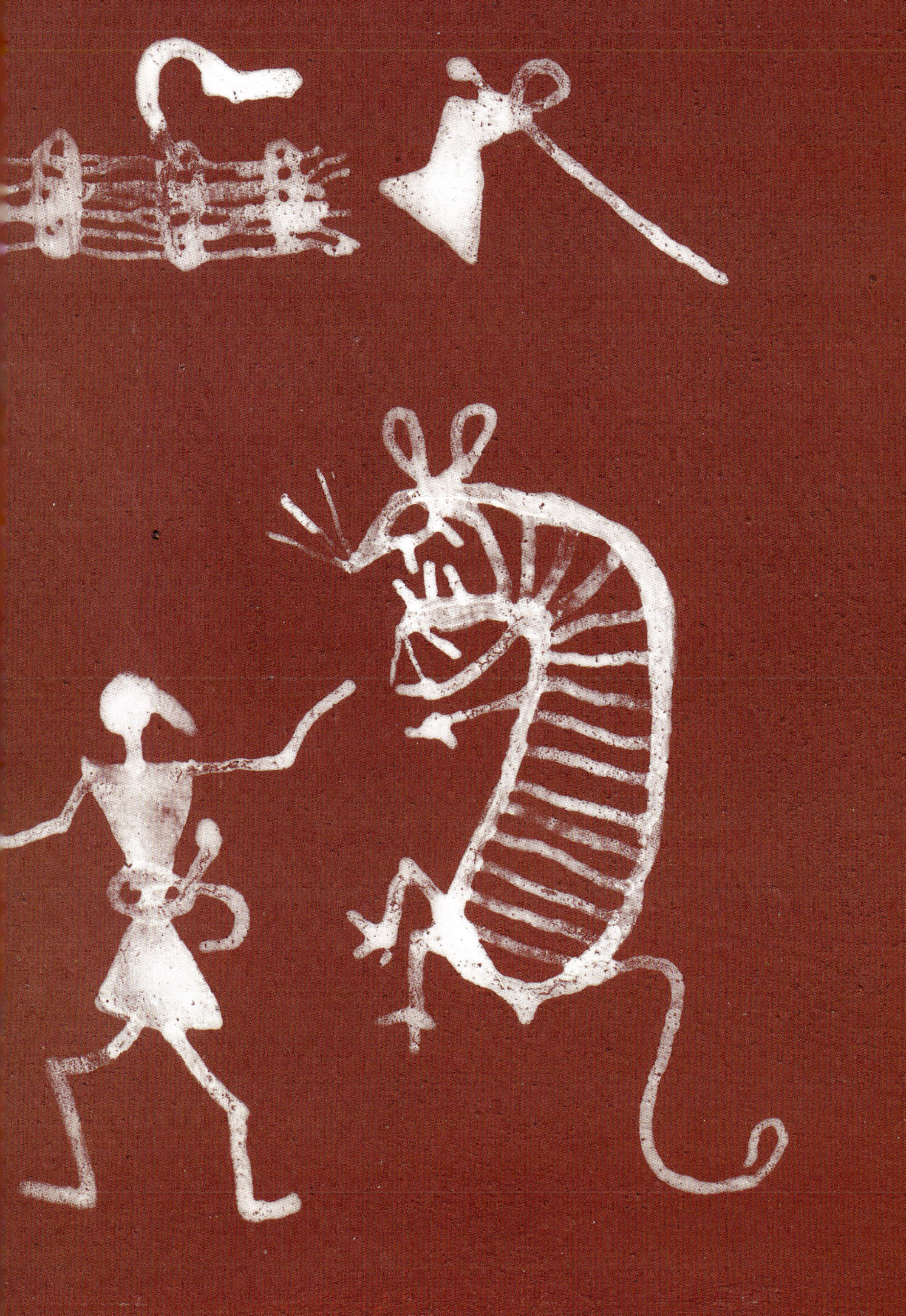

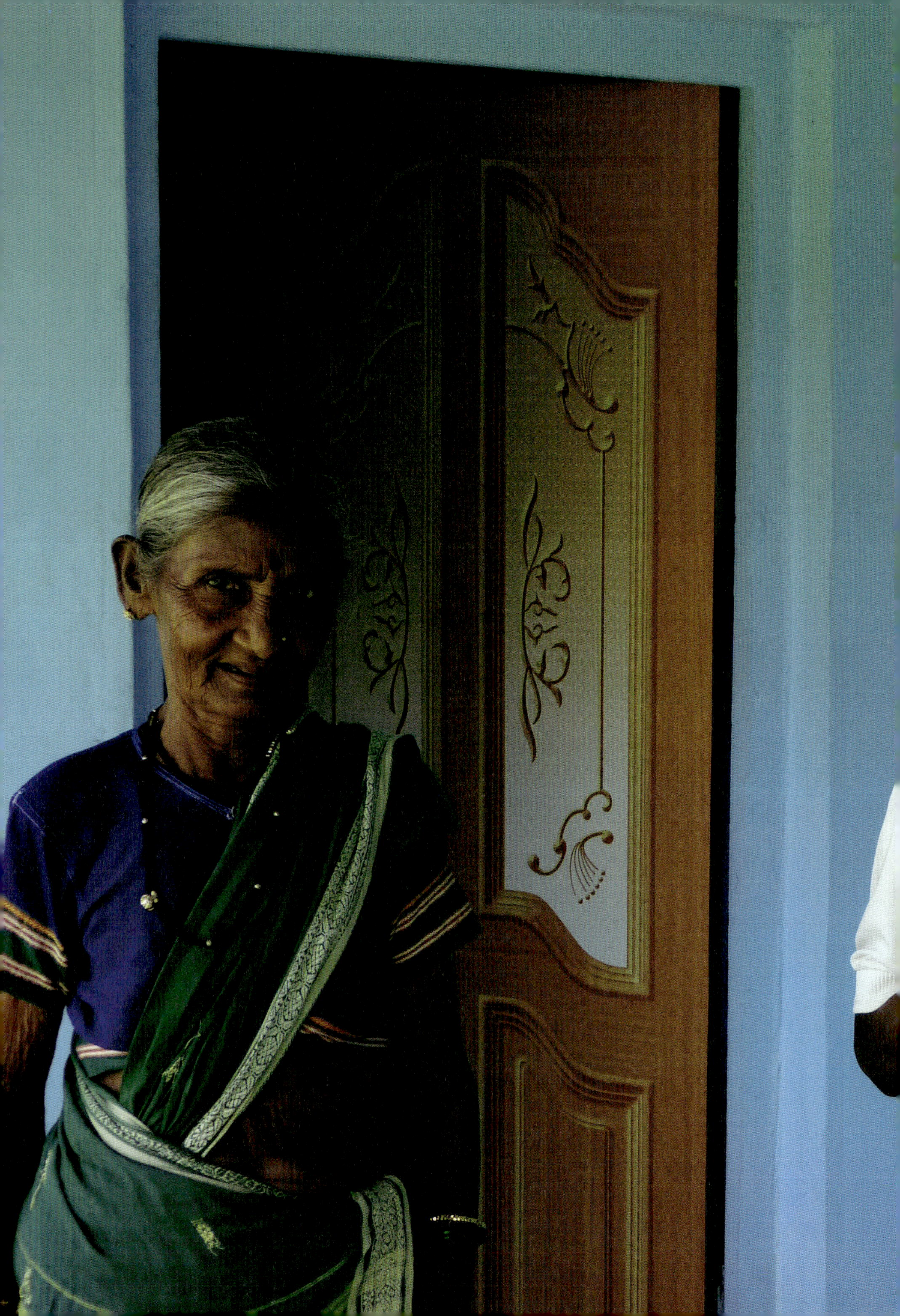

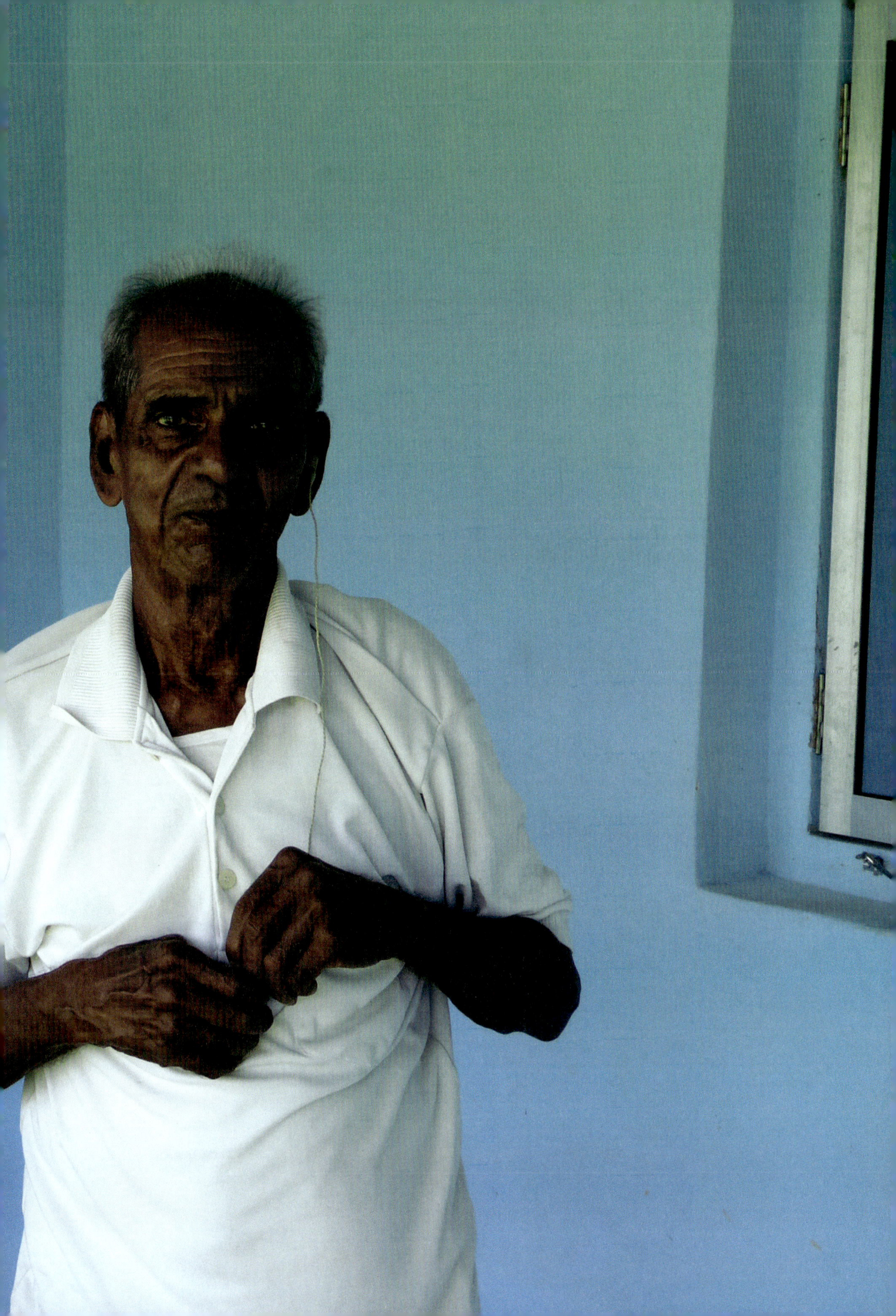

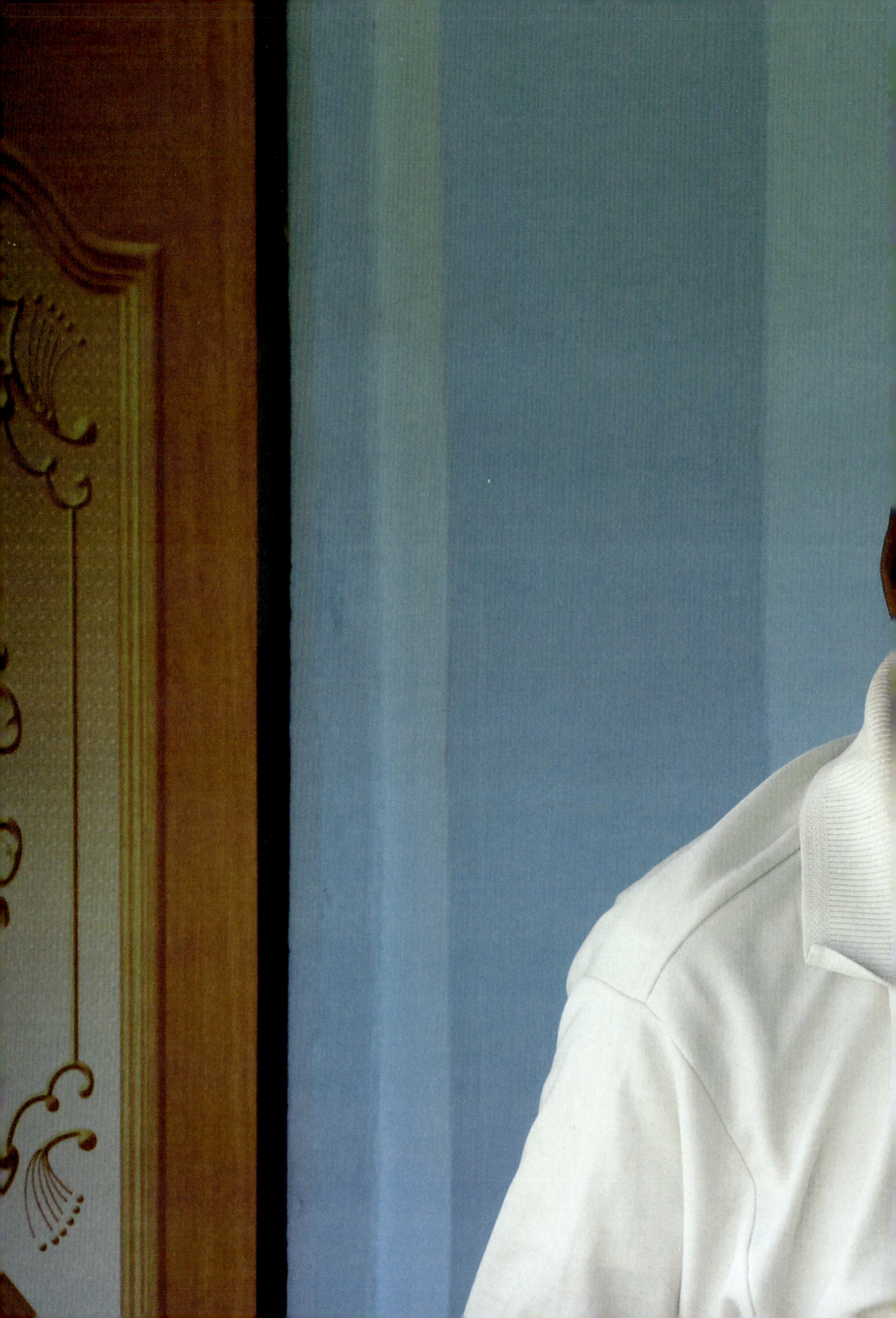

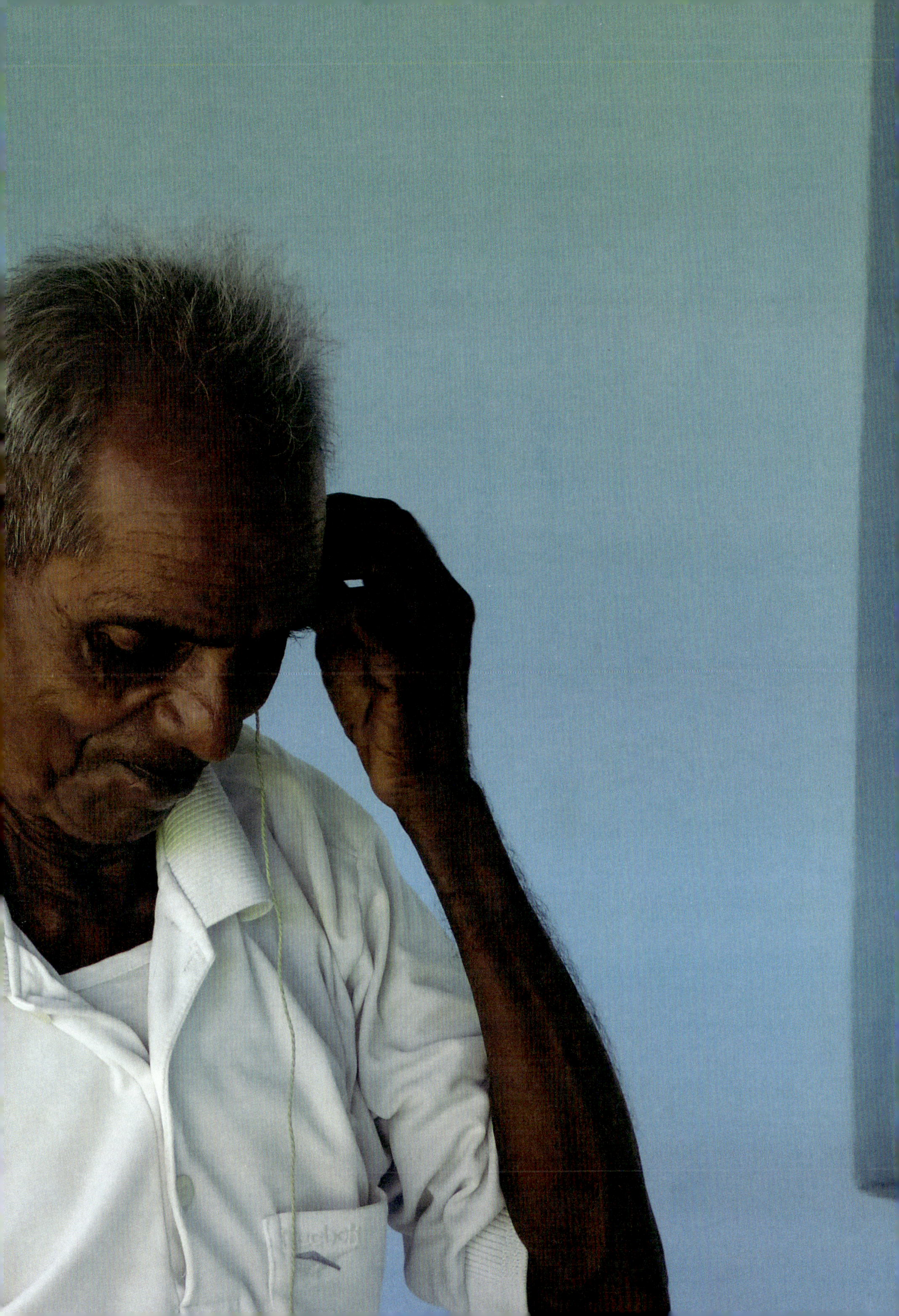

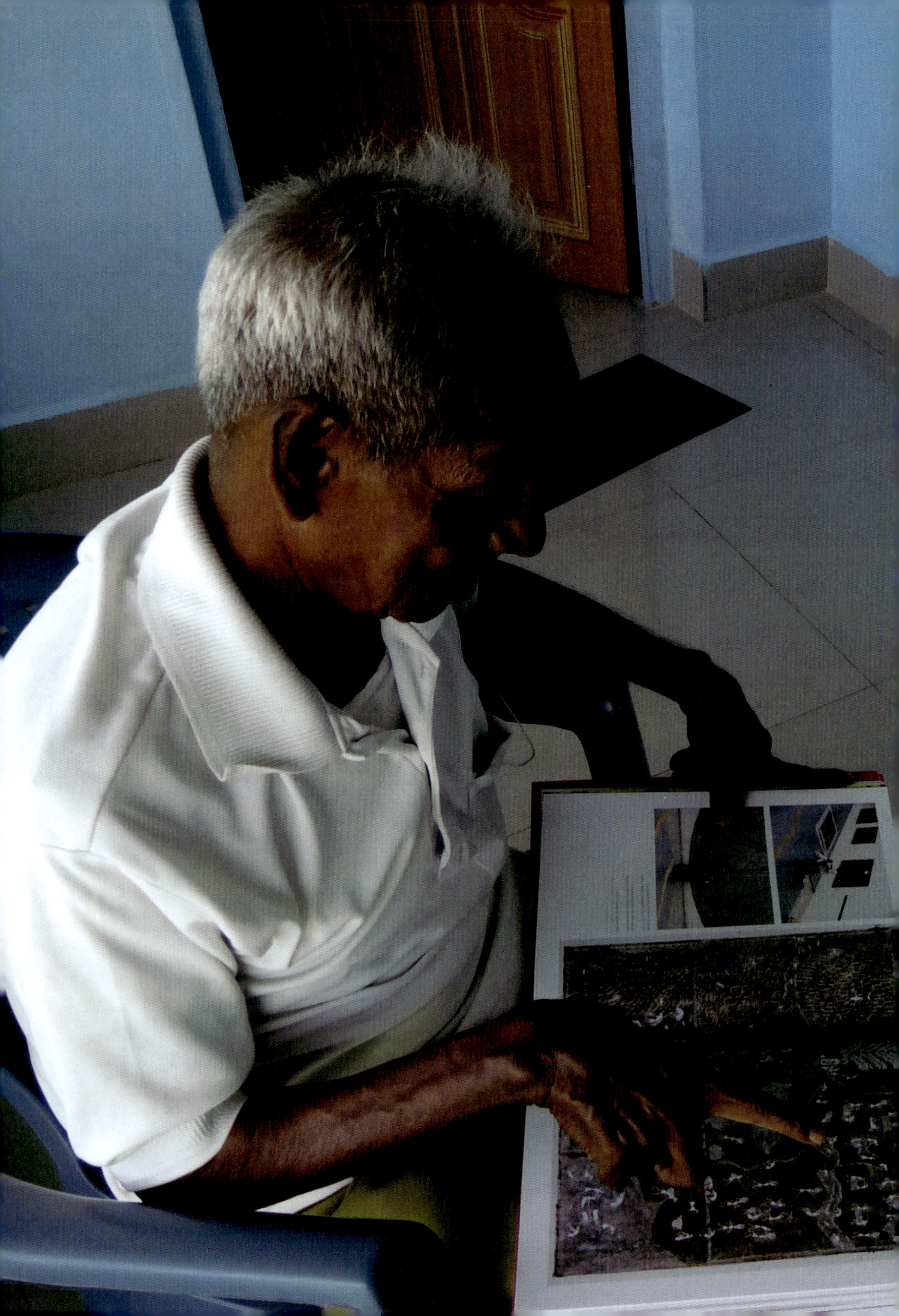

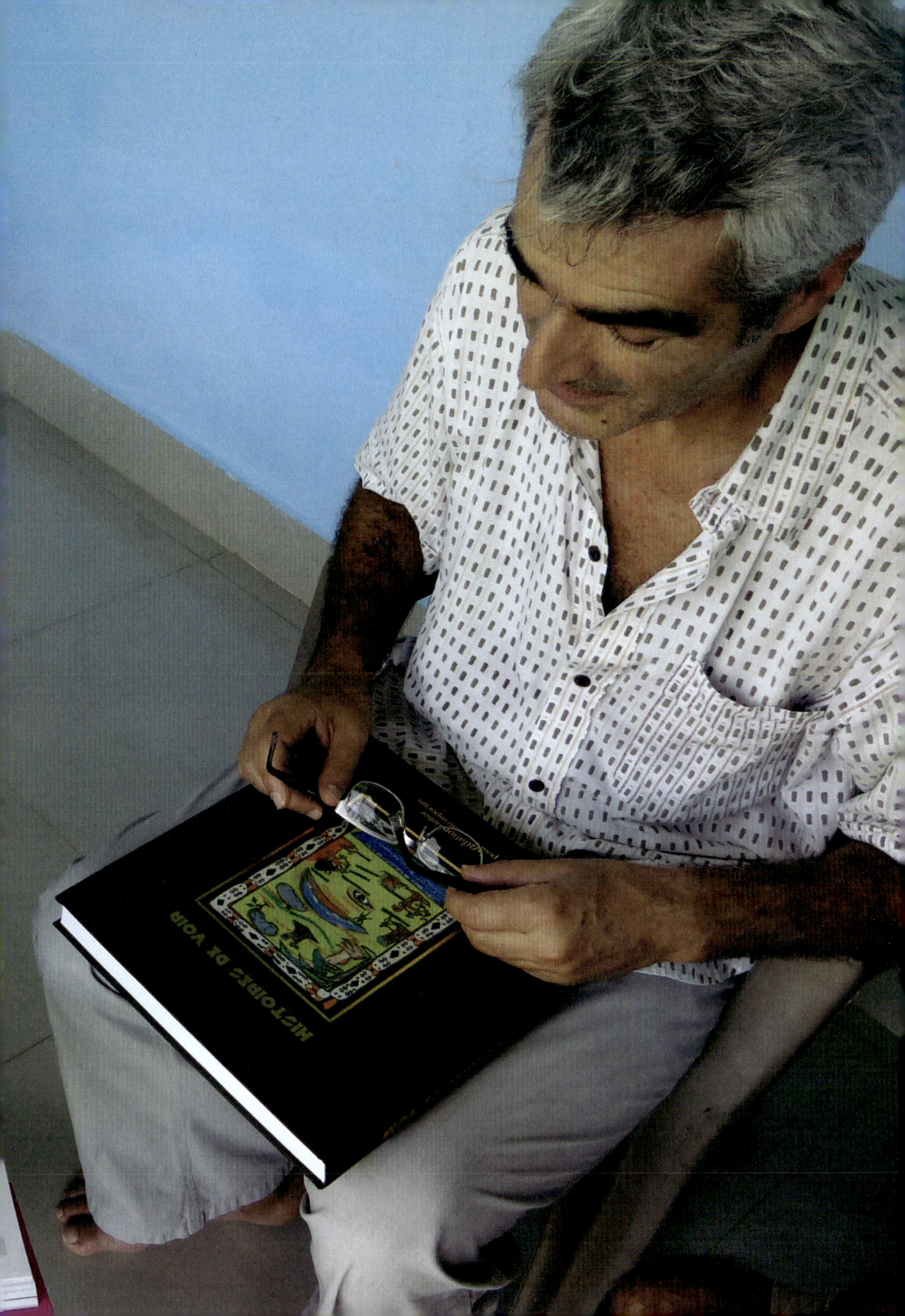
HISTOIRES DE VOIR

THE WANDERING TRIBES
LES TRIBUS VAGABONDES

Narandev was lord of home and earth, fields and forest. Every year farmers would place his image in a basketful of paddy and offering prayers. They would ask, 'Will the rains be good this year?' The lord has a simple way of answering them. If the rains were to be good, the basket would be too heavy to lift. If they were to fail, the basket would lift easily. And so they would go about their annual labours, prepared alike for prosperity or hardship.

Narandev thought he should improve their lot. He slipped in unseen as the weather gods assembled in the heavens and slipped out, armed with foreknowledge. 'Good people all', he said to the assembled tribe. 'This year it will rain farther east. Move in to lands in that direction.' From that day on, they tilled wherever the promised rains came, Narandev guiding them every year to new fields and strange pastures, away from their homeland.

The village gods got together. 'Our people have abandoned us and wander like gypsies. The earth cries out of their labours as she lies fallow and neglected.' They decided to catch hold of Narandev and brand him. 'The marks will betray him as he slips in to the assembly of the weather gods.' And so they did. Narandev could no longer bring back weather forecasts and the wandering tribes trekked back to their original lands, farming them in good years as in bad, as they had always done. The village gods were happy. And so was Narandev.

Narandev était le seigneur de la maison et de la terre, des champs et des forêts. Tous les ans, les fermiers plaçaient son image dans un panier de riz et demandaient, par leurs prières, si les pluies seraient bonnes. Le seigneur leur répondait simplement : « Si le panier est trop lourd, les pluies seront bonnes. S'il est facile à soulever, les pluies seront mauvaises. » Et c'est ainsi qu'ils s'acquittaient de leur labeur annuel, préparés aussi bien à la prospérité qu'aux difficultés.

Un jour, Narandev s'avisa qu'il devait améliorer leur fortune. Il se glissa sans être vu dans le ciel où les dieux du climat s'étaient réunis, et en ressortit armé de prescience. « Cette année, la pluie tombera plus à l'est. Allez vous installer sur les terres situées du côté est. » Depuis ce jour-là, ils travaillèrent les terres où tombaient les pluies promises, Narandev les guidant chaque année vers des terres et pâturages qu'ils ne connaissaient pas, loin de leur terre natale.

Alors, les dieux du village se réunirent : « Notre peuple nous a abandonnés et erre comme des nomades. La terre négligée, en jachère, réclame leur labeur. » Ils décident donc d'attraper Narandev et de le marquer au fer rouge : « Ces marques le trahiront lorsqu'il se glissera dans l'assemblée des dieux du climat. » Et c'est ce qu'ils firent. Narandev ne pouvant plus rapporter les prévisions météorologiques, les tribus nomades retournèrent sur leurs terres, les cultivèrent bon an mal an, comme elles l'avaient toujours fait. Les dieux du village en furent heureux. Et Narandev aussi.

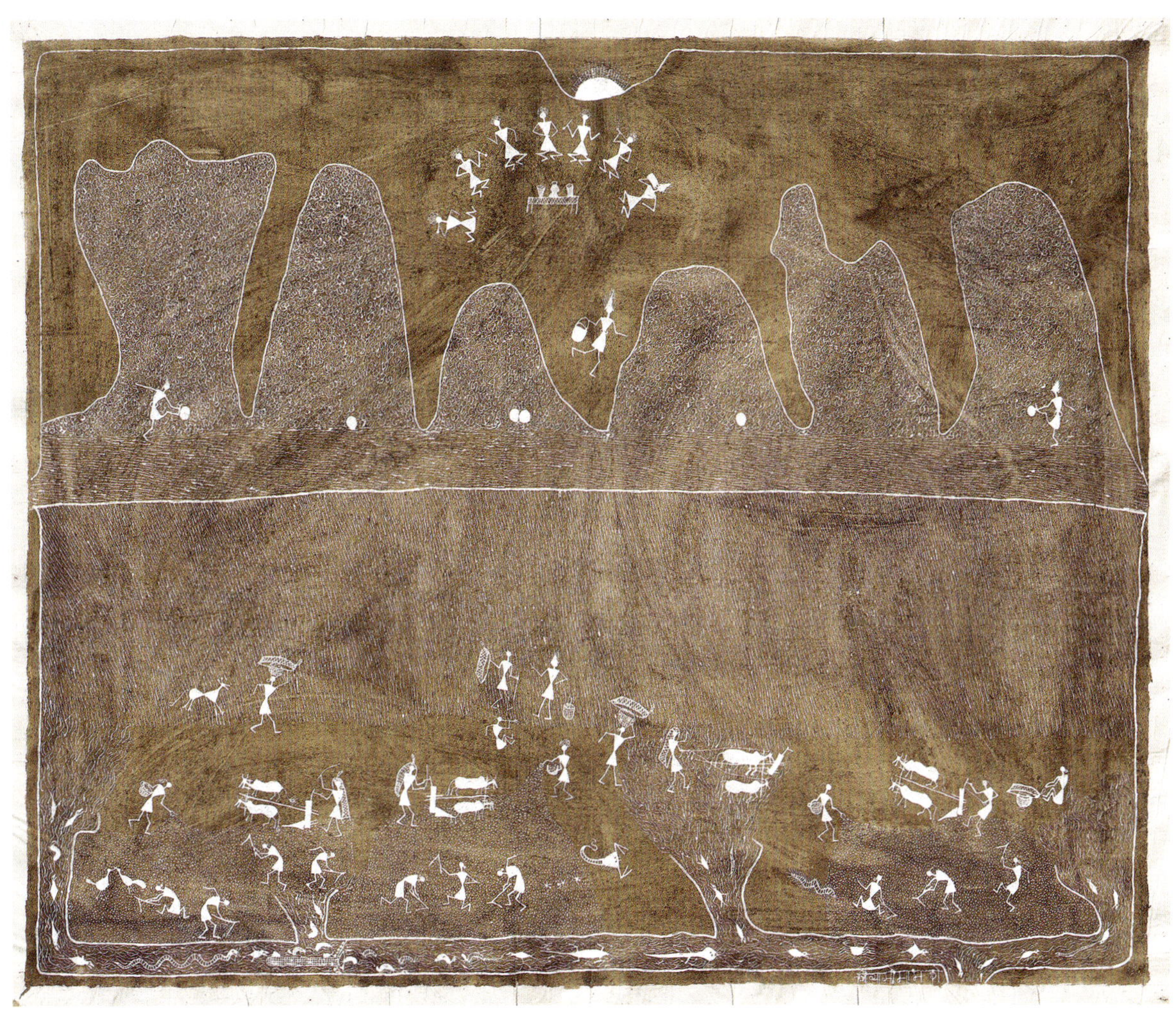

Pages 102–103
Jivya Soma Mashe and his wife at home,
Ganjad (Maharashtra, India), 2012.
Photo by T. Venkanna.

Pages 104–107
Jivya Soma Mashe and Hervé Perdriolle browsing the book *Indian Contemporary Art* (Hervé Perdriolle, 5 Continents Editions, 2012) and the exhibition catalogue *Histoires de voir, Show and Tell* (Fondation Cartier pour l'art contemporain, Paris, 2012).
Photo T. Venkanna.

Jivya Soma Mashe, *The Wandering Tribes*, 2017,
acrylic and cow dung on canvas,
100 × 125 cm; 39.37 × 49.21 in. (*details on pages* 110–117)
Collection Amrita Jhaveri.
Photo Christian Baraja.

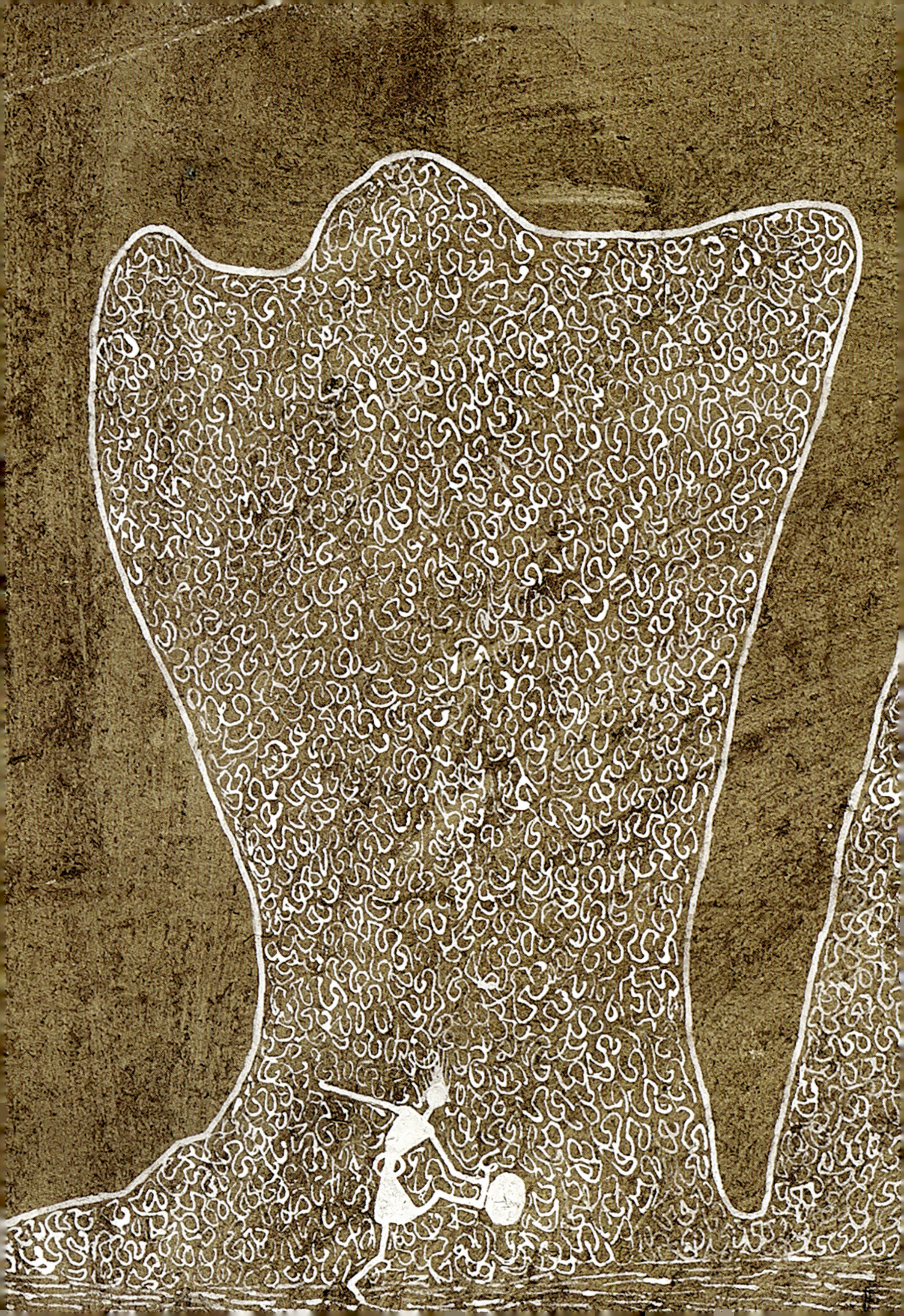

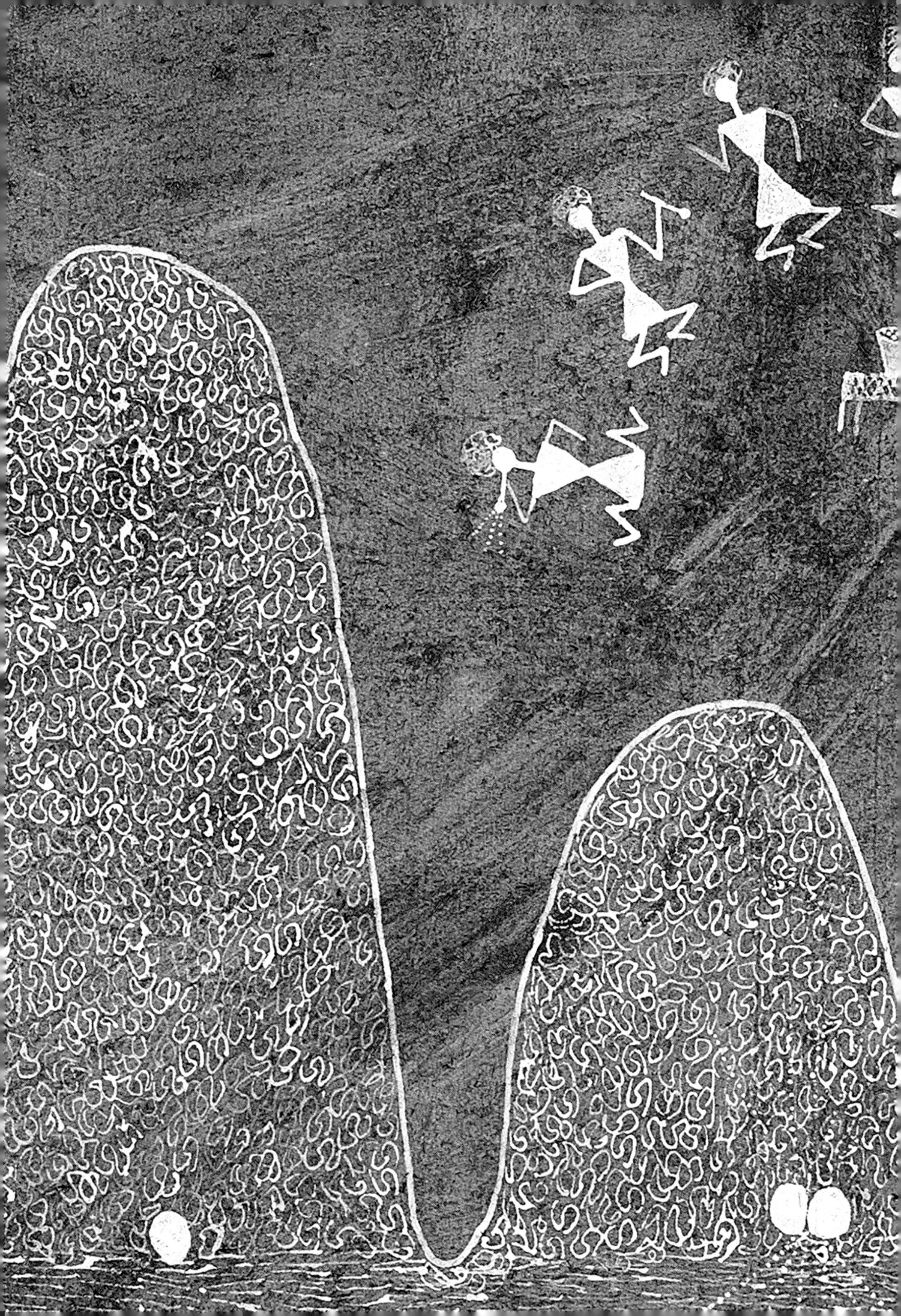

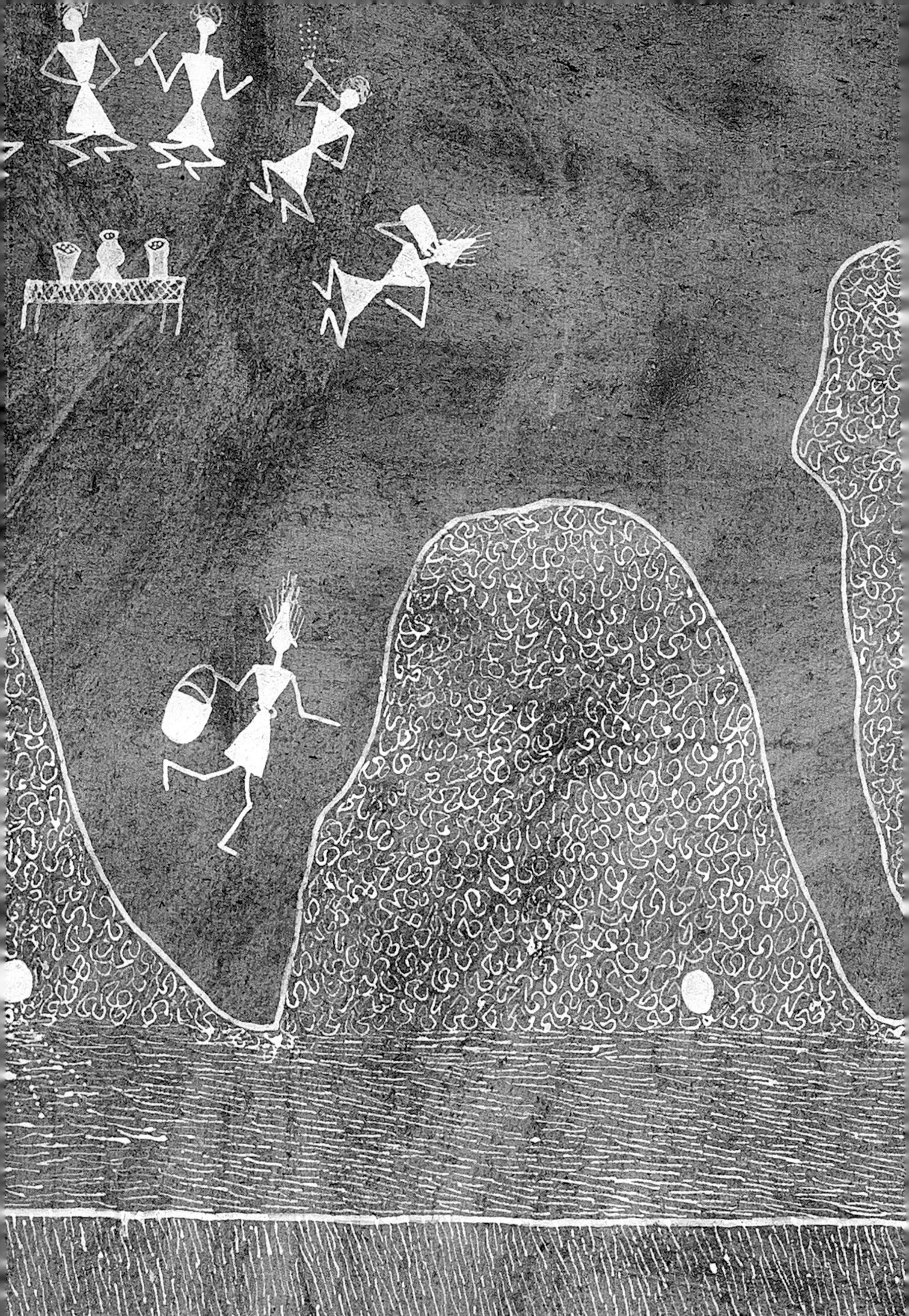

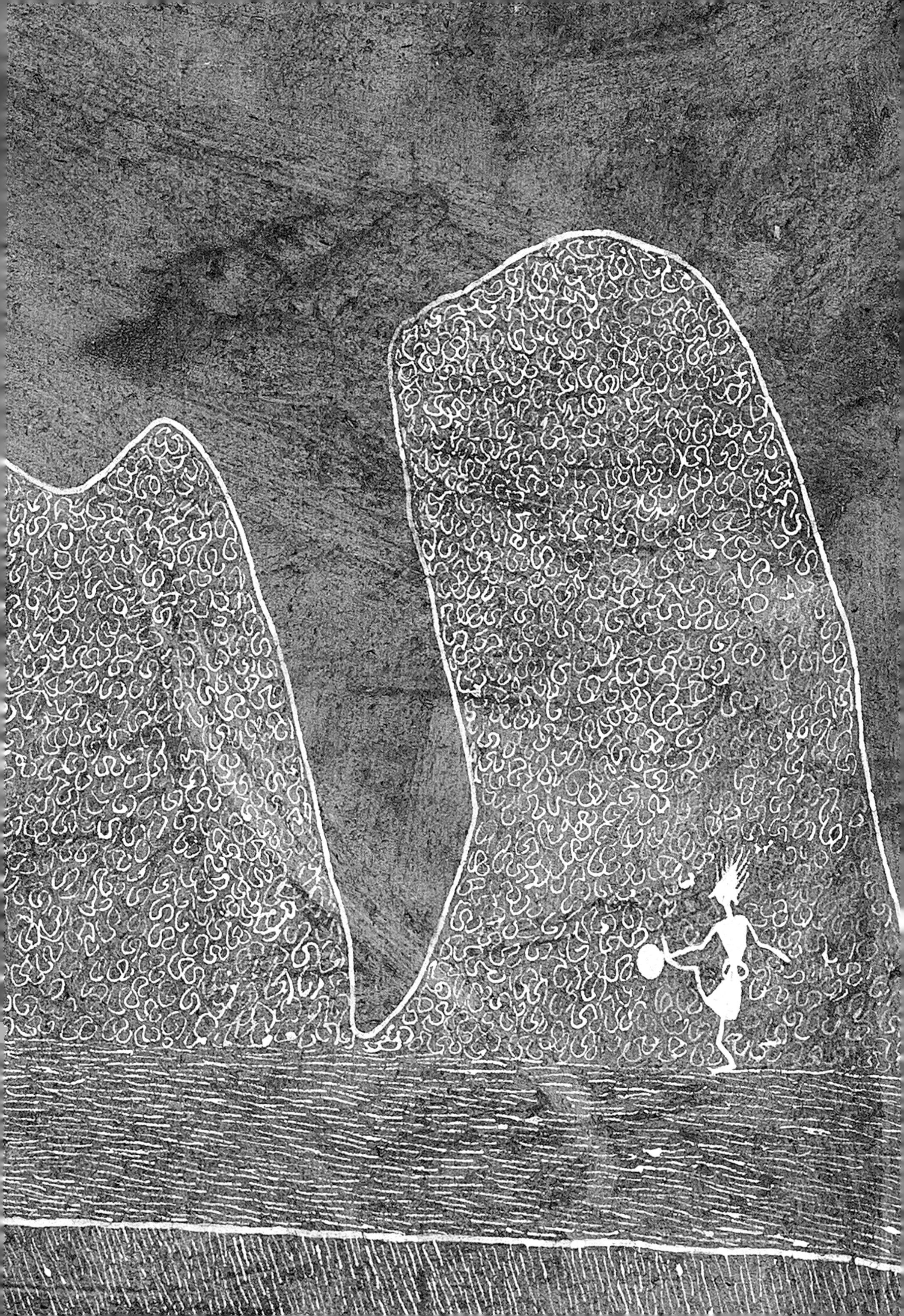

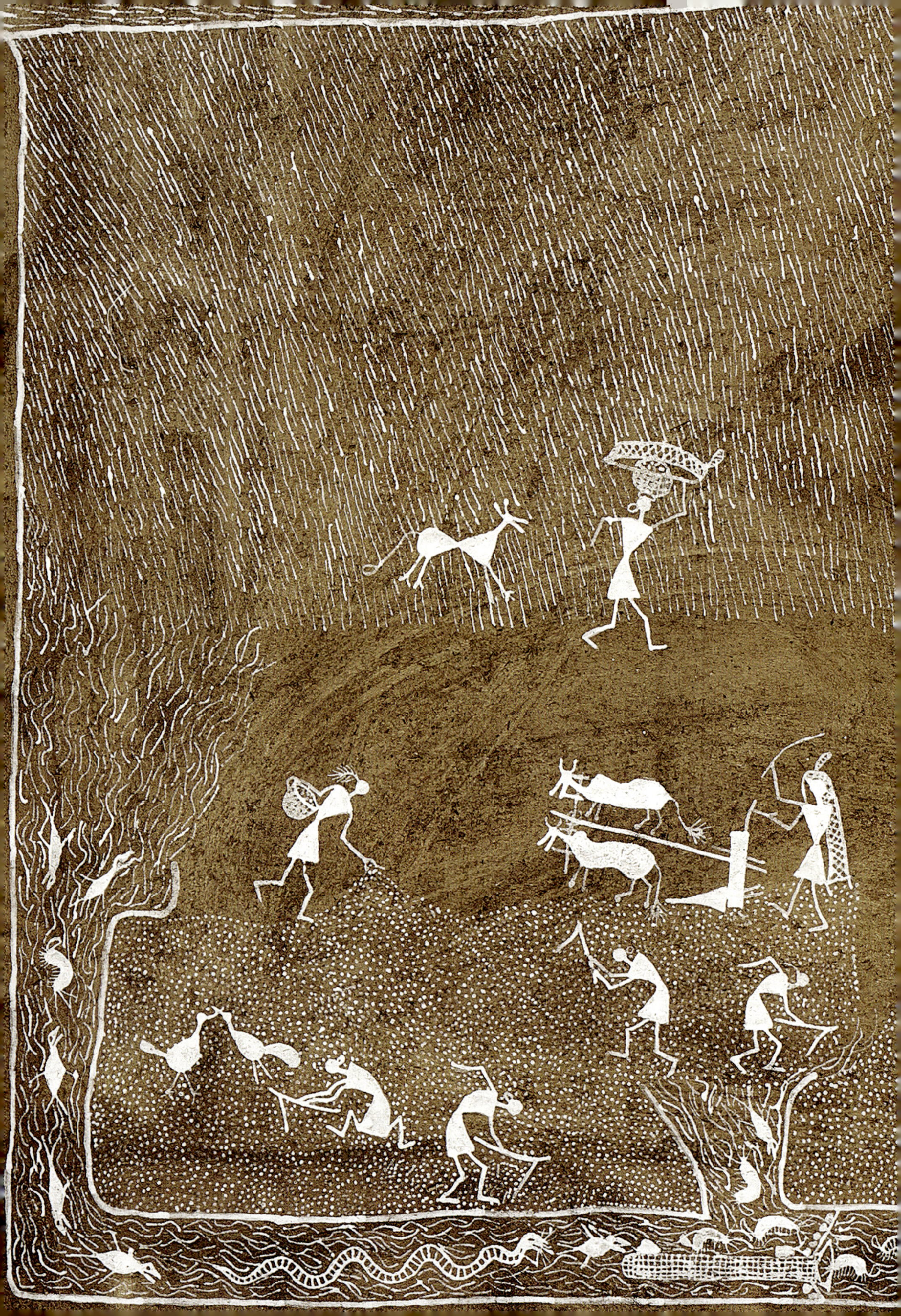

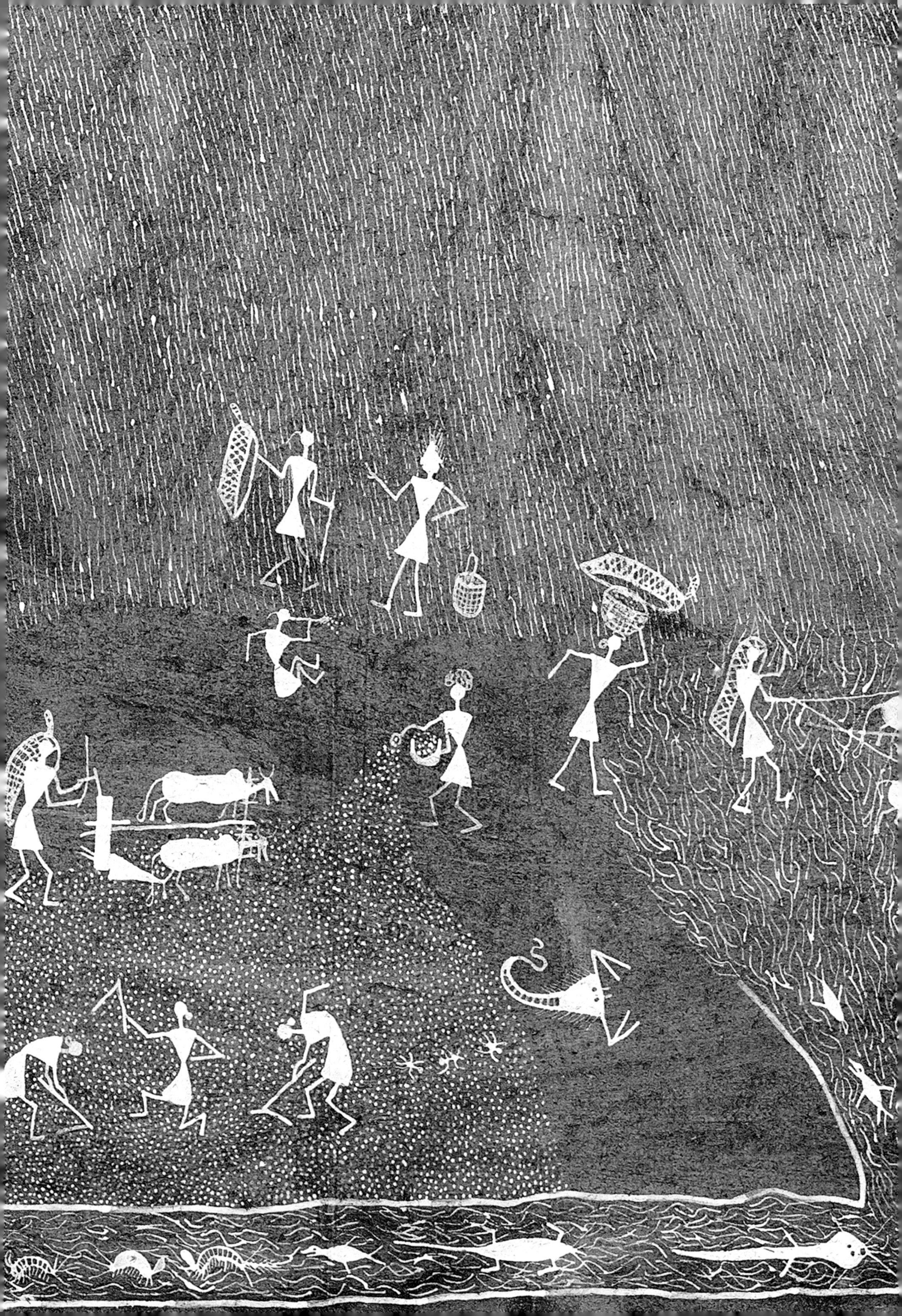

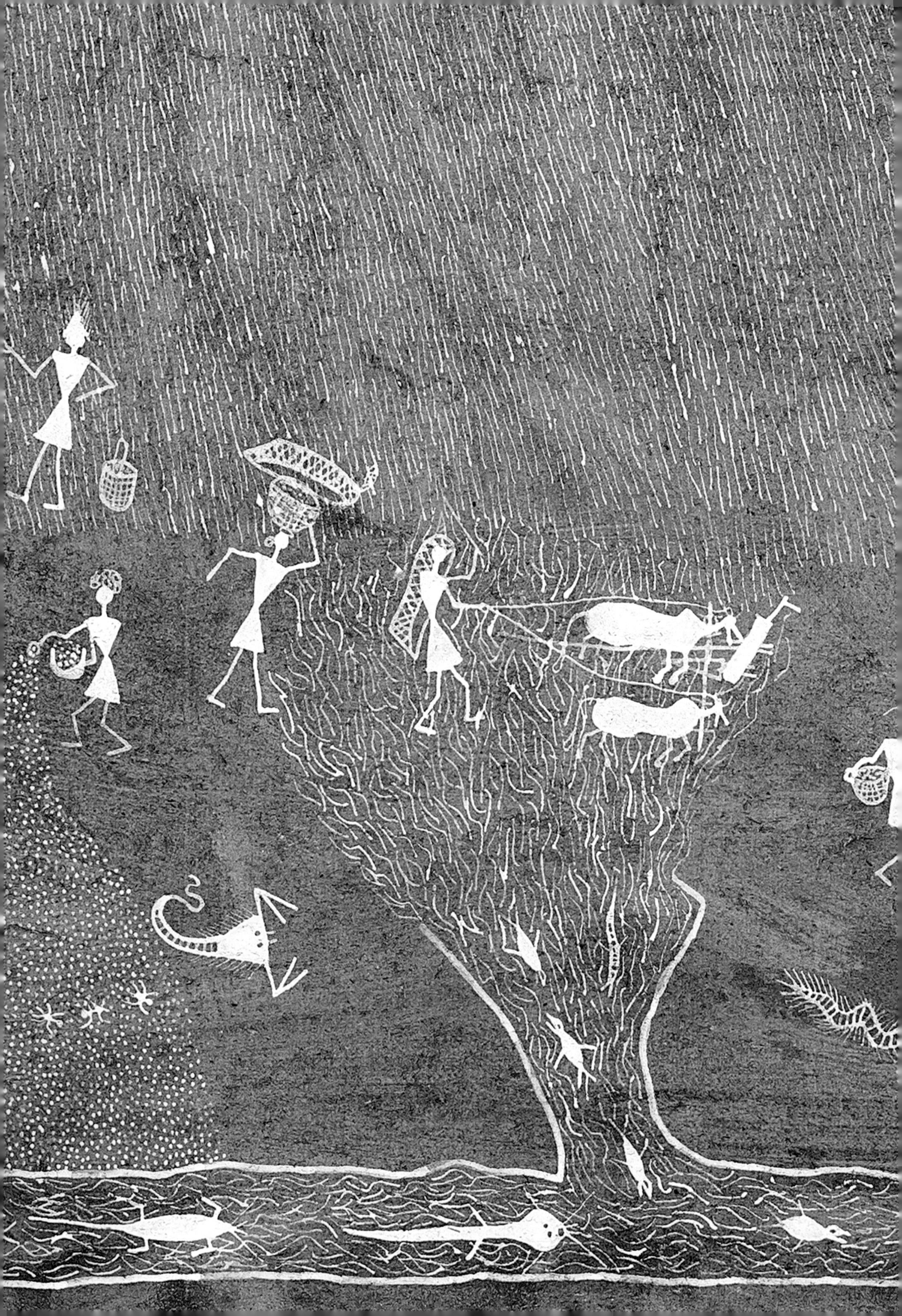

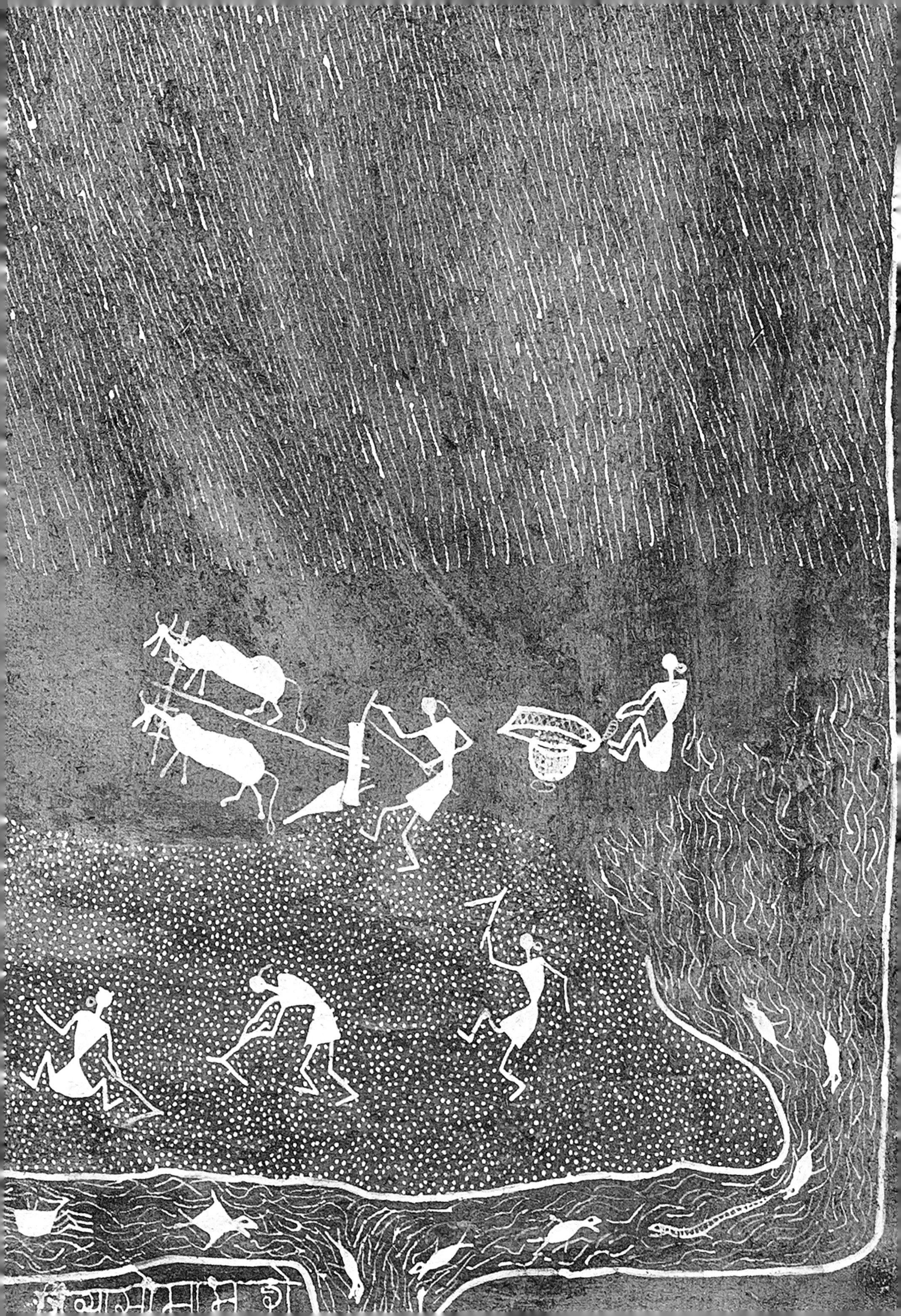

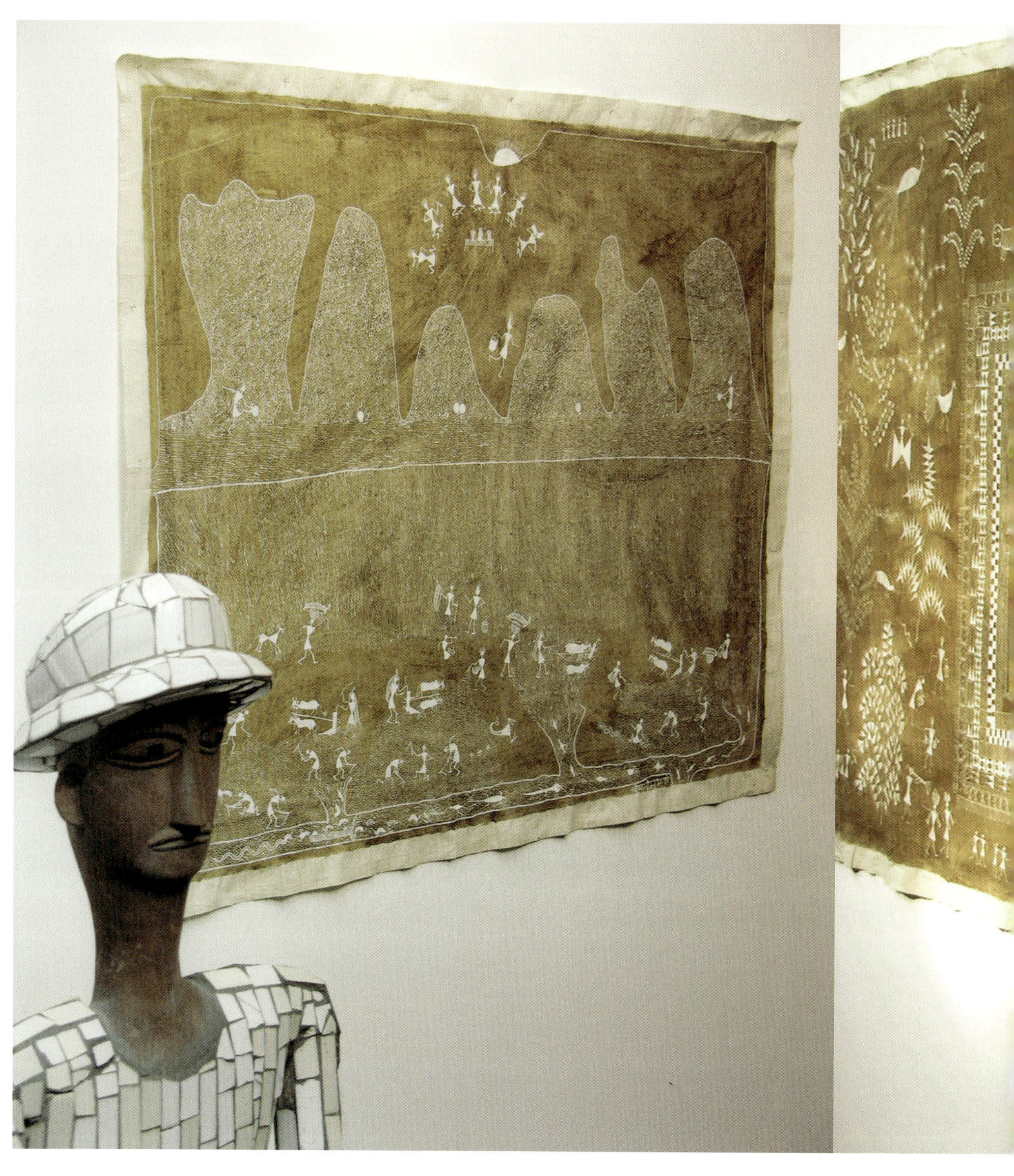

Views of the exhibition *India / Nek Chand / Jivya Soma Mashe* at Halle Saint-Pierre, Paris, 2007.

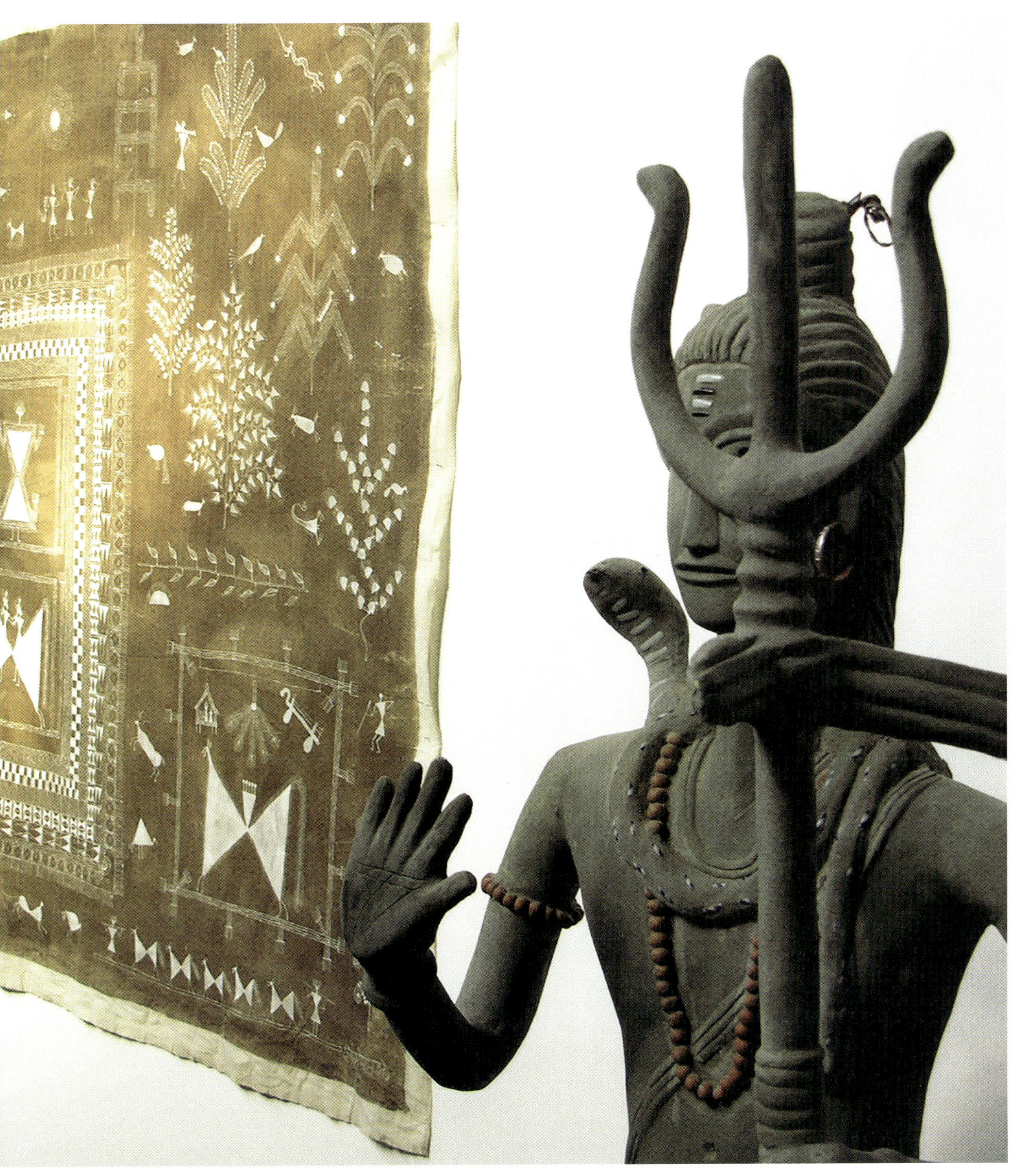

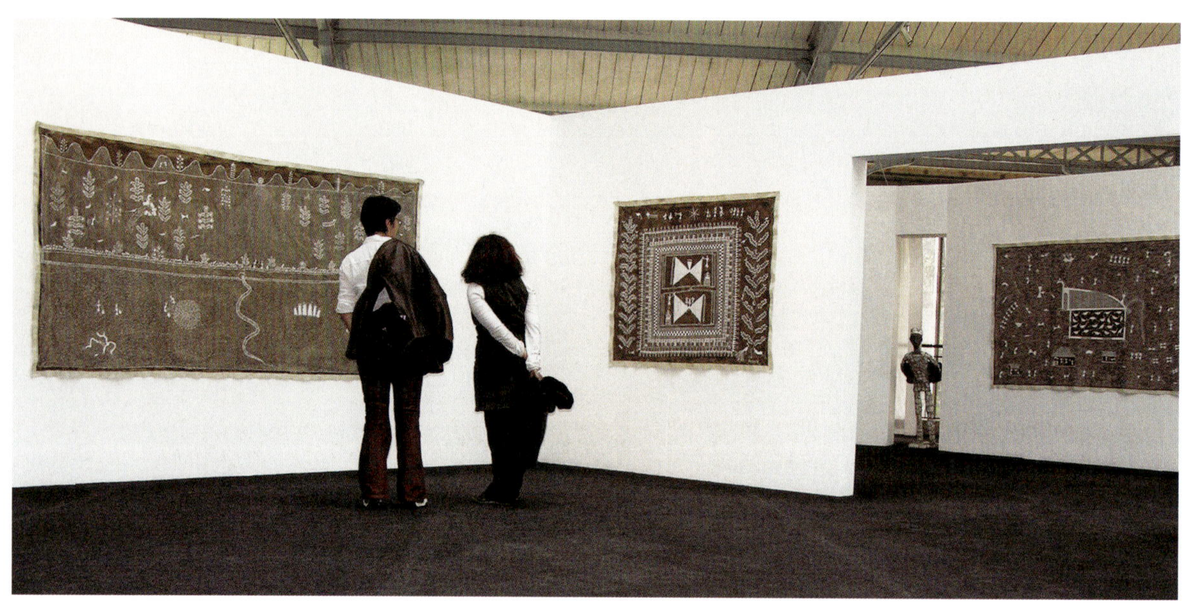

View of the exhibition *India / Nek Chand / Jivya Soma Mashe* at Halle Saint-Pierre, Paris, 2007.

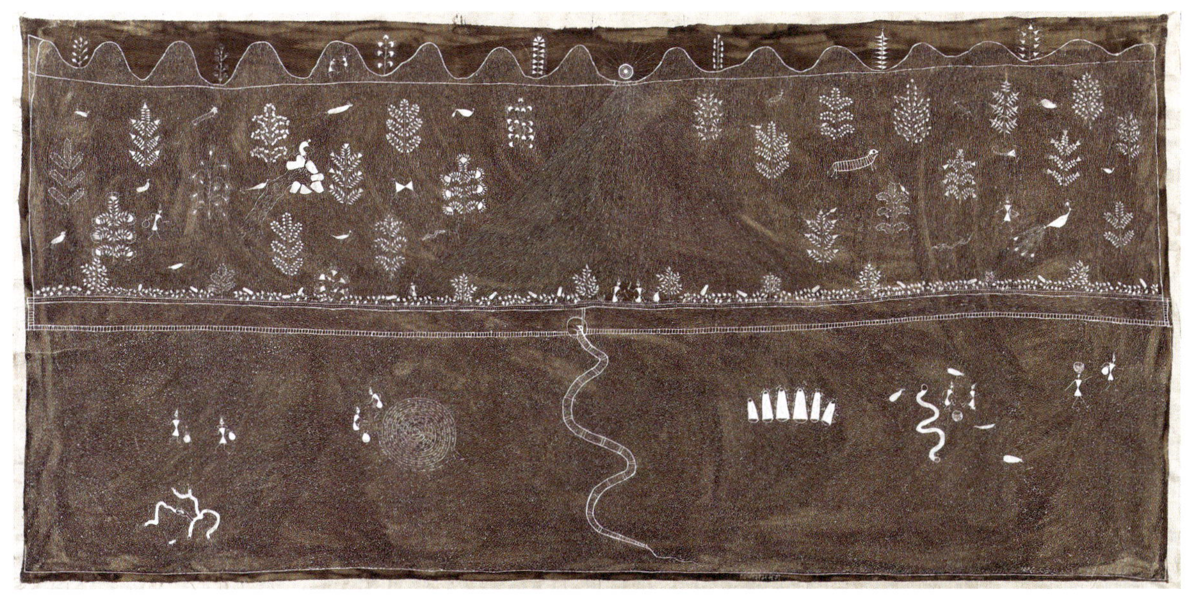

Jivya Soma Mashe, *Untitled*, 1999,
acrylic and cow dung on canvas,
138 × 290 cm; 54.33 × 114.17 in. (*details on pages* 122–129)
Fondation Cartier pour l'art contemporain Collection.
Photo by André Morin.

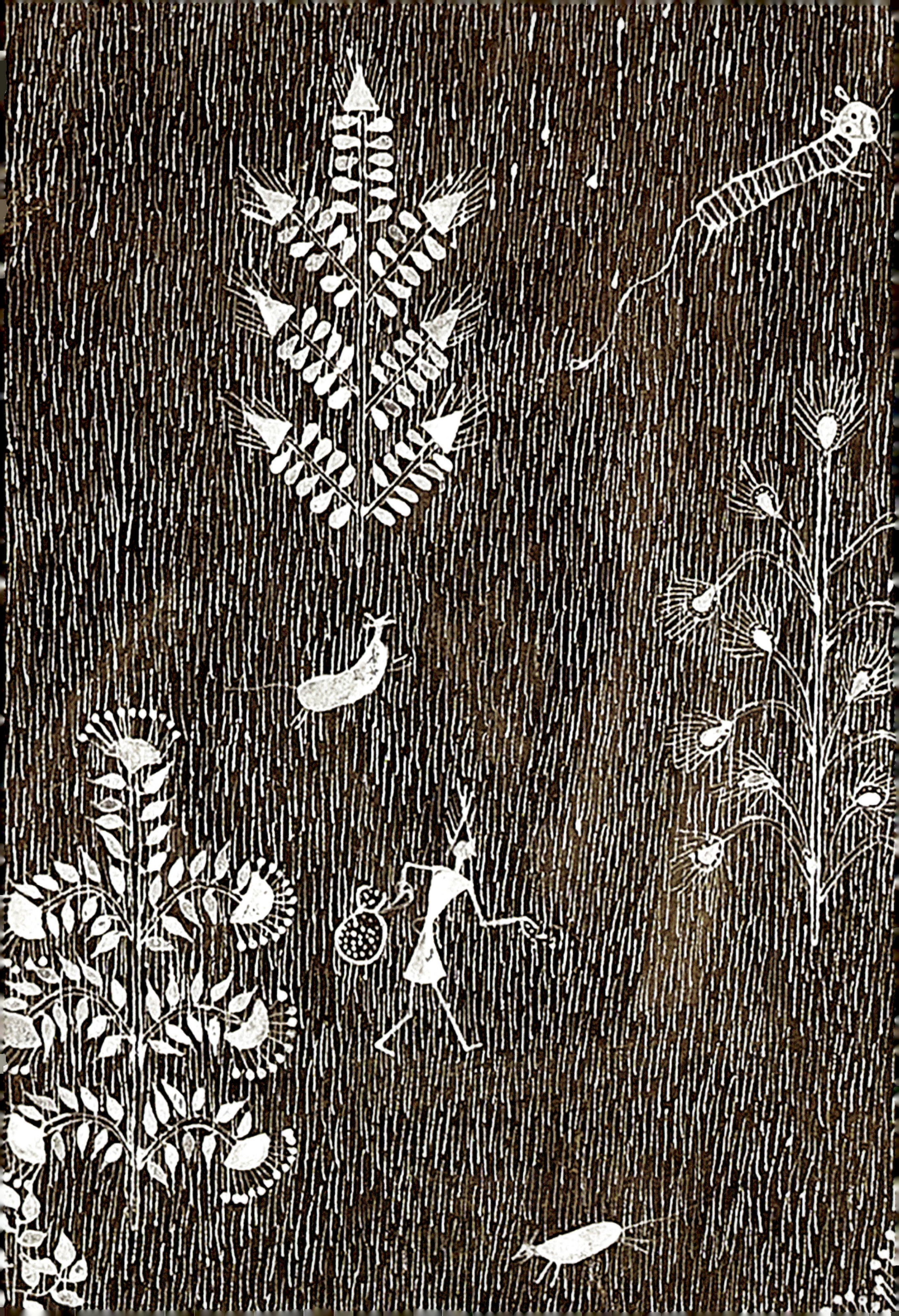

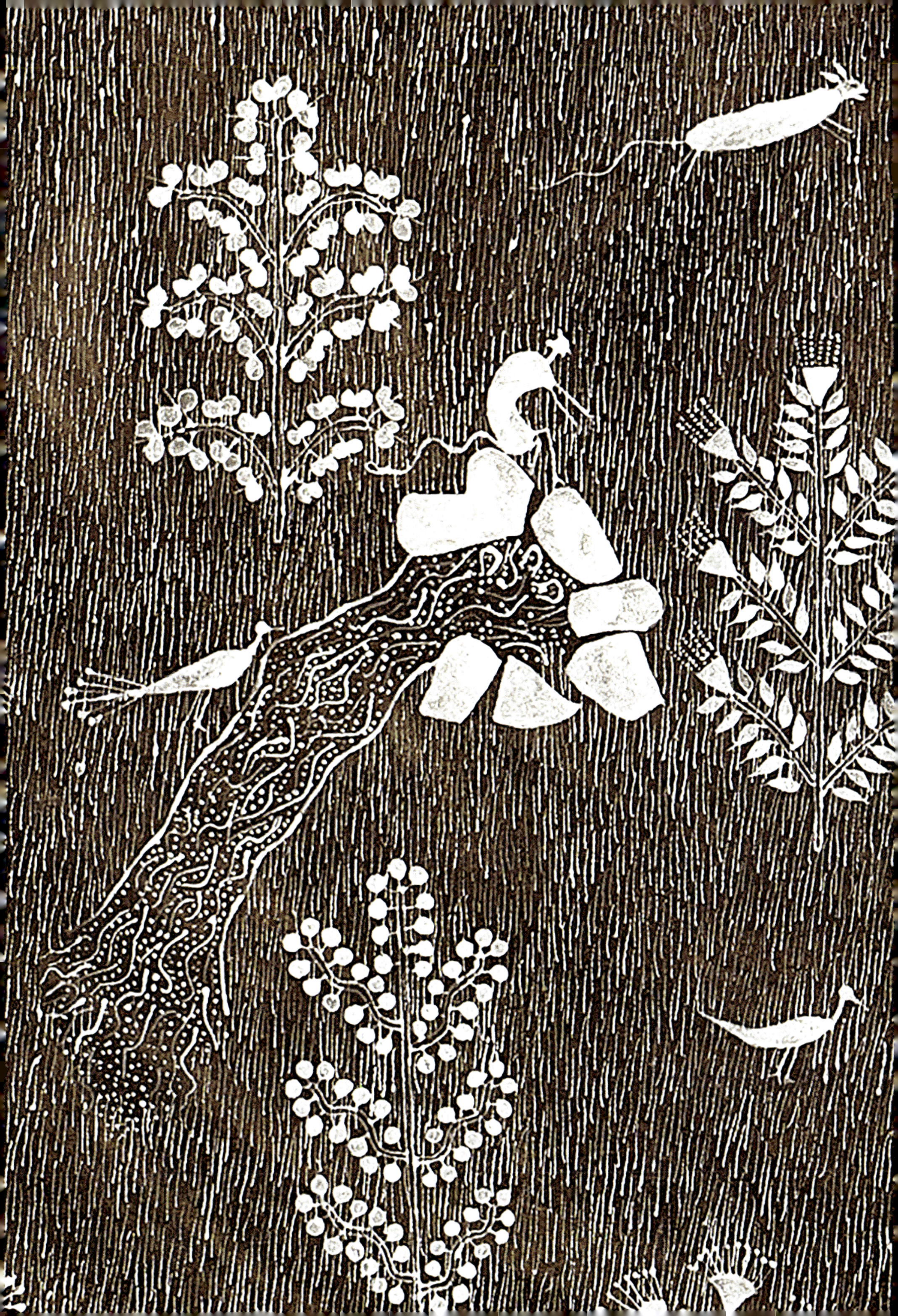

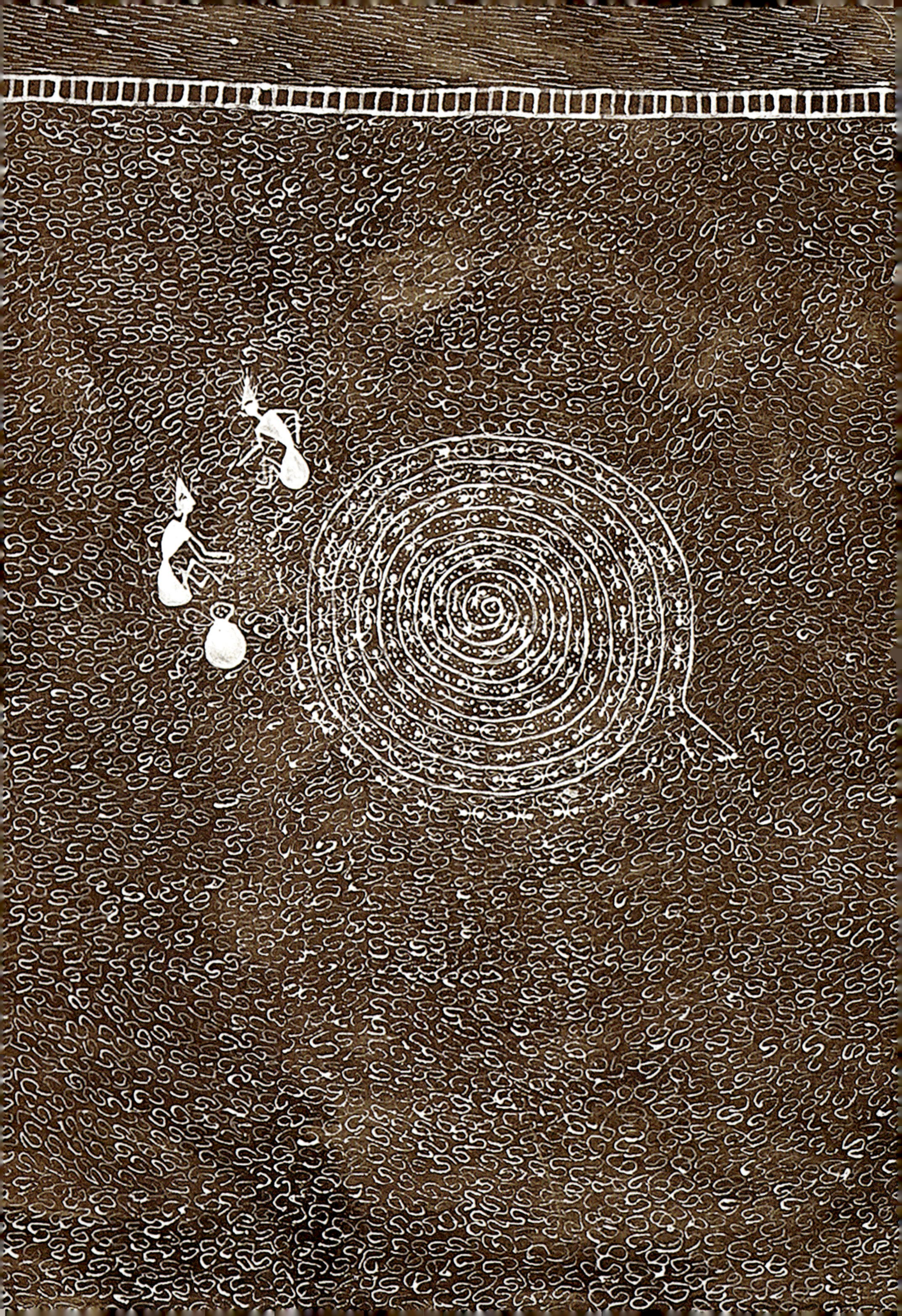

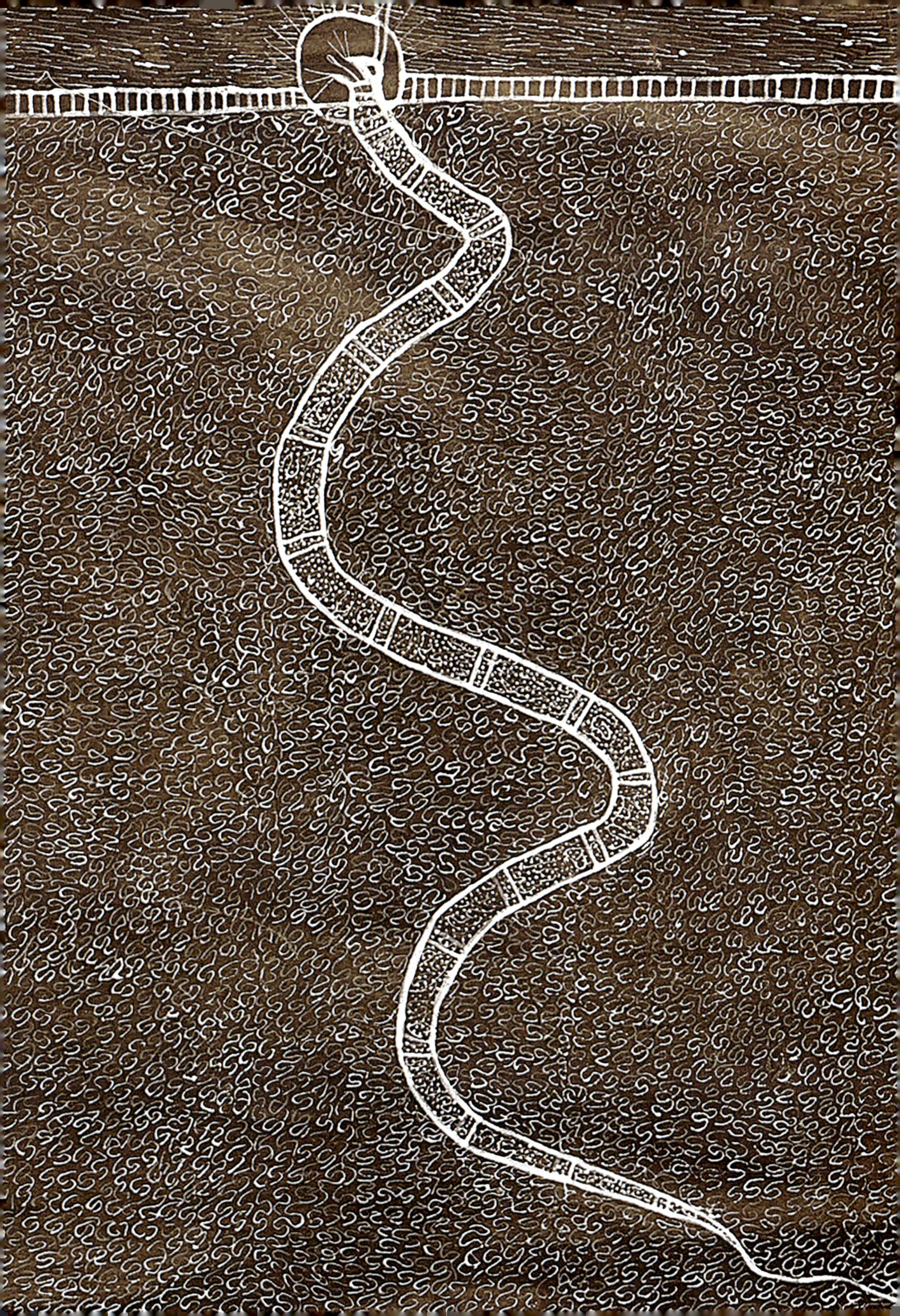

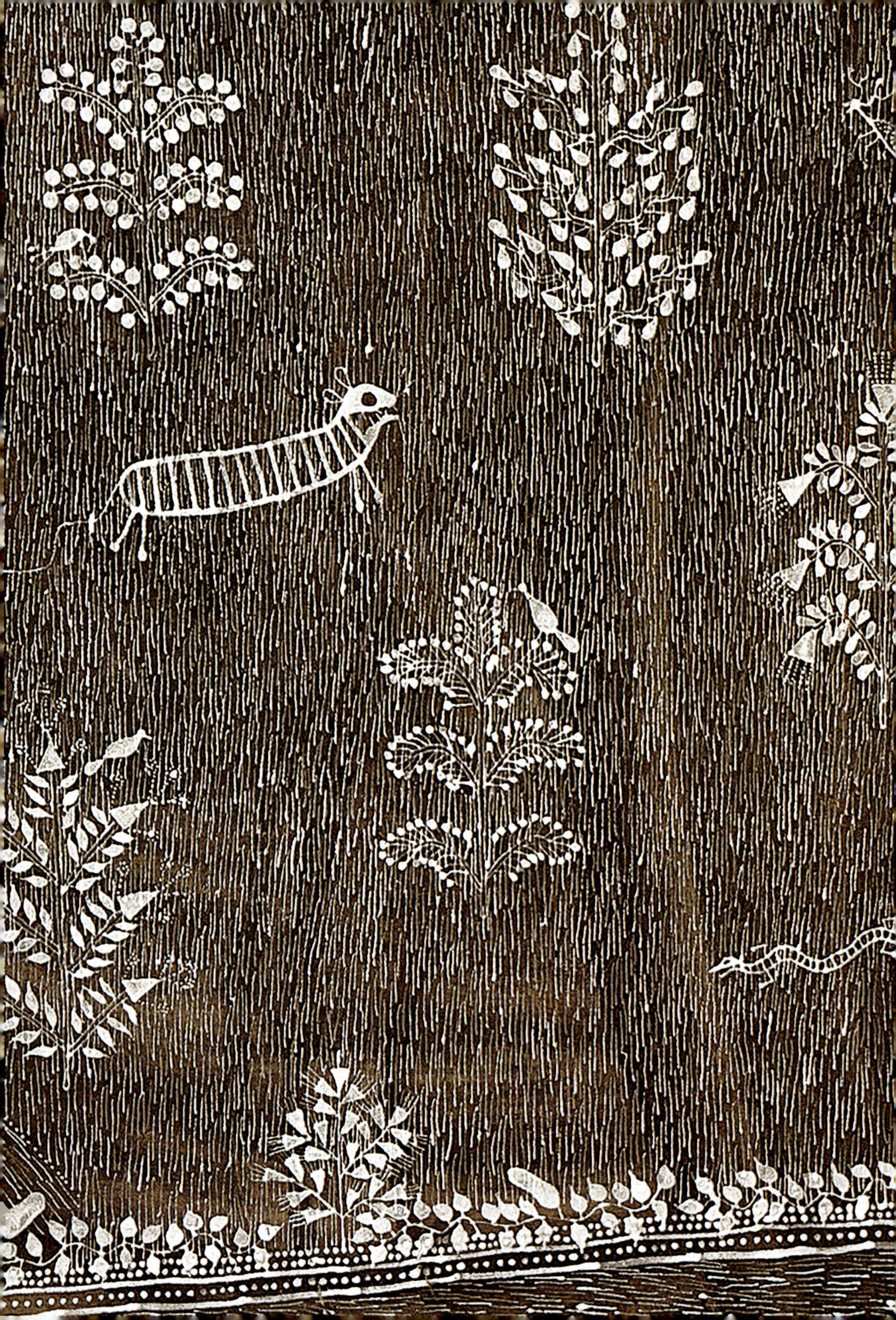

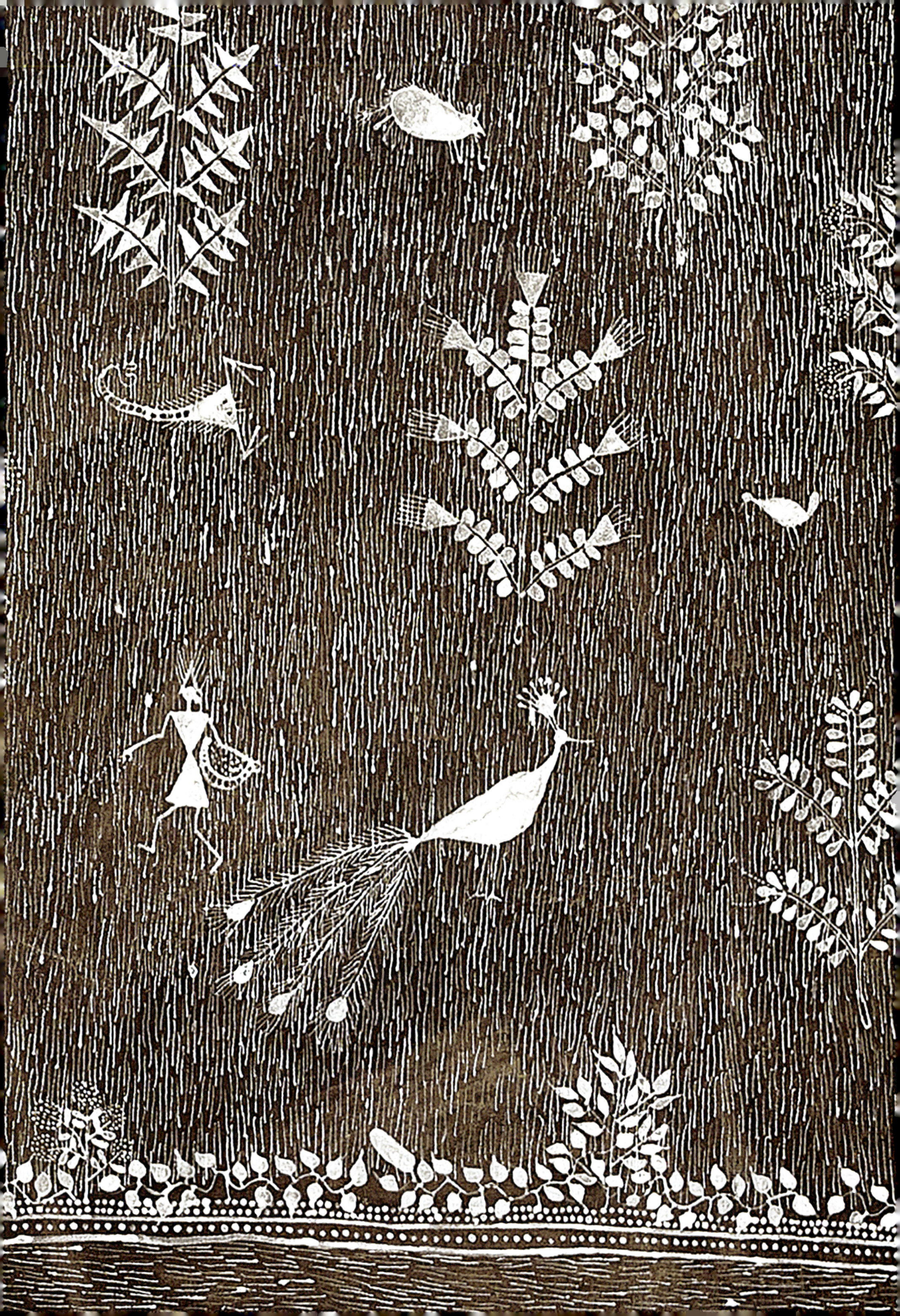

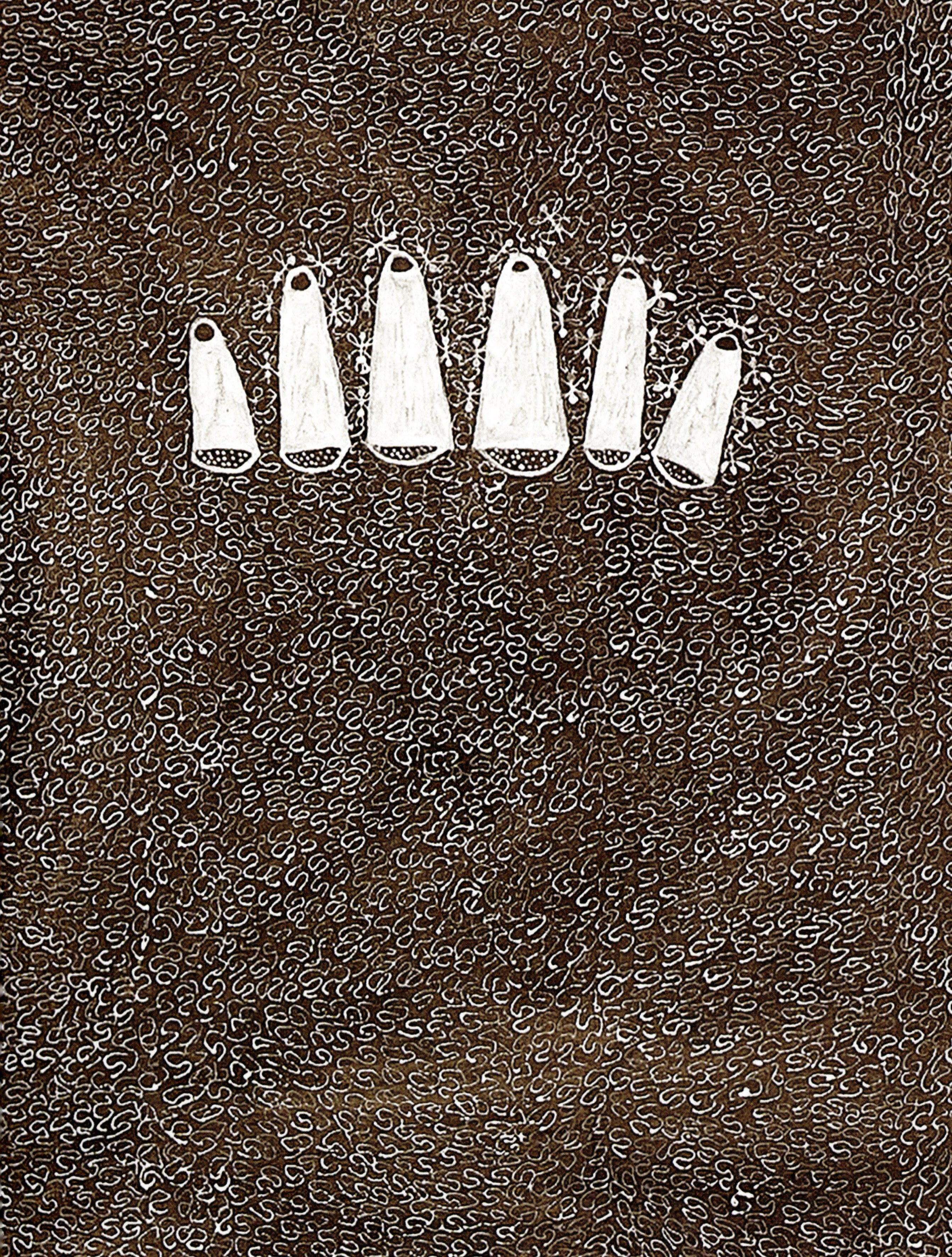

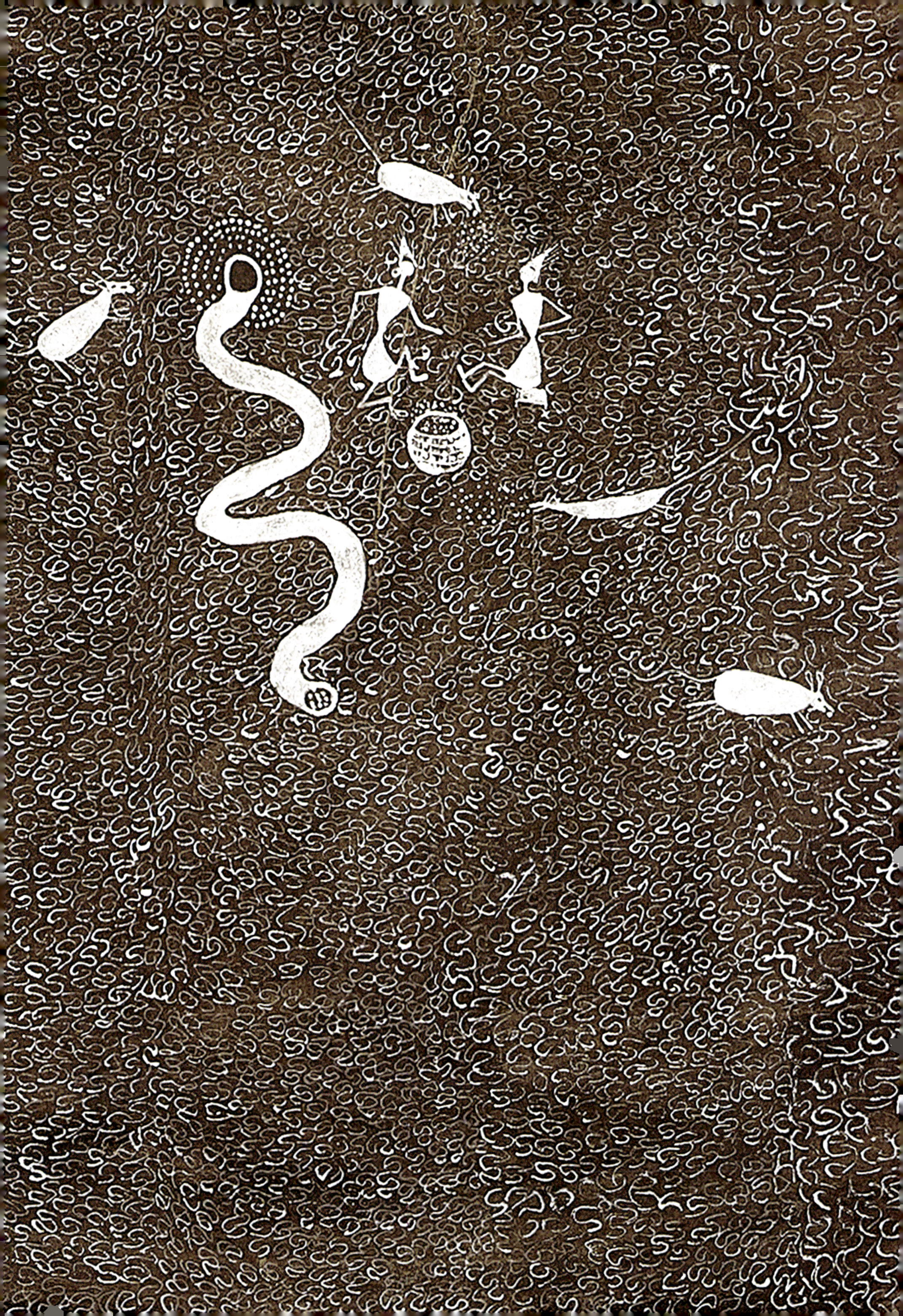

Based on the circle, triangle, and square, the pictography of the Warli people speaks to us of ancient times when the forms were inspired by the observation of nature: the circle by the moon and sun, and the triangle representing mountains, particularly the sacred mountain with its pointed summit, or trees that point skywards. Only the square does not seem to have been derived from the observation of nature, and thus appears to be a human invention that indicates a sacred enclosure or piece of land.

The form of primitivism used in modern Western art, which is progressively moving away from the use of geometric forms (Cézanne, Kandinsky, Mondrian, Malevich) inspired by the observation of nature, seems to be reaching maturity with the exclusive use of the square. Modern art appropriated art, just as primitive man had appropriated nature, and uses the square to define a purely mental, conceptual space.

Basée sur le rond, le triangle et le carré, la pictographie de la tribu warli nous parle des temps les plus anciens où les formes naissaient de l'observation de la nature, le rond de l'observation de la lune et du soleil, le triangle de celle de la montagne et des arbres aux cimes pointées vers le ciel. Seul le carré ne semble pas être le fruit de cette observation, mais apparaît alors comme une création de l'homme pour désigner l'enclos sacré, la parcelle de terrain.

Autre primitivisme, celui de l'art moderne occidental qui délaisse progressivement l'emploi de formes géométriques (Cézanne, Kandinsky, Mondrian, Malevitch) nées de l'observation de la nature et semble atteindre sa maturité avec l'utilisation exclusive du carré. L'art moderne s'approprie l'art, comme l'homme primitif s'était approprié la nature, en utilisant le carré pour délimiter un espace purement mental, conceptuel.

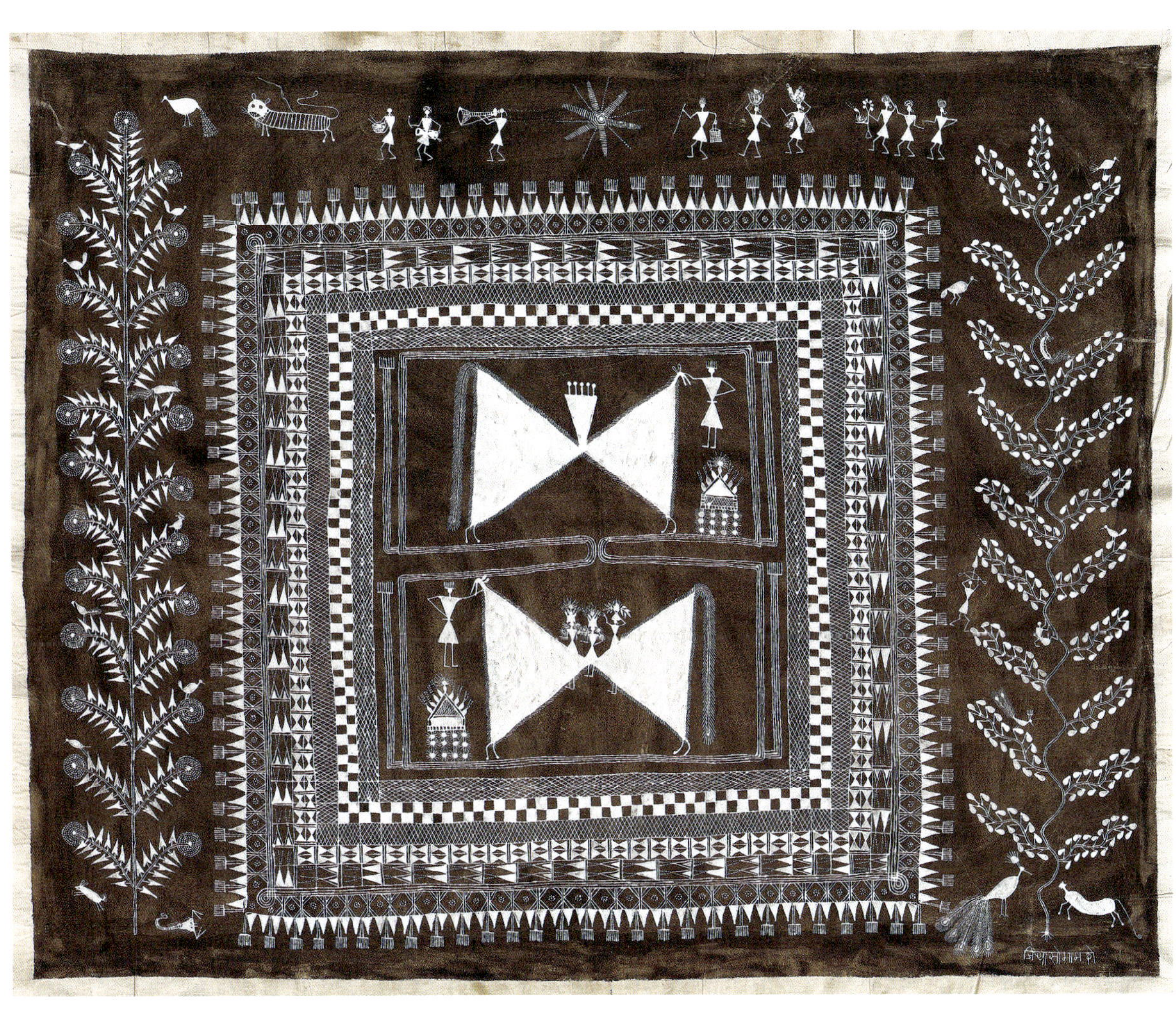

Jivya Soma Mashe, *Cauk*, 1997,
acrylic and cow dung on canvas,
116 × 145 cm; 45.66 × 57.08 in. (*detail on pages* 132–133)
Collection Hervé Perdriolle.
Photo by Christian Baraja.

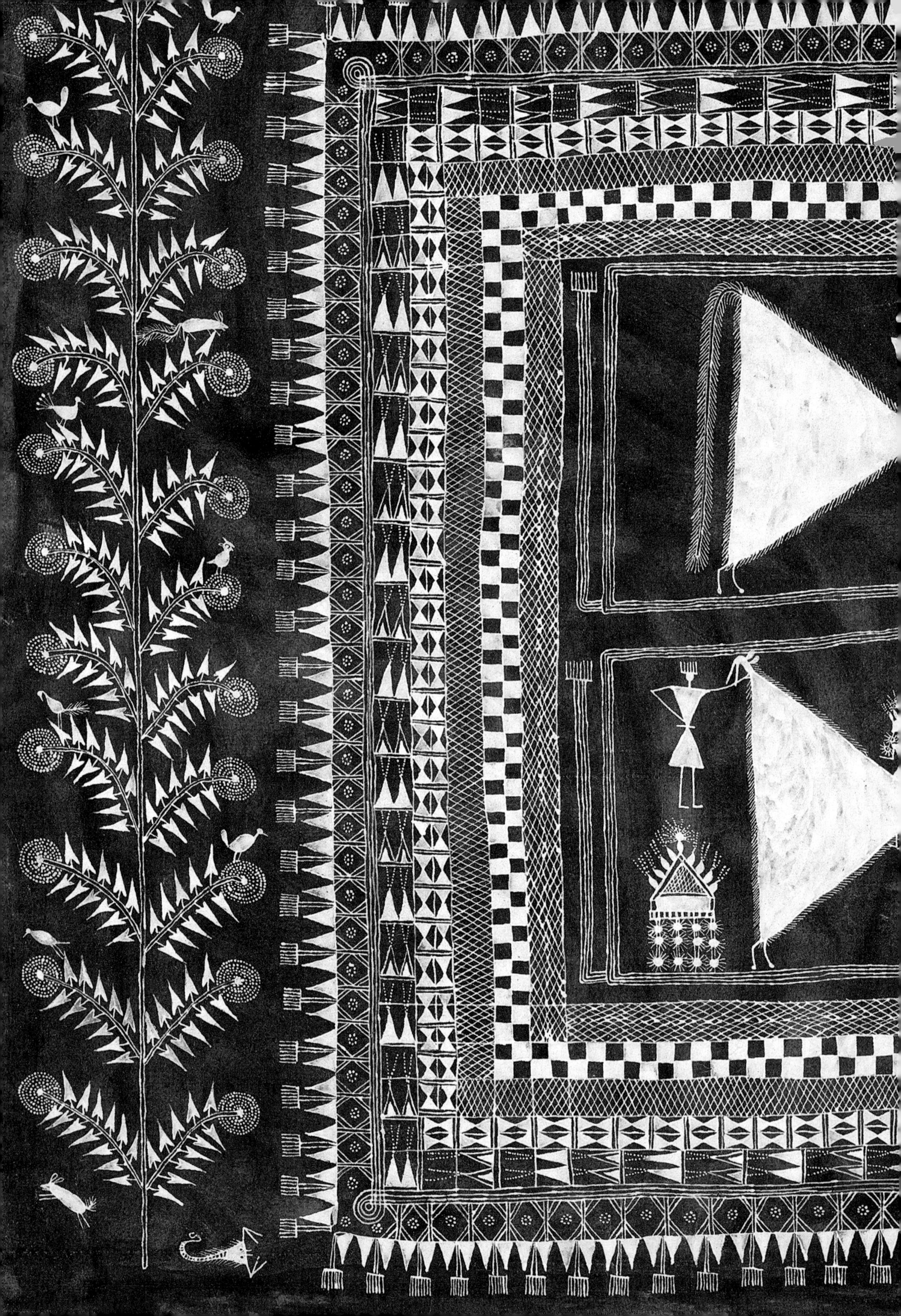

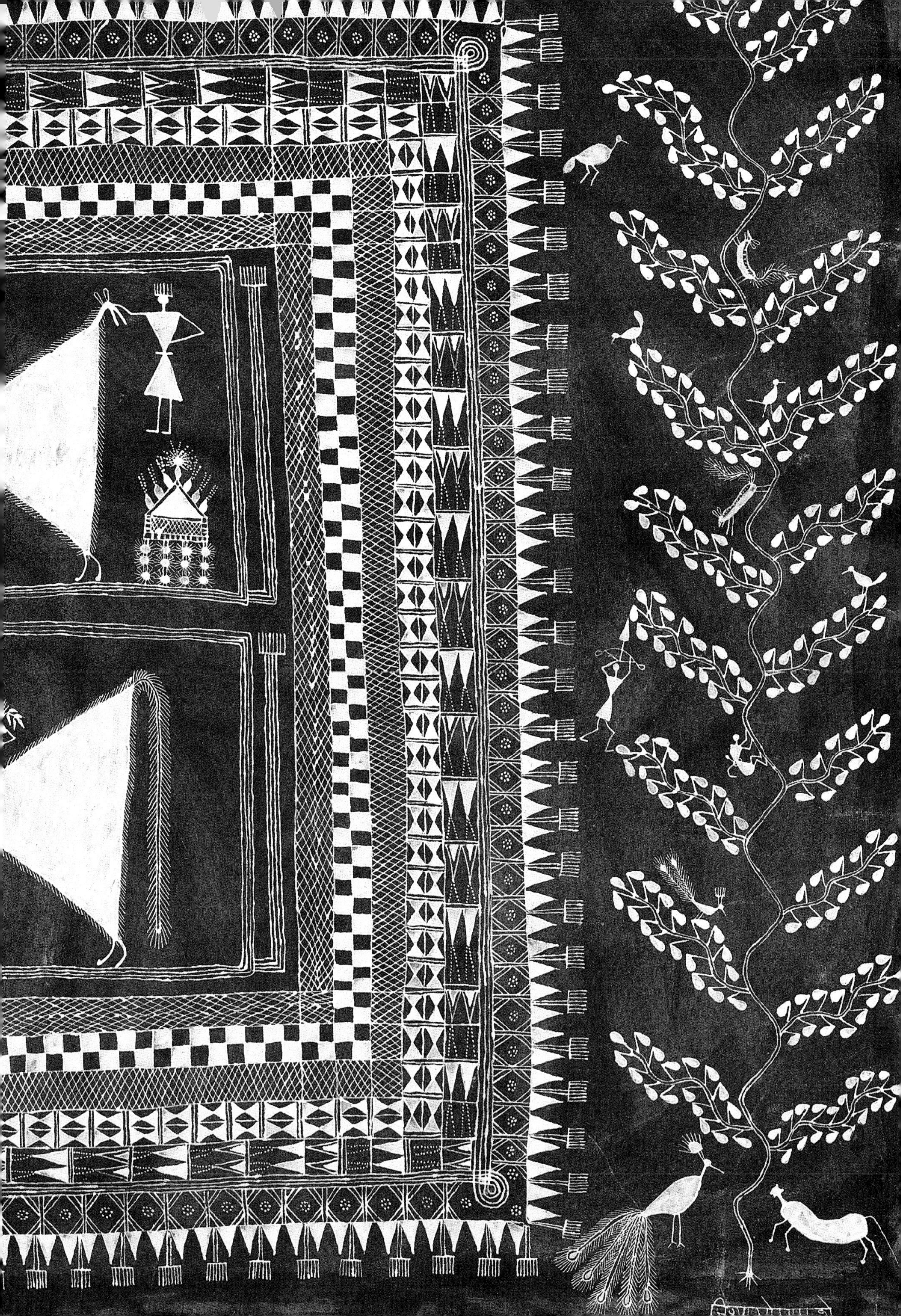

Cauk/Chauk, *chaukat*, or *chowk* is the name given to the ritual painting of marriage in the Warli community. I had always seen it executed collectively by several women of different generations (as can be seen in the photographs of Yashodhara Dalmia's book: *see page* 19). It is the most ancient pictorial expression to have been recorded in written and photographic documents. The square indicates the sacred enclosure. At its centre, Palagatha, the mother goddess and goddess of fertility, is represented by two triangles joined at their tips, a fundamental form in Warli pictography.

In this painting, Palagatha is replaced by secular scenes depicting, in particular, the bride and groom on horseback. Around the *cauk*, scenes of daily life can be seen, below are the bridal headdresses, and in the top left corner, the 'monkey tree'. This is a tree whose leaves are highly prized by monkeys–so much so that none remain, leaving only the monkeys themselves. Hence its name, the monkey tree, with the monkeys having effectively become the tree's foliage motif.

Cauk, *Caughat* ou encore *Chowk* est la peinture rituelle de mariage propre à la communauté warli. Je l'ai toujours vue réaliser collectivement par plusieurs femmes de toutes générations (comme en témoignent les photos du livre de Yashodhara Dalmia : *voir page* 19). C'est l'expression picturale la plus ancienne consignée par écrit et dans des documents photographiques. Le carré désigne l'enclos sacré. En son centre Palagatha, la déesse mère, la déesse de la fertilité et de la fécondité, représentée par les deux triangles réunis à leurs sommets opposés qui sont à la base de la pictographie warli.

Dans cette peinture, Palagatha est remplacée par des scènes profanes représentant, notamment, les mariés à cheval. Autour du Cauk, des scènes de la vie quotidienne, au-dessous, les coiffes des mariés, et en haut à gauche l'arbre à singes. Il s'agit d'un arbre dont les feuilles sont très prisées par les singes. À tel point qu'il n'y reste plus aucune feuille, juste les singes. D'où son nom d'arbre à singes, ceux-ci étant devenus le motif végétal de l'arbre.

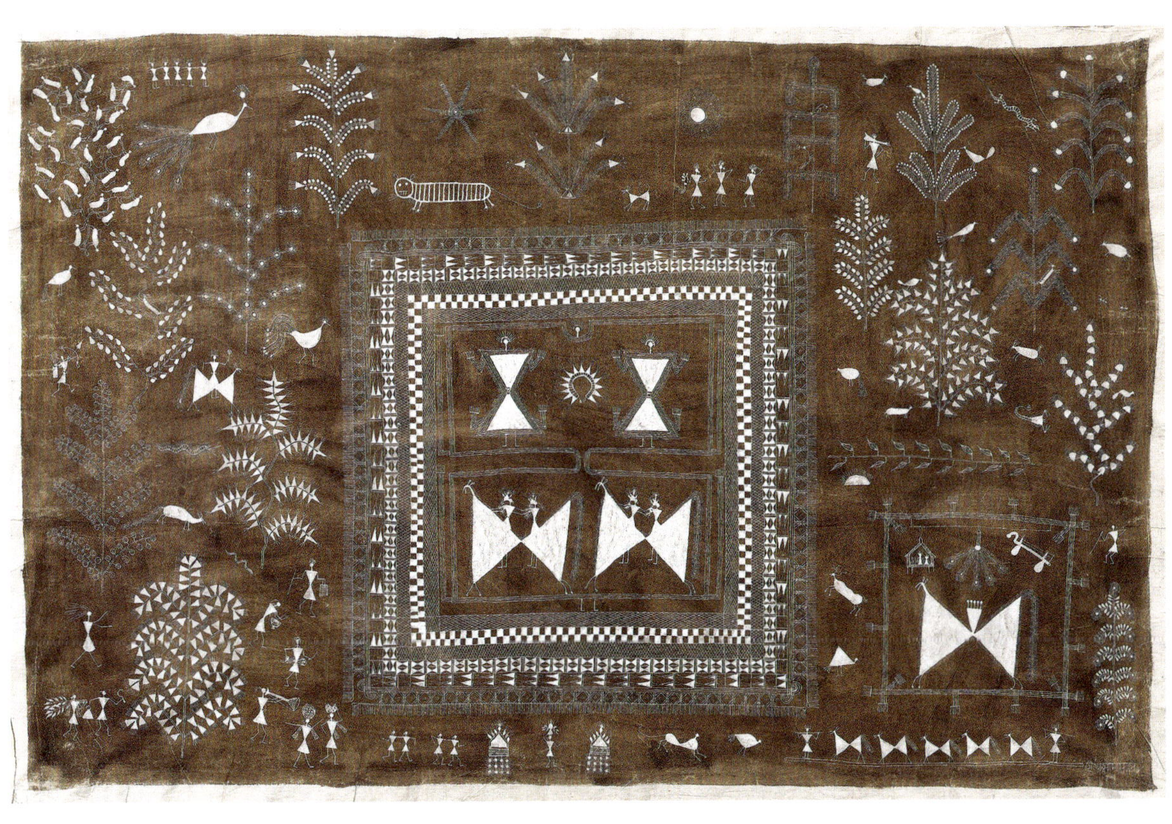

Jivya Soma Mashe, *Cauk*, 1999,
acrylic and cow dung on canvas,
145 × 230 cm; 57.08 × 90.55 in. (*detail on pages* 136–137)
Collection Hervé Perdriolle.
Photo by Christian Baraja.

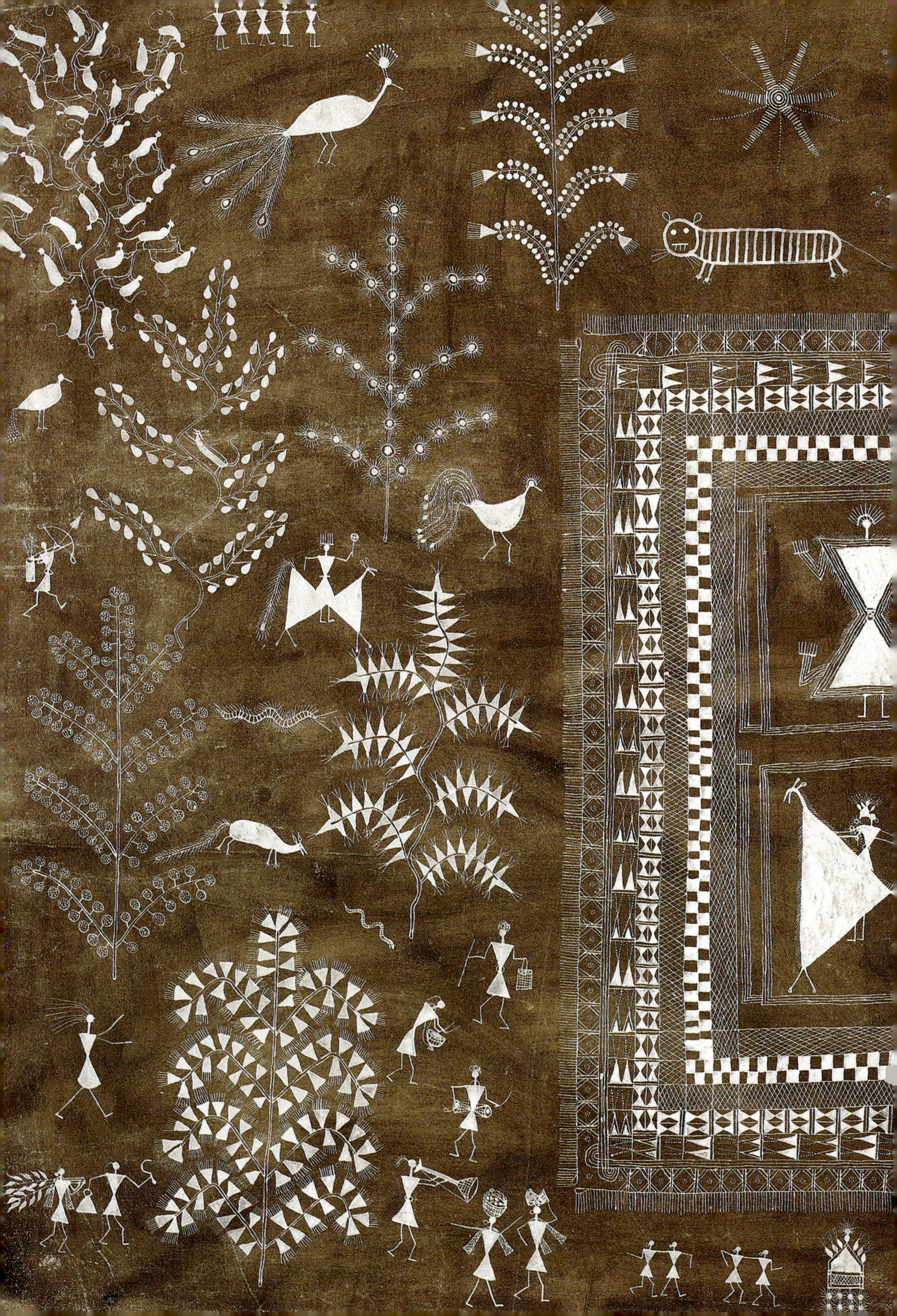

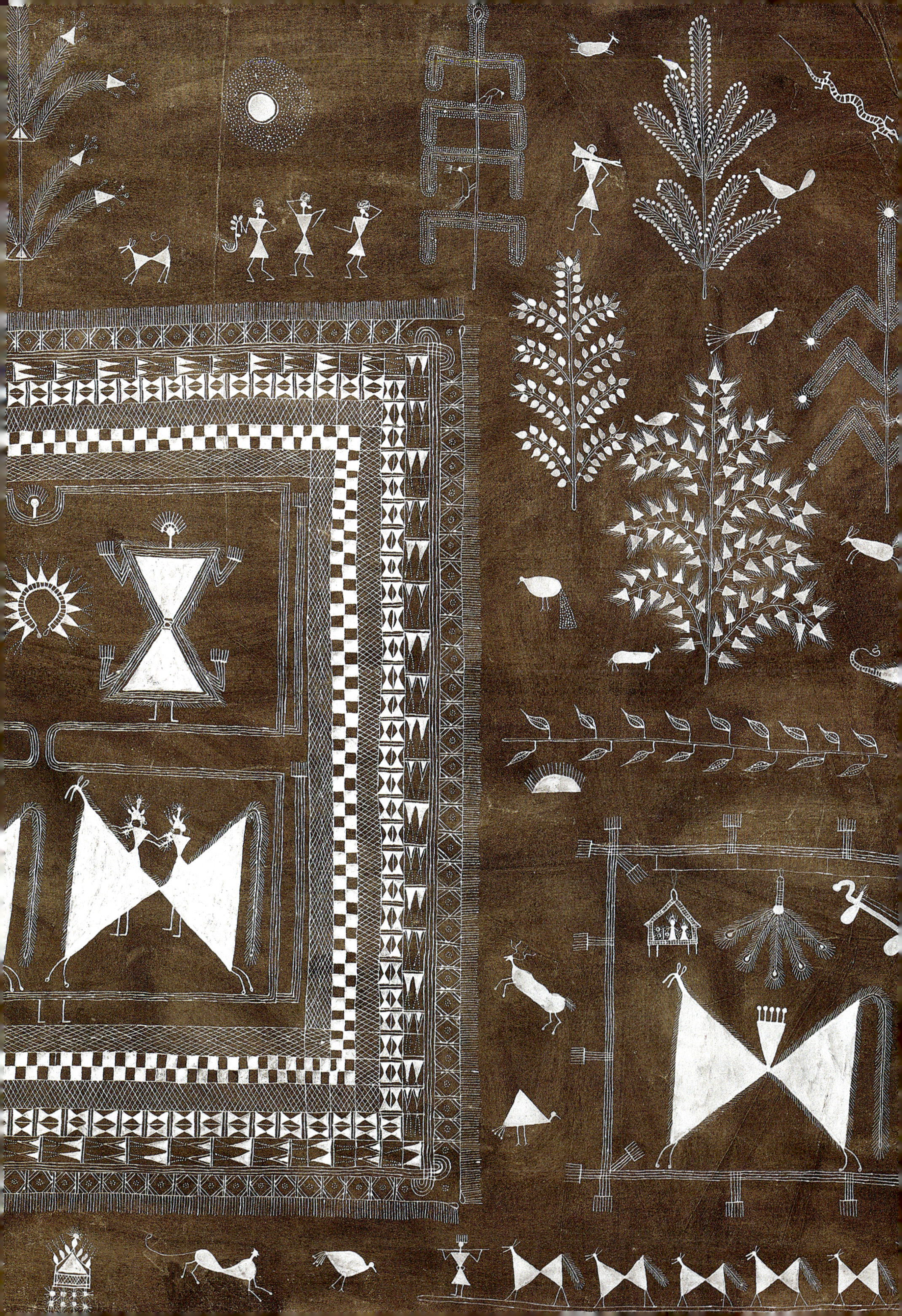

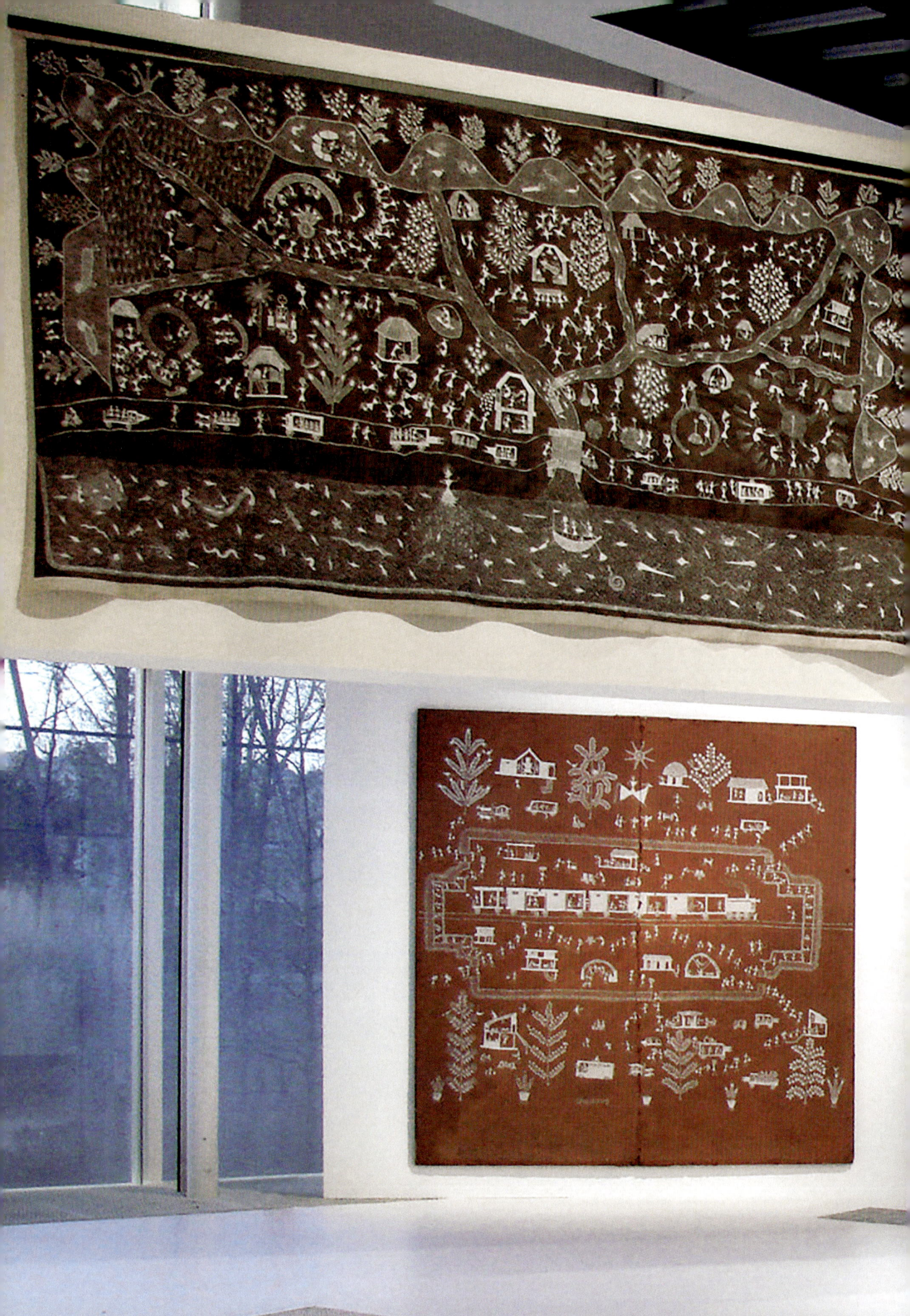

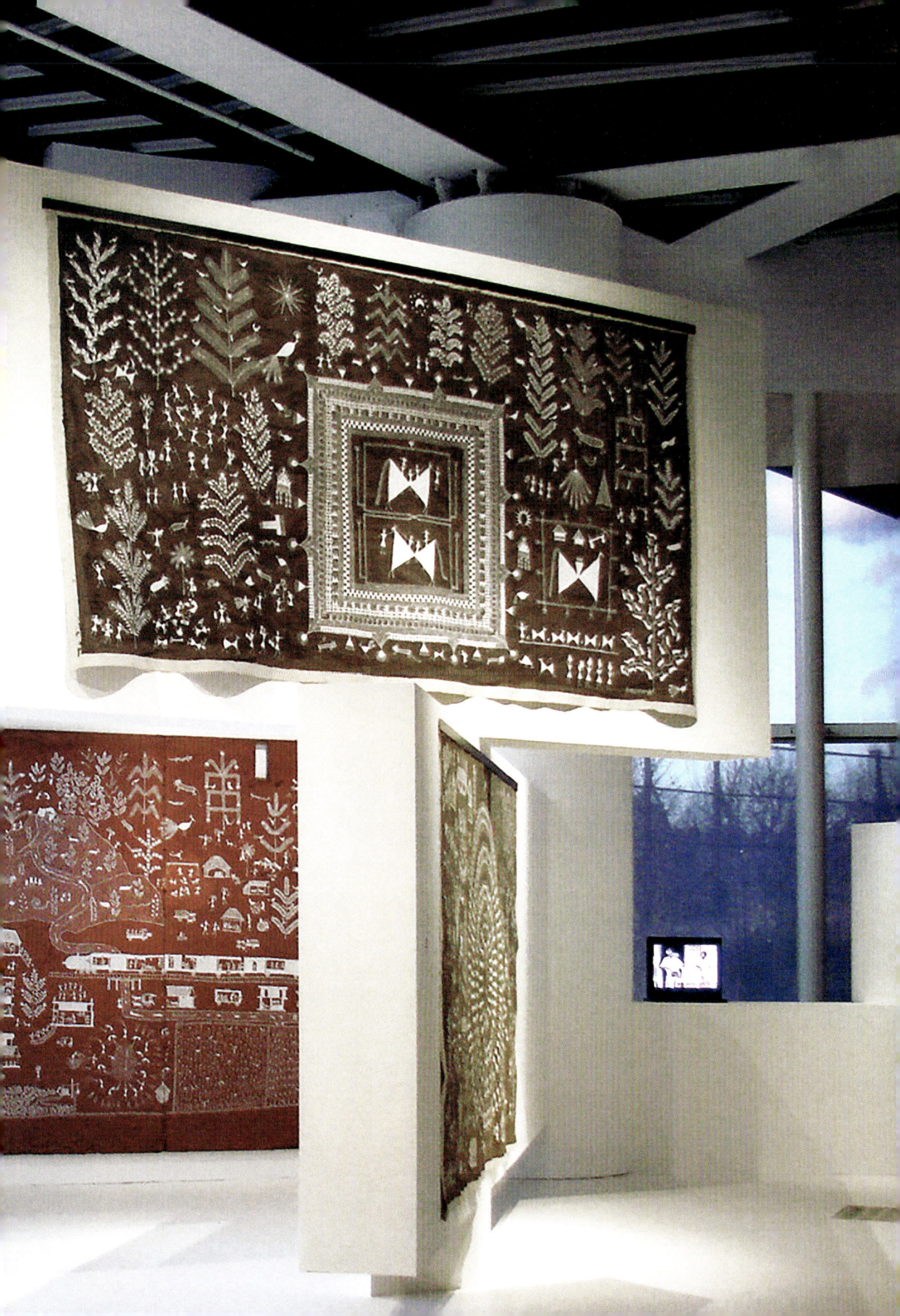

The Tarpana

The Tarpana is a recurrent motif in Warli art. It represents a ritual dance performed by young girls and boys around a player of the *tarpa*, a wind instrument that supposedly sounds like the growling of a tiger. The dance is performed in a spiral around the musician. I lived in Quimper in Brittany for four years and, curiously, the *tarpa* player reminded me of players of the *biniou* (a Breton bagpipe) and the dancers in the Fest-Deiz and Fest-Noz music festivals, in the way they struck the ground with their clogs each time they moved. I found among the Warli people the same telluric connection as among the Celts, this relationship with the earth that is cadenced, rhythmic, and resonant, as if to merge with and dance with the earth.

Dance

Dance, which introduces the affective languages of primitive societies and is, moreover, the first to be seen in children, is simply a stylization of this need, an elementary liturgical form of 'organised communion' that elevates individual instinct to the most fervent, if not the most lucid, awareness of the higher interests of the community. In tribes, [. . .] it constantly reminds the community – with its powerful rhythms, ritual repetitions, and periodic returns celebrating the most solemn events of social life – of the need to preserve, in customs, the order taught to humans by the constant manifestations of the astronomical and biological universe: the regular succession of seasons, the phases of the moon, the rising and setting of the sun and stars, the migration of birds, the periodicity of sleep and hunger, the pulsing of our arteries, the rhythm of our footsteps, and even the perceptible symmetry of the two halves of the bodies of all living beings – a mysterious mechanical ensemble that gives our subconscious foundations the sensation of a regulating pendulum, whose universal presence each of us vaguely perceives within ourselves, in society, and in the world.

– Élie Faure, taken from 'L'universalité de l'art', published in 1936 in the *Encyclopédie Française*, vol. XVI.

La Tarpana

La Tarpana est un motif récurrent dans l'art des Warlis. Il s'agit d'une danse rituelle rassemblant jeunes filles et jeunes garçons autour d'un joueur de *tarpa*, un instrument à vent censé évoquer le feulement du tigre. Cette danse se développe autour du joueur de *tarpa* en d'incessantes spirales mouvantes. J'ai habité 4 ans à Quimper et curieusement, ce joueur de *tarpa* m'évoquait les joueurs de *biniou* (une cornemuse bretonne) et les danseurs, dans leur façon de frapper le sol à chaque déplacement, le martèlement des sabots sur le sol dans les Fest-Deiz et Fest-Noz bretons. Je retrouvais, chez les Warlis, la relation tellurique des Celtes, ce rapport à la terre cadencé, rythmé, sonore, comme pour faire corps et danser avec la terre.

La Danse

La danse, qui inaugurera les langages affectifs des sociétés primitives et qui est d'ailleurs le premier qu'on rencontre chez l'enfant, n'est qu'une stylisation de ce besoin, une forme liturgique élémentaire de « communion organisée » qui élève l'instinct individuel à la conscience la plus fervente, sinon la plus lucide, des intérêts supérieurs de la collectivité. Dans les tribus [...] elle rappelle sans cesse à cette collectivité, par ses rythmes puissants, par ses répétitions rituelles, par ses retours périodiques qui célèbrent les évènements les plus solennels de la vie sociale, qu'il convient de sauvegarder dans les mœurs l'ordre qu'enseignent aux hommes les manifestations constantes de l'univers astronomique et biologique : la succession régulière des saisons, les phases de la lune, le lever et le coucher du soleil et des étoiles, la migration des oiseaux, la périodicité du sommeil, de la faim, le battement de nos propres artères, le bruit cadencé de nos pas et jusqu'à la symétrie sensible des deux moitiés du corps de tous les êtres vivants – mystérieux ensemble mécanique qui donne à nos assises subconscientes la sensation d'un balancier régulateur dont chacun de nous perçoit confusément en lui, dans la société et le monde, l'universelle présence.

Élie Faure, extrait de « L'universalité de l'art » publié en 1936 dans l'*Encyclopédie Française*, Tome XVI

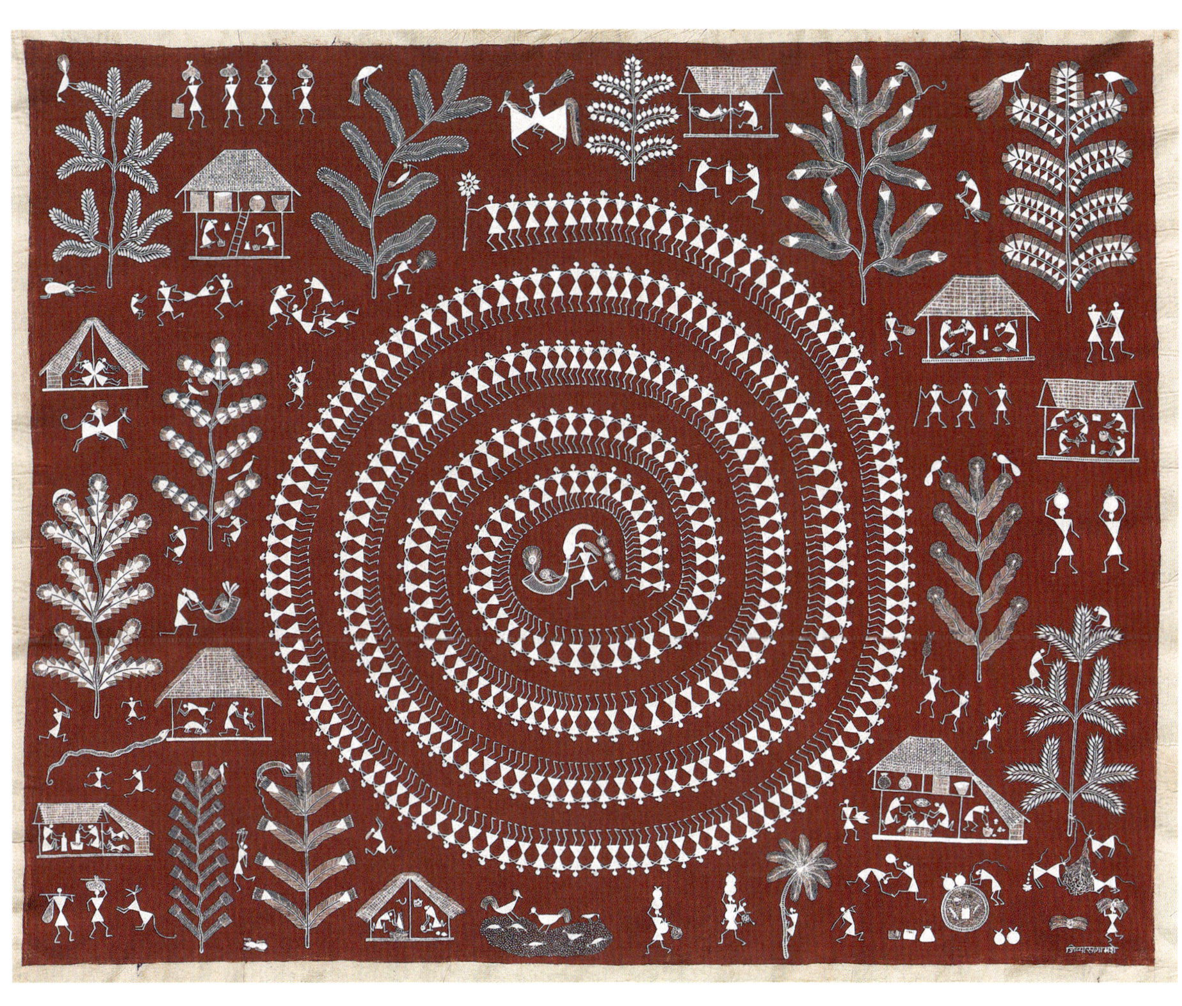

Pages 138–139
View of the exhibition *Autres maîtres de l'Inde – Other Masters of India*, curator Jyotindra Jain, Musée du quai Branly – Jacques Chirac, Paris, 2010.

Jivya Soma Mashe, *Tarpana*, 1998,
acrylic on canvas,
120 × 145 cm; 47.24 × 57.28 in.
Collection Charles-Eric Bauer.
Photo by Christian Baraja.

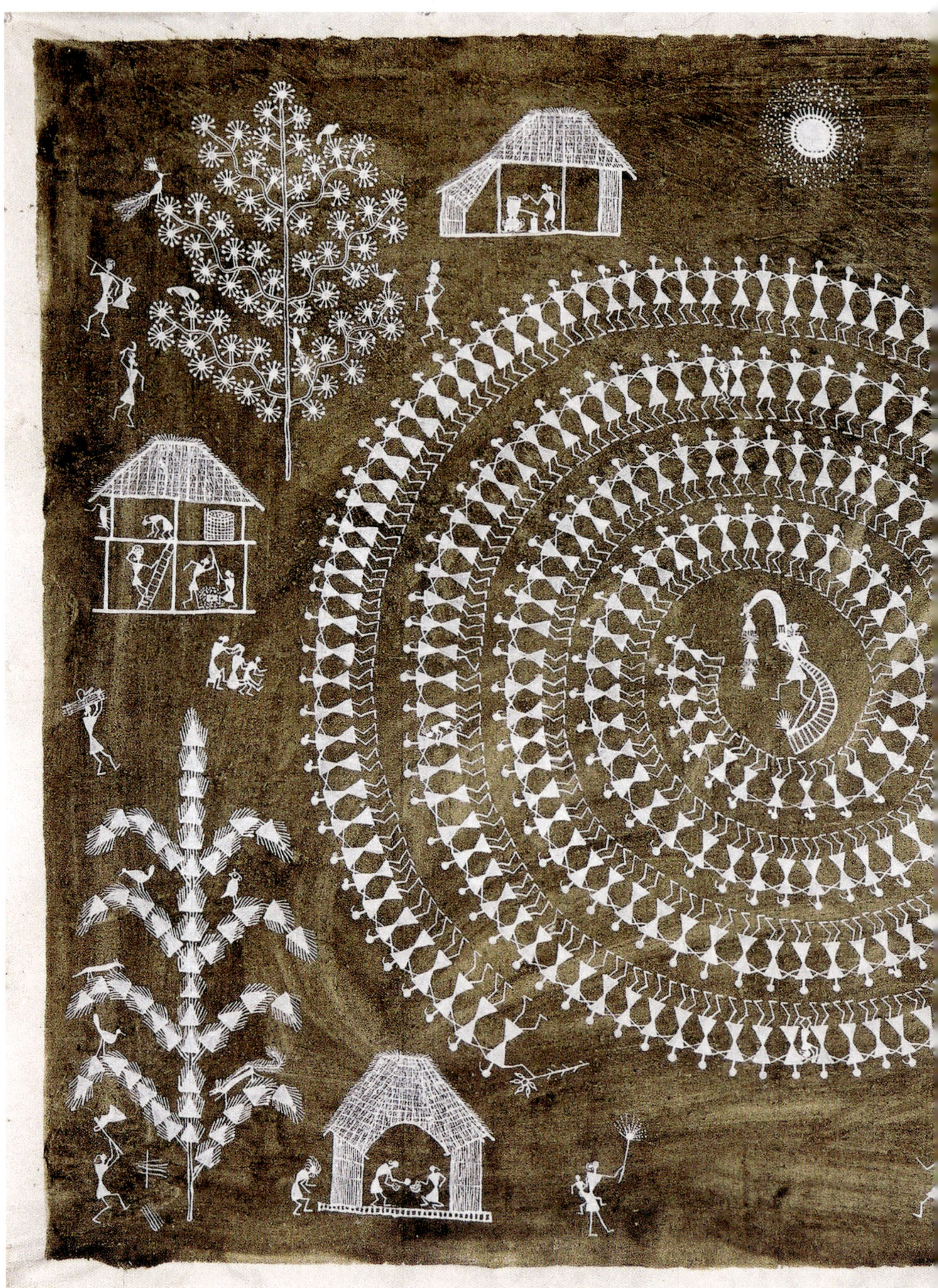

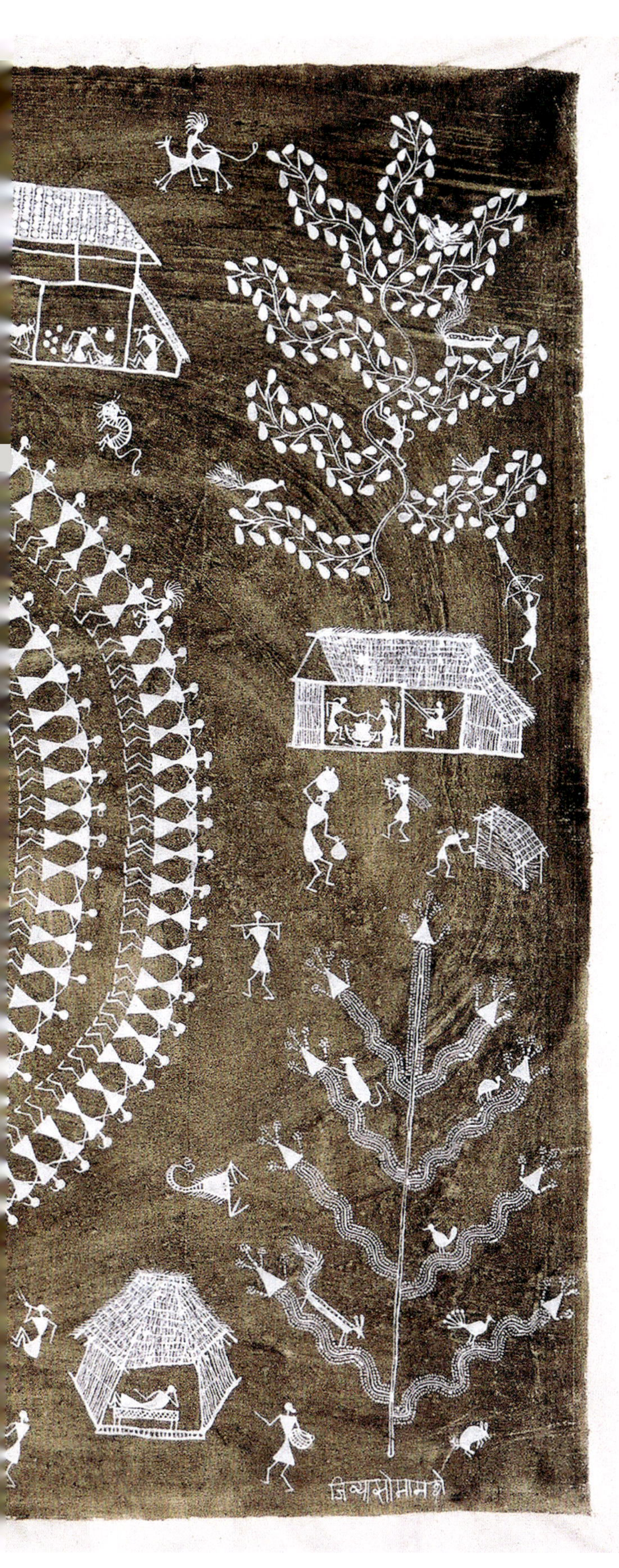

Jivya Soma Mashe, *Tarpana*, 1998,
acrylic and cow dung on canvas,
99 × 125 cm; 38.97 × 49.21 in.
Collection Alain-Dominique Perrin.

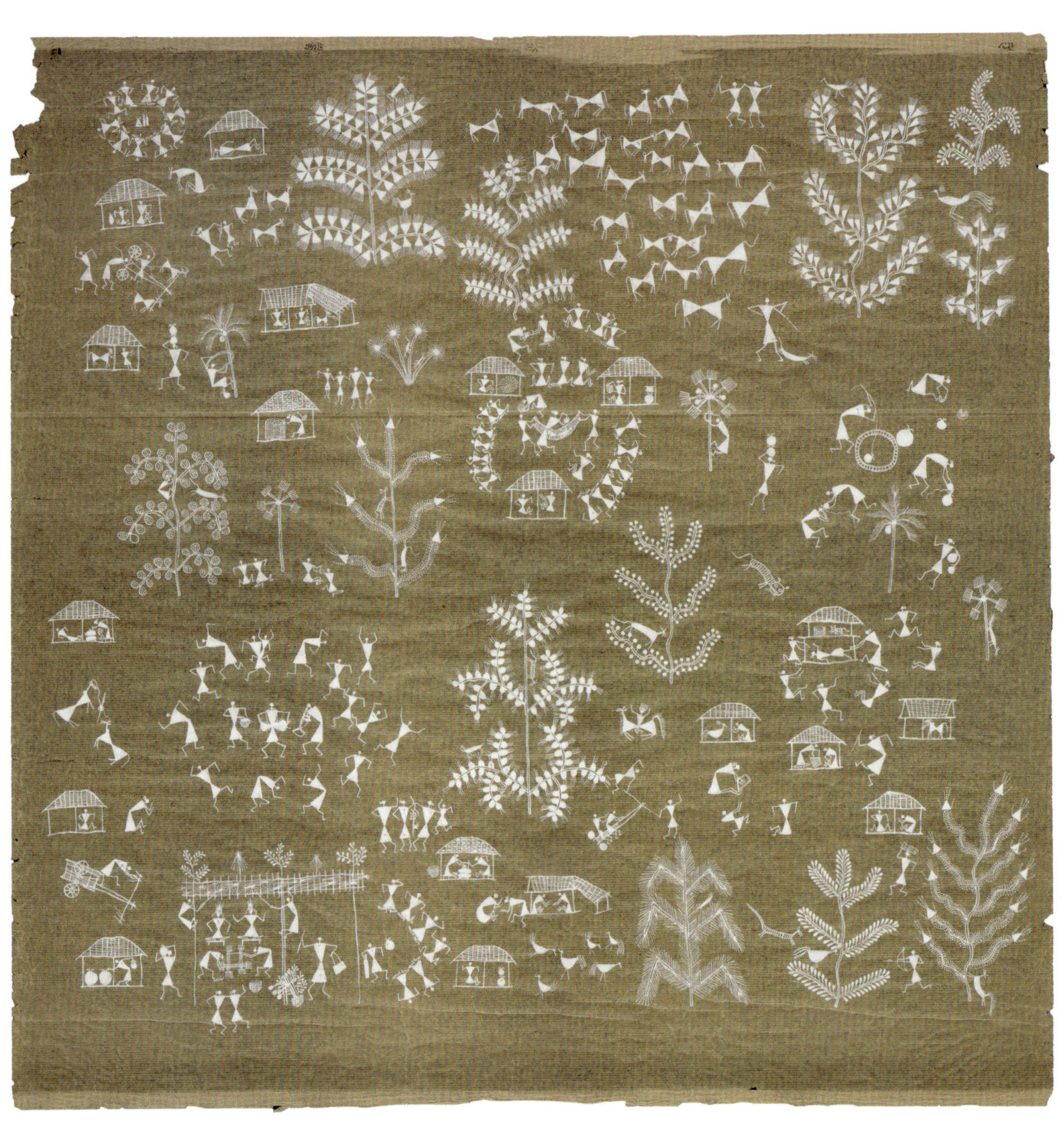

Jivya Soma Mashe, *Untitled*, circa 1970,
acrylic on tarred kraft paper,
111 × 111 cm; 43.70 × 43.70 in.
Photo by Christian Baraja.

This painting on kraft paper was purchased in Bombay during the 1970s by Rena and Jean-Louis Dumas of the French company Hermès. It was the only artwork that remained uninterruptedly on the wall of the office of Rena Dumas, a fact that attests her attachment to it.

A while after her death, a team from Hermès, who were aware of my dedication to Indian contemporary tribal art, asked me to identify the work, whose artist had until then remained unknown. Almost convinced that it was one of Jivya Soma Mashe's early works, I offered to show a photograph of it to the painter the next time I made a trip to India. On the following double-page, we see Jivya Soma Mashe and his grandson Kishore when they were shown the Hermès scarf created from a painting by George Lilanga. It was Hermès' wish that this lovely story should be accompanied by the production of a Jivya Soma Mashe scarf. Coming soon . . .

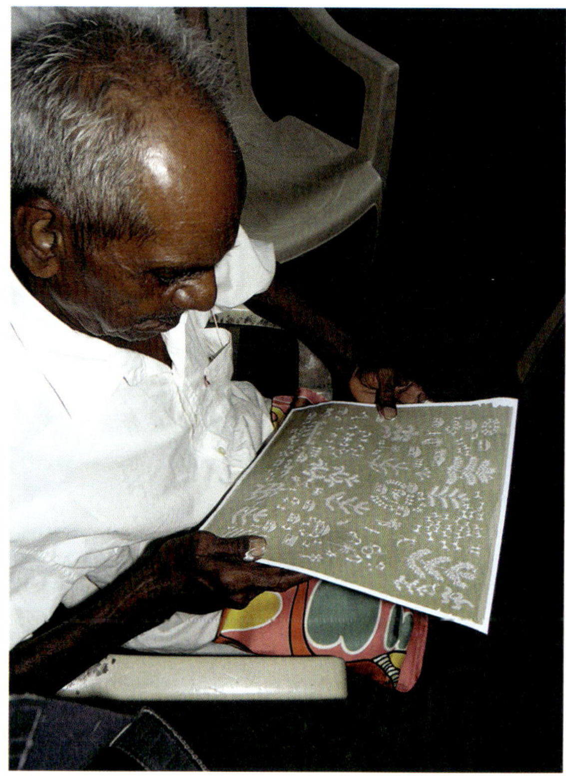

Cette peinture sur papier kraft a été acquise par Rena et Jean-Louis Dumas, de la maison française Hermès, dans les années 1970 à Bombay. Elle fut la seule œuvre à rester en permanence accrochée sur les murs du bureau de Rena Dumas, témoignant de la sorte son attachement à cette peinture singulière.

Quelque temps après la disparition de Rena Dumas, une équipe d'Hermès, connaissant ma passion pour l'art tribal contemporain indien, me demanda d'identifier cette œuvre jusque-là restée dans l'anonymat. Quasiment persuadé qu'il s'agissait là d'une œuvre des premières heures de Jivya Soma Mashe, je leur proposai de prendre avec moi la photo de cette peinture et de la faire authentifier par l'artiste lors d'un de mes prochains voyages en Inde. On voit sur la double page suivante Jivya Soma Mashe et son petit-fils Kishore découvrir le Carré Hermès créé d'après l'œuvre de George Lilanga. Le souhait d'Hermès a été d'accompagner cette belle histoire par l'édition d'un Carré Jivya Soma Mashe. À découvrir prochainement…

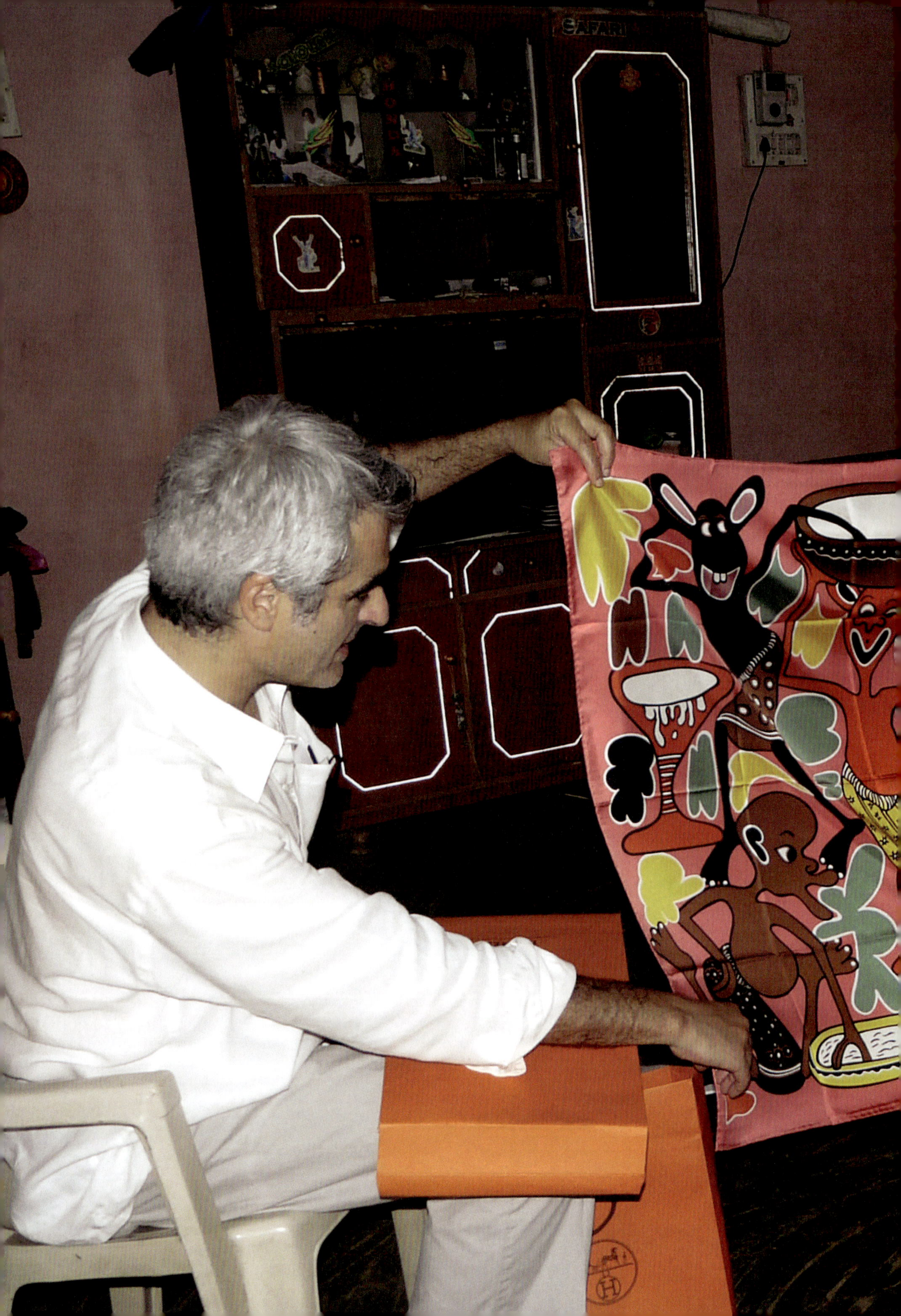
SAFARI

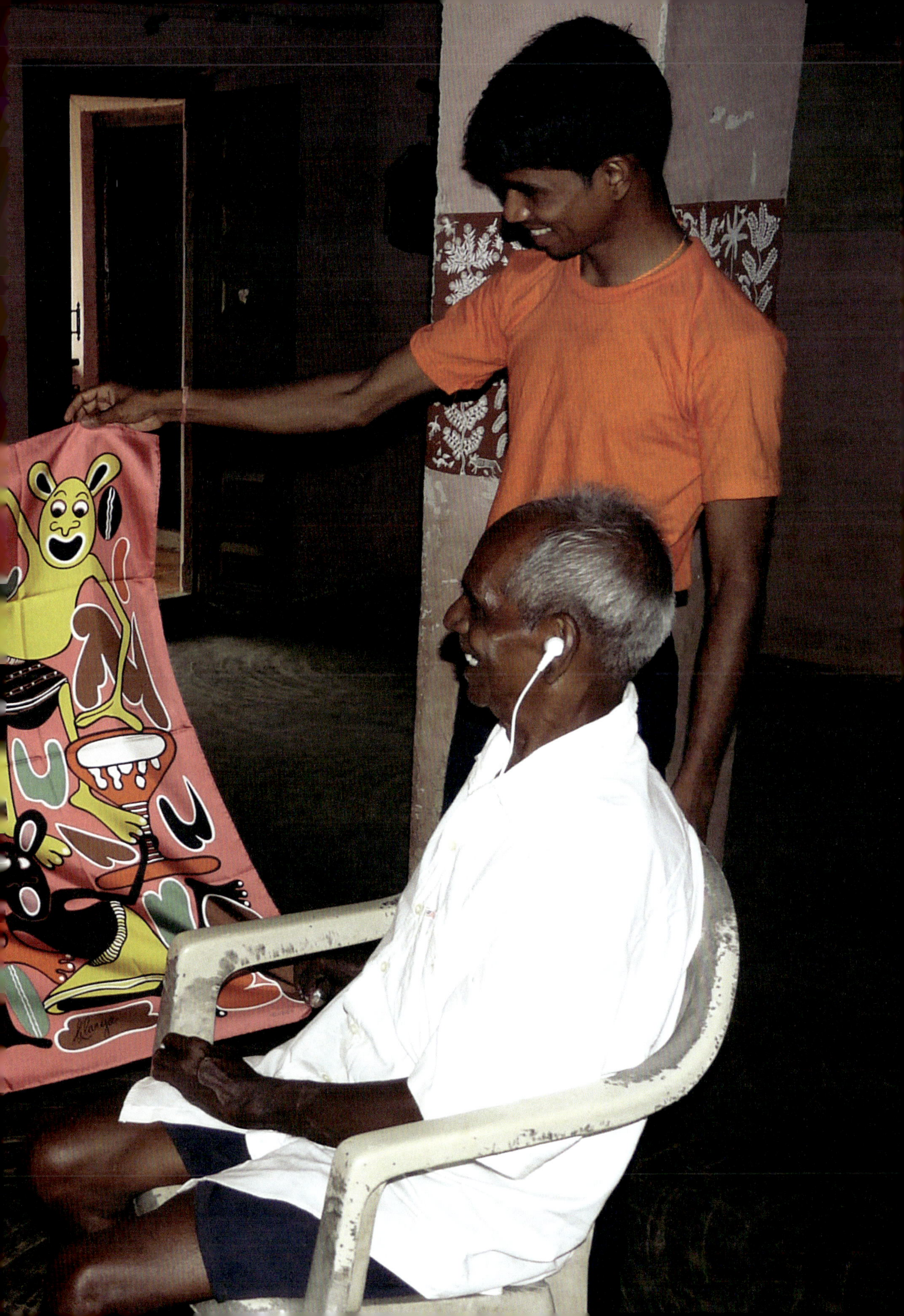

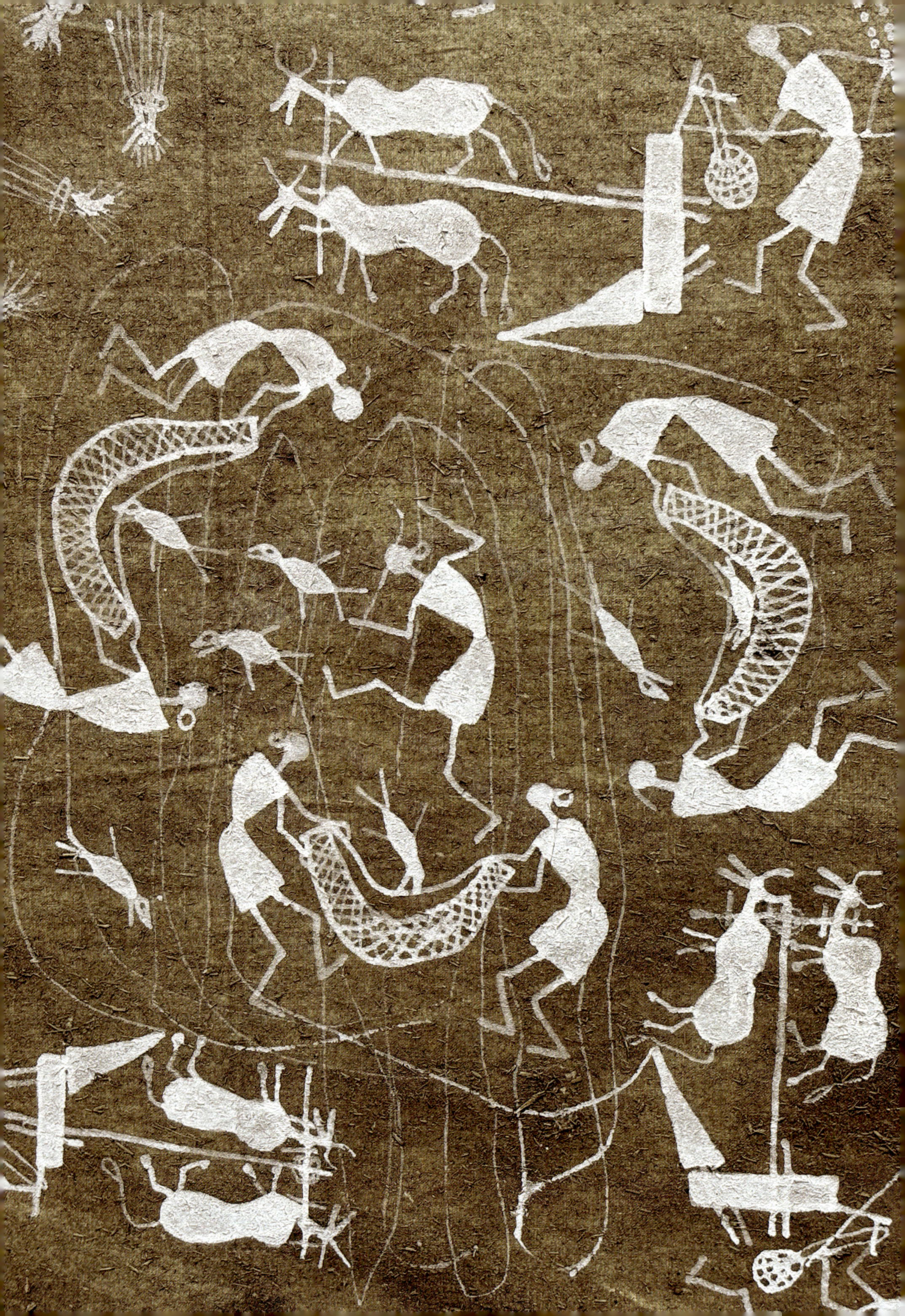

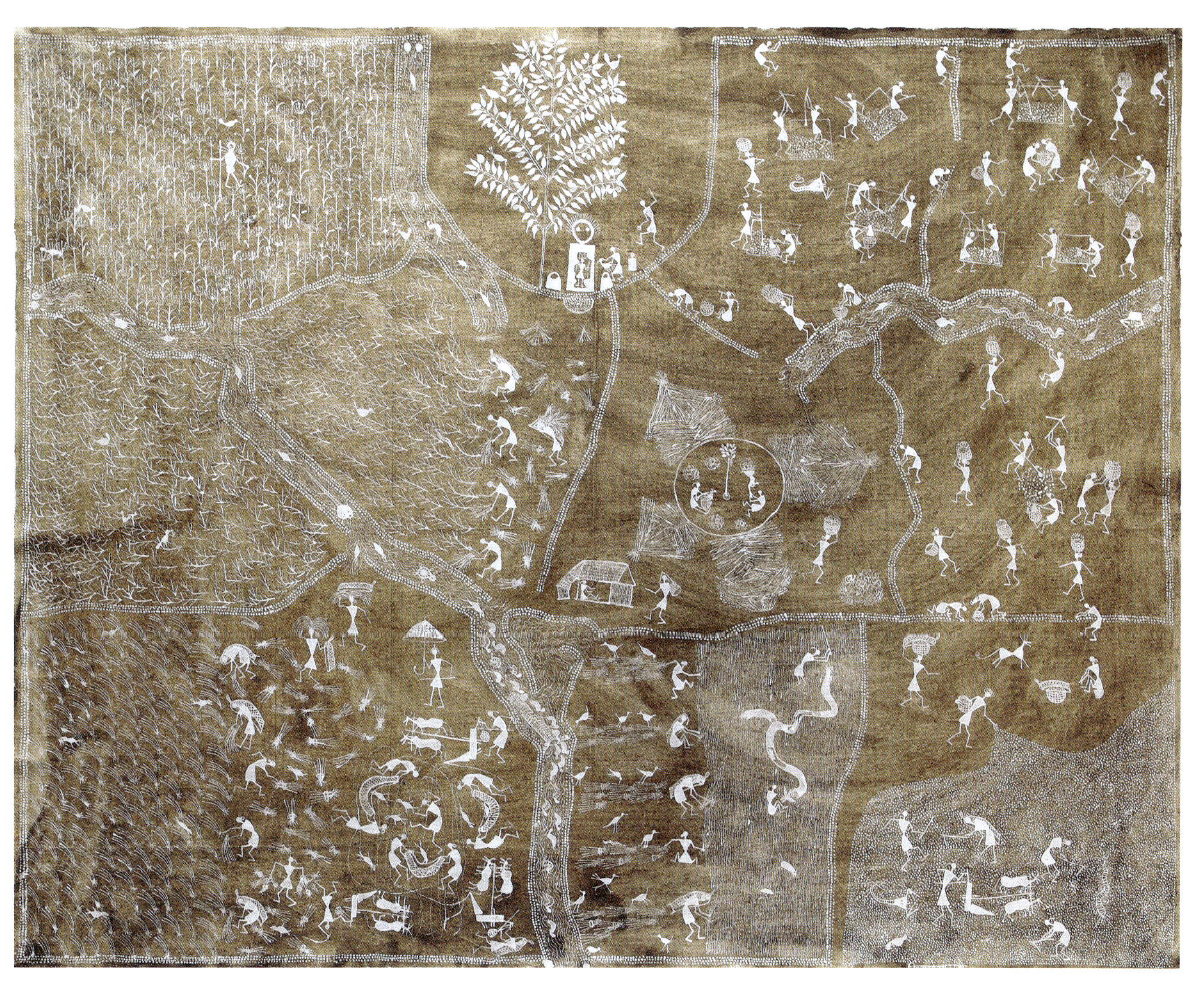

Jivya Soma Mashe, *Untitled*, 1999,
acrylic and cow dung on canvas,
100 × 125.5 cm; 39.37 × 49.40 in. (*detail on page* 148)
Collection Hervé Perdriolle.

THE MAN WHO DIDN'T WANT TO WORK
L'HOMME QUI NE VOULAIT PAS TRAVAILLER

Once upon a time, a very poor elderly couple lived in an abandoned village. The old man didn't want to work and left his wife to toil in the fields. One day, as she was working there, she found an earthenware jar buried in the soil but, even though she used all her strength, she couldn't shift it. She asked her husband for help but he was not interested in an old abandoned jar. Dispirited, she went to the closest village to ask assistance from the first men she came across. On seeing the jar, the men took fright and claimed that the place was undoubtedly full of snakes and scorpions. Once she was alone again, the old woman mustered up all her courage and succeeded in digging up, though not without great effort, the strange jar. She dragged it to her hut and, by the light of the stars, opened it, whereupon she found a treasure trove of gold and silver coins.

Il était une fois un vieux couple démuni vivant dans un village abandonné. Le vieil homme ne voulait pas travailler, laissant à sa femme tous les travaux des champs. La vieille femme, travaillant la terre, découvre une jarre enfouie. Malgré tous ses efforts, elle ne parvient pas à la dégager. Elle demande de l'aide à son mari, lequel n'a que faire d'une vielle jarre abandonnée. Dépitée, elle va au village le plus proche solliciter de l'aide auprès des premiers hommes qu'elle rencontre. À la vue de cette jarre, les hommes prennent peur et déclarent que celle-ci est certainement pleine de serpents et de scorpions. Une fois seule, la vieille femme prend son courage à deux mains et déterre, non sans peine, l'étrange jarre.

Après l'avoir traînée jusqu'à sa hutte, elle entreprend, à la lueur des étoiles, de l'ouvrir et y découvre alors un trésor de pièces d'or et d'argent.

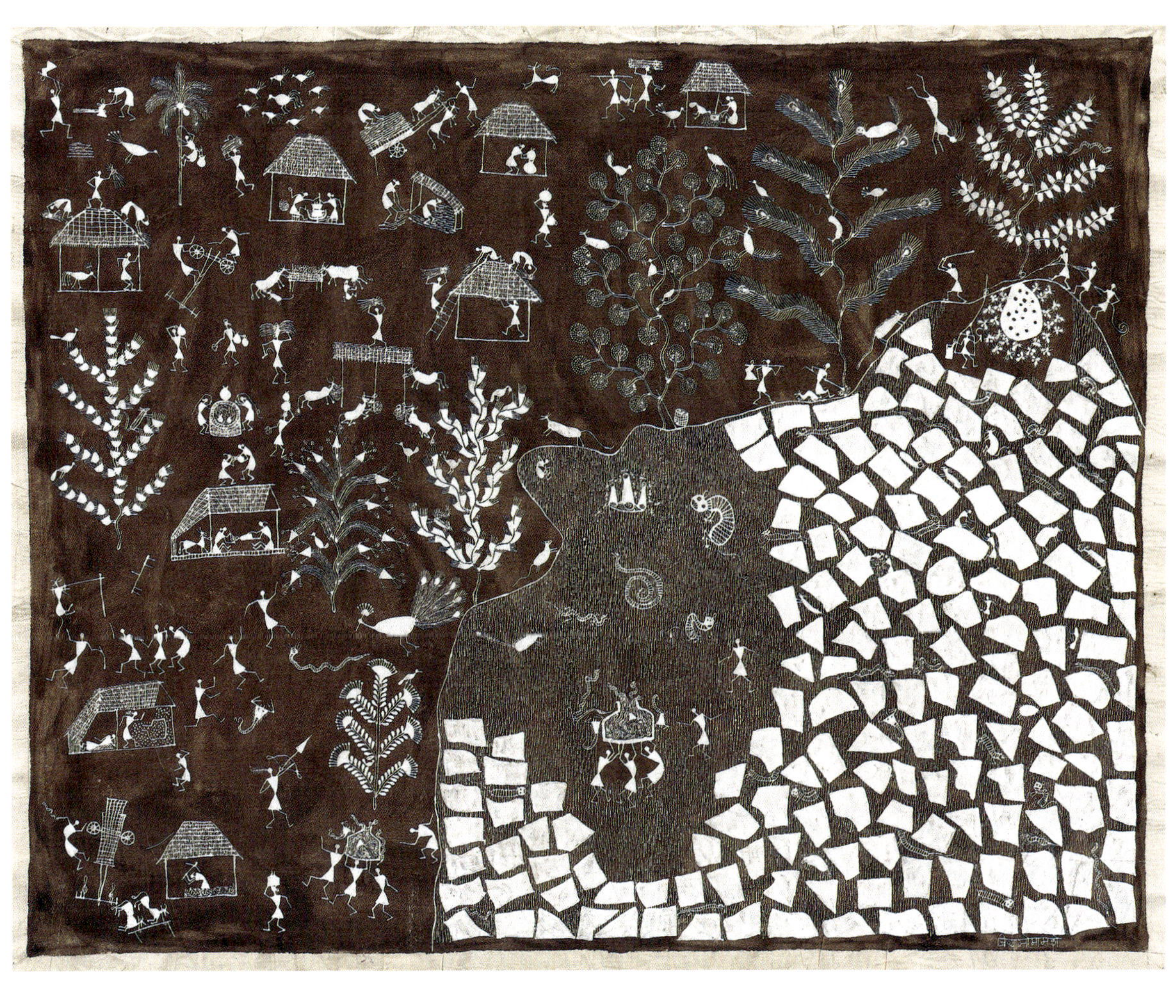

Jivya Soma Mashe, *The Man Who Would Not Work*, 1998,
acrylic and cow dung on canvas,
115 x 146 cm; 45.27 x 57.48 in. (*detail on pages* 152–153)
Collection Hervé Perdriolle.
Photo by Christian Baraja.

Pages 154–155
View of the exhibition *Richard Long – Jivya Soma Mashe*, PAC – Padiglione d'Arte Contemporanea, Milan, 2004.
In the foreground, a spiral created by Richard Long using Milan street cobblestones, titled *Warli Spiral*. In the background, paintings by Richard Long and Jivya Soma Mashe.
Photo by Mario Tedeschi.

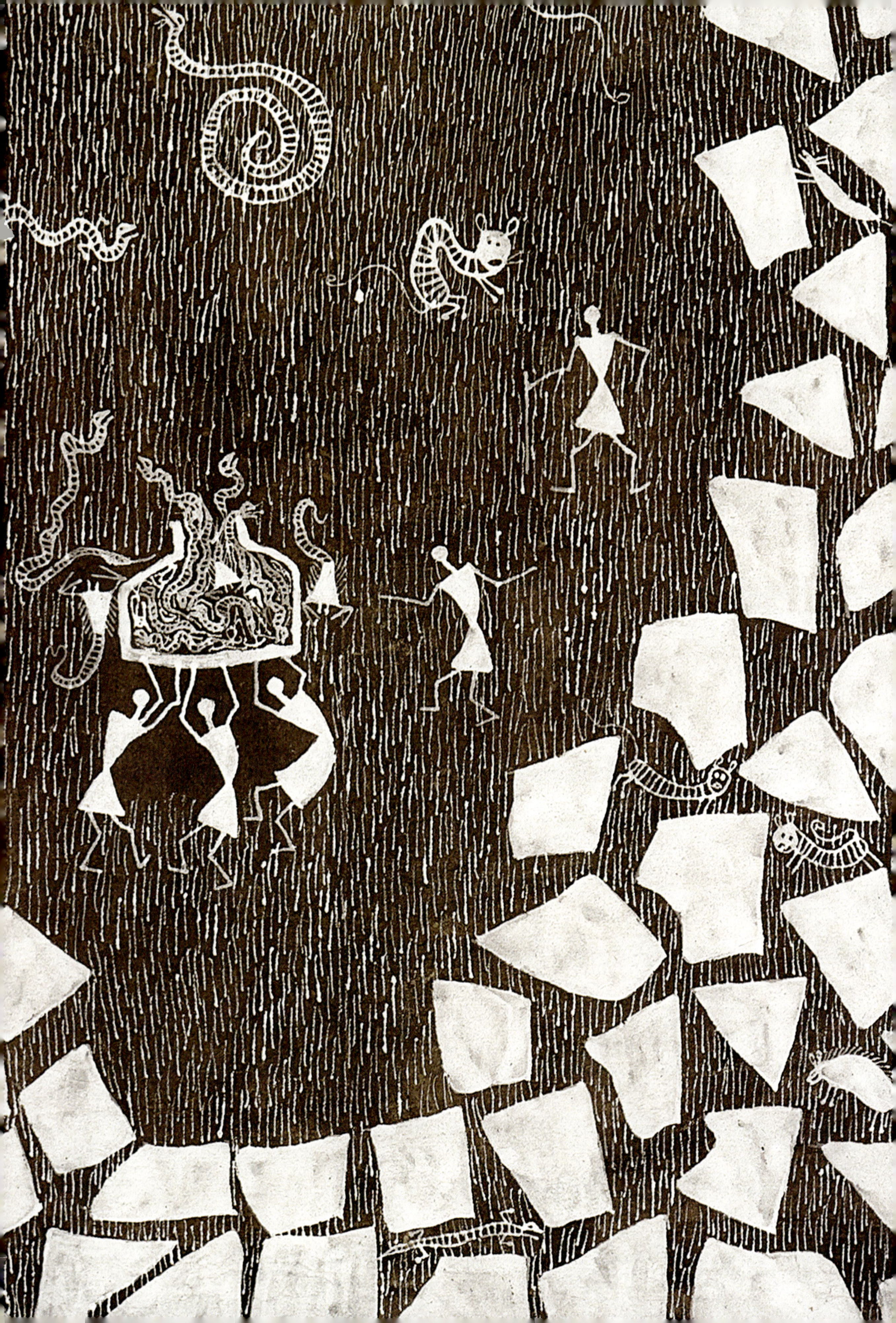

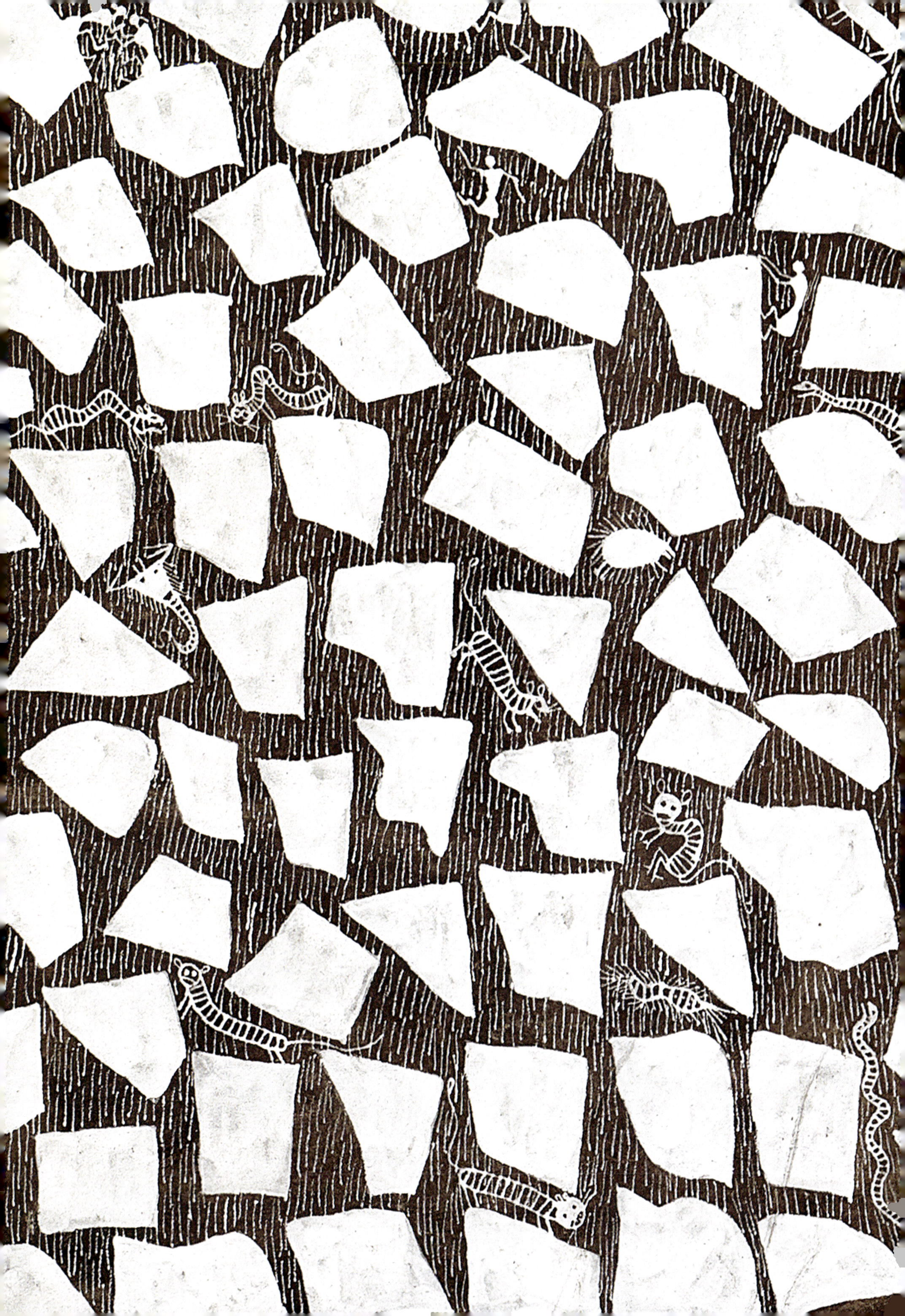

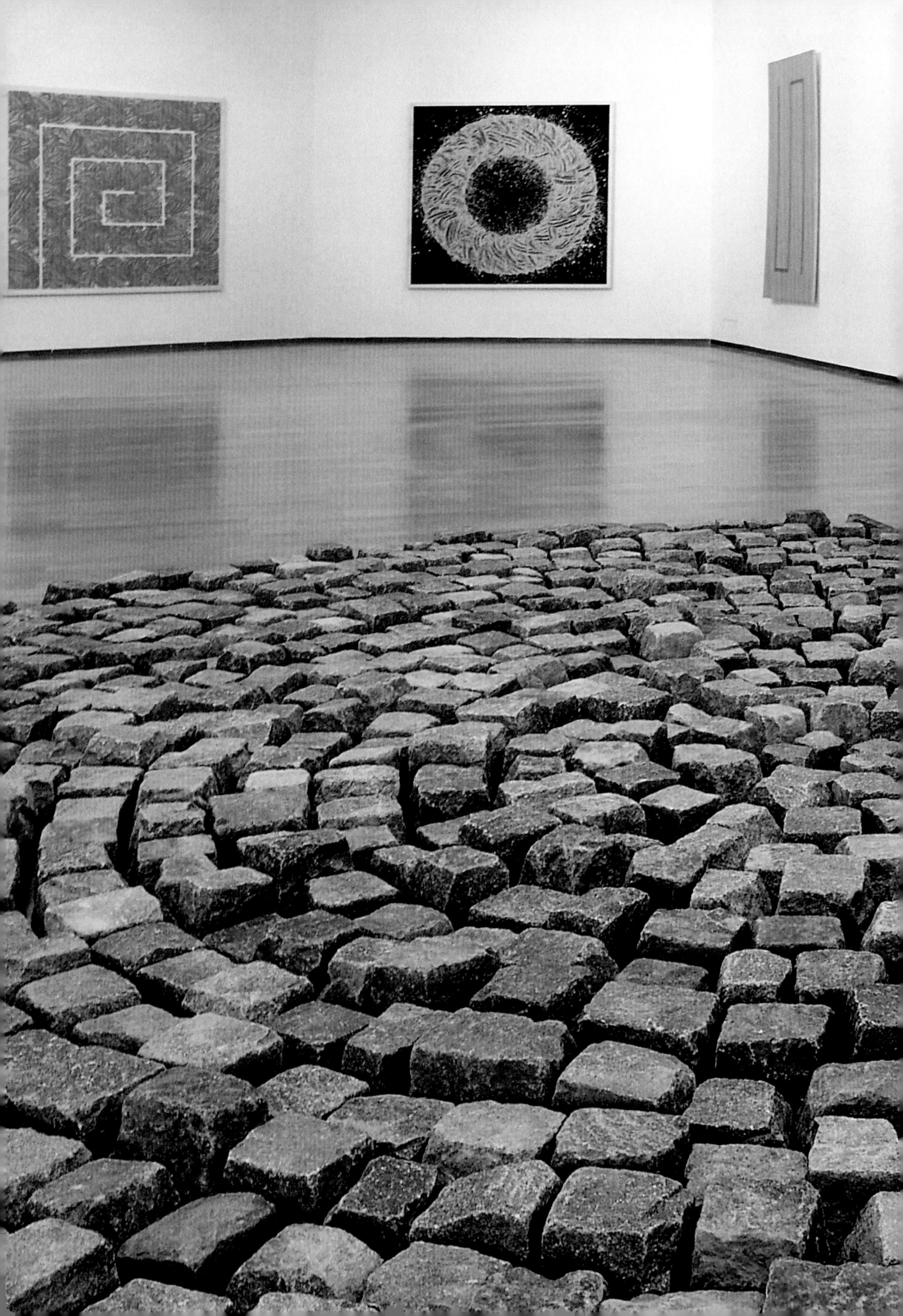

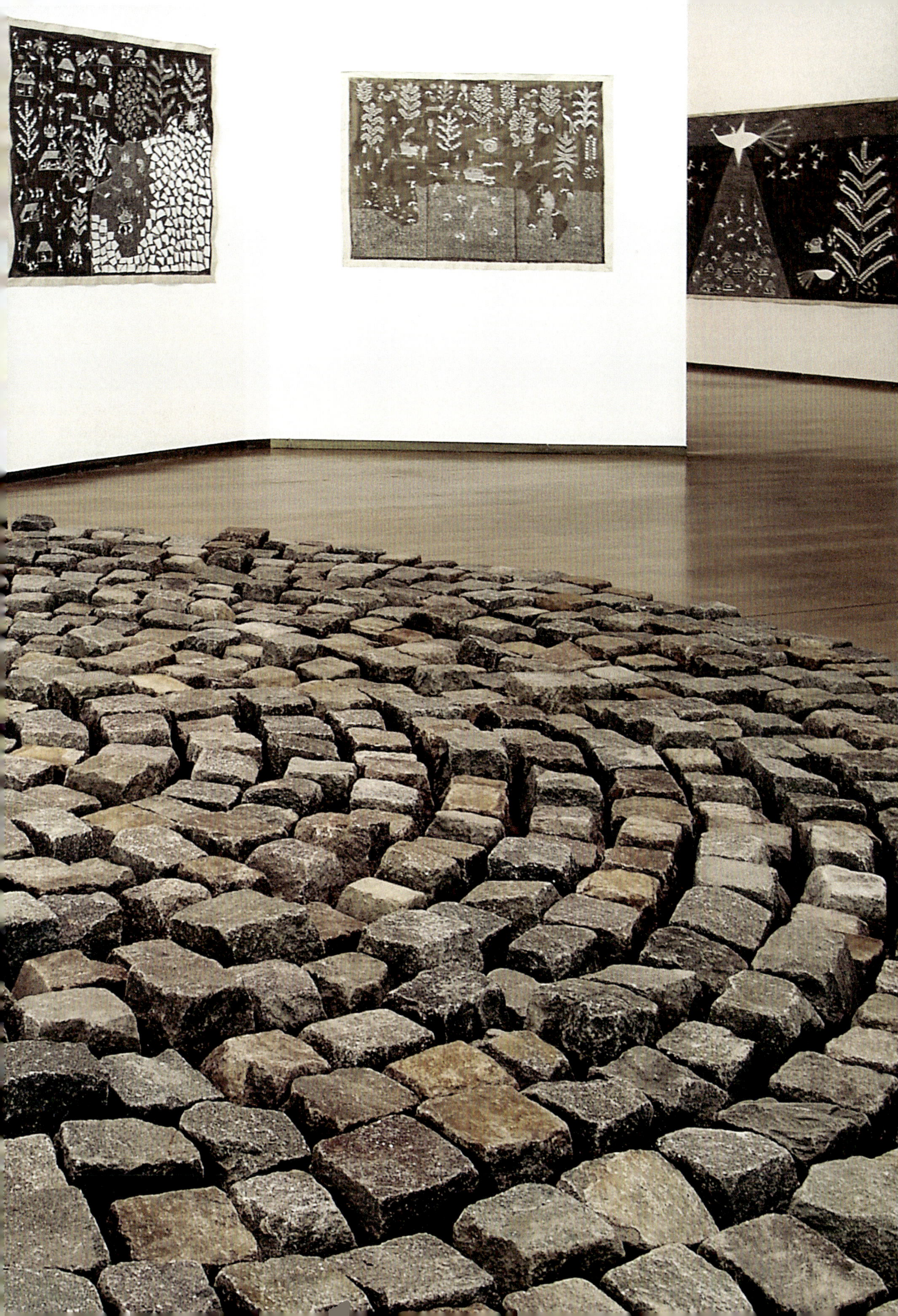

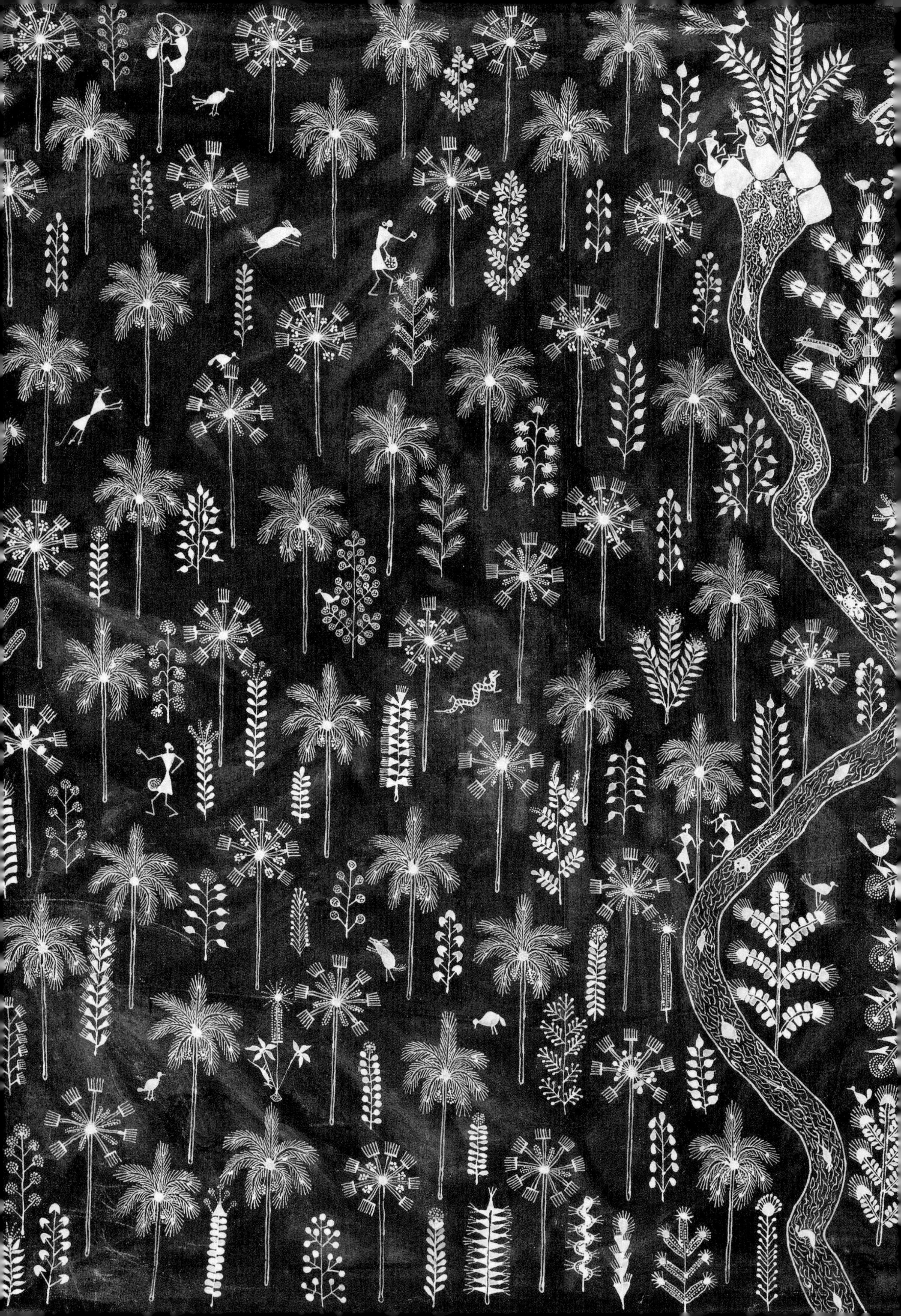

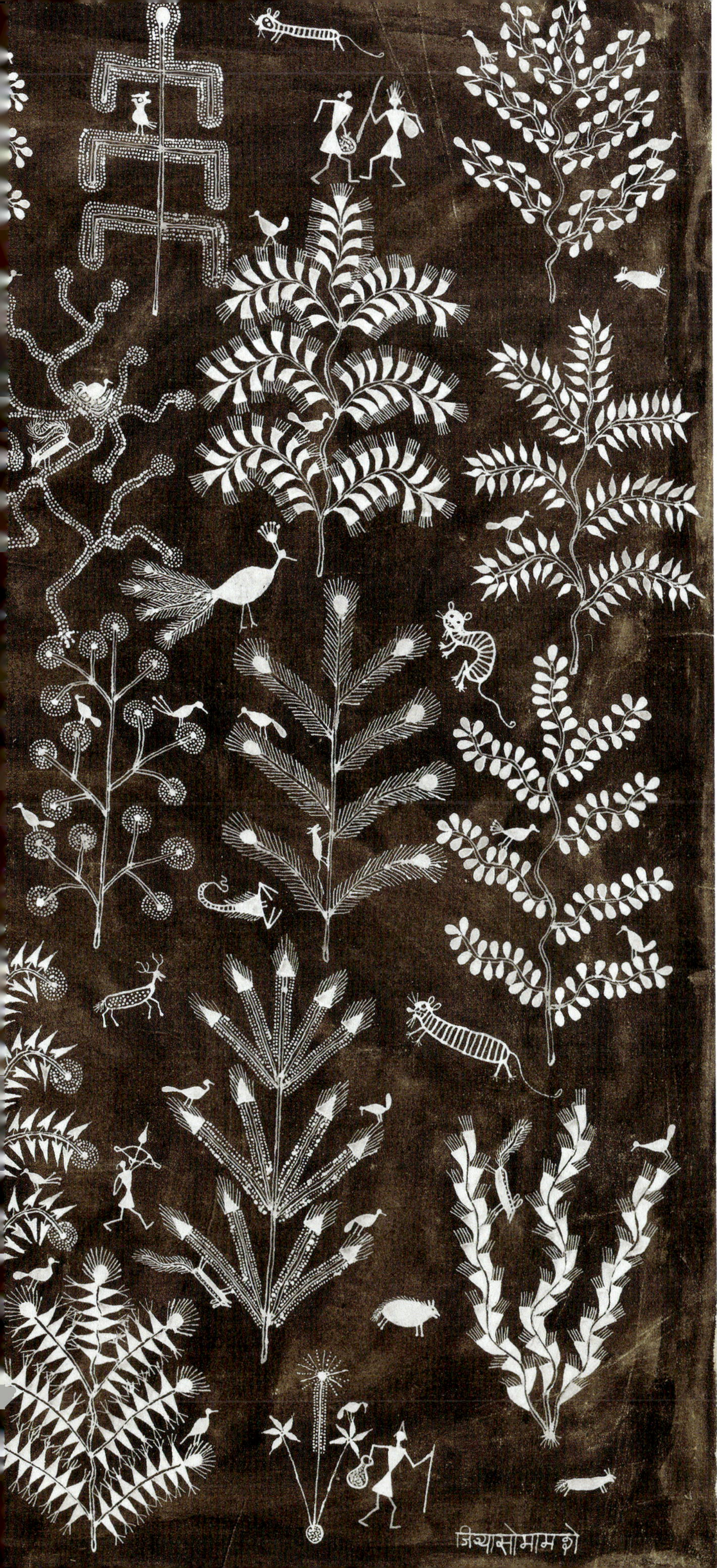

The Warlis think that trees are inhabited by spirits. Each tree is treated with the greatest care to give it its own visual identity.

Les Warlis pensent que les esprits habitent les arbres. Aussi, chaque arbre est traité avec la plus grande attention, conférant à chacun d'entre eux une identité visuelle propre.

Jivya Soma Mashe, *Untitled*, 1998, acrylic and cow dung on canvas, 115 × 146 cm; 45.27 × 57.48 in. Collection Hervé Chandès. Photo by André Morin.

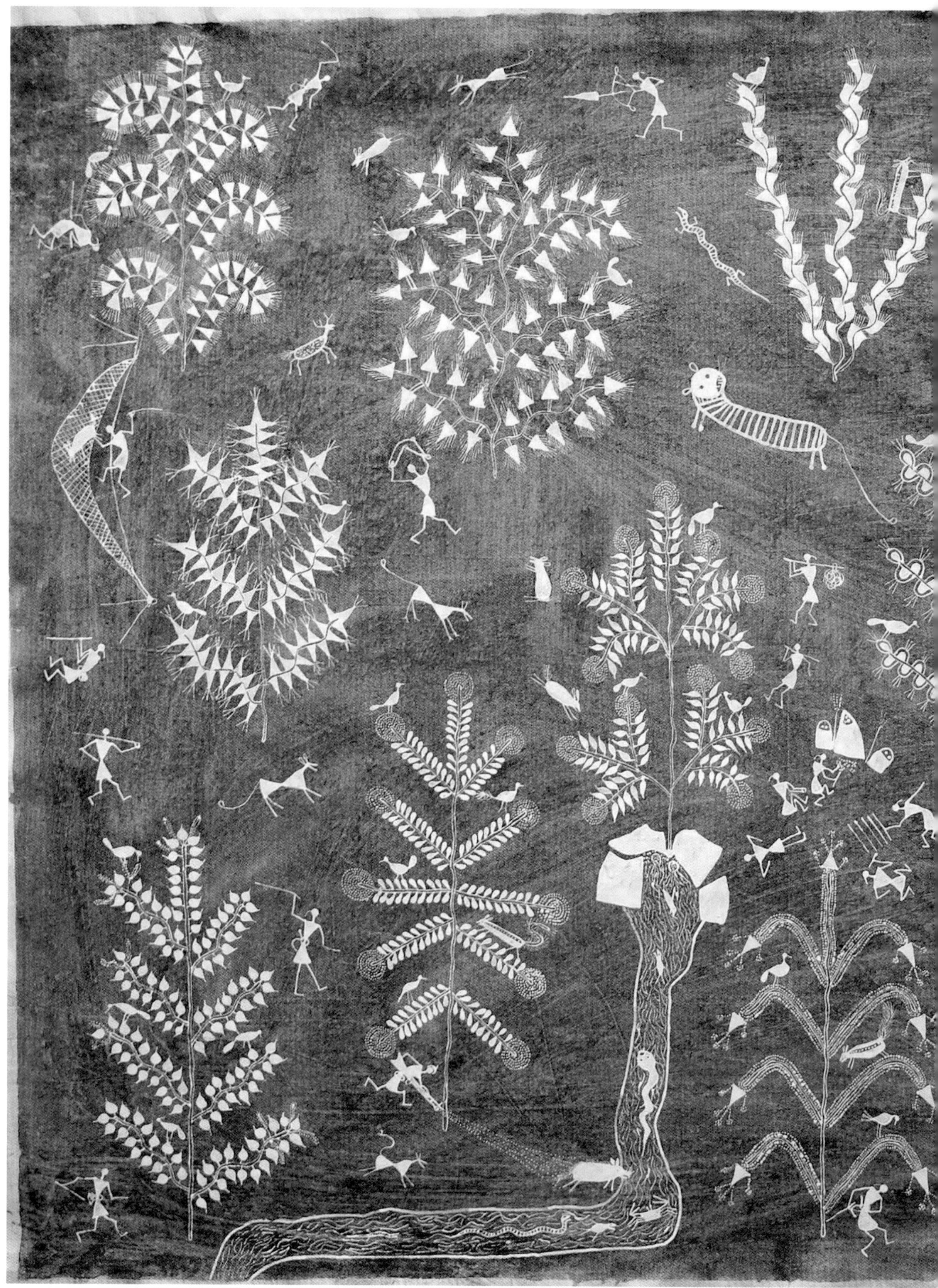

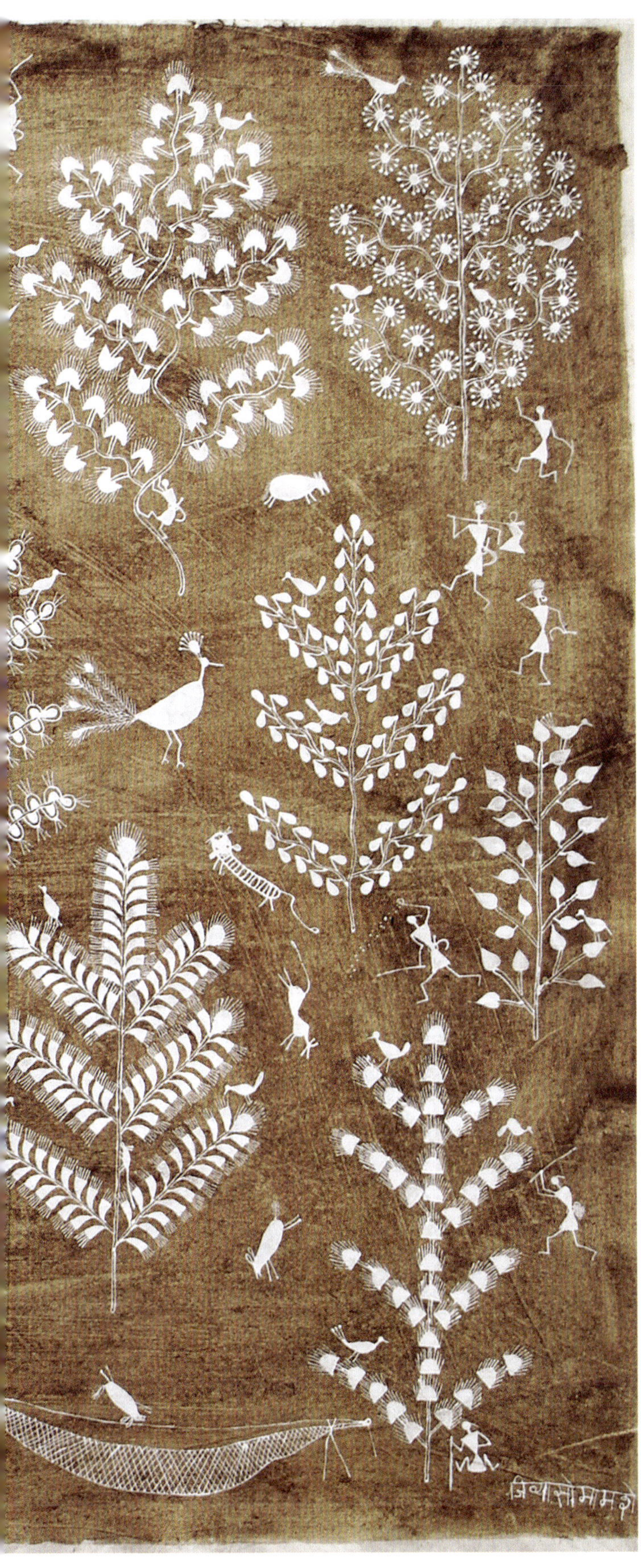

Jivya Soma Mashe, *Untitled*, 1997,
acrylic and cow dung on canvas,
100 × 125 cm; 39.37 × 39.37 in.
Collection Florence and Daniel Guerlain.
Photo by Christian Baraja.

Pages 160–161
Jivya Soma Mashe, *Untitled*, 1997,
acrylic and cow dung on canvas,
100 × 125 cm; 39.37 × 39.37 in.
Collection Lucile Allanche.
Photo by Christian Baraja.

Pages 162–163
Jivya Soma Mashe, Ganjad (Maharashtra, India), 2012.
Photo by T. Venkanna.

Pages 164–165
Jivya Soma Mashe, Hervé Perdriolle, and Abhay Maskara,
Ganjad (Maharashtra, India), 2012.
Photo by T. Venkanna.

Pages 166–167
Sadashiv and Jivya Soma Mashe showing a painting
by Jivya Soma Mashe acquired by Richard Long,
Ganjad (Maharashtra, India), 2003.
Photo by Hervé Perdriolle.

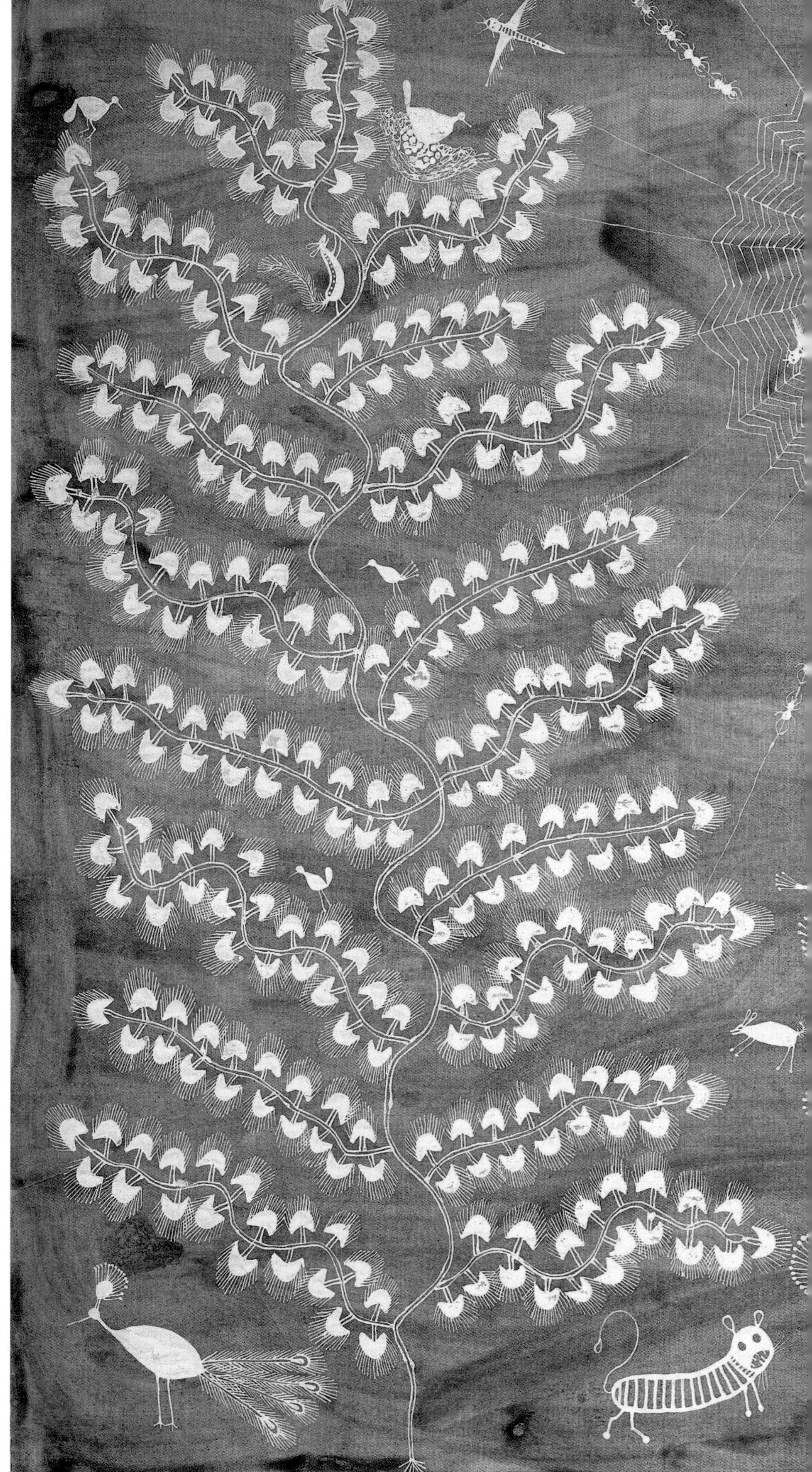

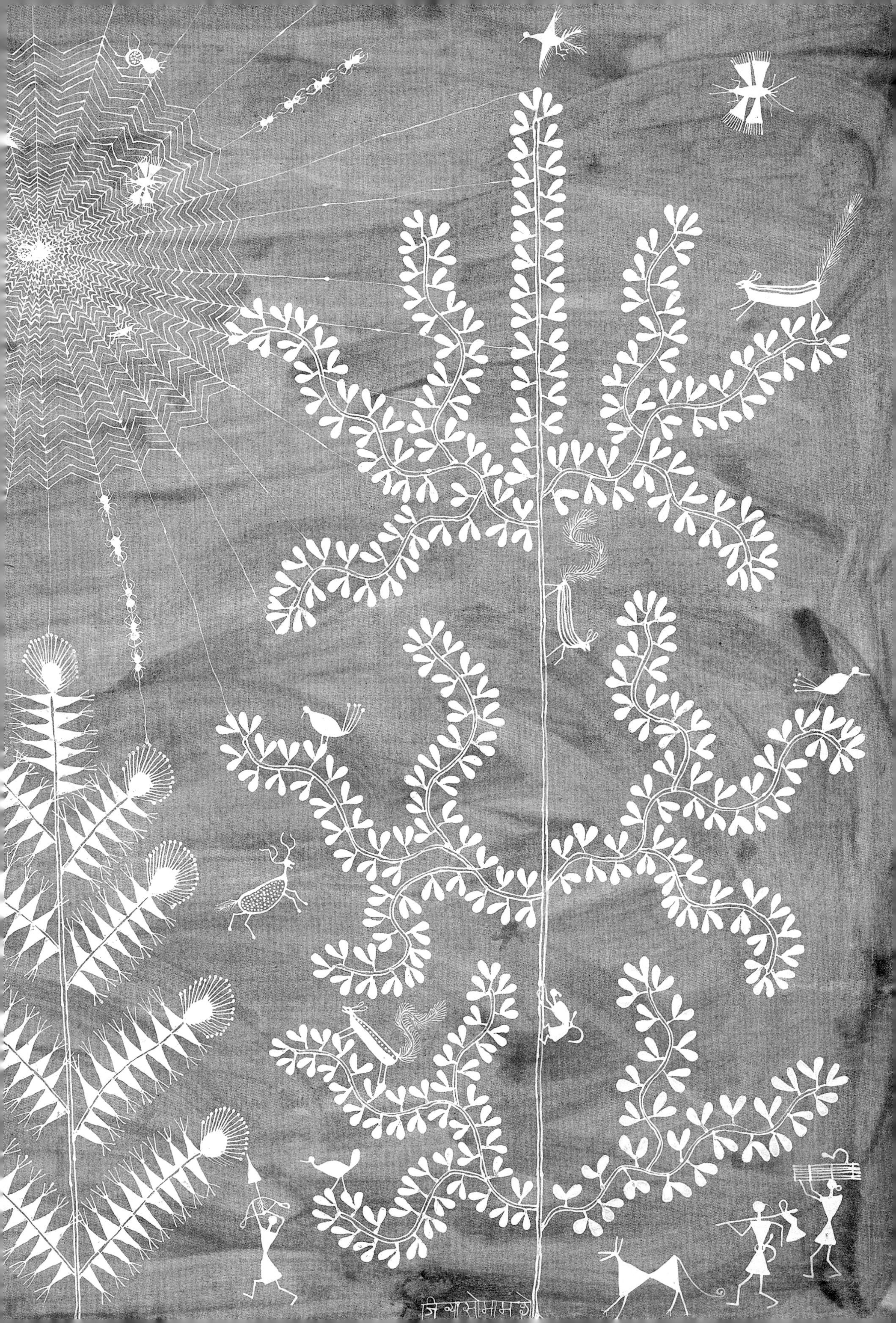
जिव्यासोमामशे

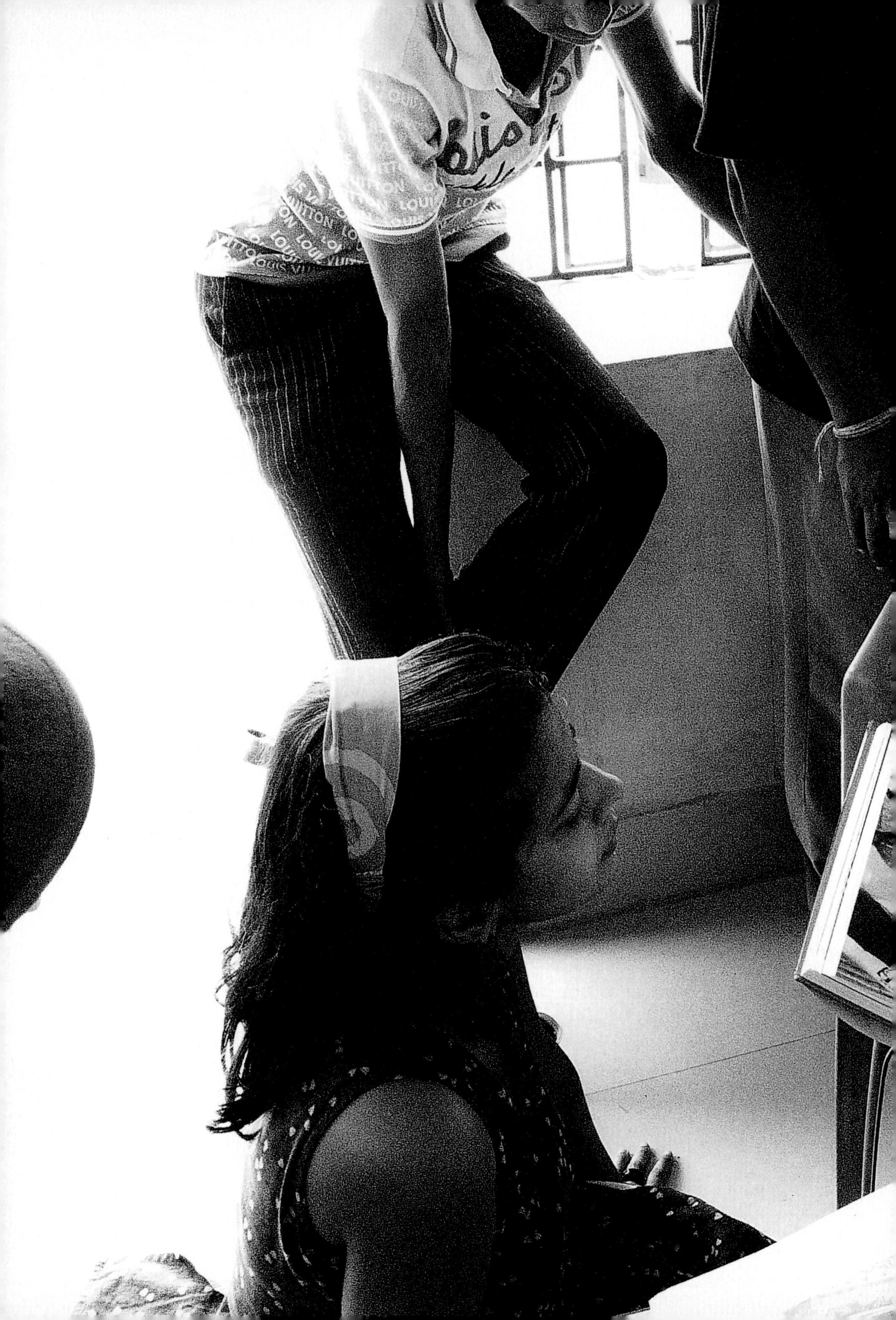

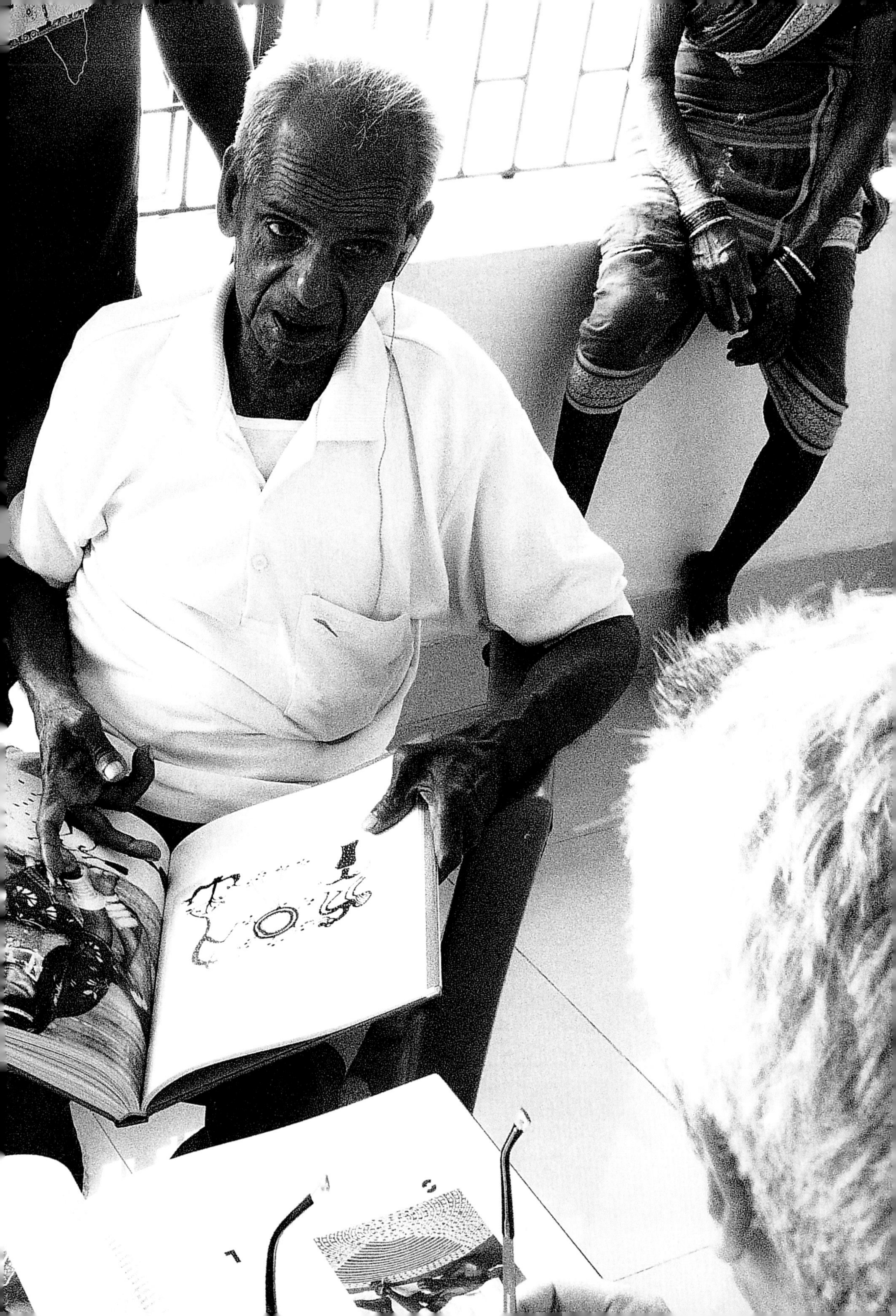

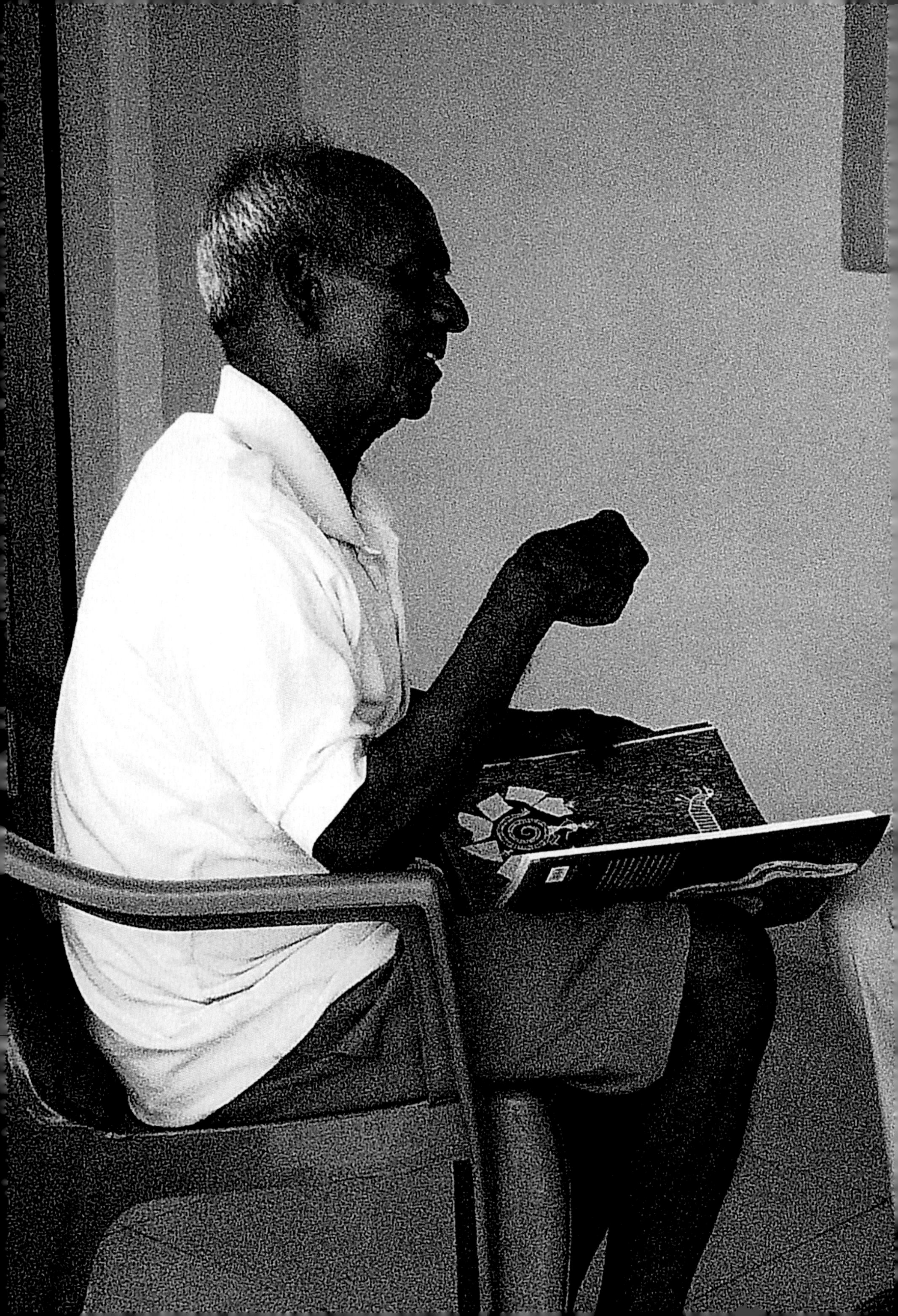

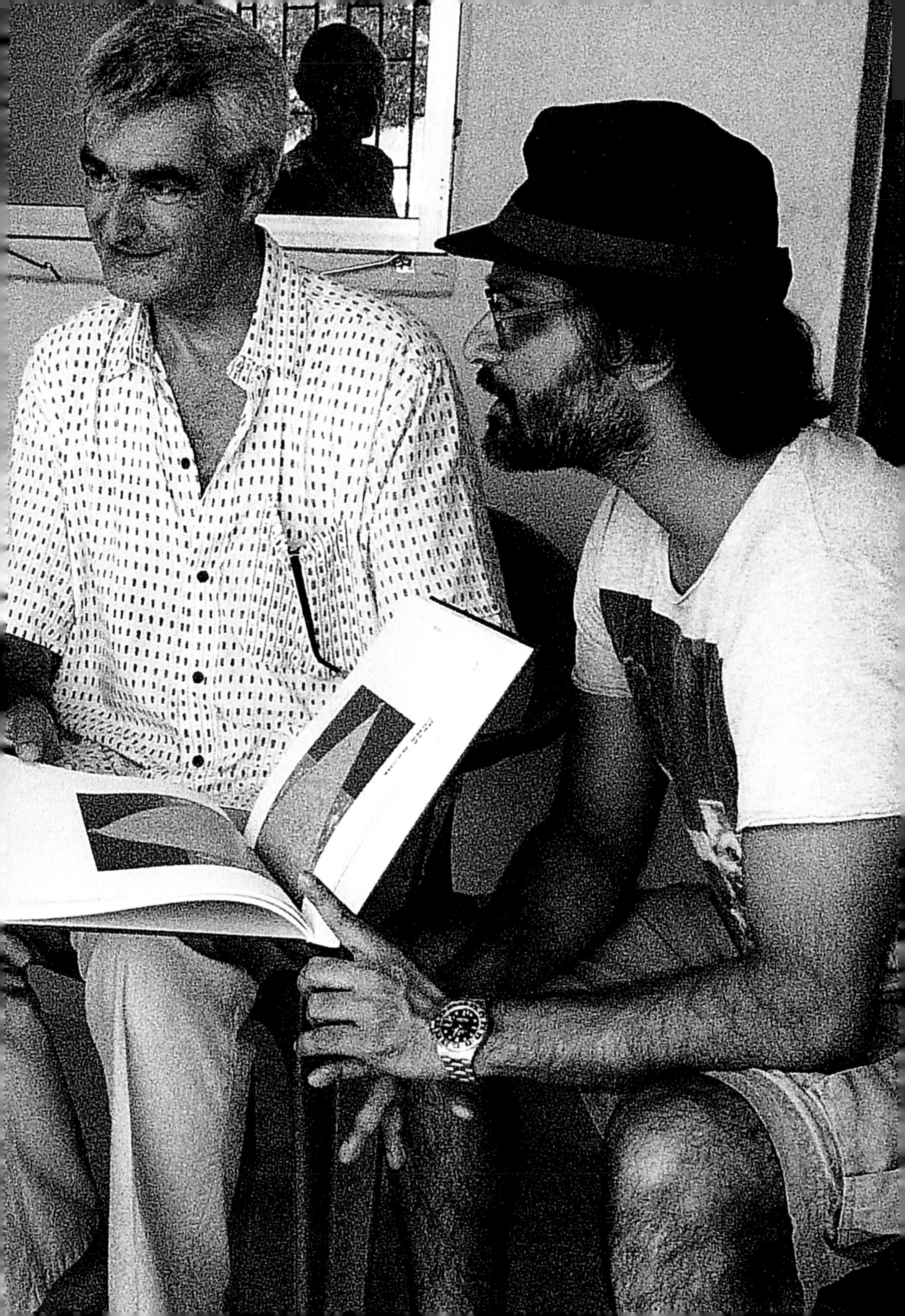

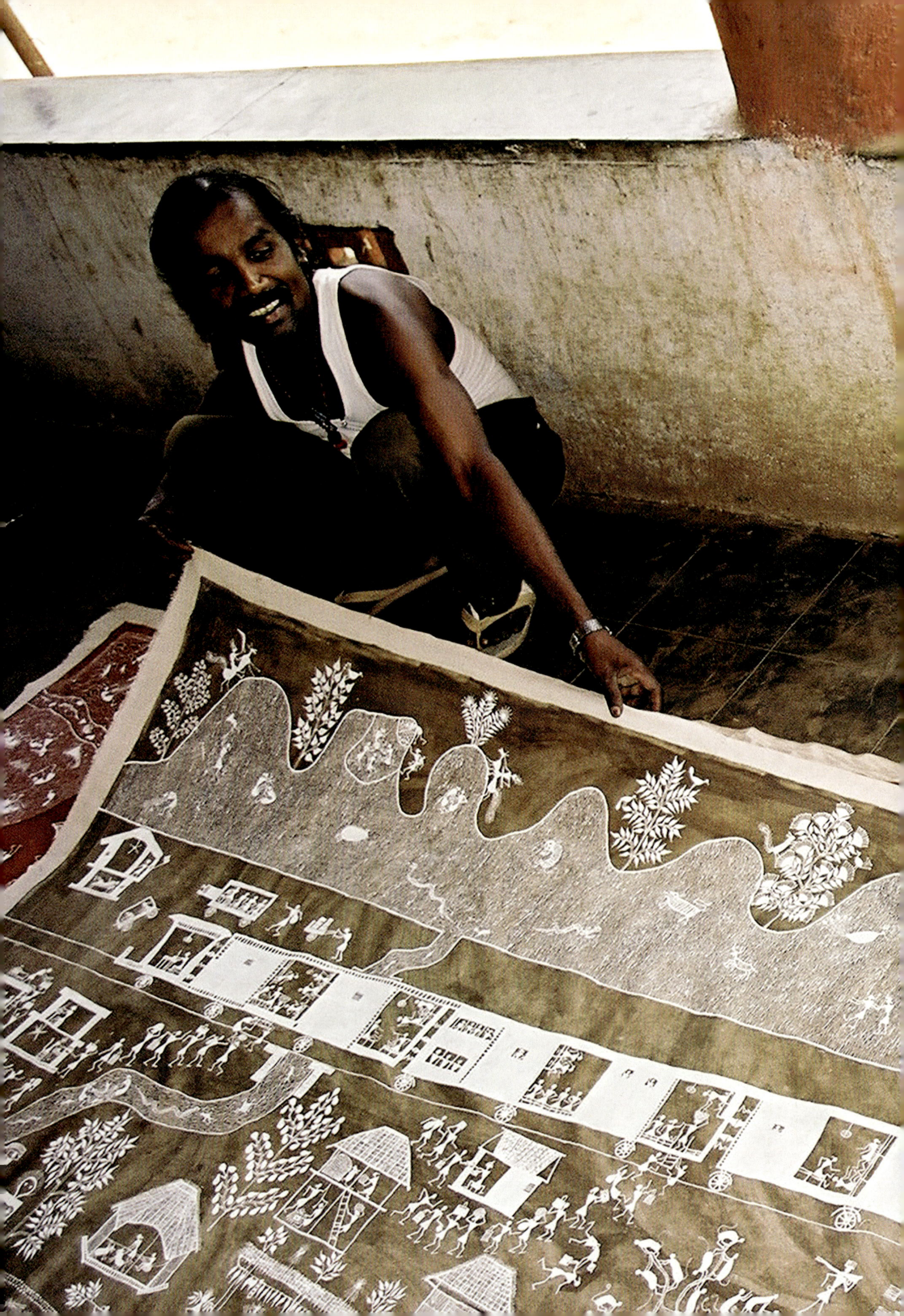

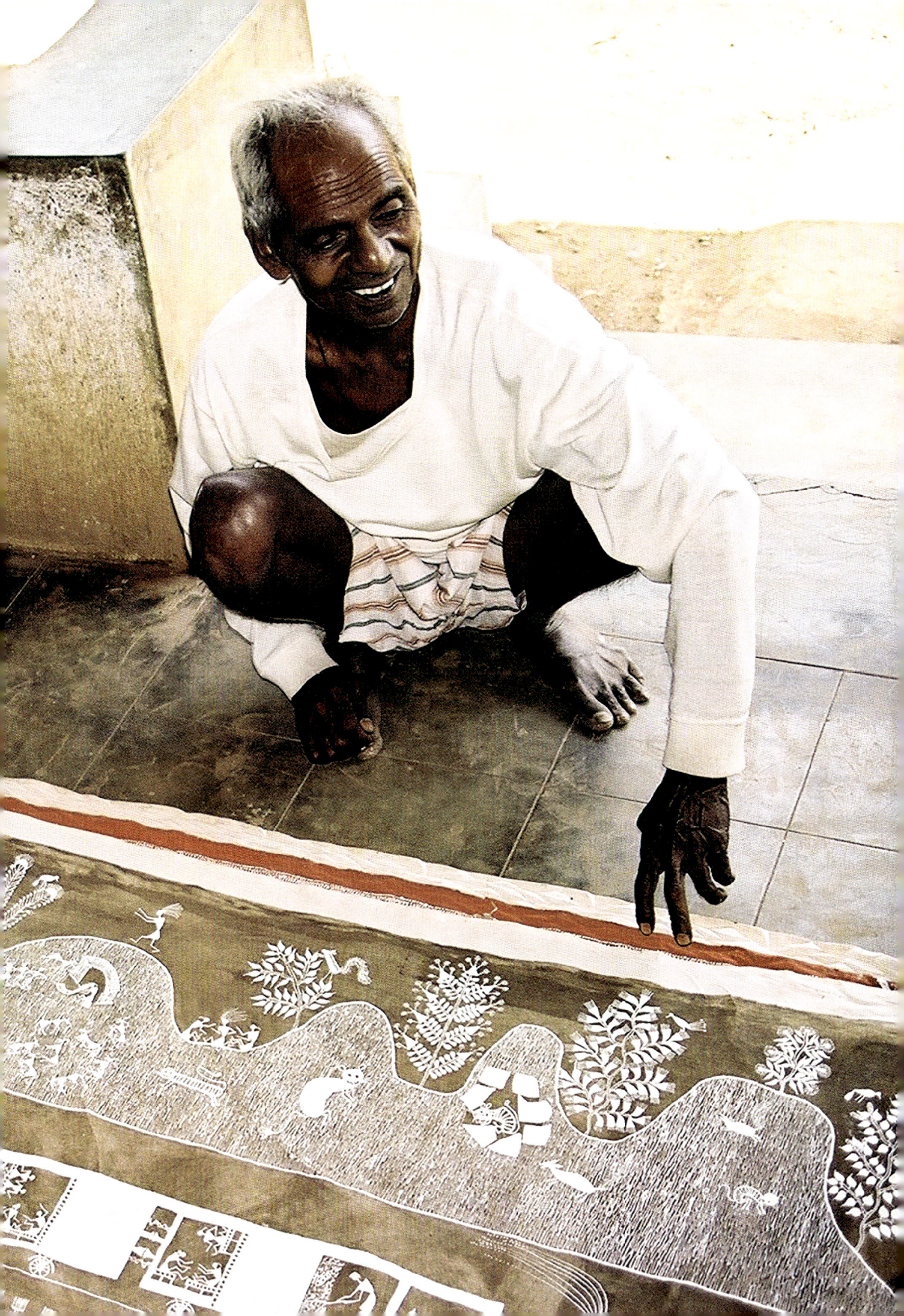

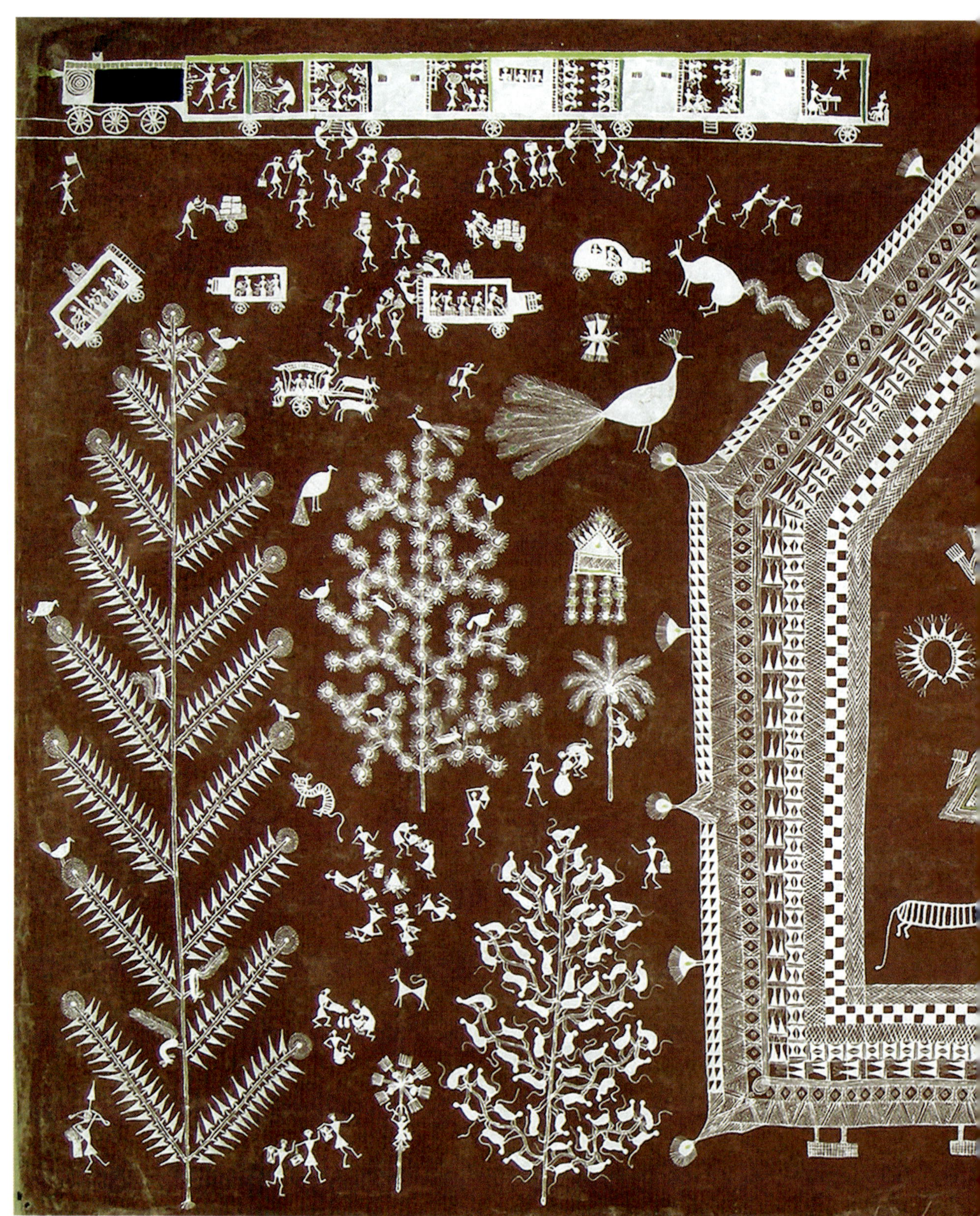

Jivya Soma Mashe, *Untitled*, 1996,
acrylic on canvas,
160 × 320 cm; 62.99 × 125.98 in.
Collection Daniel Simonin.

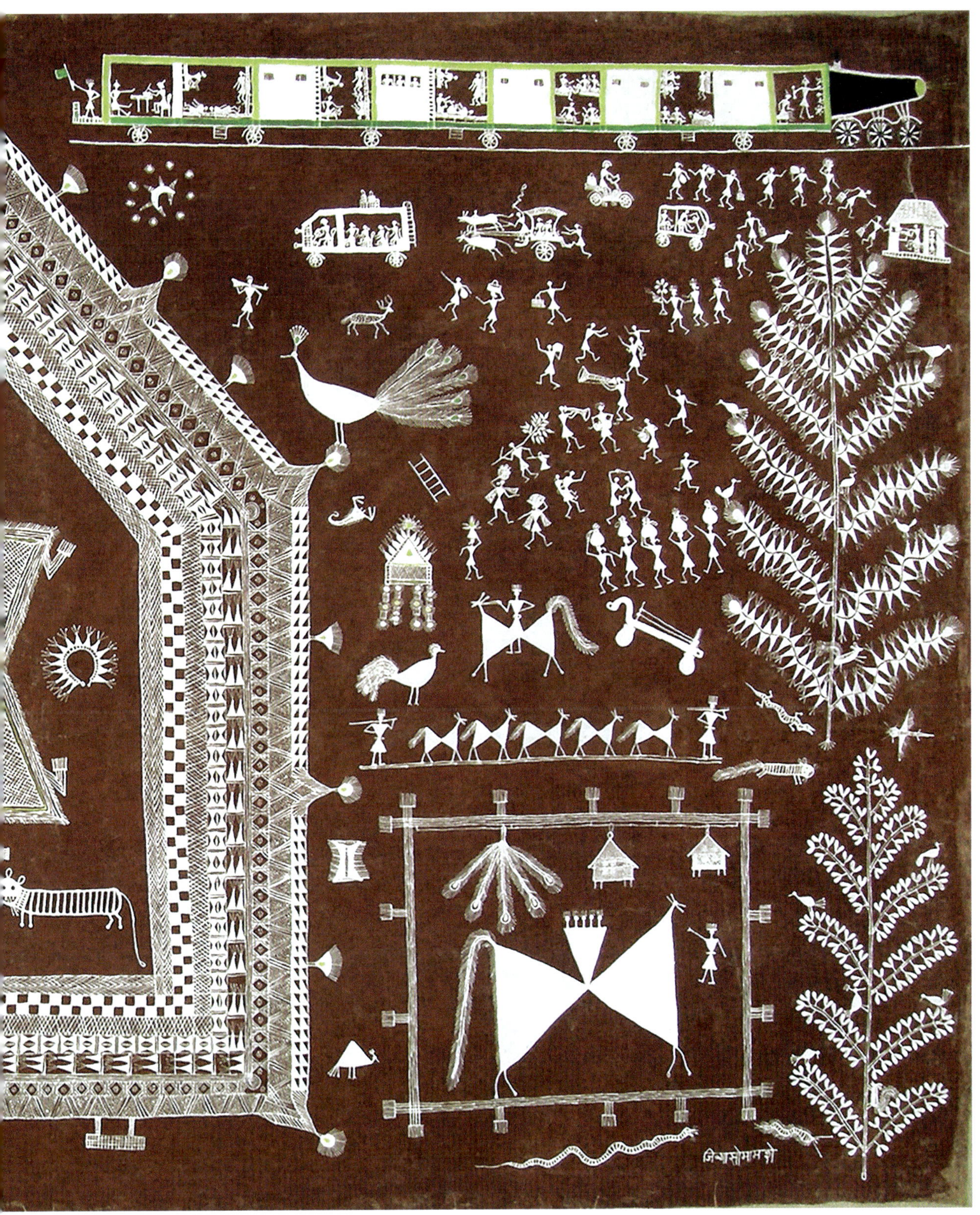
जिव्यासोमामशे

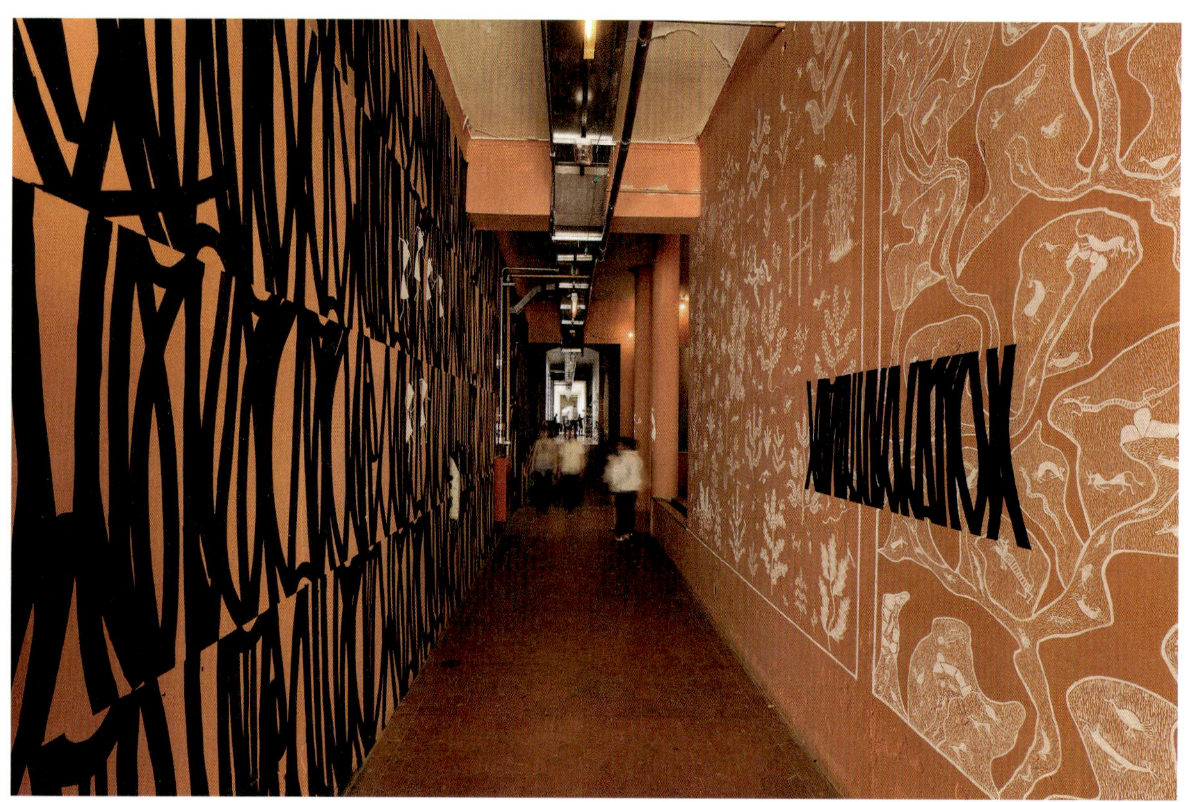

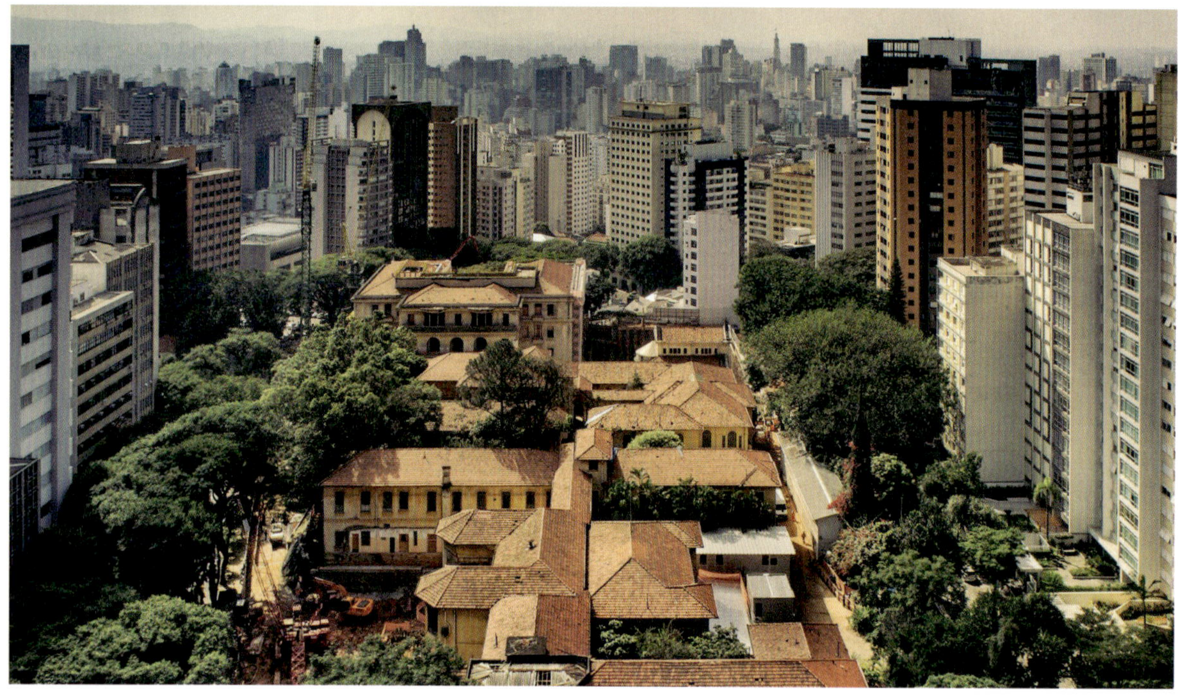

Mural paintings by Caligrapixo and the Warli tribe
for the show *Made by… Feito por Brasileiros*, São Paulo, 2014.
Photo by Ding Musa.

Two of Jivya Soma Mashe's sons, Balu and Sadashiv, are also painters and farmers, as are three of his grandsons, Kishore, Pravin, and Vijay, some of whom have often accompanied Jivya on his many trips around India and abroad. In 2013, when Jivya had grown more elderly and wished to travel less or not at all, I had the pleasure of inviting Sadashiv and Kishore to create frescoes on the walls of each floor of the new Maison de l'Inde building, designed by the Lipsky+Rollet architecture firm, in the Cité Universitaire in Paris. One of my most wonderful and stimulating trips was the one to Brazil in 2014 with Balu, Sadashiv, and Kishore Mashe, as well as Shantaram Gorkana, a neighbour, friend, and excellent painter.

We had been invited by François Allard and Marc Pottier to paint immense mural frescoes as part of a creative invasion to which a hundred international artists were contributing. This extraordinary project was held in the sensational setting of a disused hospital, the Cidade Matarazzo, in the heart of São Paulo. This magical place had been abandoned for decades, and was made even more impressive by the fact that nature had re-established itself in all of the buildings, which covered several thousand square metres.

To give meaning to this intervention by artists from tribal communities from India to Brazil, we conceived a dialogue with one of the city's graffiti artists, Caligrapixo. São Paulo's taggers had created their own calligraphic style based on curves and sharp angles that had an unusual affinity with the art of the Warlis, who, as their dialect was not written, had invented a pictography based on the triangle, circle, and square.

Deux des fils de Jivya, Balu et Sadashiv, sont également peintres et paysans, comme plusieurs de ses petits-fils, Kishore, Pravin et Vijay. Les uns où les autres ont souvent accompagné Jivya dans ses nombreux voyages en Inde et à l'étranger. Lorsque Jivya est devenu plus âgé et qu'il souhaitait moins ou ne plus voyager, j'ai eu le plaisir de pouvoir inviter en 2013 Sadashiv et Kishore à réaliser des fresques murales à chaque étage du nouveau bâtiment de la Maison de l'Inde conçu par le studio d'architecture Lipsky+Rollet à la Cité Universitaire de Paris. L'un des plus beaux et excitants voyages fut celui que je fis au Brésil en 2014 en compagnie de Balu, Sadashiv et Kishore Mashe, auxquels s'était joint Shantaram Gorkana, un de leurs voisins, ami et excellent peintre.

Nous y étions invités par François Allard et Marc Pottier pour réaliser d'immenses fresques murales dans le cadre d'une invasion créative réunissant une centaine d'artistes internationaux. Ce projet inouï allait prendre place en plein cœur de São Paulo, dans le cadre époustouflant d'un ancien hôpital désaffecté, la Cidade Matarazzo. Un lieu magique, abandonné depuis des décennies, où la vétusté des lieux était magnifiée par la nature reprenant ses droits en chaque recoin de ses bâtiments s'étalant sur plusieurs milliers de mètres carrés.

Pour donner du sens à cette intervention d'artistes issus de communautés tribales de l'Inde au Brésil, nous imaginions un dialogue avec un graffeur de São Paulo, Caligrapixo. Les graffeurs de São Paulo ont inventé leur propre style sous la forme d'une calligraphie spécifique avec des courbes et des angles vifs. Elle trouve ici un écho singulier avec l'art des Warlis qui, parlant un dialecte sans écriture, ont inventé une pictographie commune à toute la tribu basée sur le triangle, le cercle et le carré.

Pages 172–173
Mural paintings by Balu, Sadashiv, and Kishor Mashe accompanied by Shantaram Gorkana for the show *Made by... Feito por Brasileiros*, Cidade Matarazzo, São Paulo, 2014. Photo by Ding Musa.

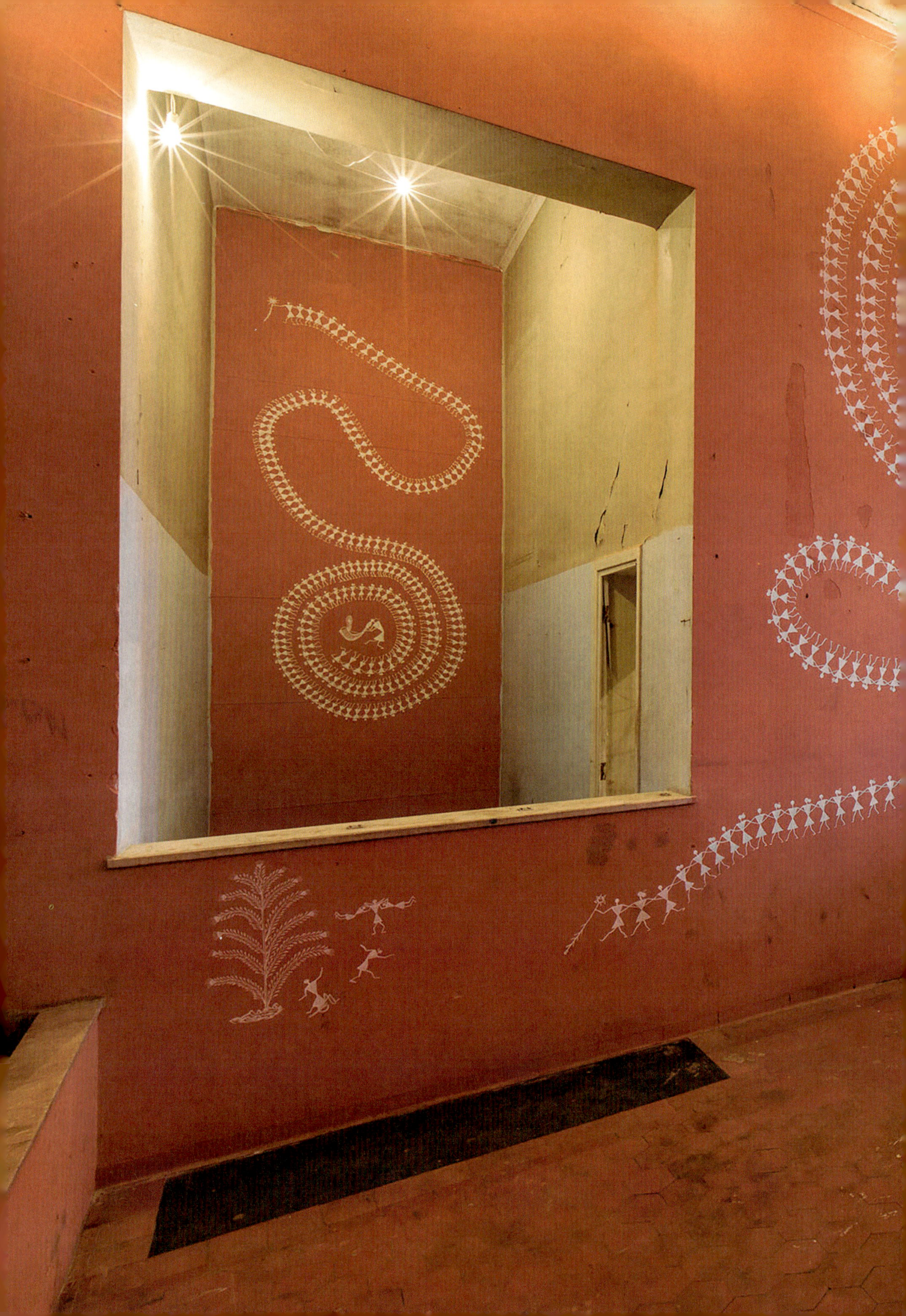

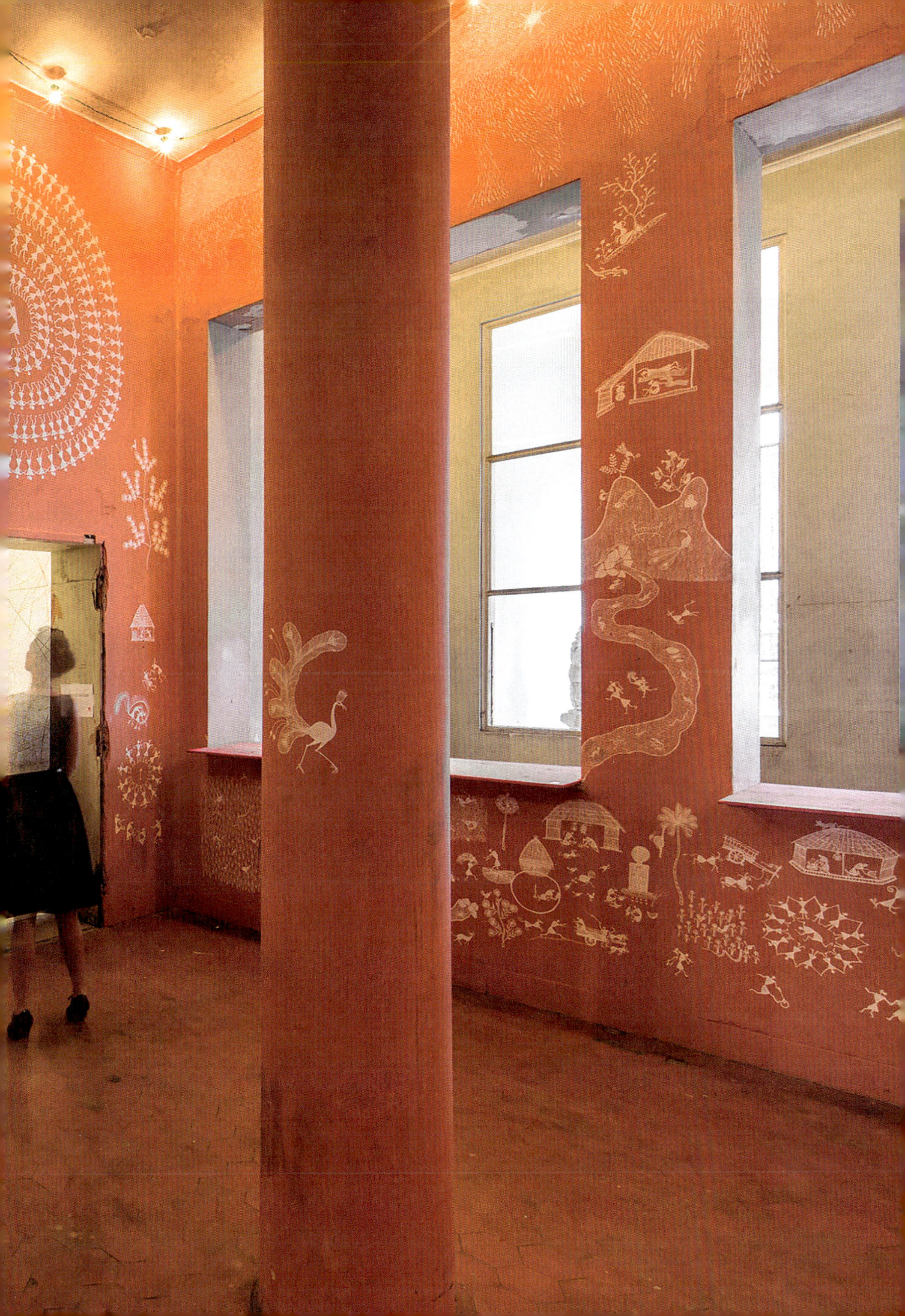

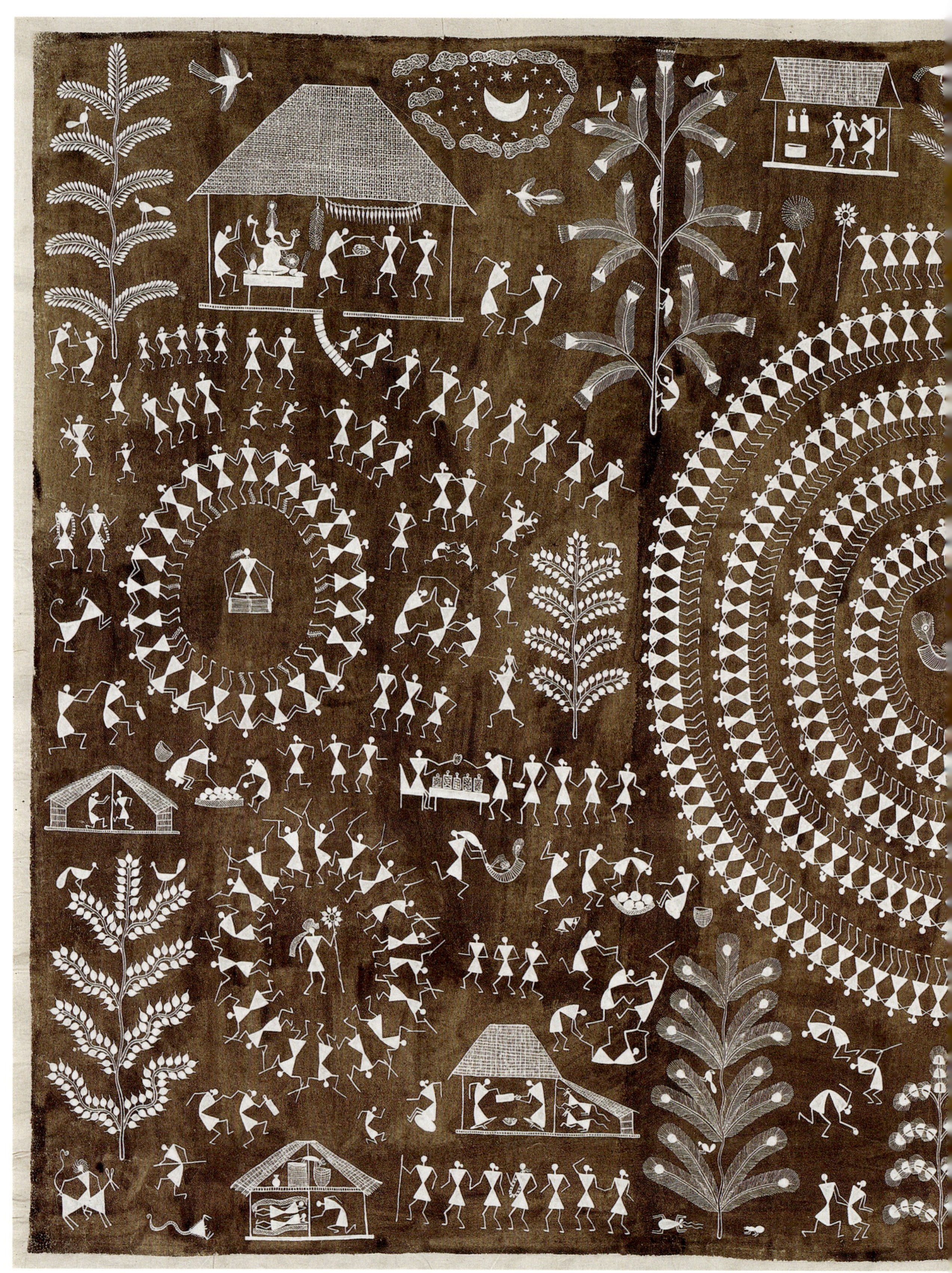

Jivya Soma Mashe, *Ganesh Festival*, 1999, acrylic and cow dung on canvas, 138 × 230 cm; 54.33 × 90.55 in.

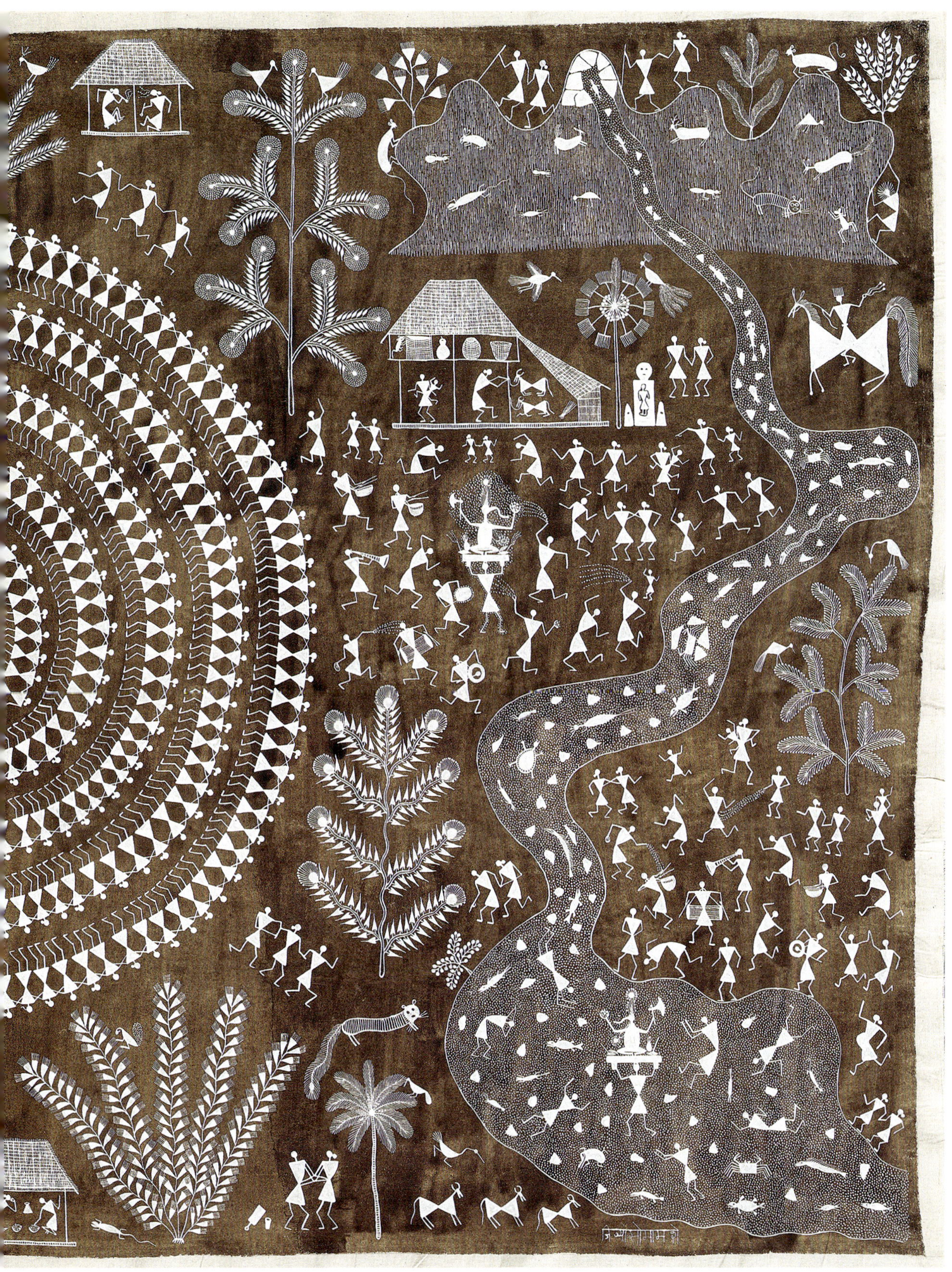

Collection of Hervé Perdriolle. Photo by Christian Baraja.

FISHING NET
FILET DE PÊCHE

The fishing net is Jivya Soma Mashe's favourite motif. In forty years of painting, Jivya must have created around thirty, all in different formats. The artist reinterprets this theme, which evokes the miraculous catch. Also apparent is an evocation of the roof of the world specifically related to the Warli tribe, with the depiction of their pointed sacred mountain. The meticulous repetition of the meshes of these nets in thousands of small overlapping circles, like the links of a chain, creates a lace-like effect. There is no sense of monotony in this repetition. The circles are neither inflexible nor rendered precise by a craftsman's technique. Every circle feels as though it is generated by the artist's experience. They resonate with the rhythm of inspiration. This way of endlessly modulating a single pure form is like the recitation of a mantra, an exercise in meditation.

A spirit resides in each of these fishing nets, and is represented by the same system as all other Warli human figures, based on the principle of two mirrored triangles. The only difference from a human figure is the spirit's long hair. The spirit ensures that Warli fishermen return small fish to the water. Humans' dependence on nature, what we now call ecology, is a feeling that moves the Warli soul.

Le filet de pêche est le thème de prédilection de Jivya Soma Mashe. En quarante ans de peinture, Jivya a dû en réaliser une trentaine, tous de formats différents. L'artiste réinterprète ce sujet qui évoque celui de la pêche miraculeuse. On peut y voir également une évocation du toit du monde, en l'occurrence pour la tribu warli l'évocation de la montagne sacrée au sommet acéré. La répétition à l'infini des mailles de ces filets comme des milliers de petits cercles, se superposant tels les maillons d'une chaîne, donne un effet visuel proche de celui de la dentelle. On ne perçoit aucune lassitude dans cette répétition. Les cercles ne sont pas figés. Ils n'ont pas la rigueur de l'application du travail de l'artisan. Chacun de ces cercles semble vécu. Ils vivent au rythme de l'inspiration. Cette façon de moduler à l'infini une même forme épurée pourrait évoquer le principe du mantra, un exercice de méditation.

Dans chacun de ces filets de pêche se trouve un esprit. Celui-ci a le même système de représentation que toutes les autres figures humaines, basé sur le principe de deux triangles inversés. La seule différence qui permet de l'identifier est le fait qu'il possède une longue chevelure. Cet esprit veille à ce que les pêcheurs rejettent à l'eau les petits poissons. La dépendance de l'homme à la nature, que l'on nomme écologie aujourd'hui, est un sentiment qui anime l'âme warli.

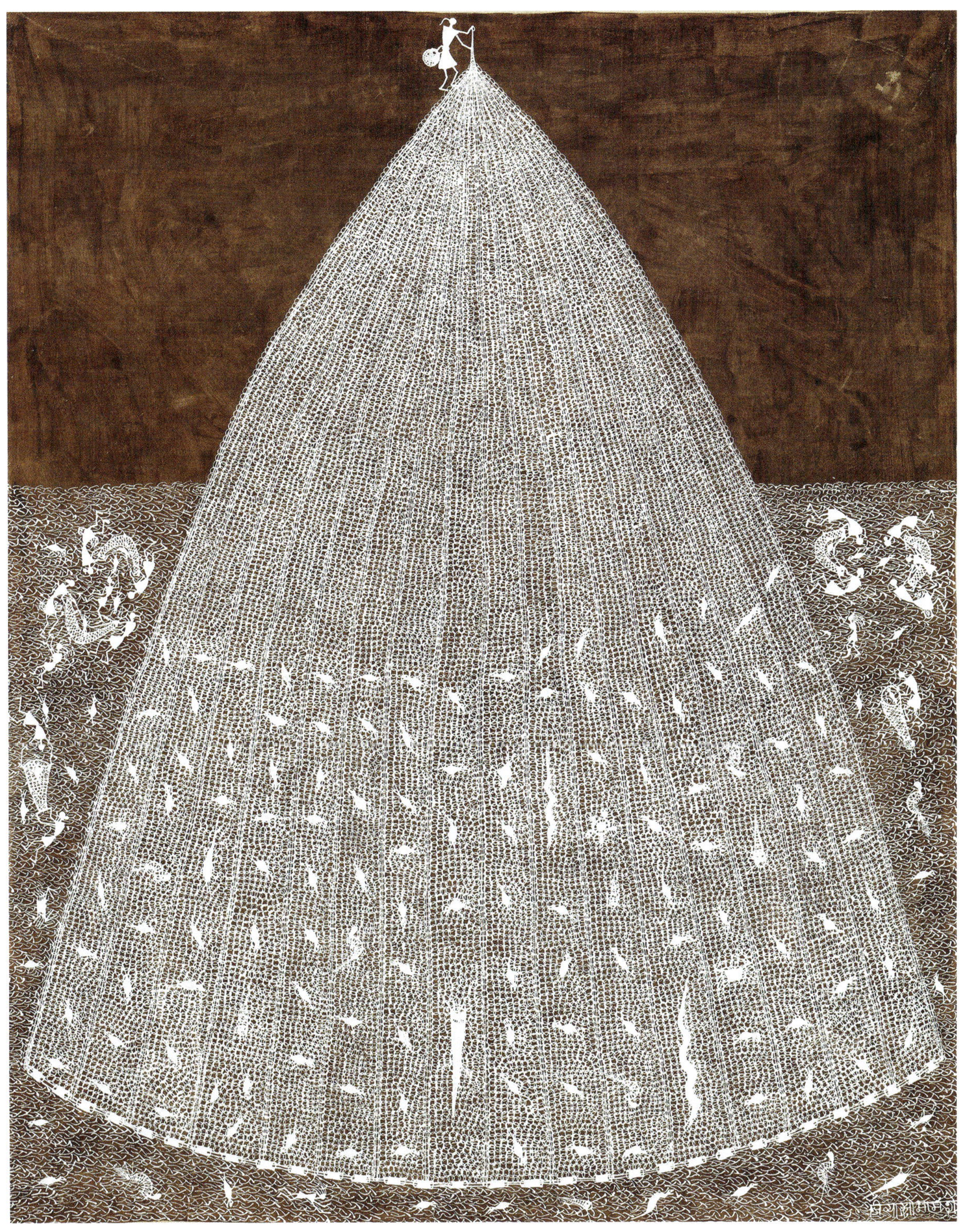

Jivya Soma Mashe, *Fishnet*, 2011,
acrylic and cow dung on canvas,
170 × 140 cm; 66.92 × 55.11 in.
Collection Hervé Chandès.
Photo by André Morin.

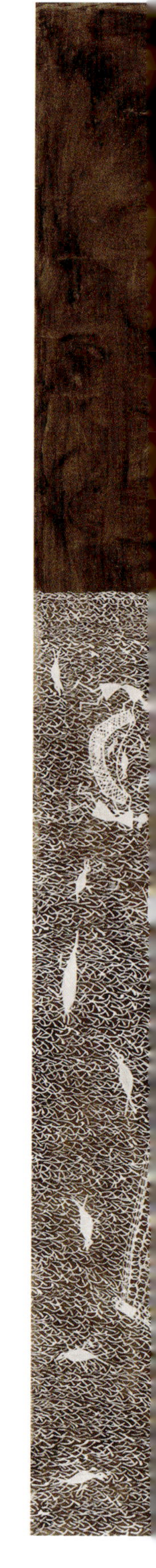

Jivya Soma Mashe, *Fishnet*, 2016,
acrylic and cow dung on canvas,
157 × 144 cm; 61.81 × 56.69 in.
Collection Bérengère Primat.
Photo by Christian Baraja.

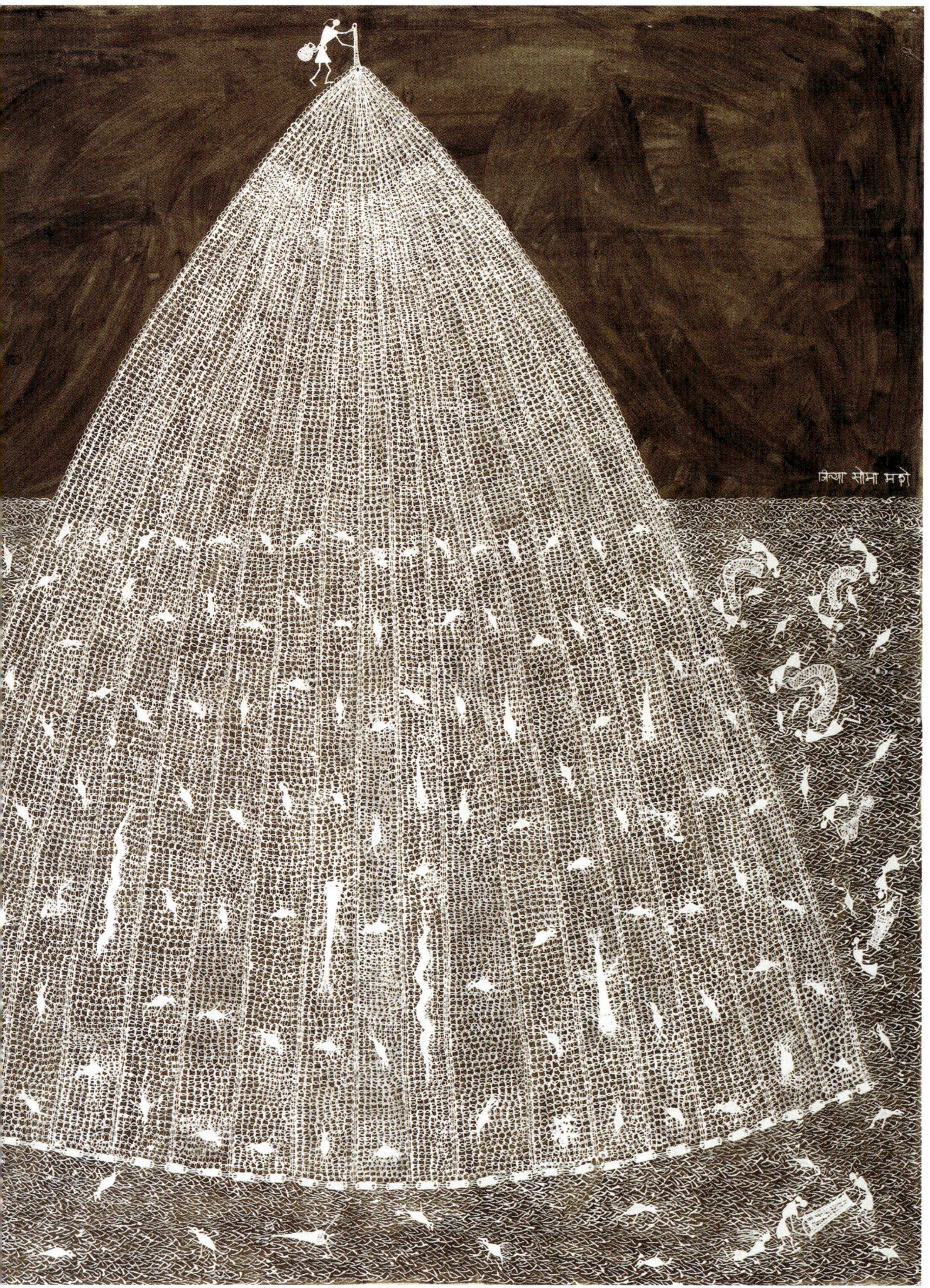
जिव्या सोमा मशे

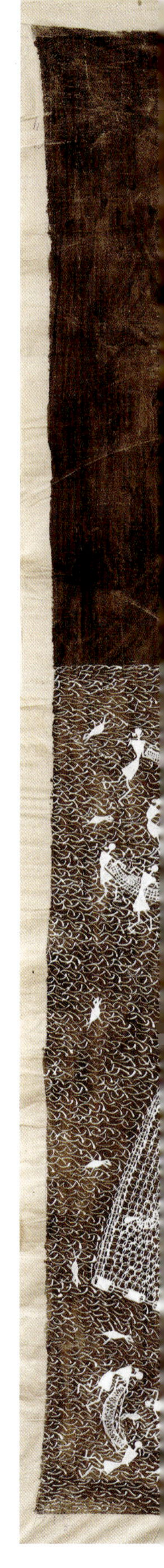

Jivya Soma Mashe, *Fishnet*, 2009,
acrylic and cow dung on canvas,
167 × 148 cm; 65.74 × 58.26 in. (*details on pages* 190–193)
Fondation Cartier pour l'art contemporain Collection.
Photo by André Morin.

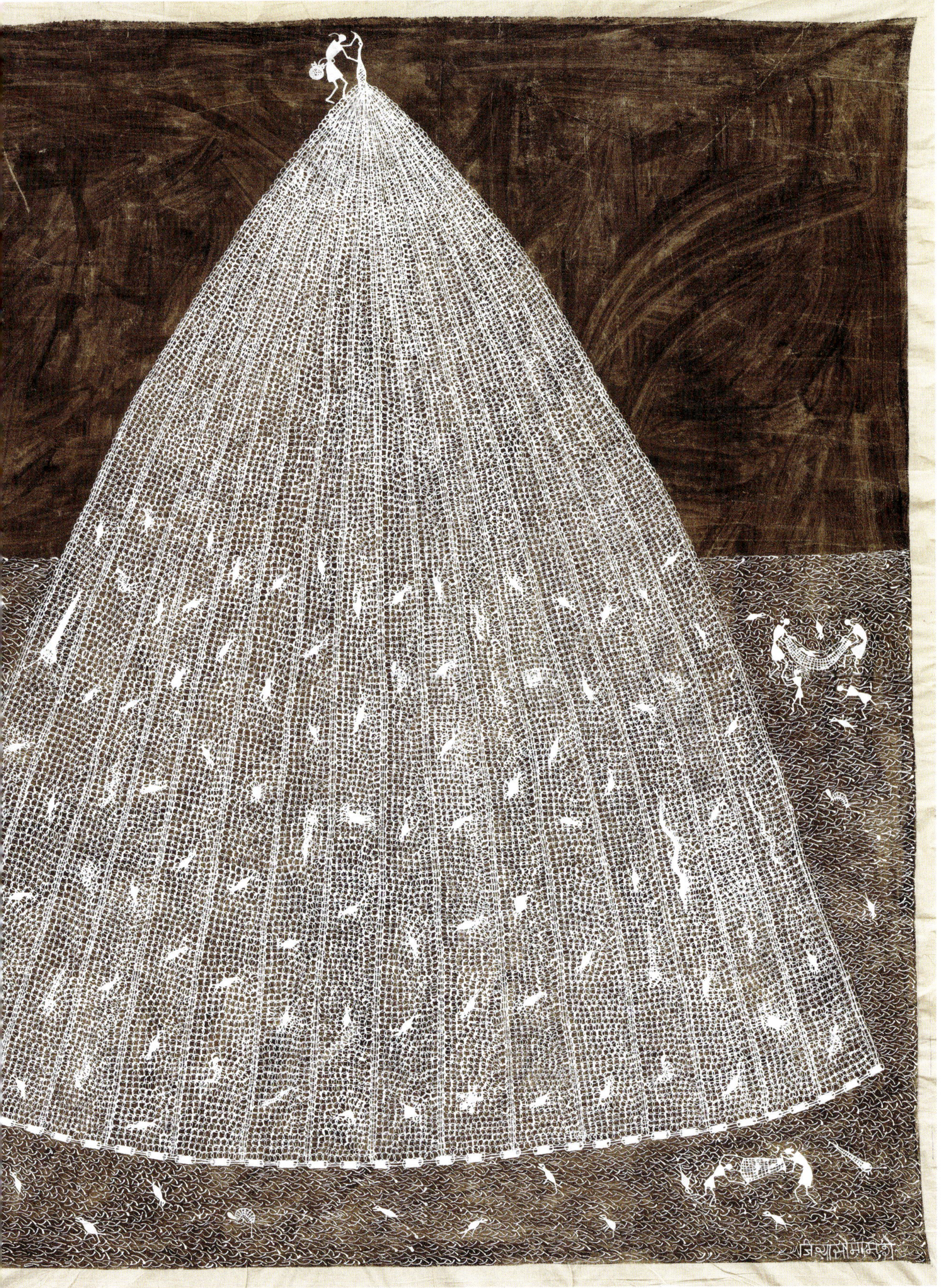

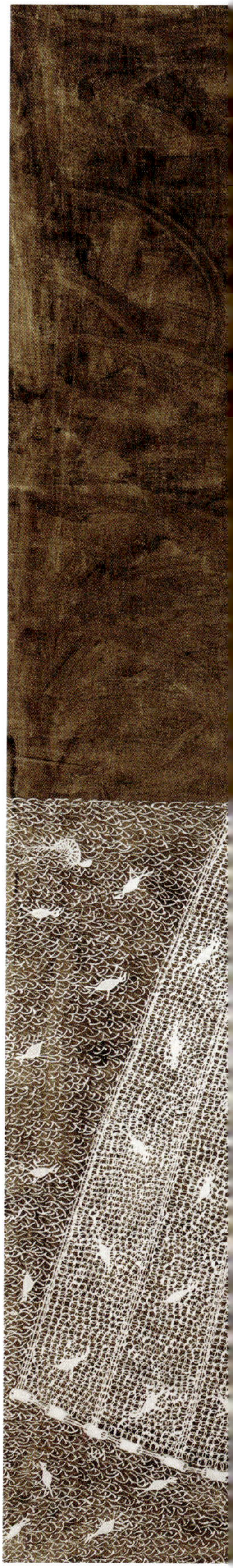

Jivya Soma Mashe, *Fishnet*, 2013,
acrylic and cow dung on canvas,
158 x 165 cm; 62.20 x 64.96 in.
Courtesy Jeanne Bucher Jaeger.
© Rodrigo Bettencourt da Câmara.

Pages 184–189
Jivya Soma Mashe making a *Fishnet* in his workshop,
Ganjad (Maharashtra, India), 2012.
Photos by Hervé Perdriolle.

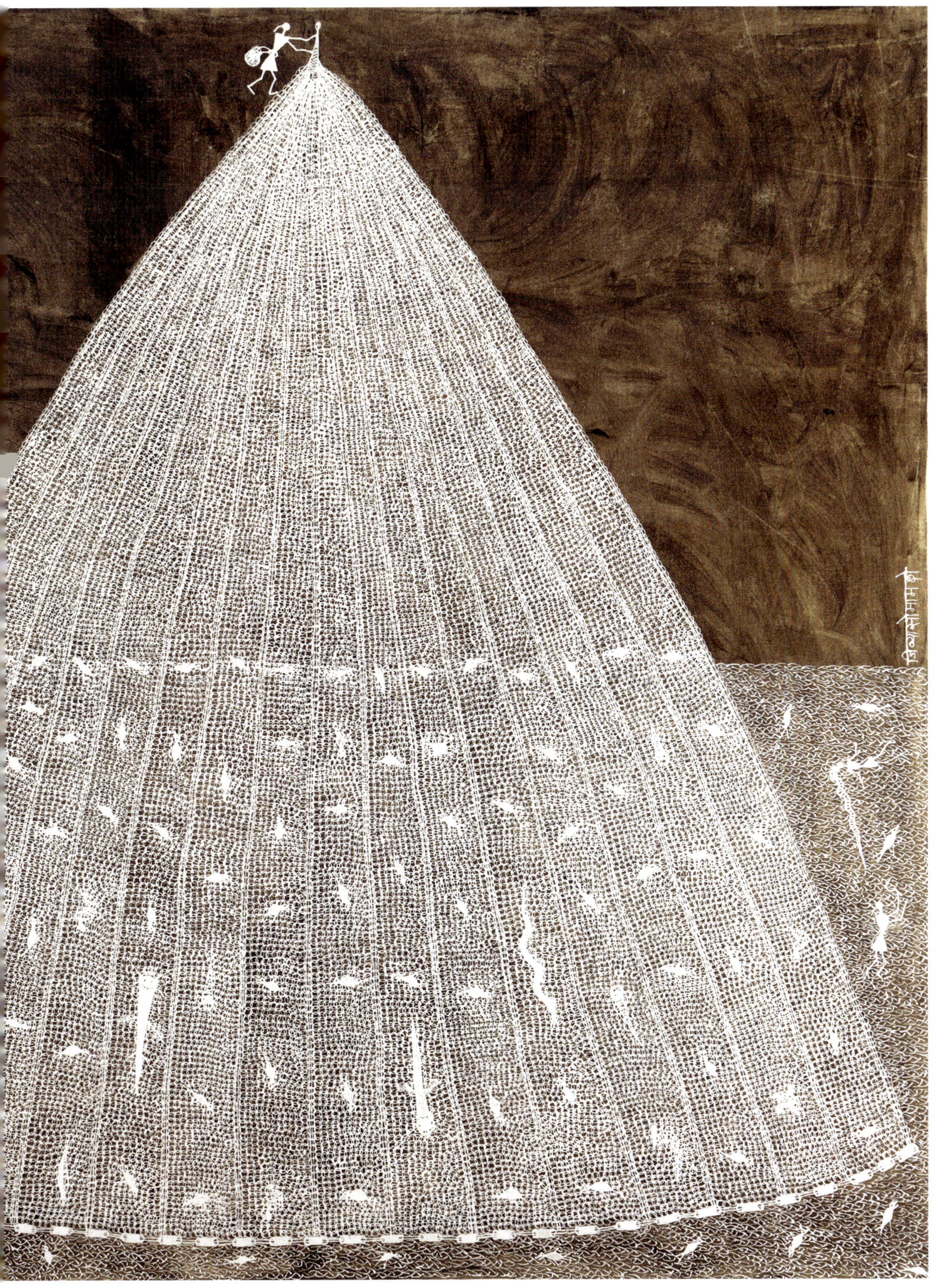

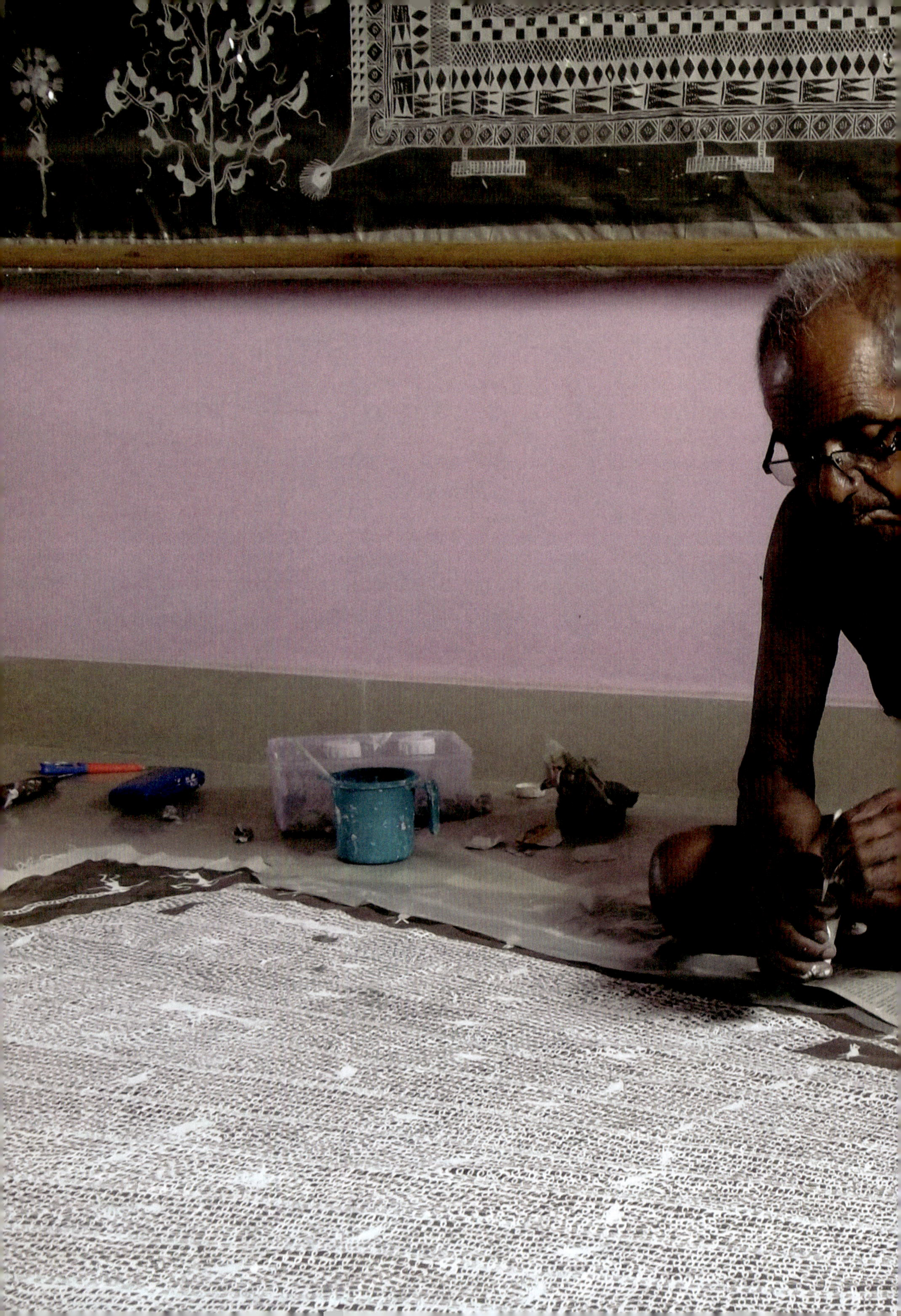

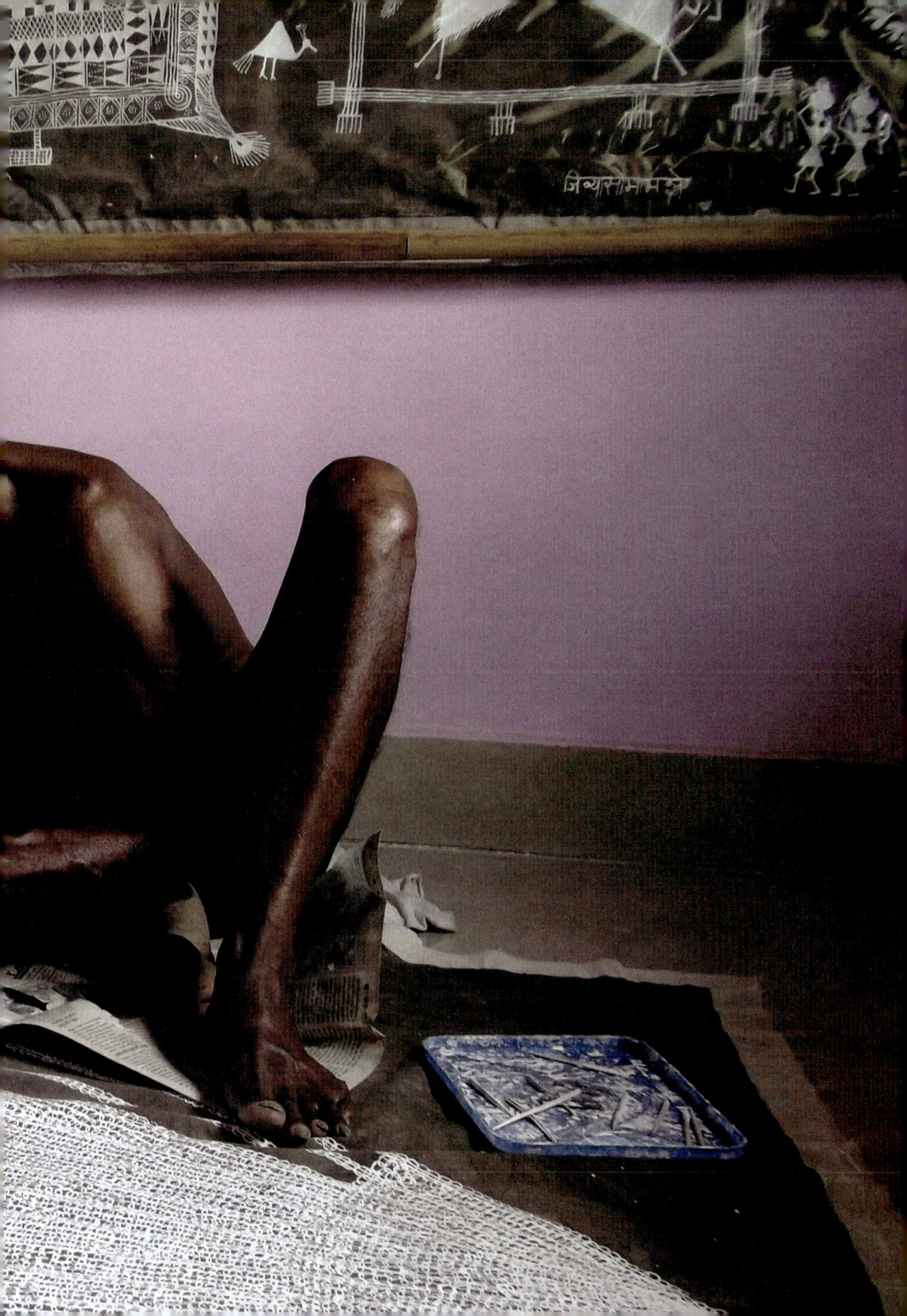

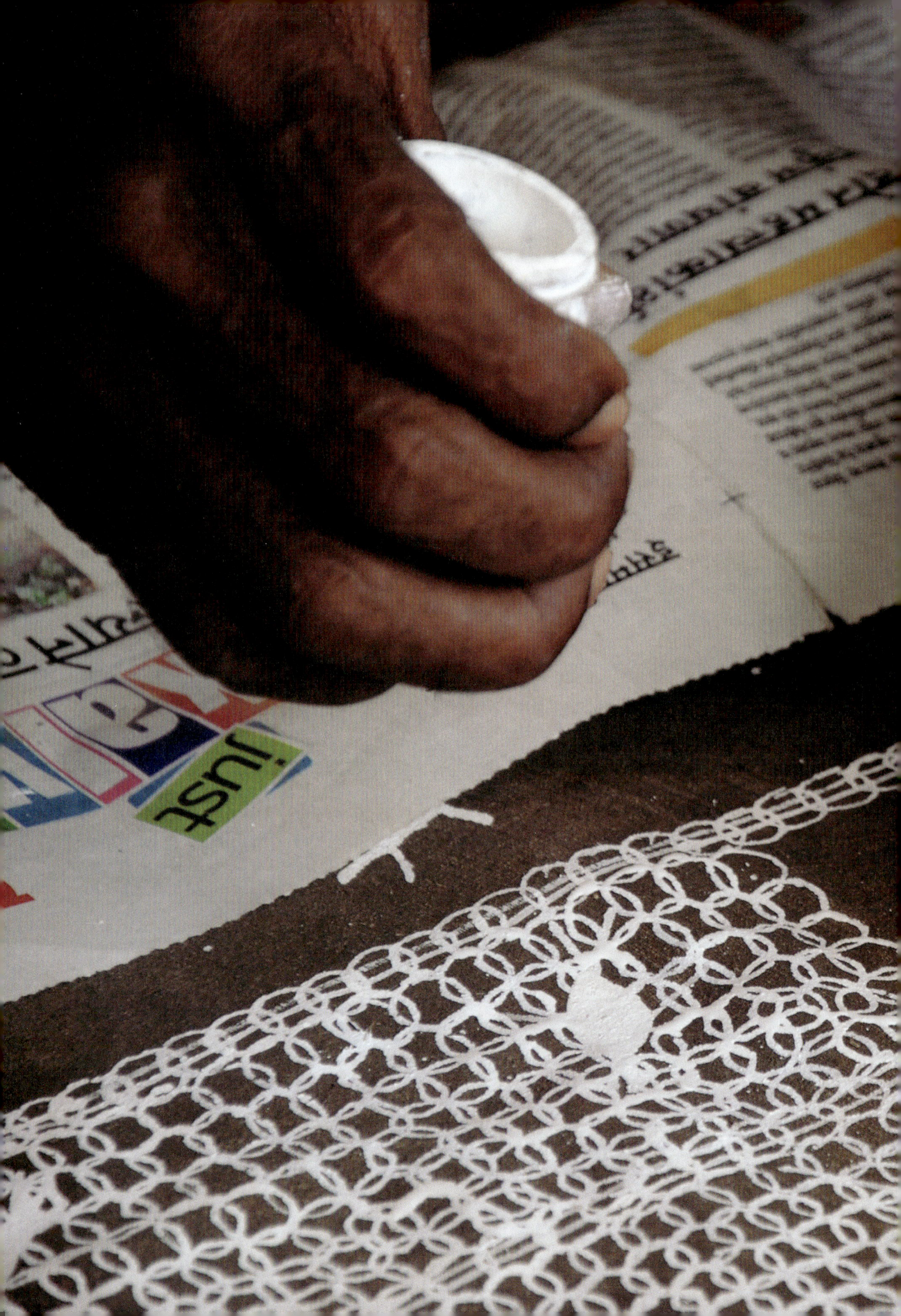
just

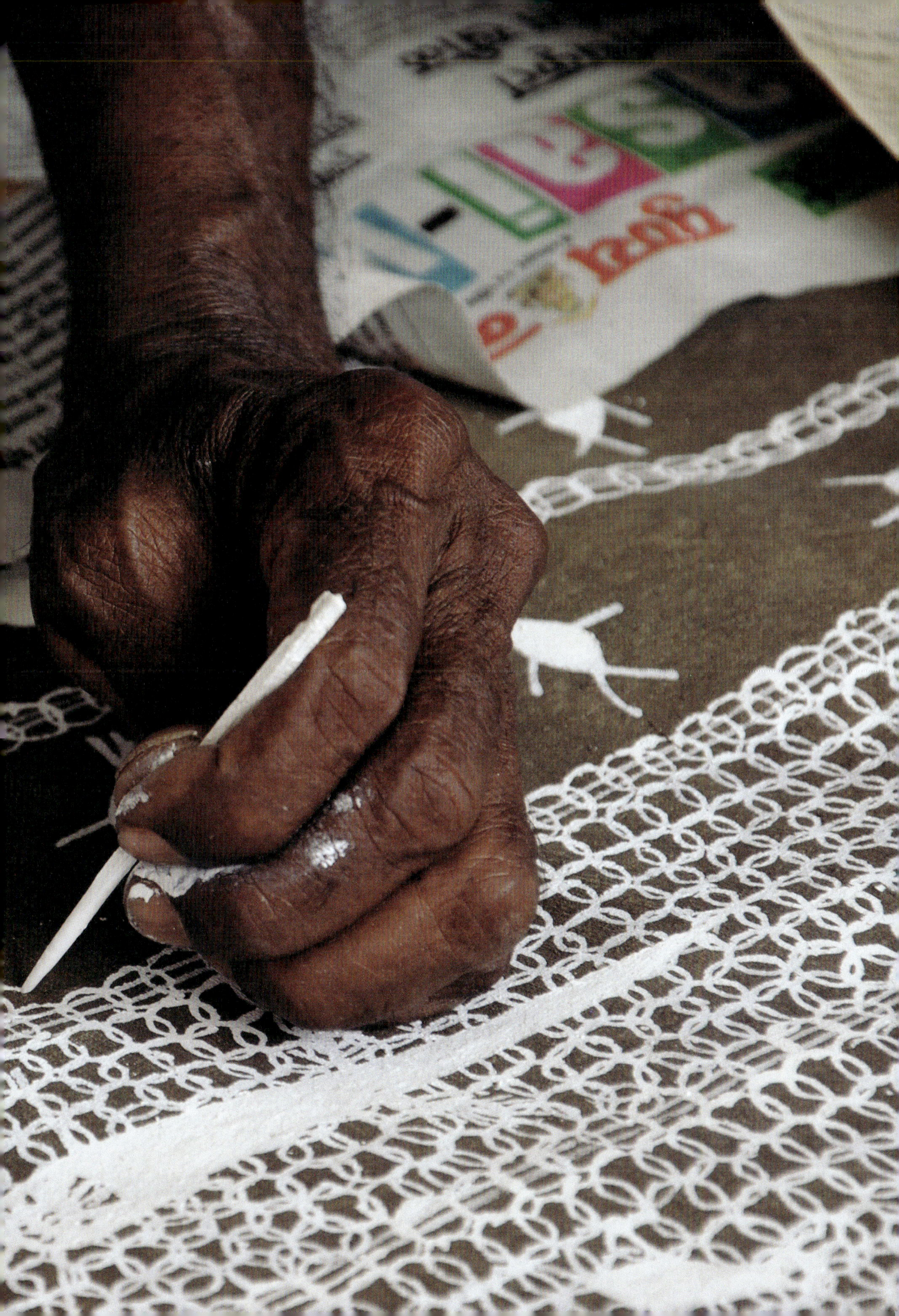

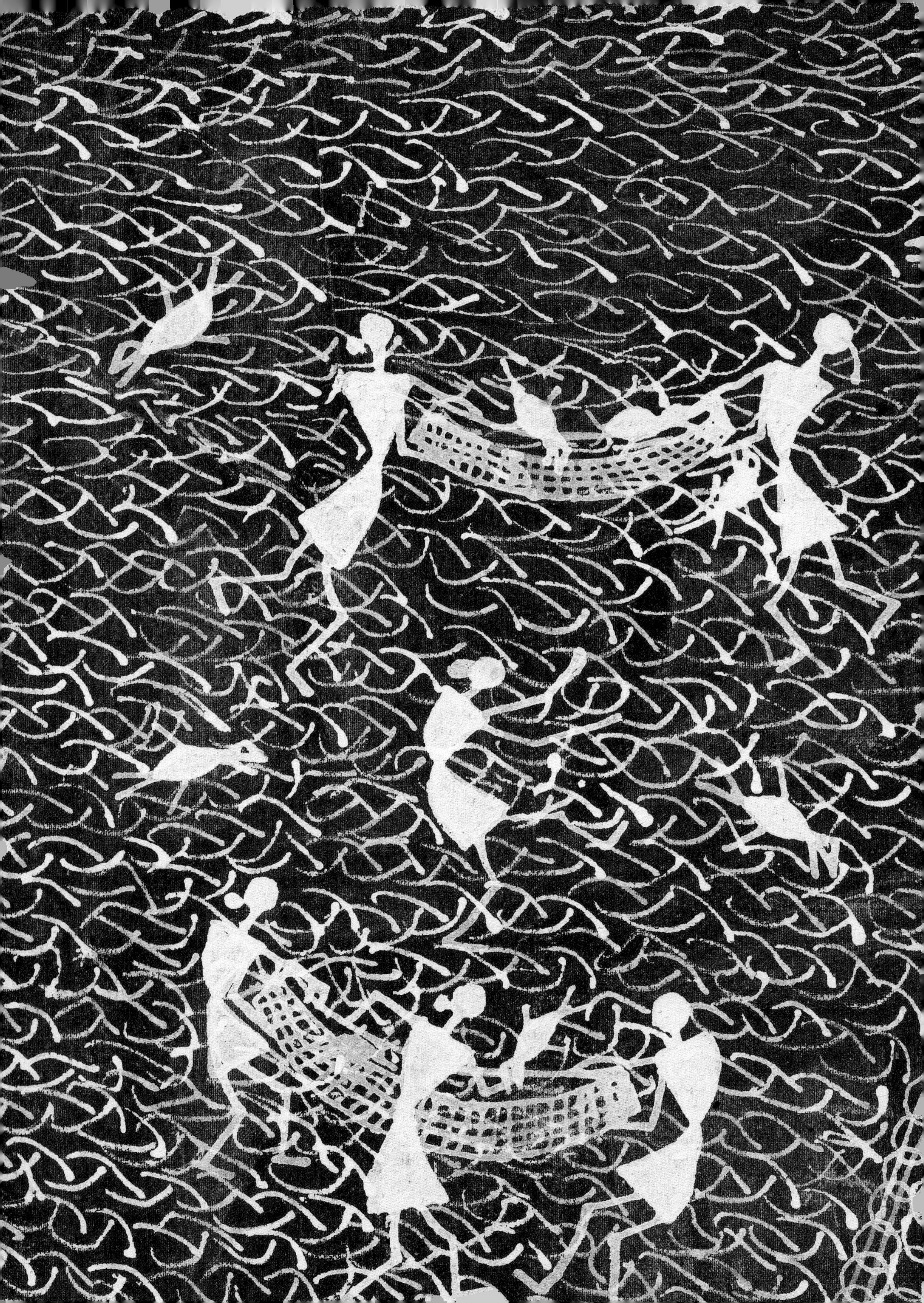

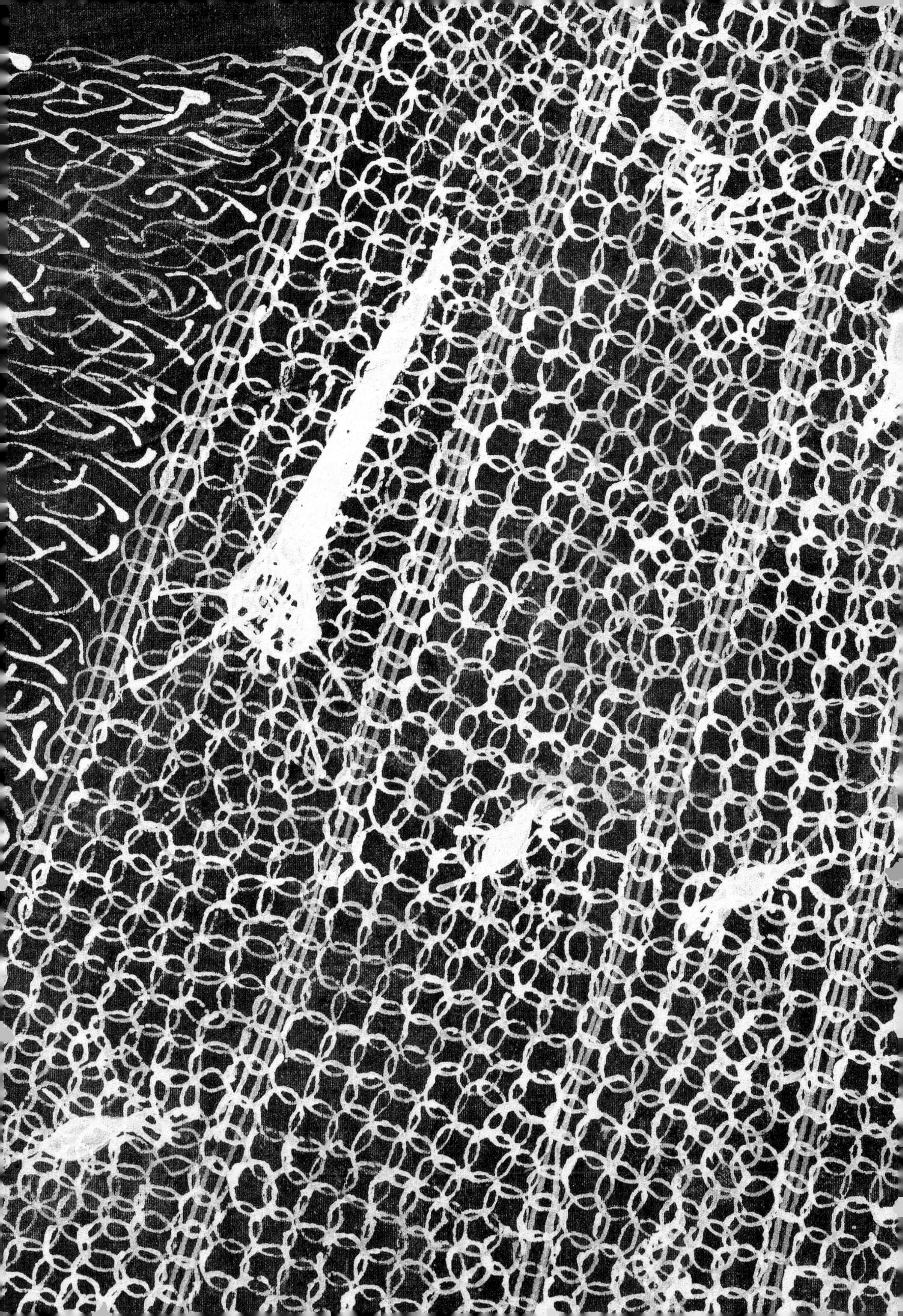

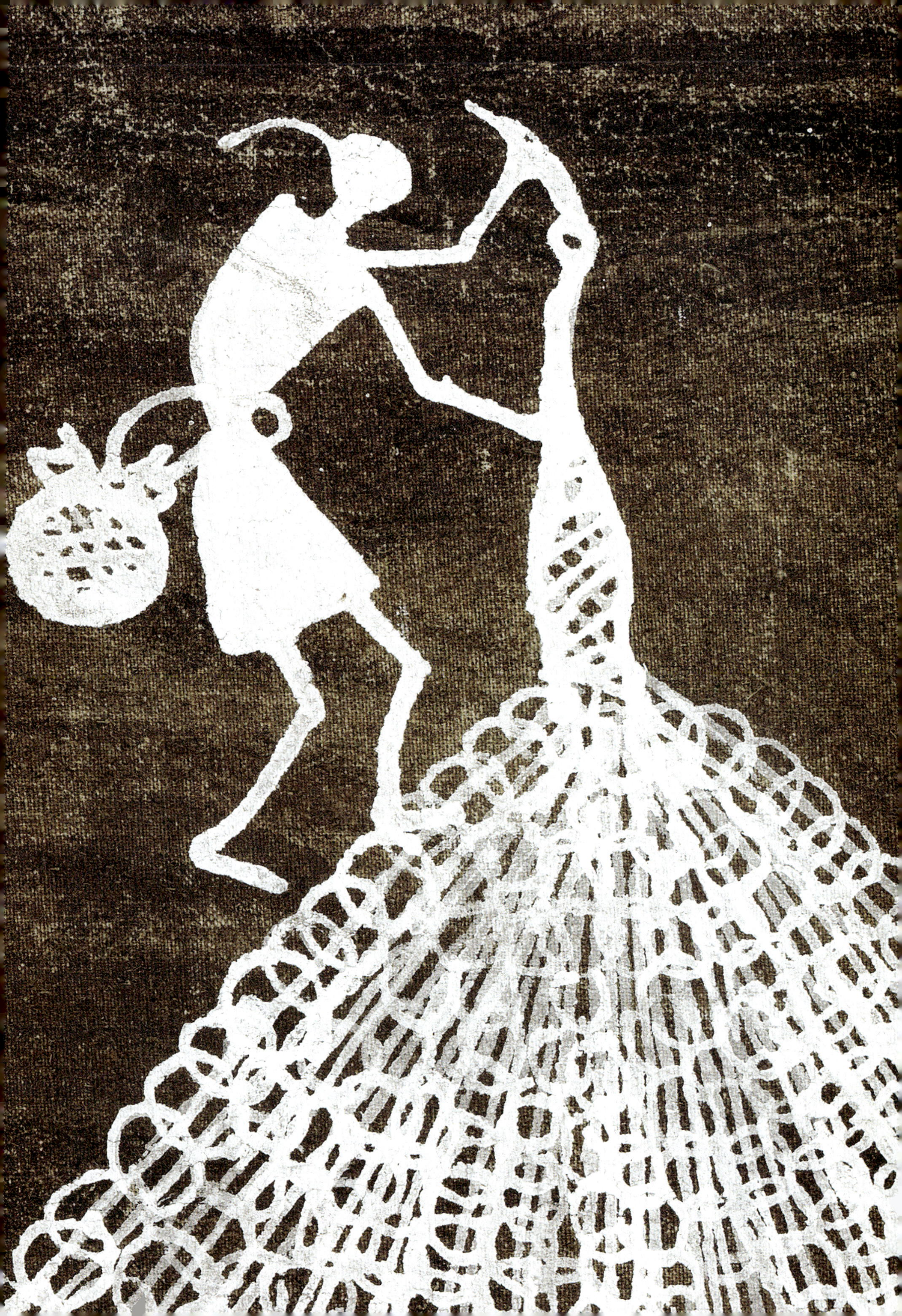

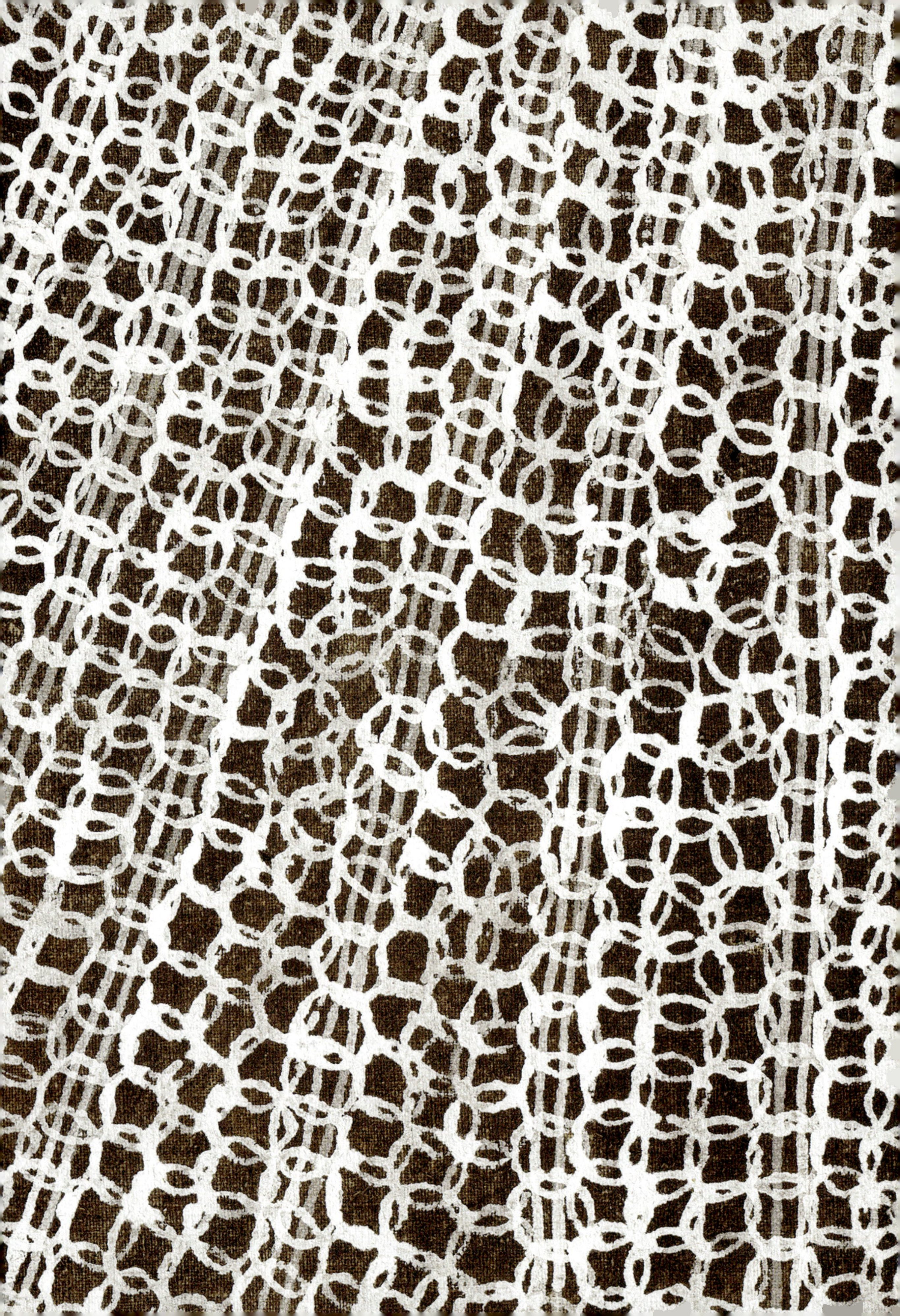

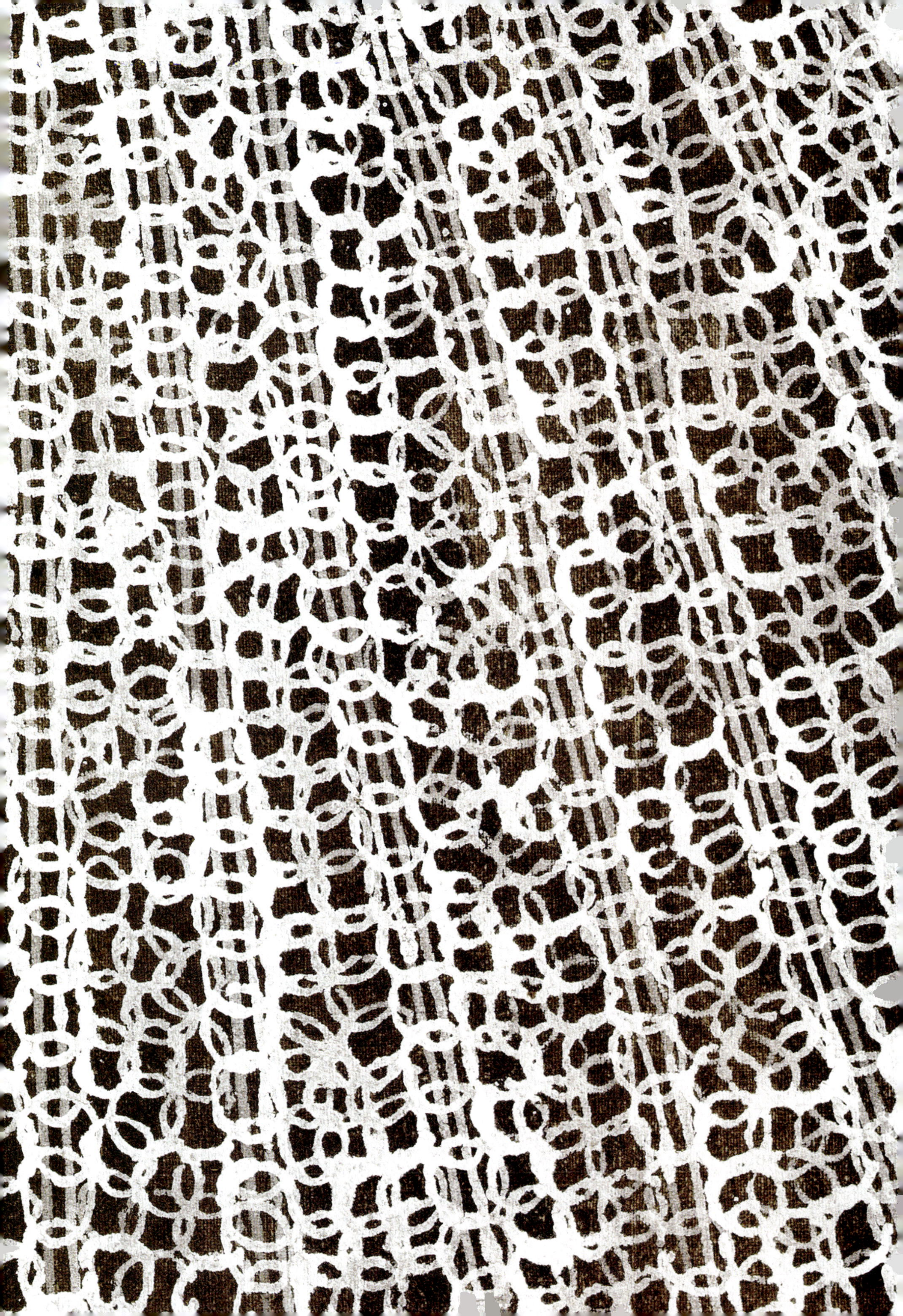

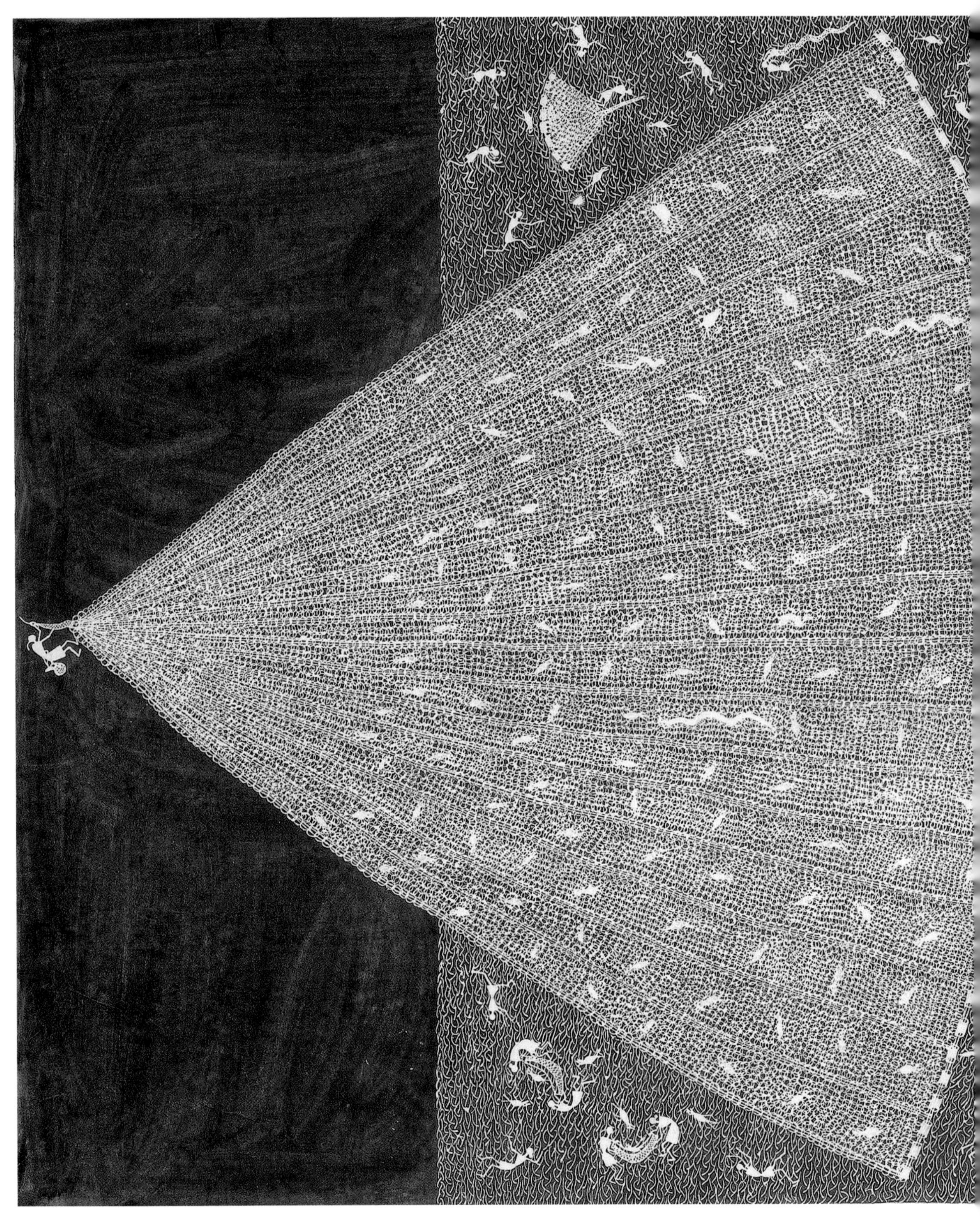

Jivya Soma Mashe, *Double Fishnet*, 2008,
acrylic on canvas,
138 x 237 cm; 54.33 x 93.30 in.
Collection Agnès B., Paris.

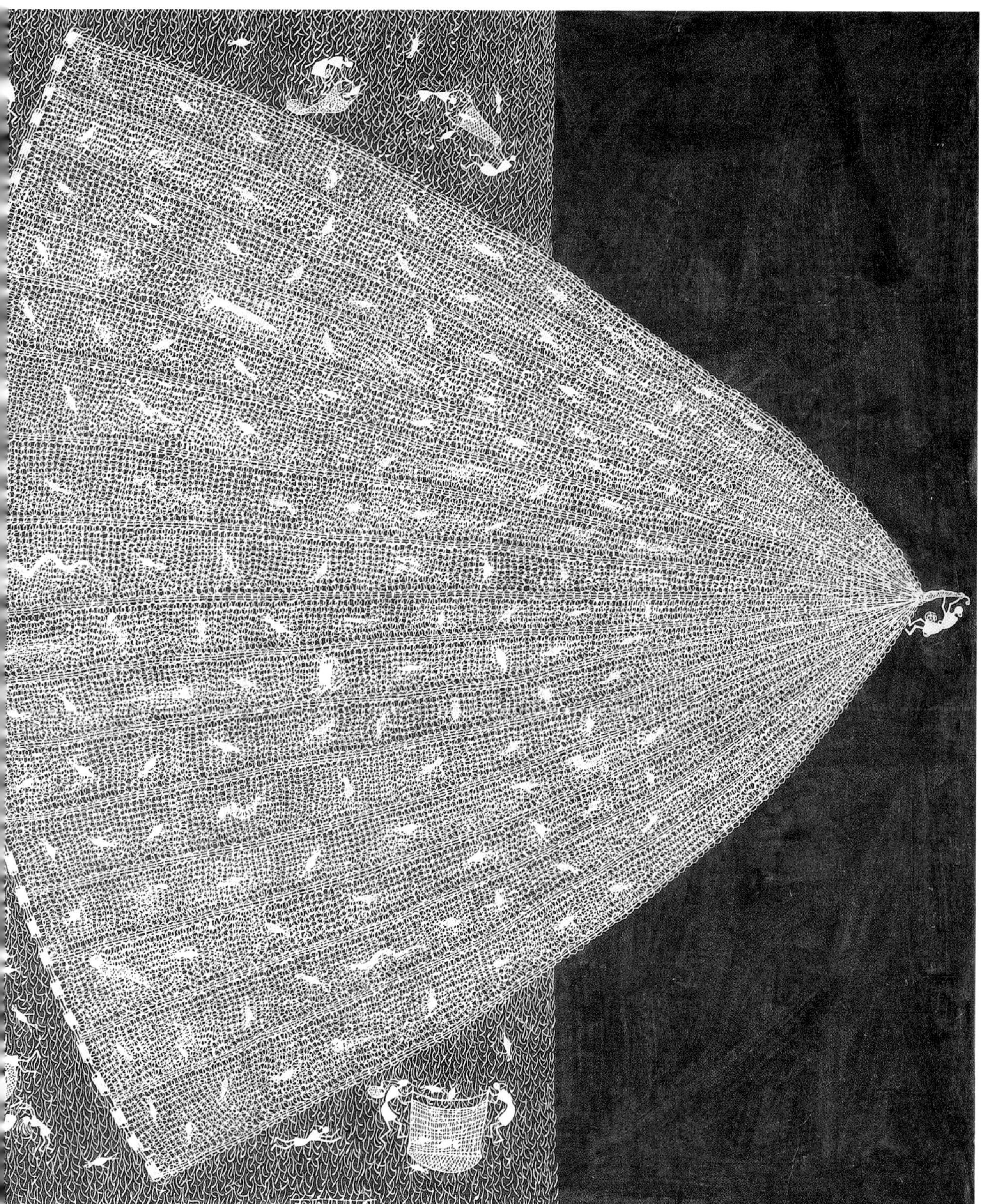

Pages 196–197
View of the exhibition *Inde*,
dedicated to the memory of Jivya Soma Mashe,
Manoir de Martigny (Switzerland), 2018.
Photo by Annik Wetter.

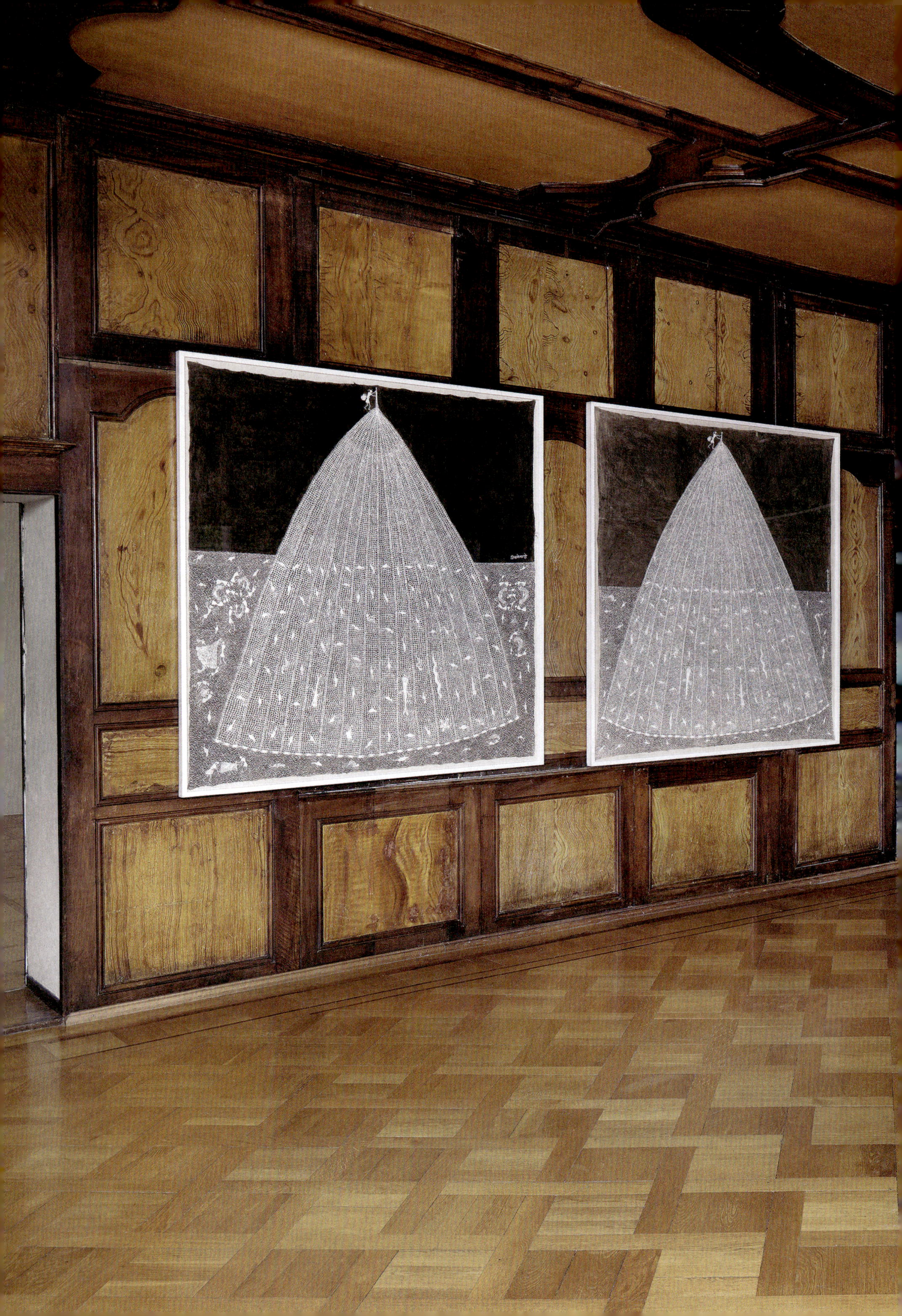

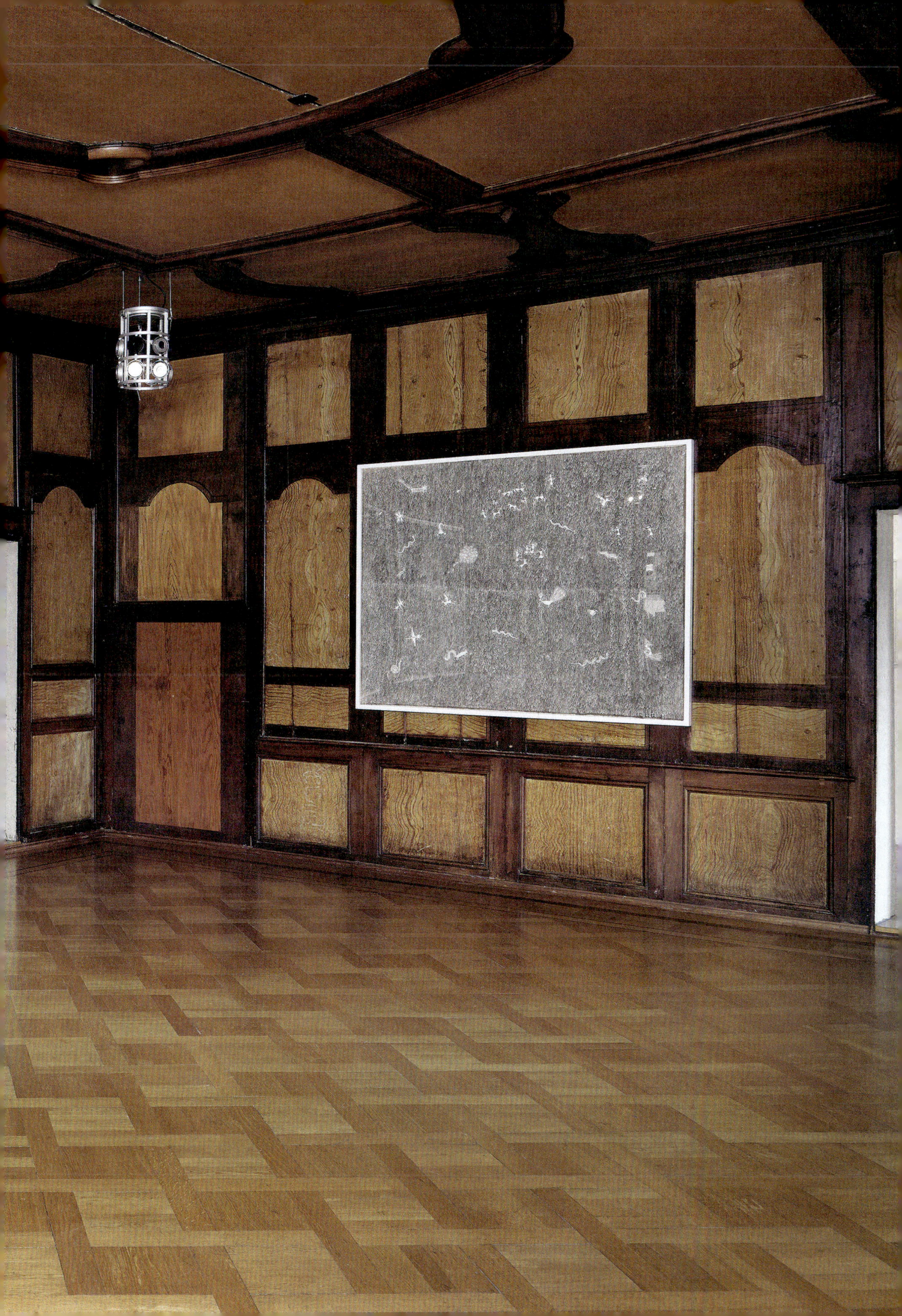

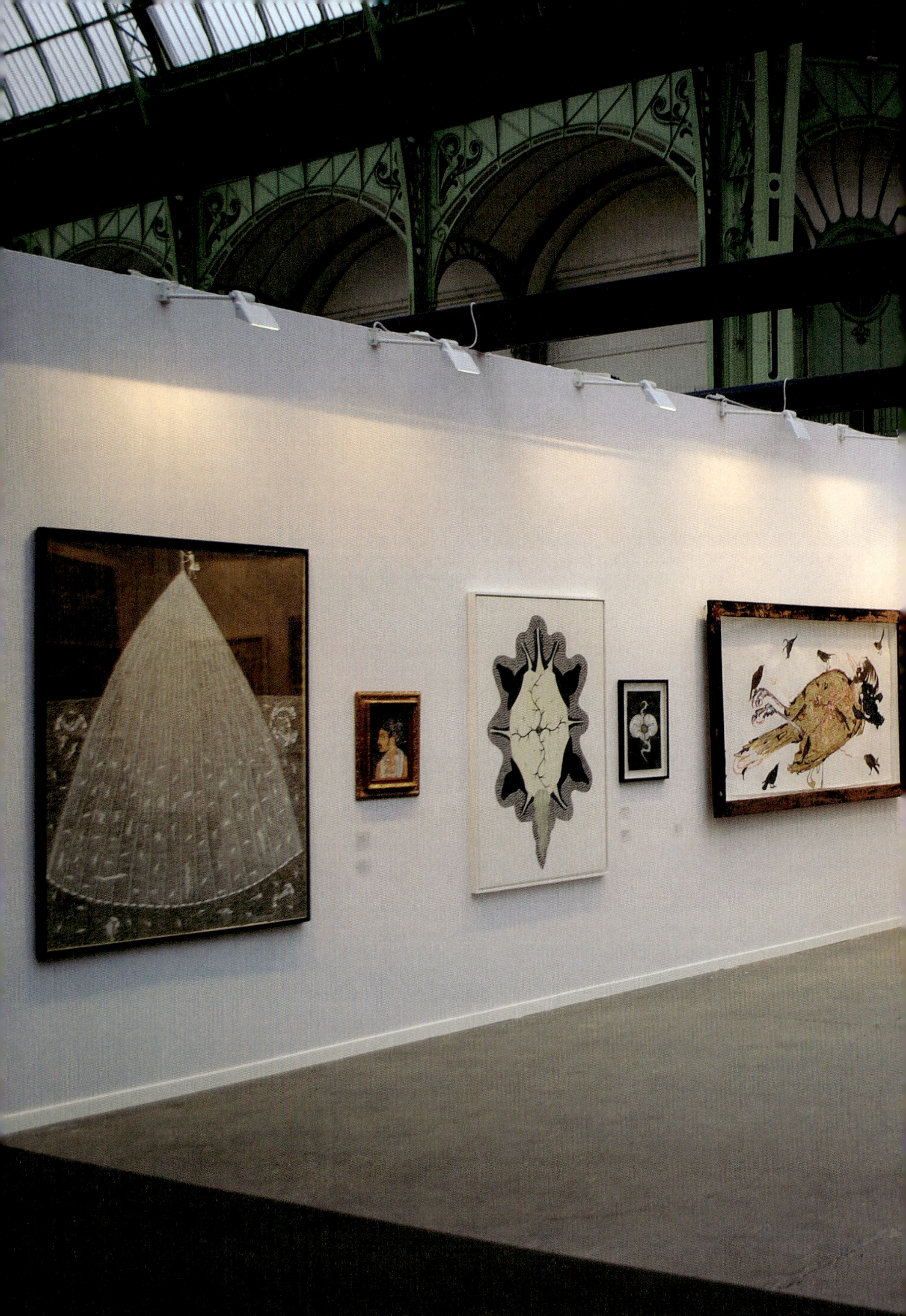

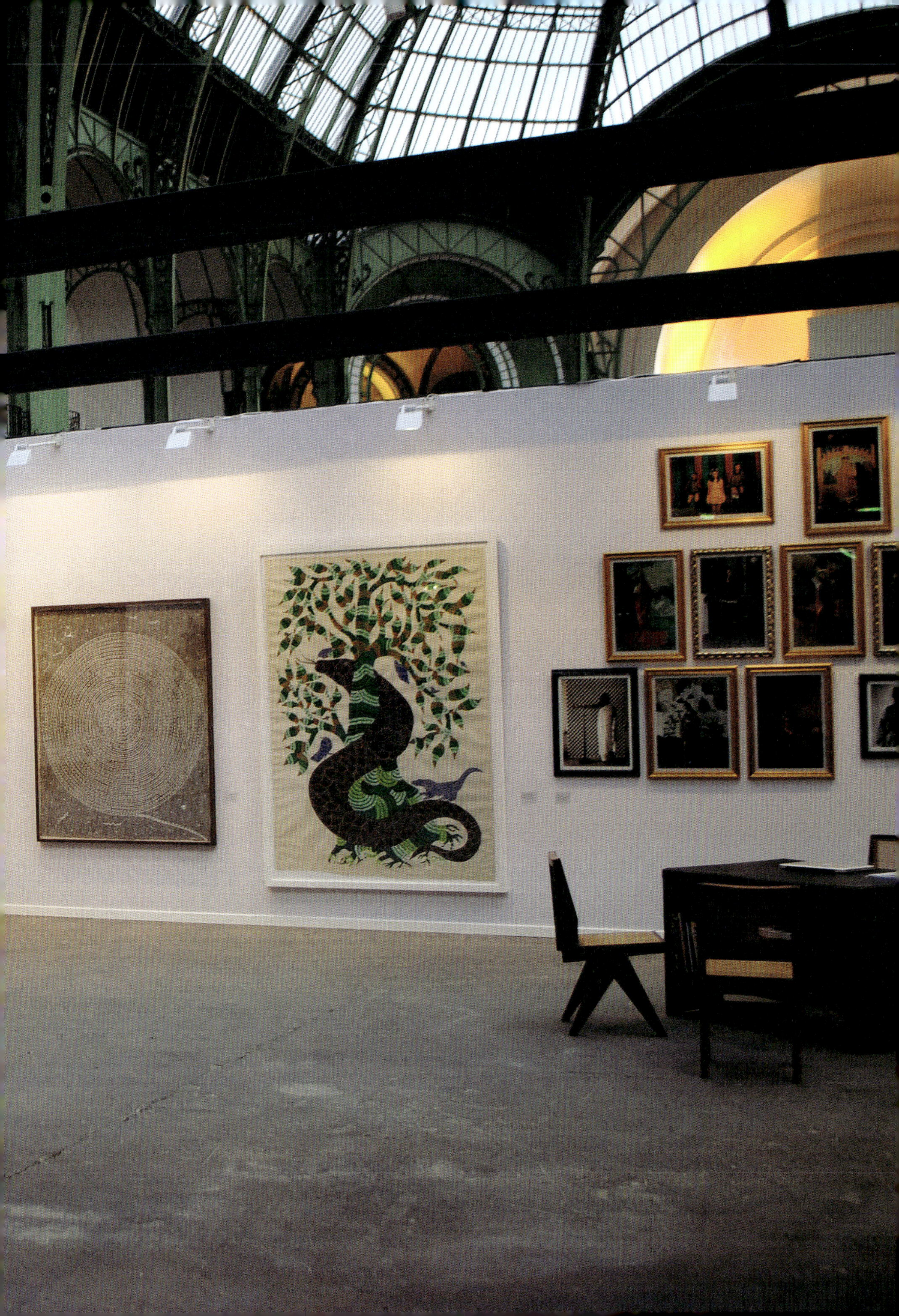

MICROCOSM AND MACROCOSM
MICROCOSME ET MACROCOSME

The infinitely small and infinitely large are notions found in all primitive arts. I remember spending time in a Warli hut in 1997; there was little to do – go out for a walk, sit with my new friends talking in a dialect I didn't know, share the present moment. Seated beneath a hut canopy, I watched water dripping and creating a channel on the beaten earth in the same way that rivers form their beds. Ants climbing over or around obstacles, the microscopic world on the ground as I waited for the clouds to clear in the sky. With nightfall, the rain stopped, allowing me to watch the sky in that unlit setting, with its innumerable stars visible in a way that is only possible today in the most isolated of spots, far from civilisation and its light pollution. It is said that art is born from the observation of nature.

The first peoples had the time to watch the infinitely small. On cloudless nights they were confronted by the spectacle of the infinitely large, which still amazes those who have the privilege of seeing it. It is easy to imagine the extent to which the infinitely large and infinitely small must have stimulated the imagination of those who did not have our scientific knowledge, and contributed to the invention of tales and legends.

L'infiniment petit et l'infiniment grand sont des notions que l'on retrouve dans tous les arts primitifs. Je me souviens d'avoir passé du temps dans une hutte de la tribu warli en 1997. Peu de choses à faire. Se promener, s'asseoir aux côtés de mes nouveaux amis parlant un dialecte que je ne connais pas. Simplement partager le temps présent. Assis sous l'auvent de la hutte à l'abri de la pluie, observer l'eau qui goutte se frayer un chemin sur la terre battue. Rigoles, qui, comme des rivières, dessinent leur lit. Des fourmis qui contournent ou surmontent les obstacles. Observer à ses pieds, sans bouger, dans l'attente d'une éclaircie, ce monde microscopique qui s'anime. La nuit tombe. La pluie s'arrête. Observer le ciel. Sans lumière parasite aucune, les étoiles sont là, innombrables, perceptibles comme encore aujourd'hui seulement dans les endroits les plus reculés, loin de toute civilisation, loin de toute lumière artificielle et de toute pollution. On dit que l'art est né de l'observation de la nature. Les peuples premiers avaient le temps d'observer l'infiniment petit. Ils étaient mis en présence, les nuits sans nuages, de ce spectacle de l'infiniment grand qui stupéfie ceux qui ont encore le privilège d'y être confronté. Il est aisé d'imaginer à quel point ces spectacles, infiniment grand et petit, sans les connaissances qui sont les nôtres, devaient être propices à l'imaginaire, au développement des contes et légendes.

Pages 198–199
View of the Hervé Perdriolle gallery booth, Art Paris, Grand Palais, 2011 (works by Jivya Soma Mashe, Rashid Rana, Mayank Shyam, Mithu Sen, Jangarh Singh Shyam, Pushpamala N., Pierre Jeanneret furniture courtesy of Galerie Jousse Entreprise Paris).

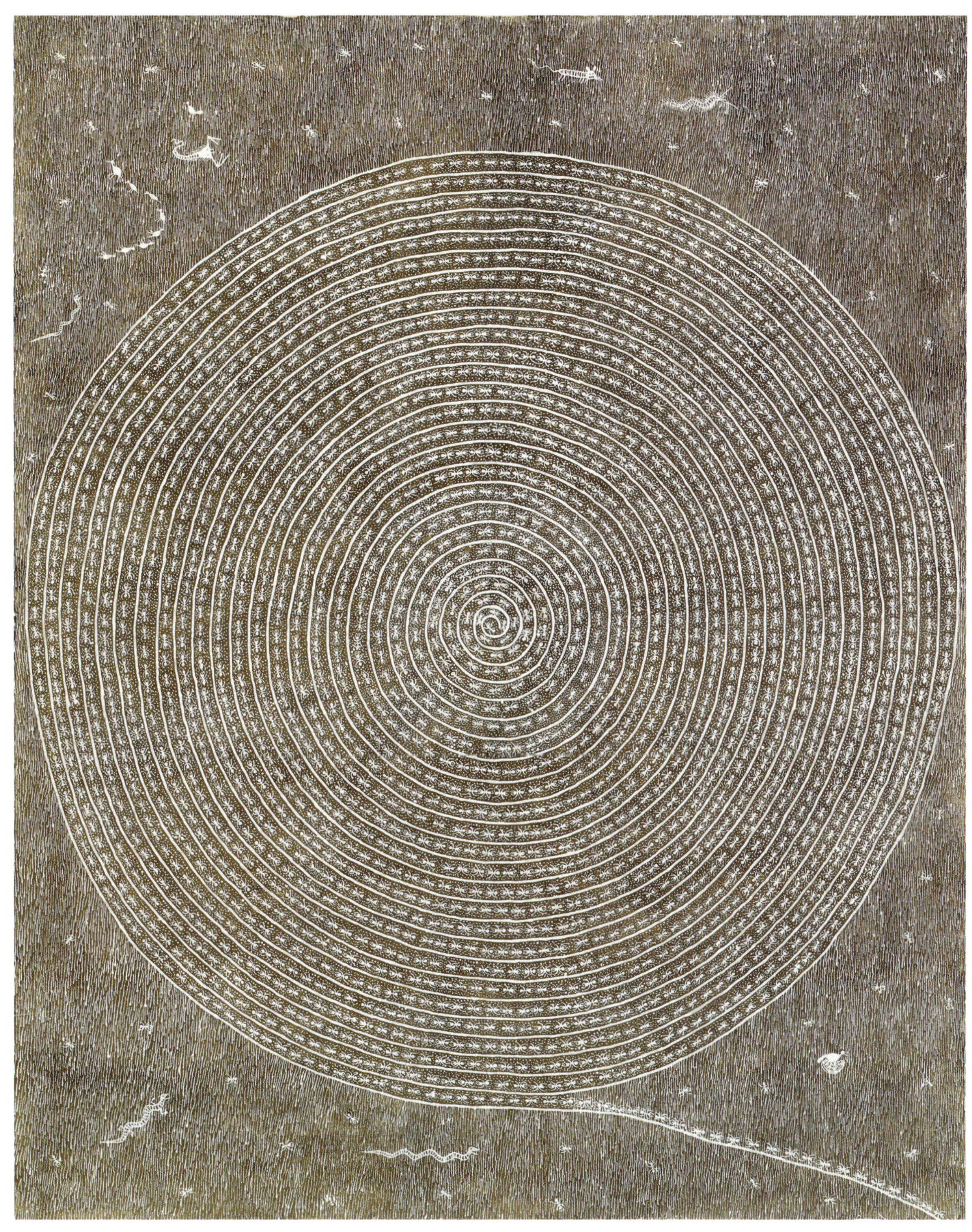

Jivya Soma Mashe, *Ants Spiral*, 2010,
acrylic and cow dung on canvas,
166 × 145 cm; 65.35 × 57.08 in. (*detail on pages* 202–203)
Garance Primat Collection.
Photo by Arthur Péquin.

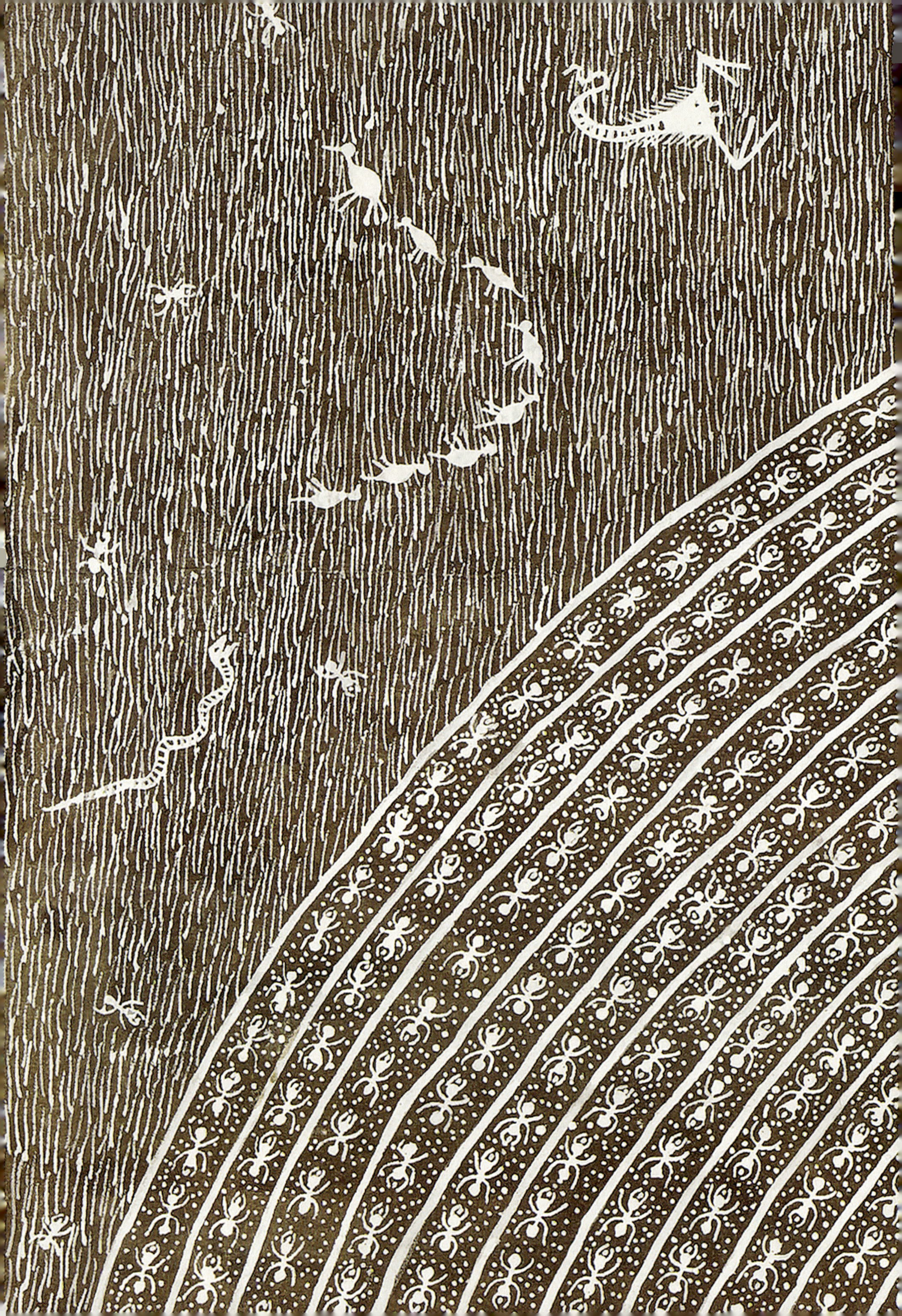

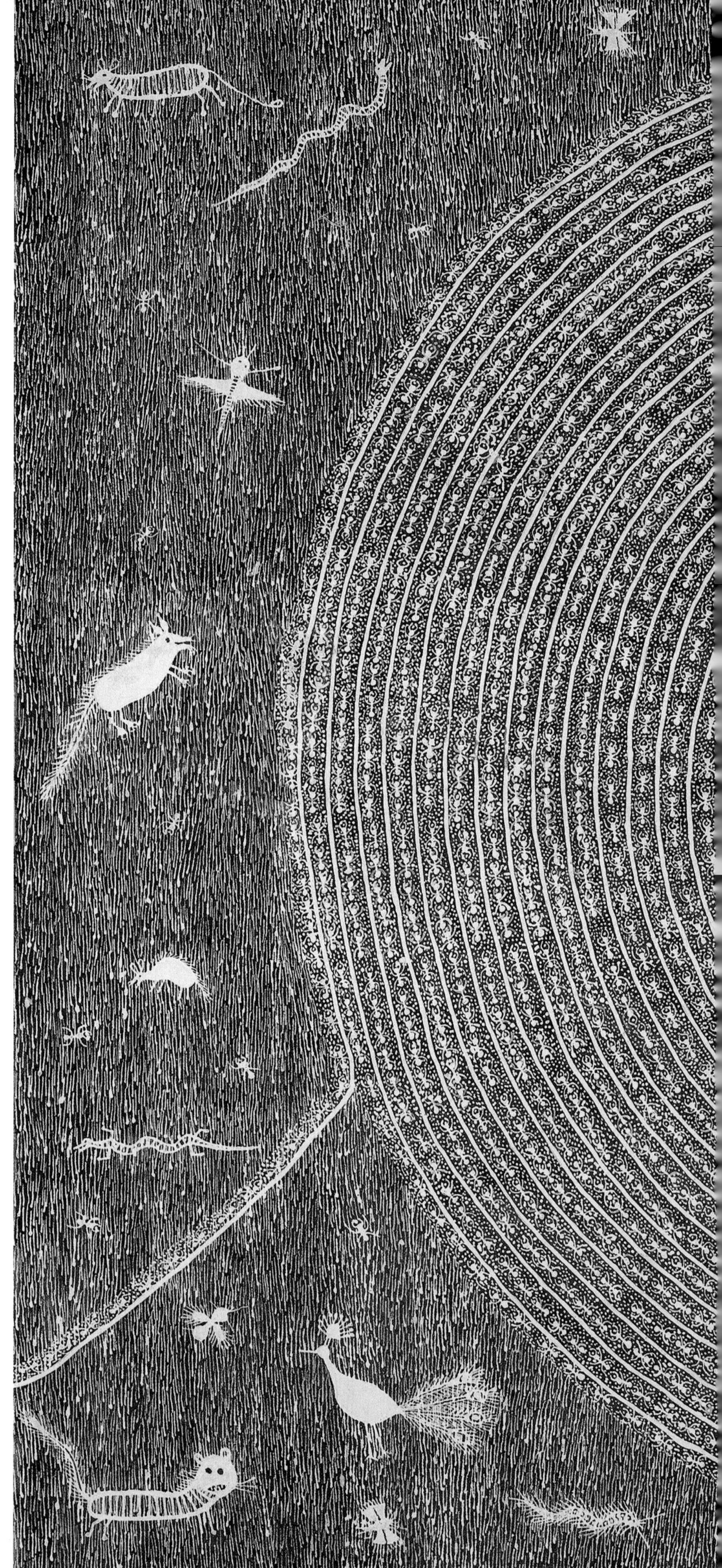

Jivya Soma Mashe, *Ants Spiral*, 2016, acrylic and cow dung on canvas, 133 × 163 cm; 52.36 × 64.17 in. (*detail on pages* 206–207) Marie-Françoise Morelli Collection. Photo by Christian Baraja.

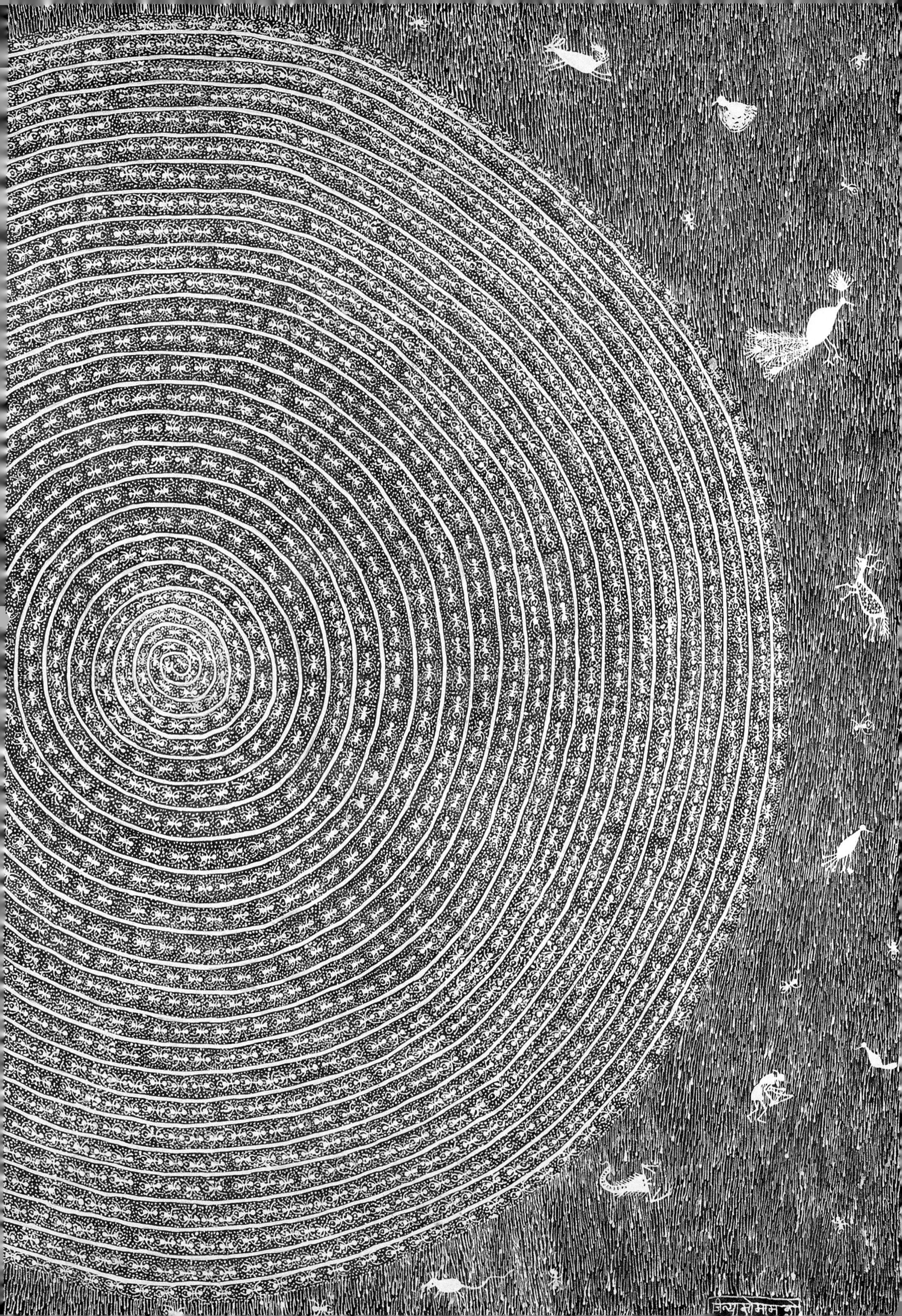

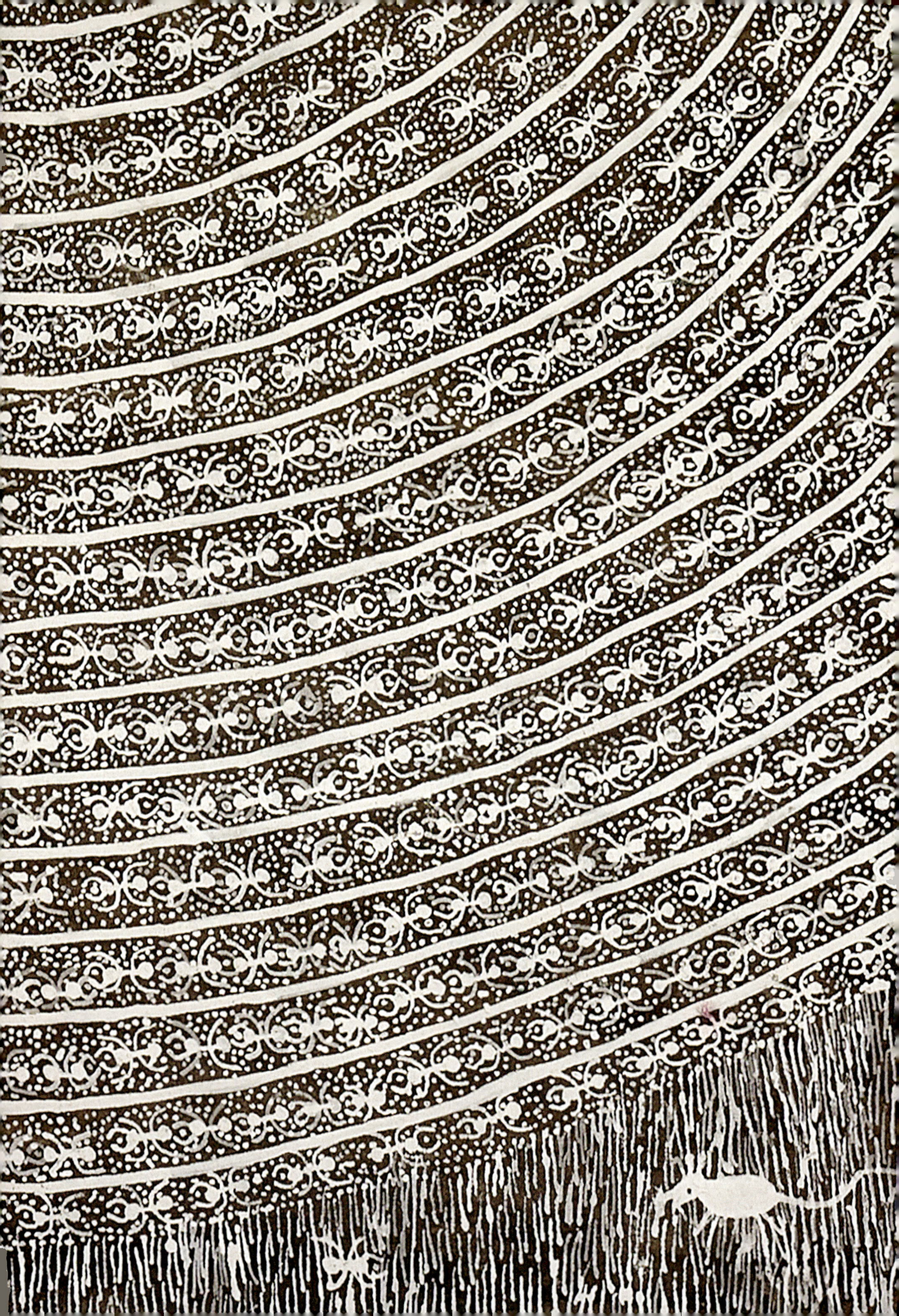

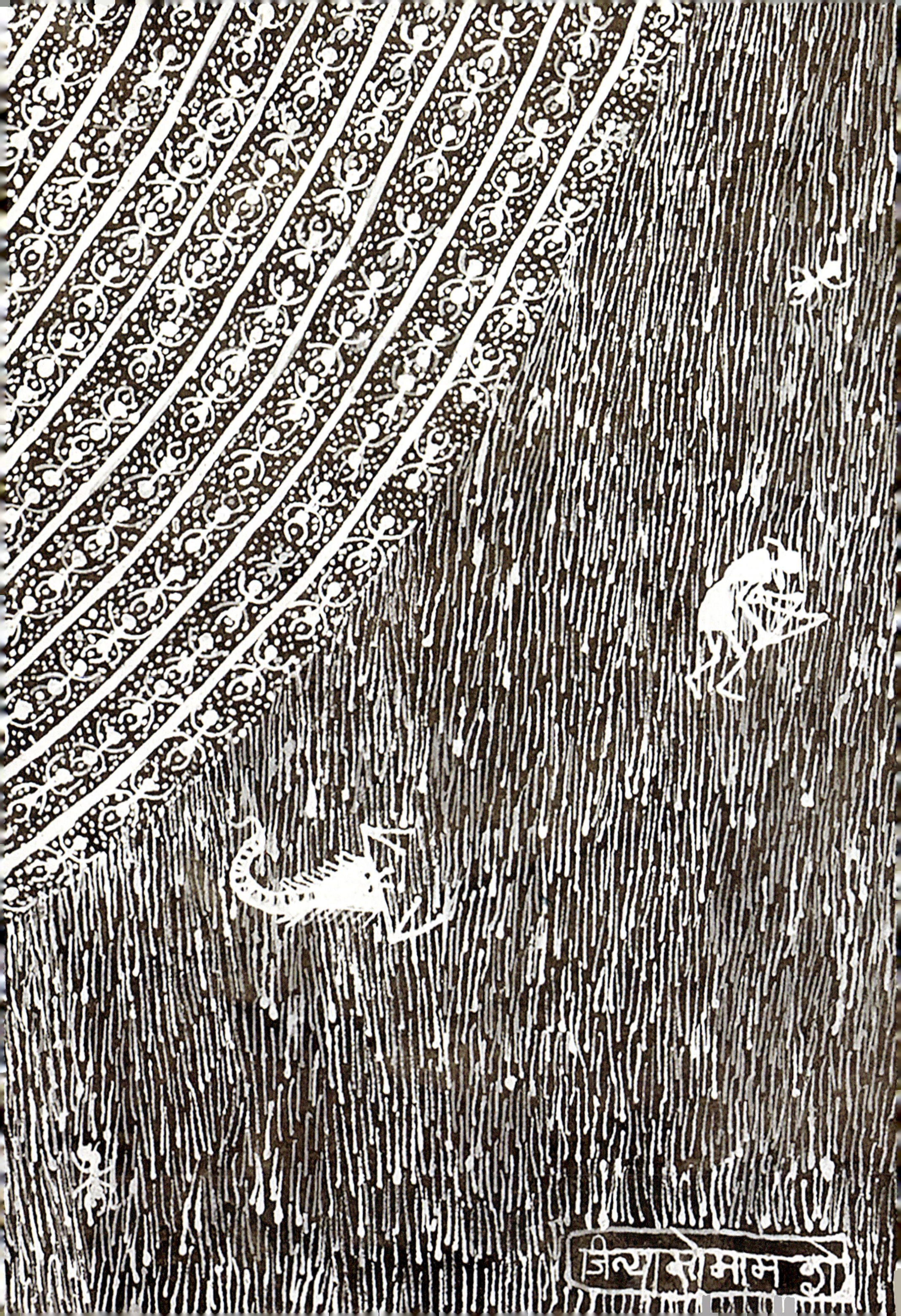
जिव्या सोमा मशे

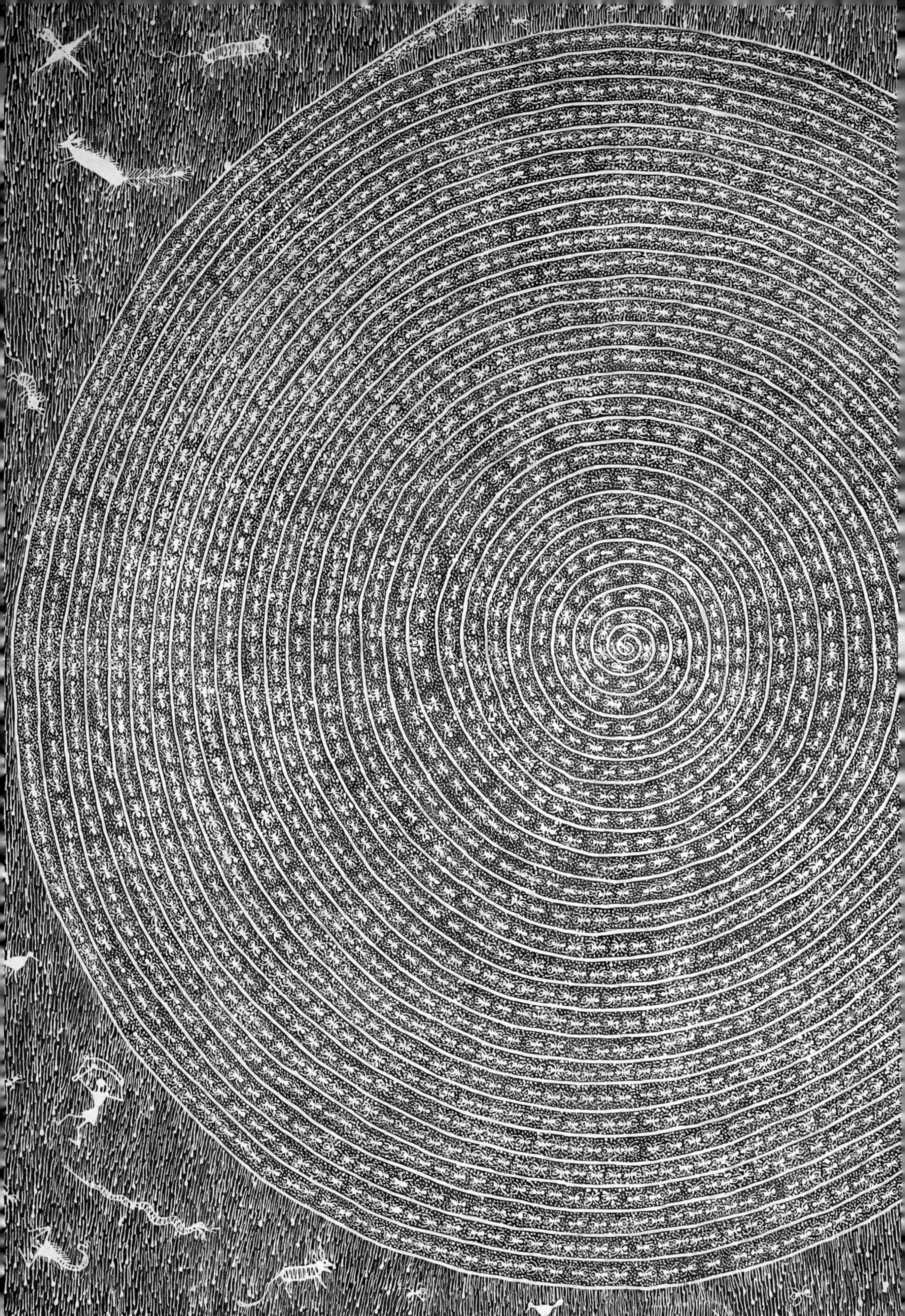

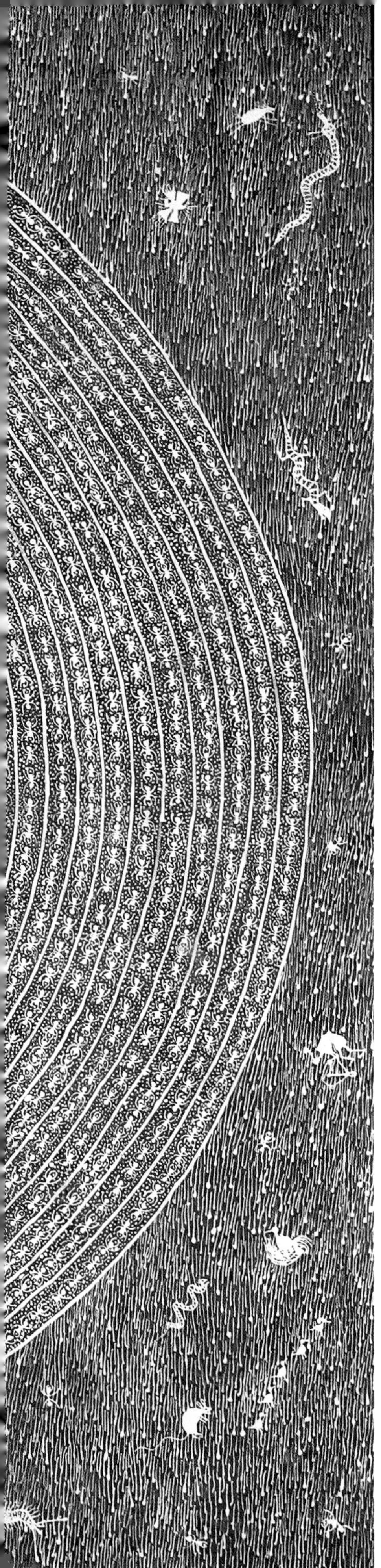

Jivya Soma Mashe, *Ants Spiral*, 2014,
acrylic and cow dung on canvas,
153 × 153 cm; 60.23 × 60.23 in.
Raj Deshpande Collection.

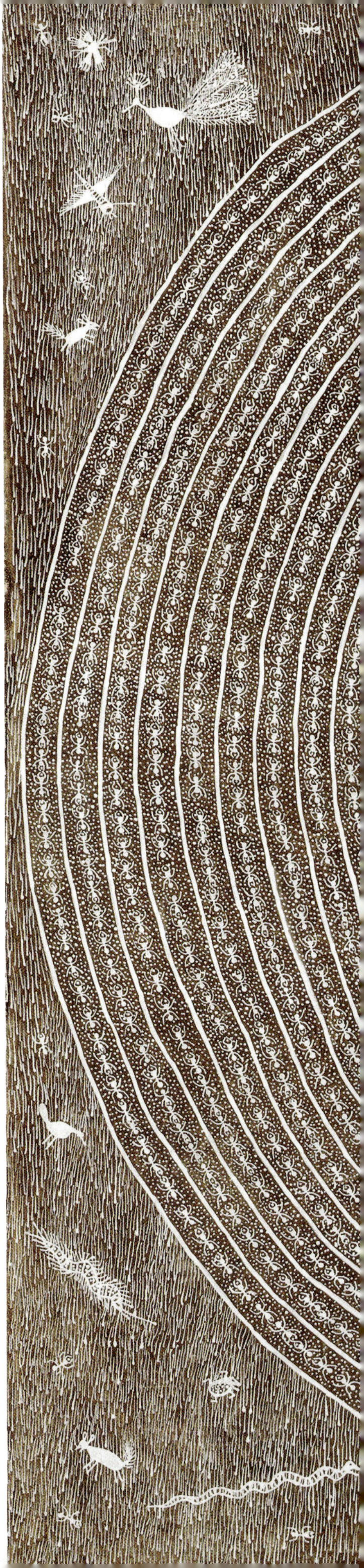

Jivya Soma Mashe, *Ants Spiral*, 2011,
acrylic and cow dung on canvas,
149 × 150 cm; 58.66 × 59.06 in.
Fondation Cartier pour l'art contemporain Collection.
Photo by André Morin.

Pages 212–213
Jivya Soma Mashe, *Ants Spiral (detail)*, 2010,
acrylic and cow dung on canvas,
85 × 95 cm; 33.46 × 37.40 in.
Courtesy Galerie Jeanne Bucher Jaeger, Paris-Lisbon.
Photo by Jean-Louis Losi.

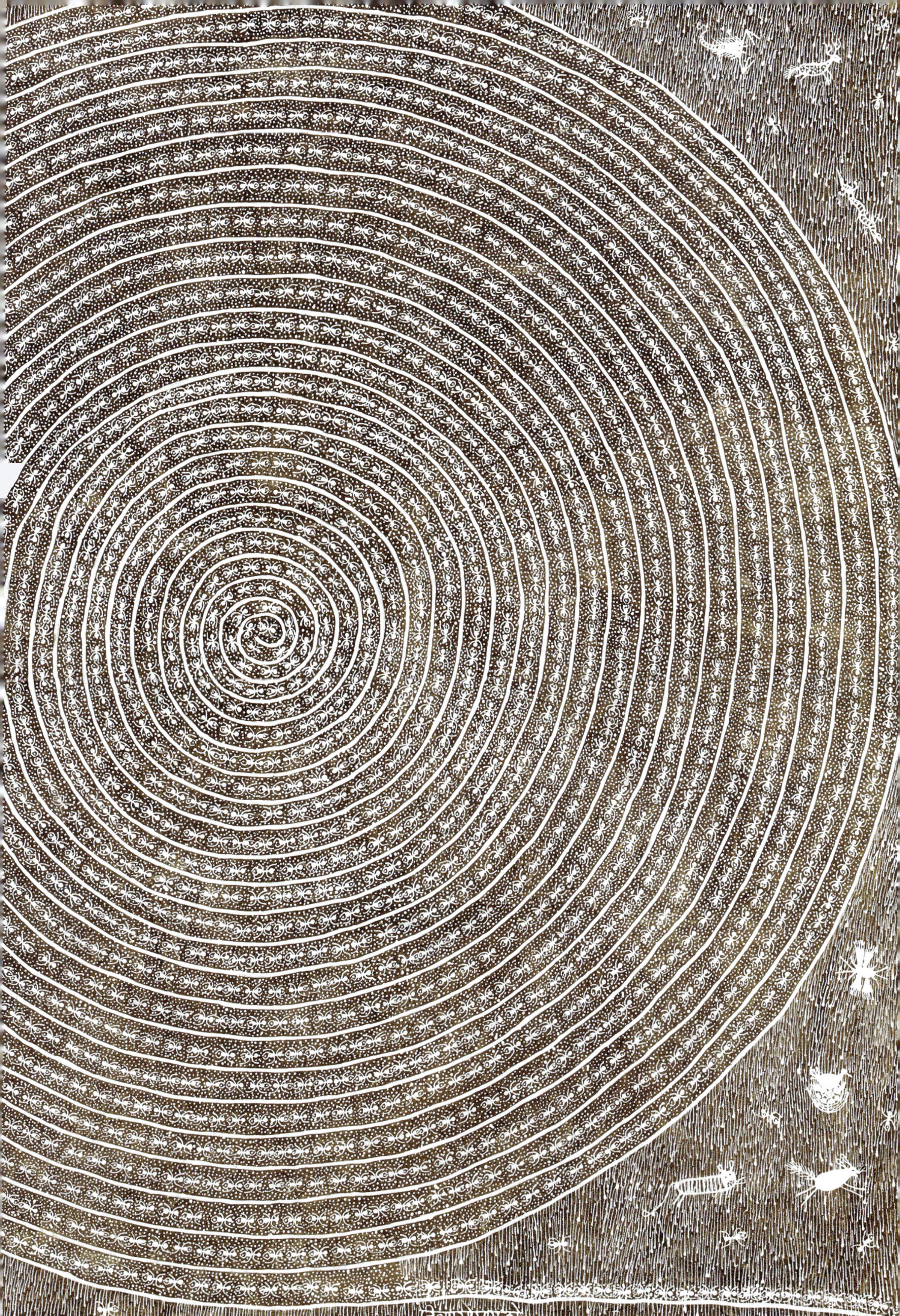

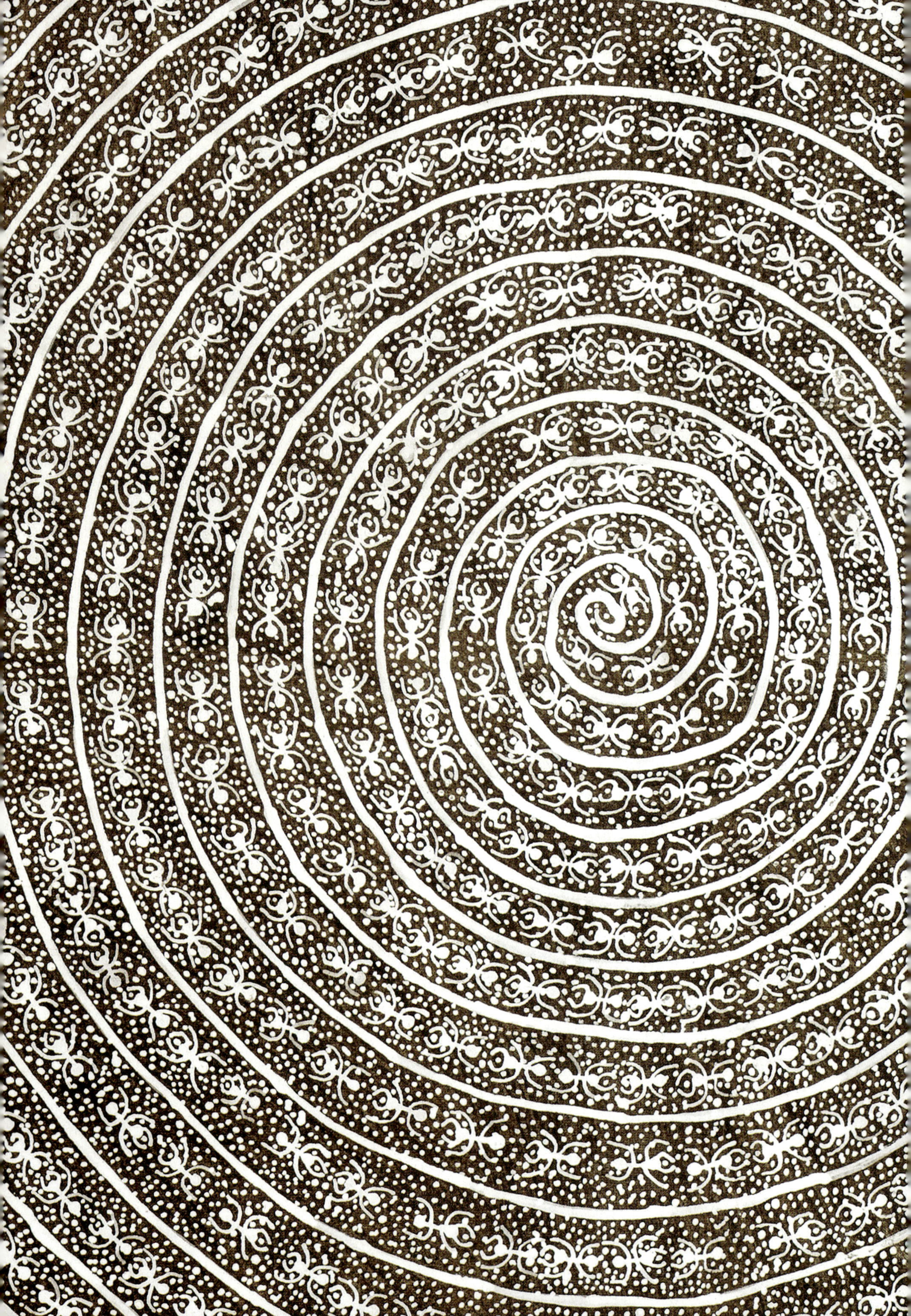

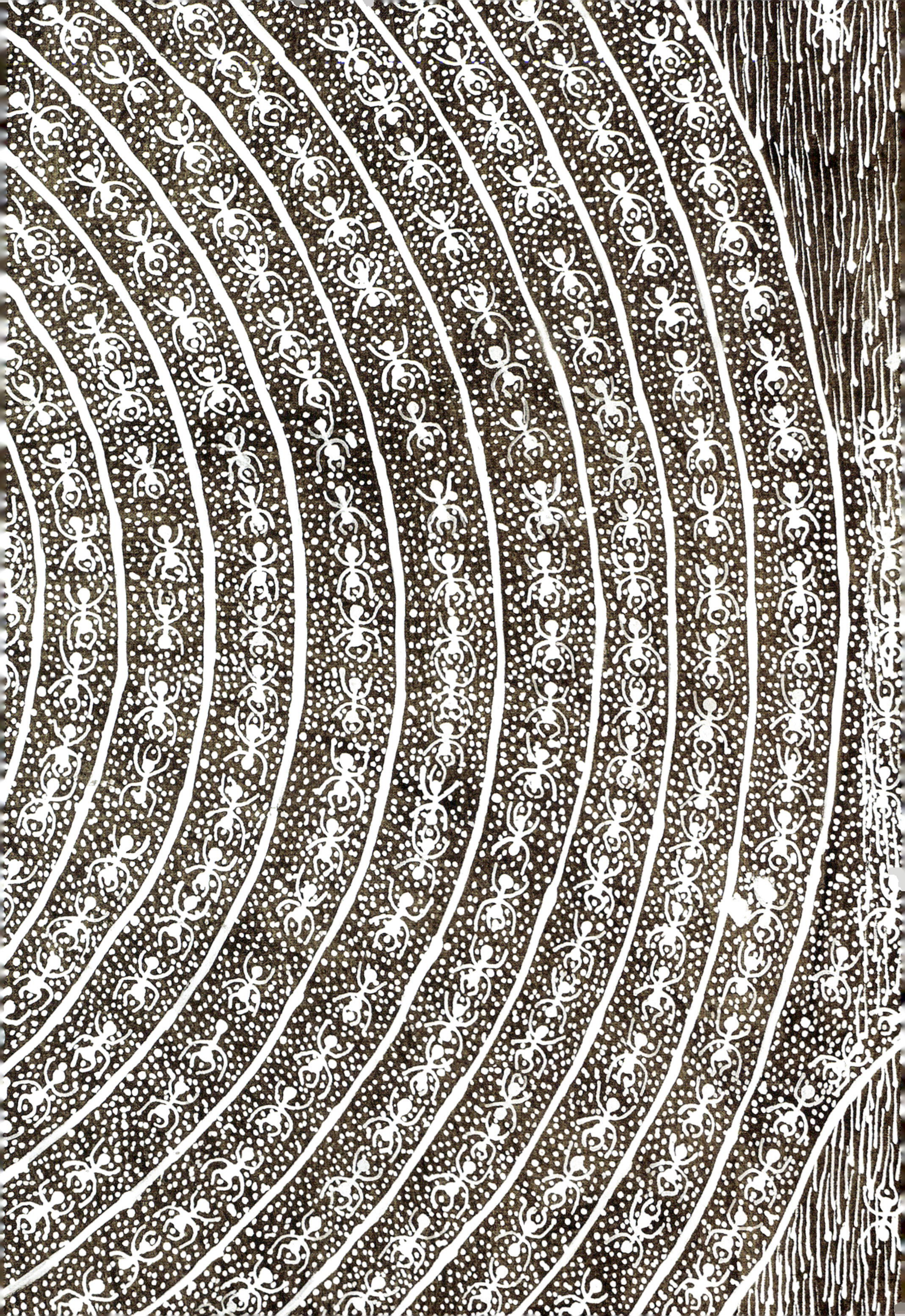

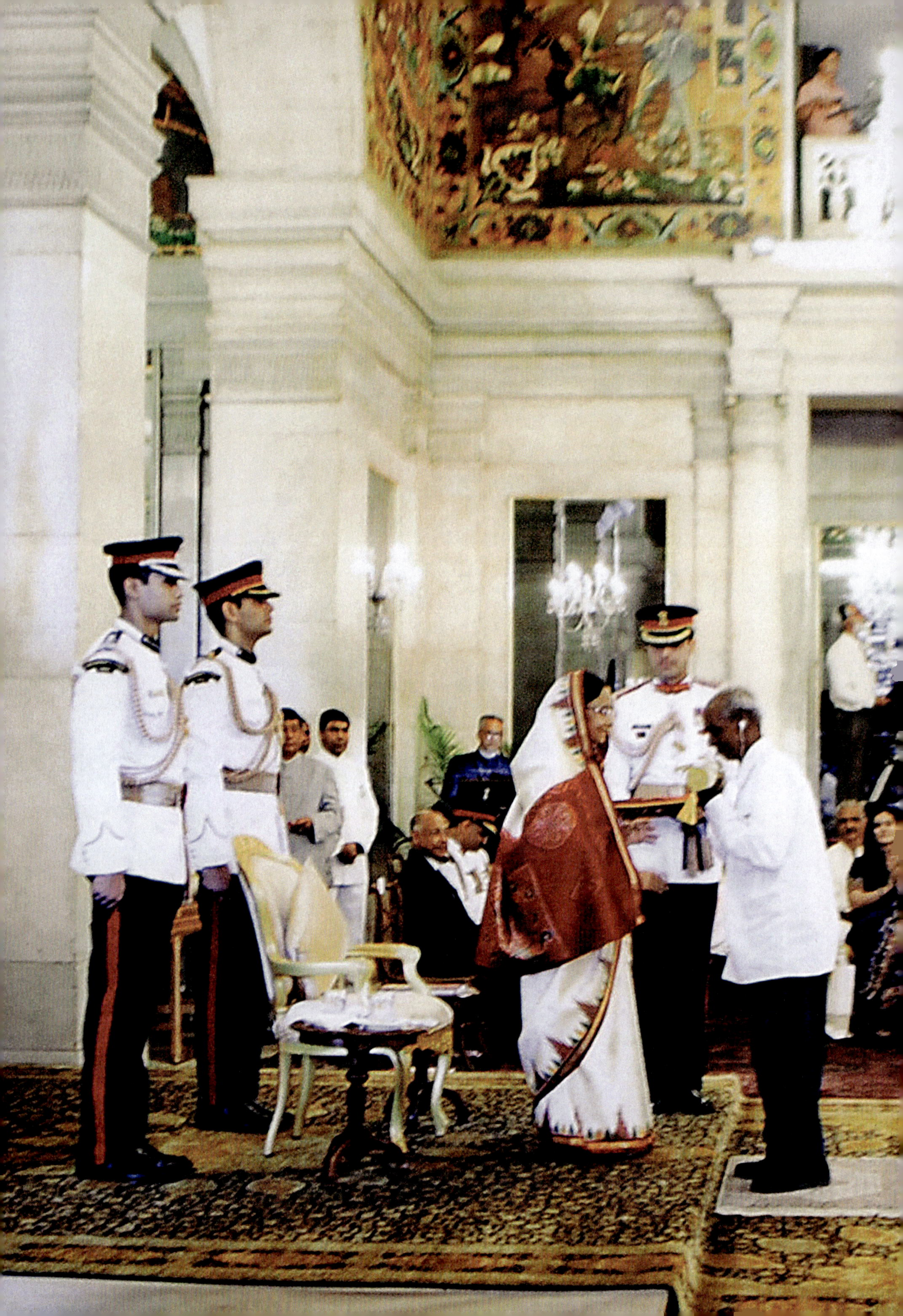

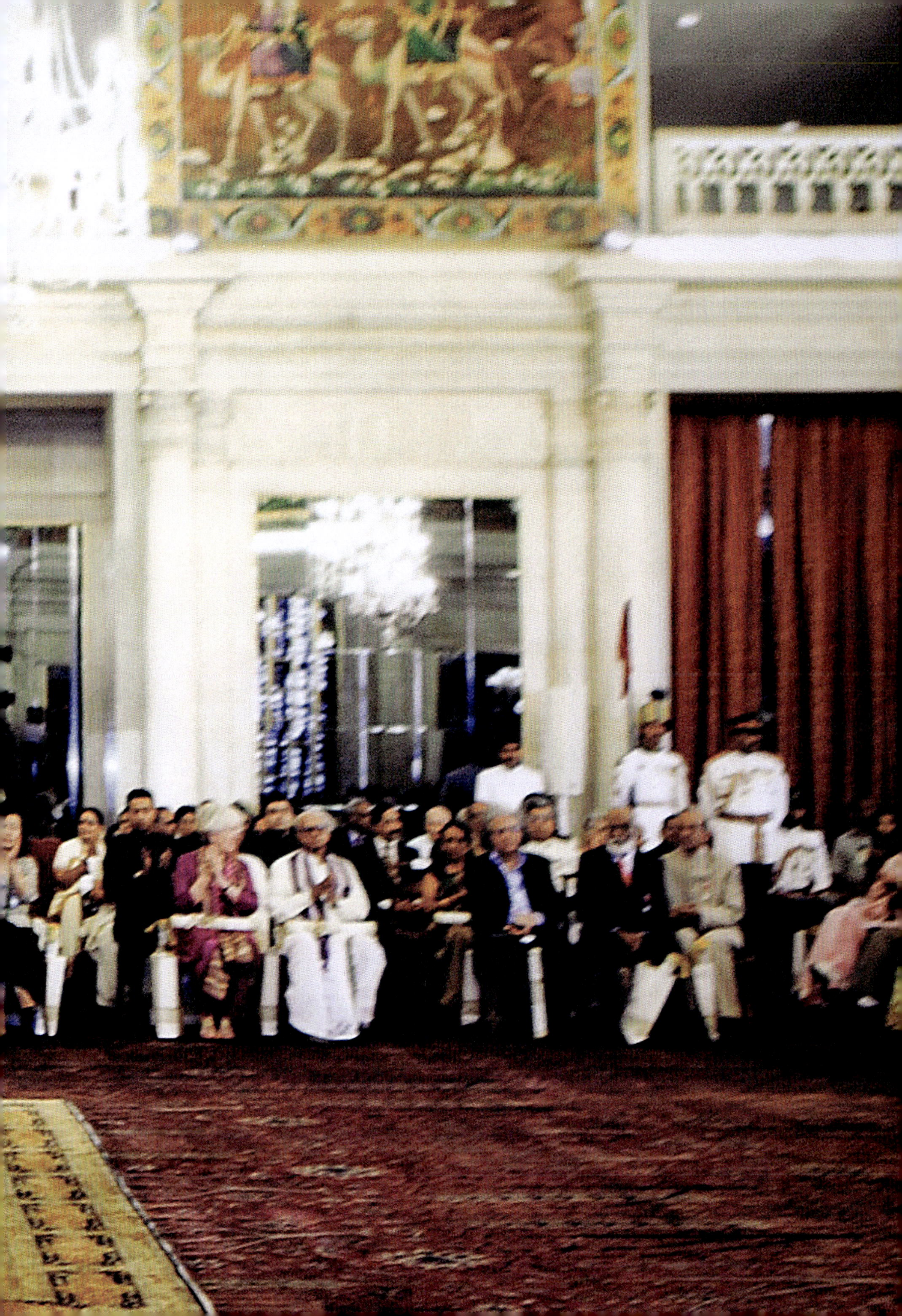

Pages 214–215
Jivya Soma Mashe receiving the *Padma Shri Award*, India's highest honorary award, from the President of India, New Delhi, 2011.

Jivya Soma Mashe, *Untitled*, 2001,
acrylic on canvas,
91.5 × 91.5 cm; 36.02 × 36.02 in.
Sonia Perrin Collection.
Photo by Christian Baraja.

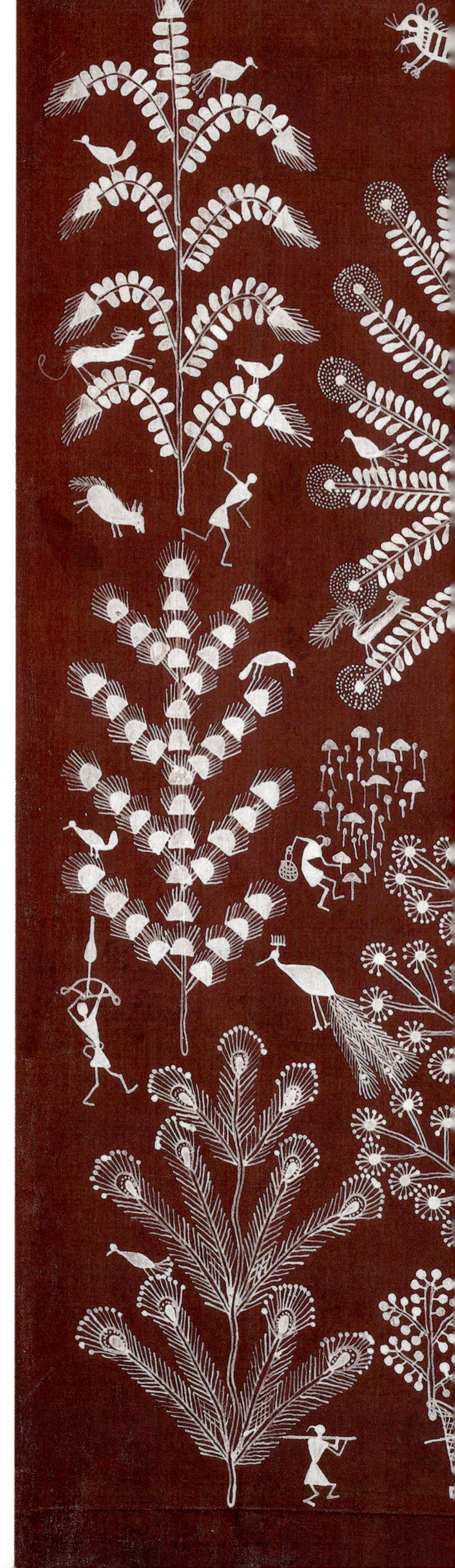

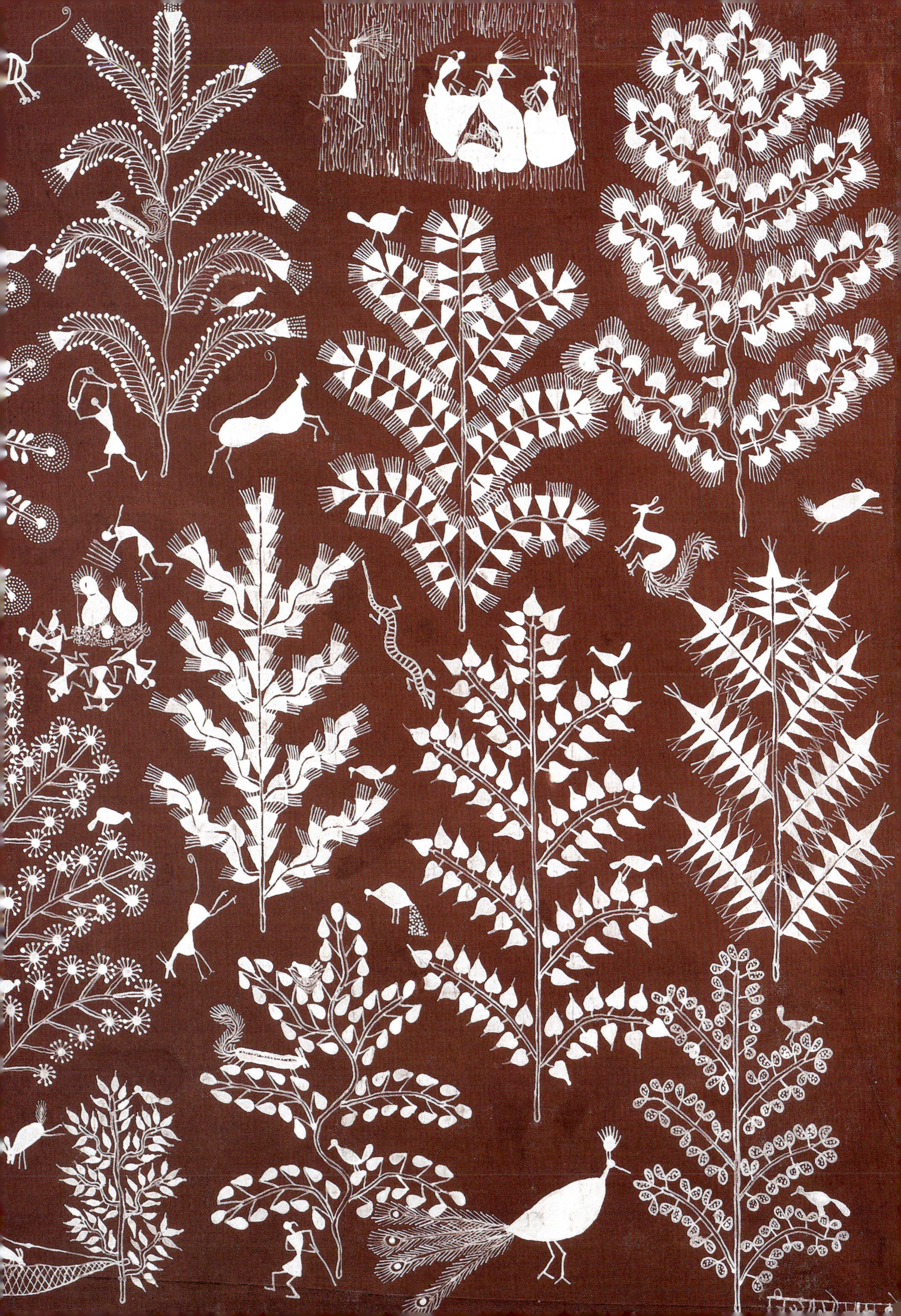

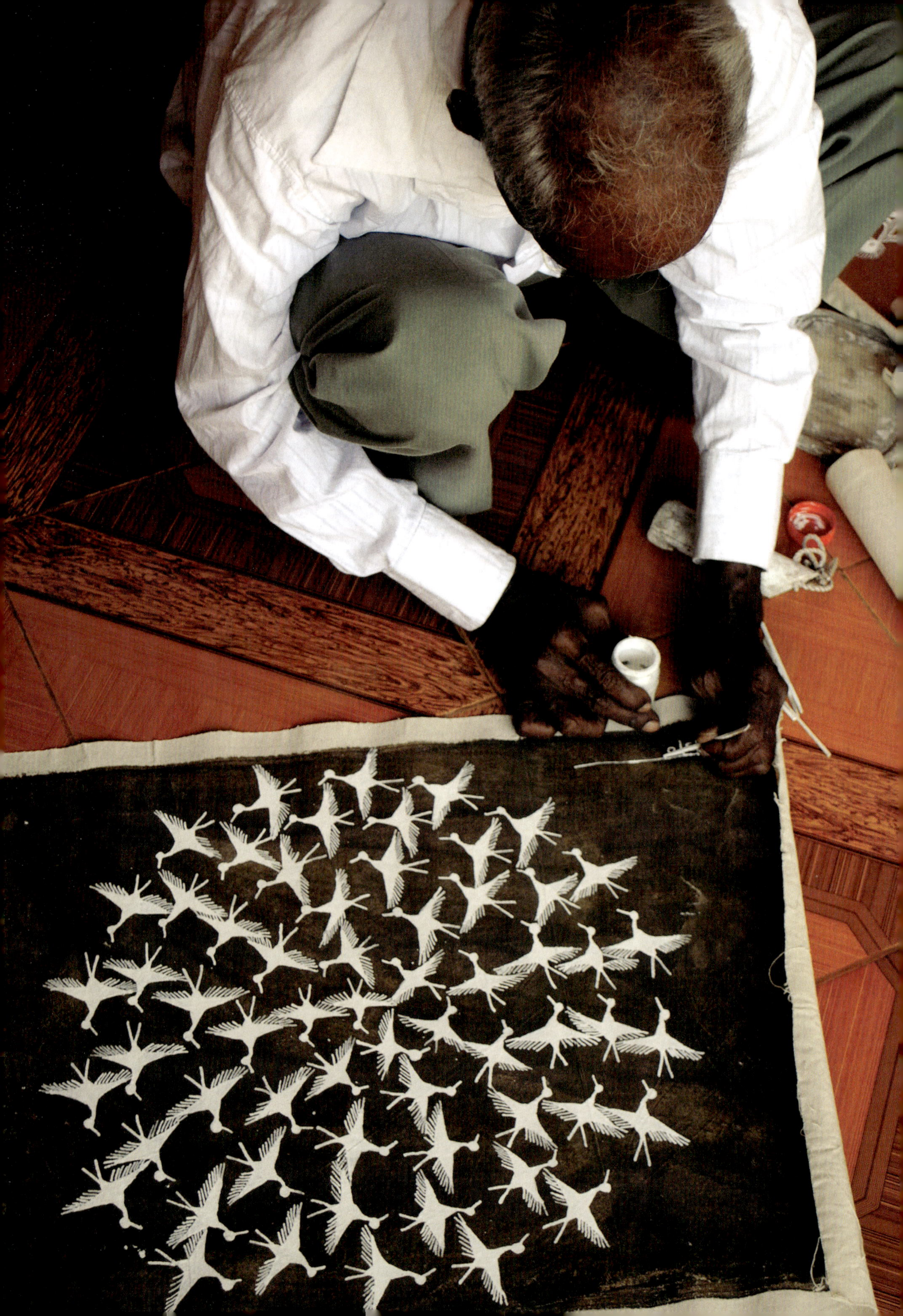

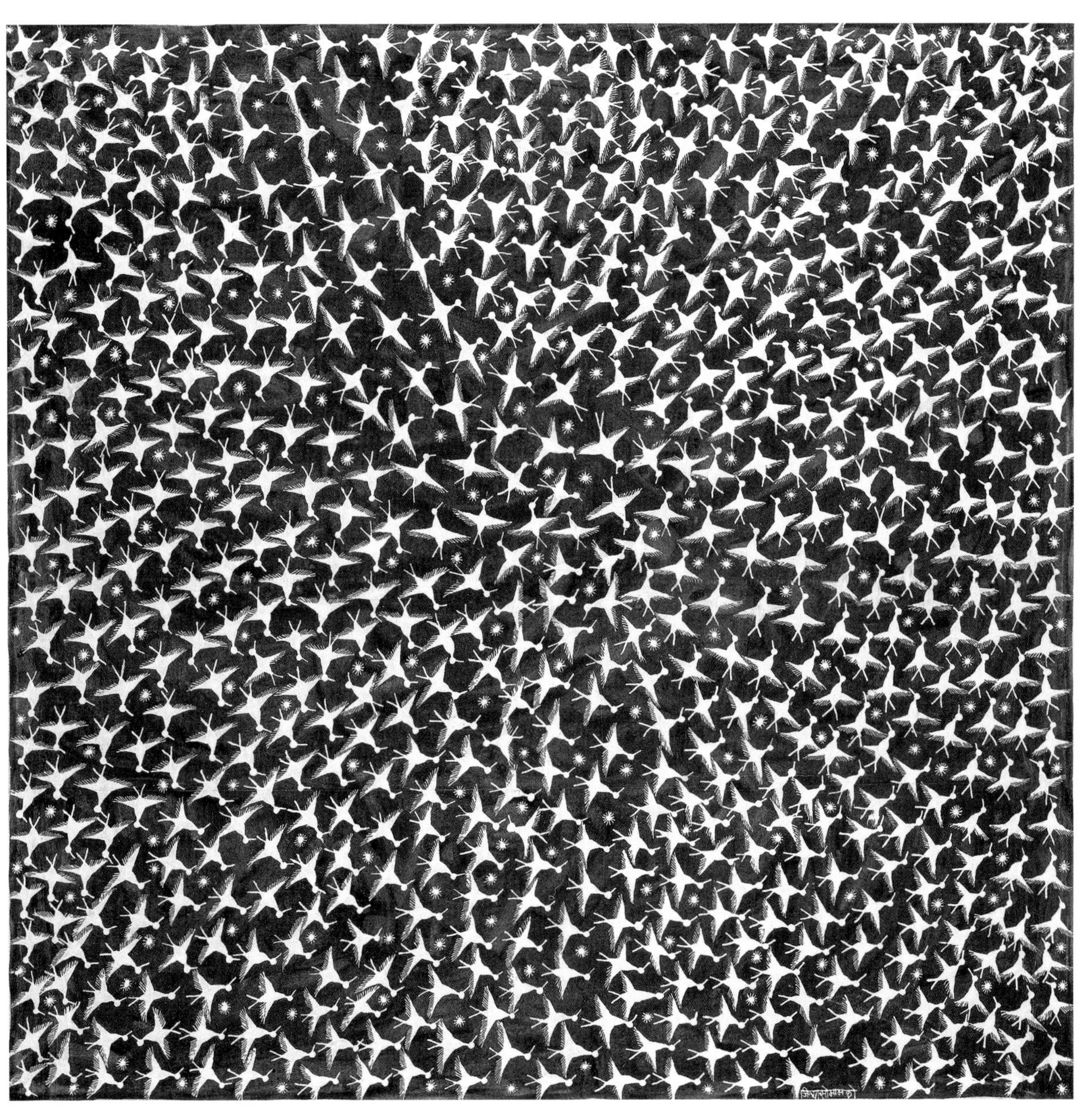

Jivya Soma Mashe, *Untitled*, 2016,
acrylic and cow dung on canvas,
141 × 136.5 cm; 55.51 × 53.74 in. (*detail on pages 220–221*)
Geneviève and Robert Combas Collection.
Photo by Christian Baraja.

Jivya Soma Mashe, Ganjad (Maharashtra, India), 2011.
Photo by Hervé Perdriolle.

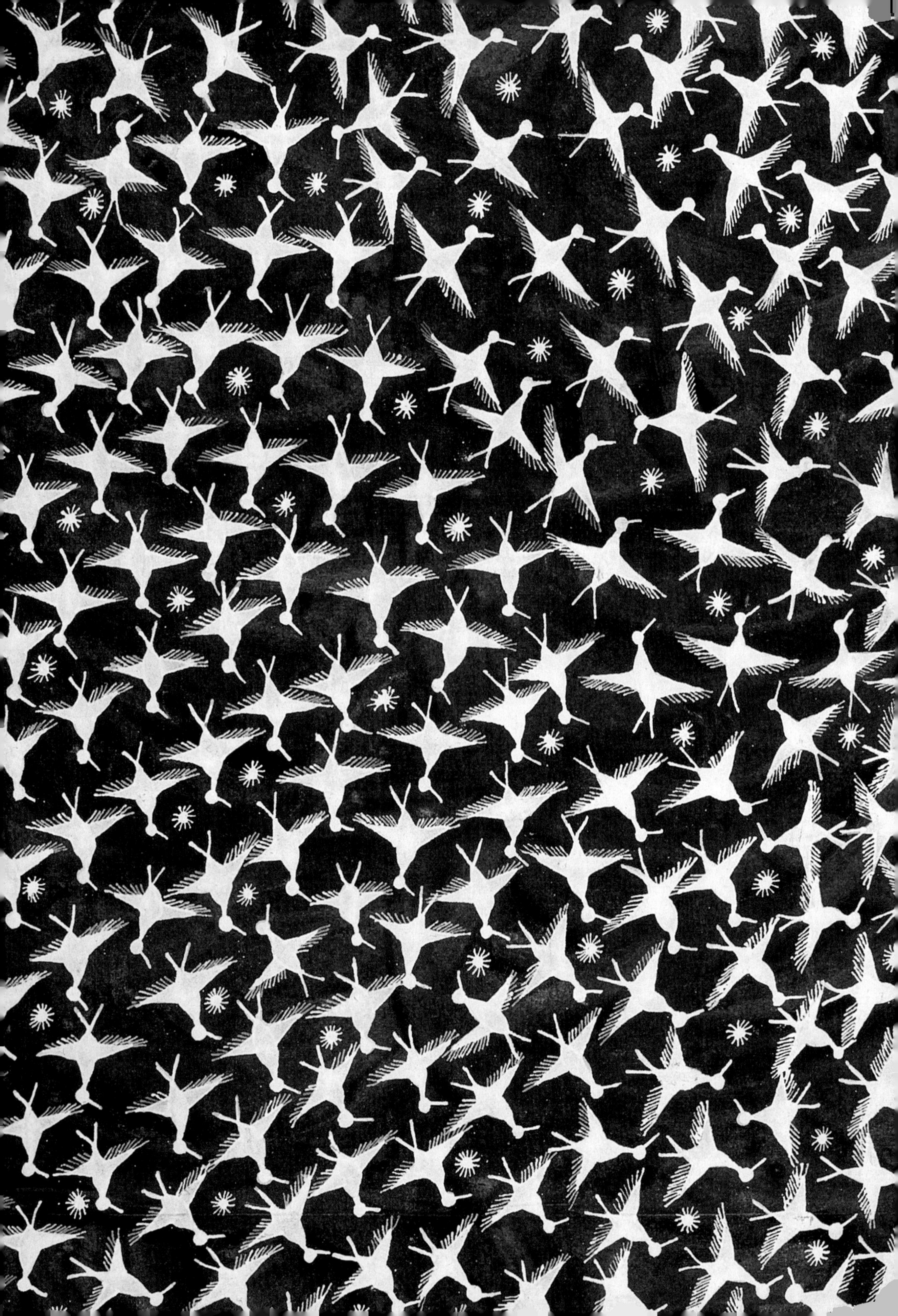

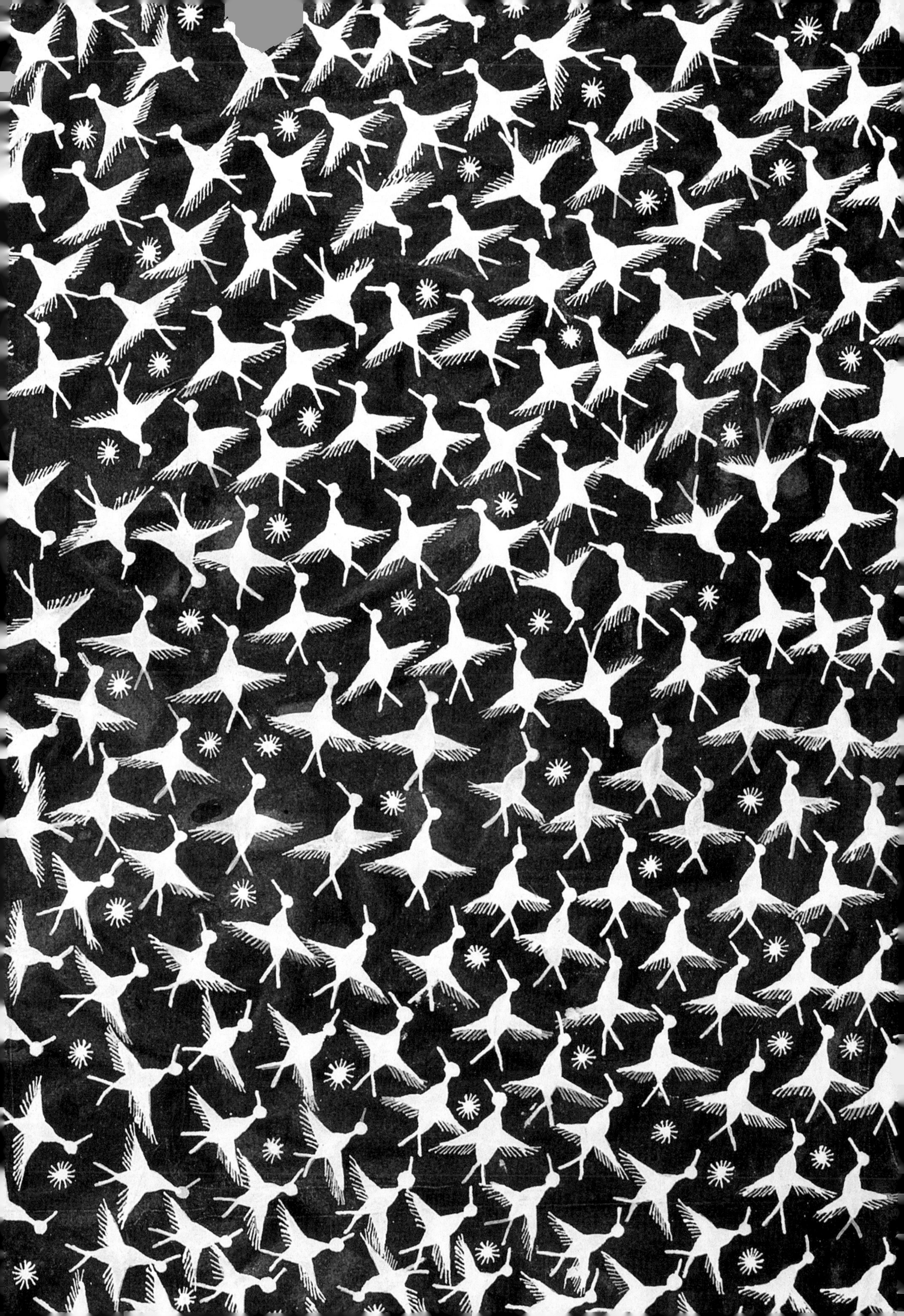

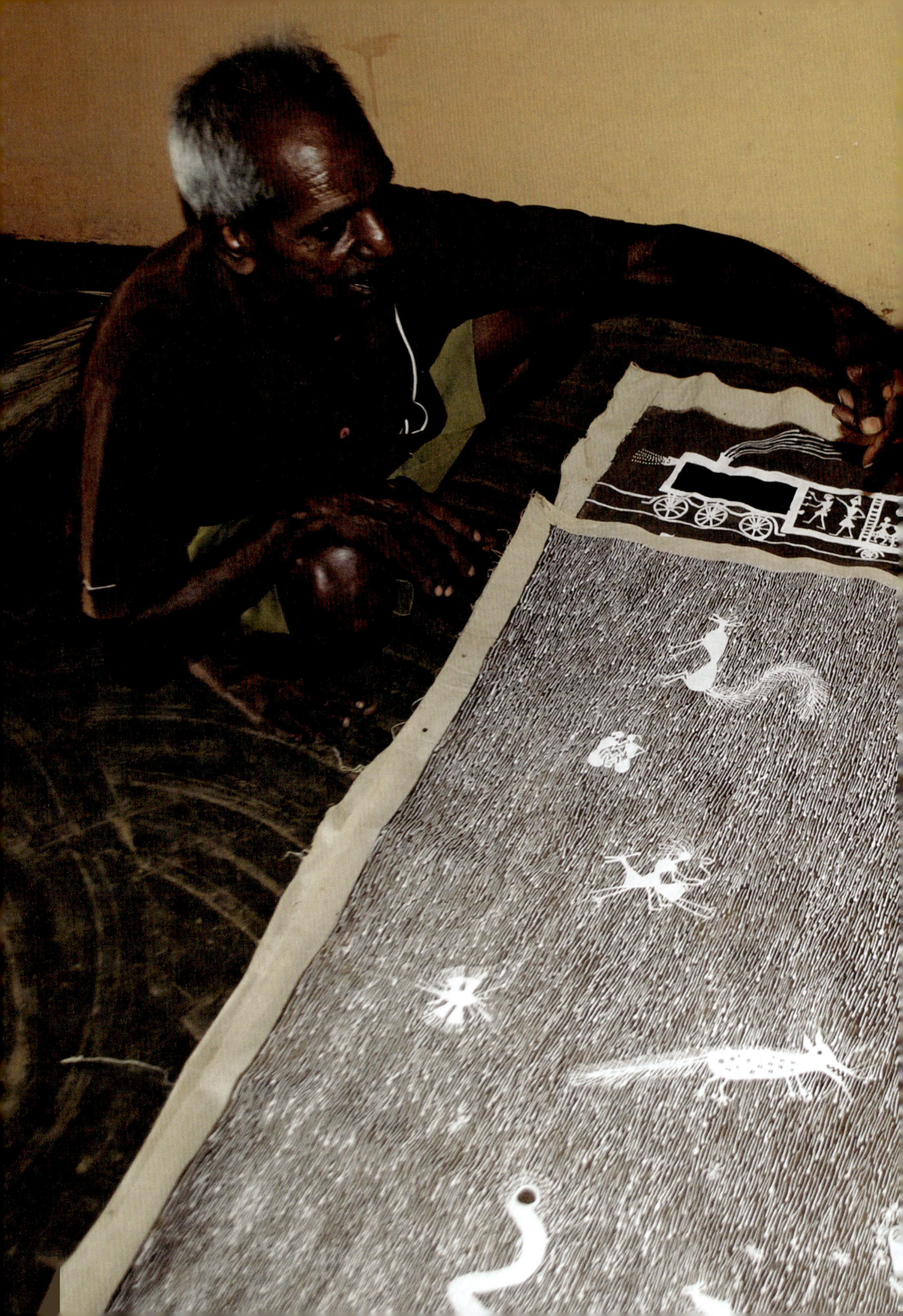

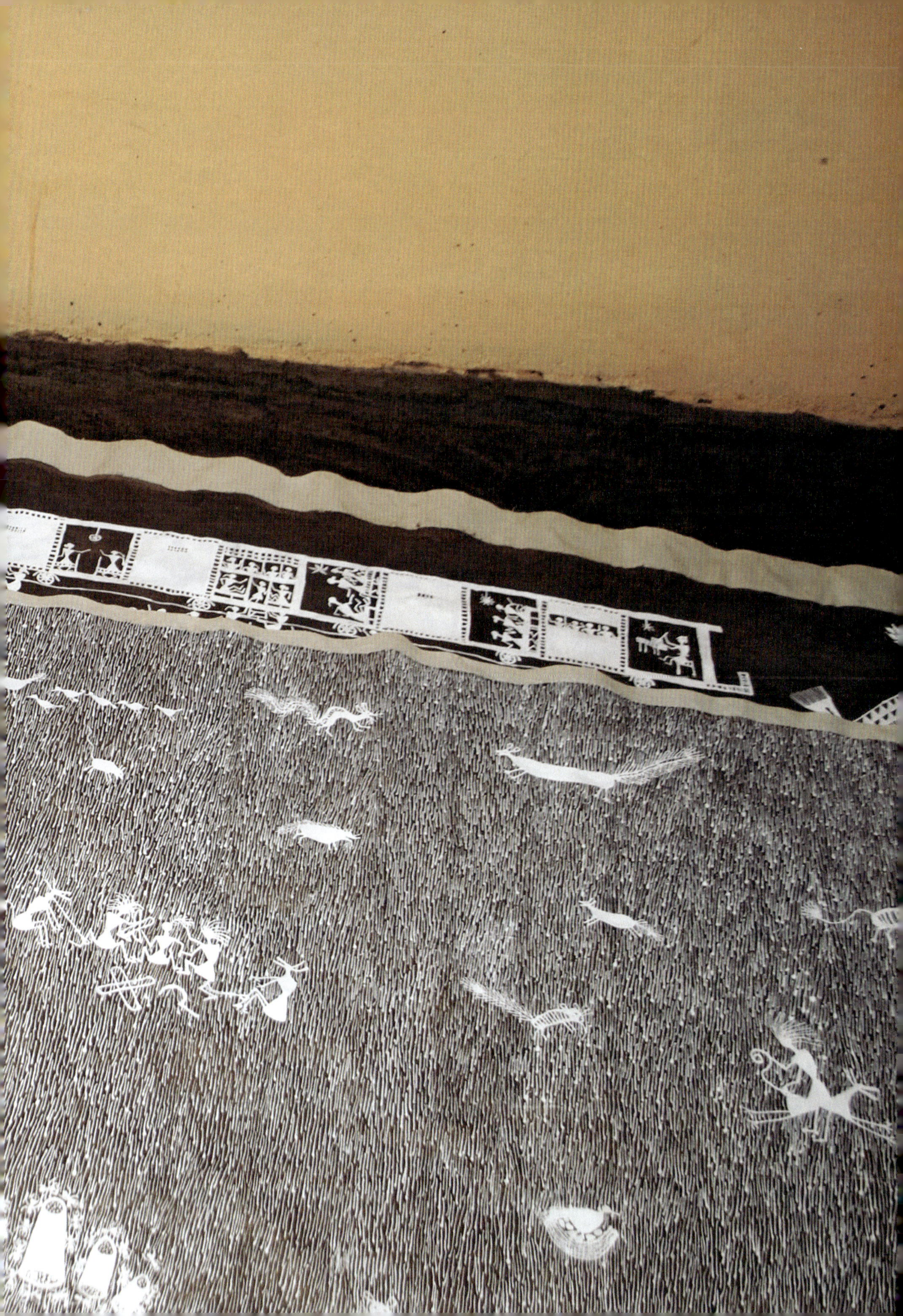

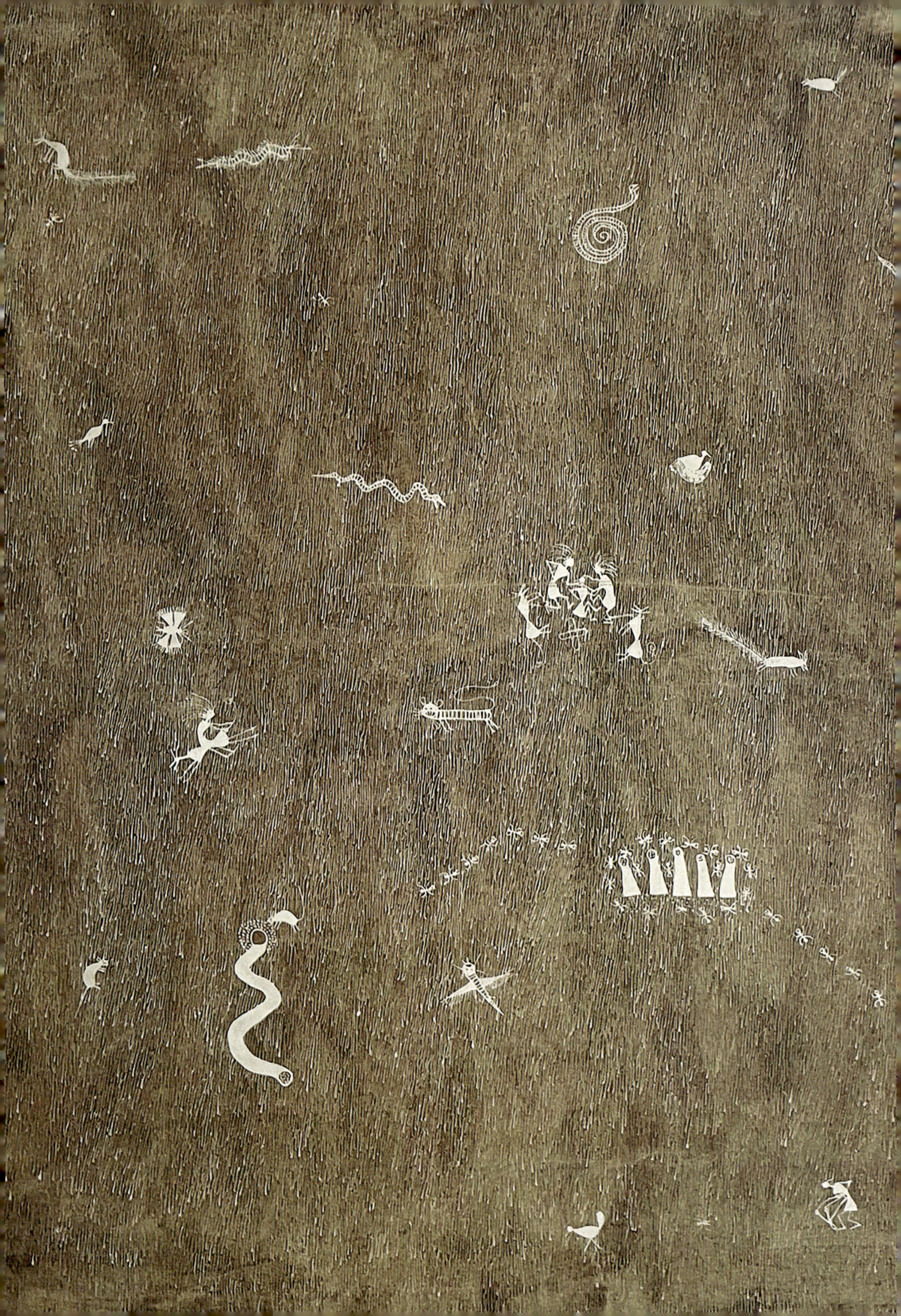

THE FARMER AND THE GHOSTS
LE FERMIER ET LES FANTÔMES

A farmer went fishing at night. Returning, he had to walk through the woods. Suddenly there was a rustle of leaves and two ghosts stood before him. 'No one walks through these woods at night', said one shadow figure. 'We are going to eat you up, you foolish man', said the other.

The man put up a brave front. 'Of course you can eat me. But there is something you have to do before my flesh is tasty and fit to eat. You have to solve this knotty problem first.' Saying this he handed them two puzzles made out of interlocked blades of grass. 'You have to take these apart without breaking the blades of grass.'

The ghosts got so busy with the puzzle that they did not notice the sky lightening. They did not realise that the night would soon be over. As day broke over the hills, the ghosts vanished and the farmer went home, safe and sound.

Un fermier était parti pêcher la nuit. Sur la route du retour, alors qu'il marche à travers bois, il entend un bruissement soudain de feuilles. Deux fantômes se dressent alors devant lui : « Personne ne se promène dans ces bois la nuit », dit l'une des ombres. « Nous allons te dévorer, pauvre idiot », dit l'autre.

Le fermier s'arme alors de courage et répond : « Bien sûr, il vous est possible de me manger. Mais avant, pour rendre ma chair savoureuse et meilleure à manger, il vous faut résoudre ce difficile casse-tête. » Et disant cela, il leur tend deux casse-têtes faits de brins d'herbe entrelacés : « Il faut les démonter sans casser les brins d'herbe. »

Si bien que les fantômes, trop occupés à démêler les casse-têtes, ne remarquèrent pas les lueurs du jour dans le ciel et ne s'avisèrent pas que la nuit touchait à sa fin. Le jour se leva sur les collines, les fantômes disparurent et le fermier rentra chez lui sain et sauf.

Pages 222–223
Soma Mashe explaining the story behind the painting
Jungle Spirit, 2011,
acrylic and cow dung on canvas,
140 × 170 cm; 55.11 × 66.92 in.
Fondation Cartier pour l'art contemporain Collection.
Photo by Hervé Perdriolle, Ganjad (Maharashtra, India), 2011.

Jivya Soma Mashe, *The Farmer and the Ghosts*, 2006,
acrylic and cow dung on canvas,
135 × 142 cm; 53.14 × 55.90 in.
Diane and Jacques-Antoine de Geffrier Collection.

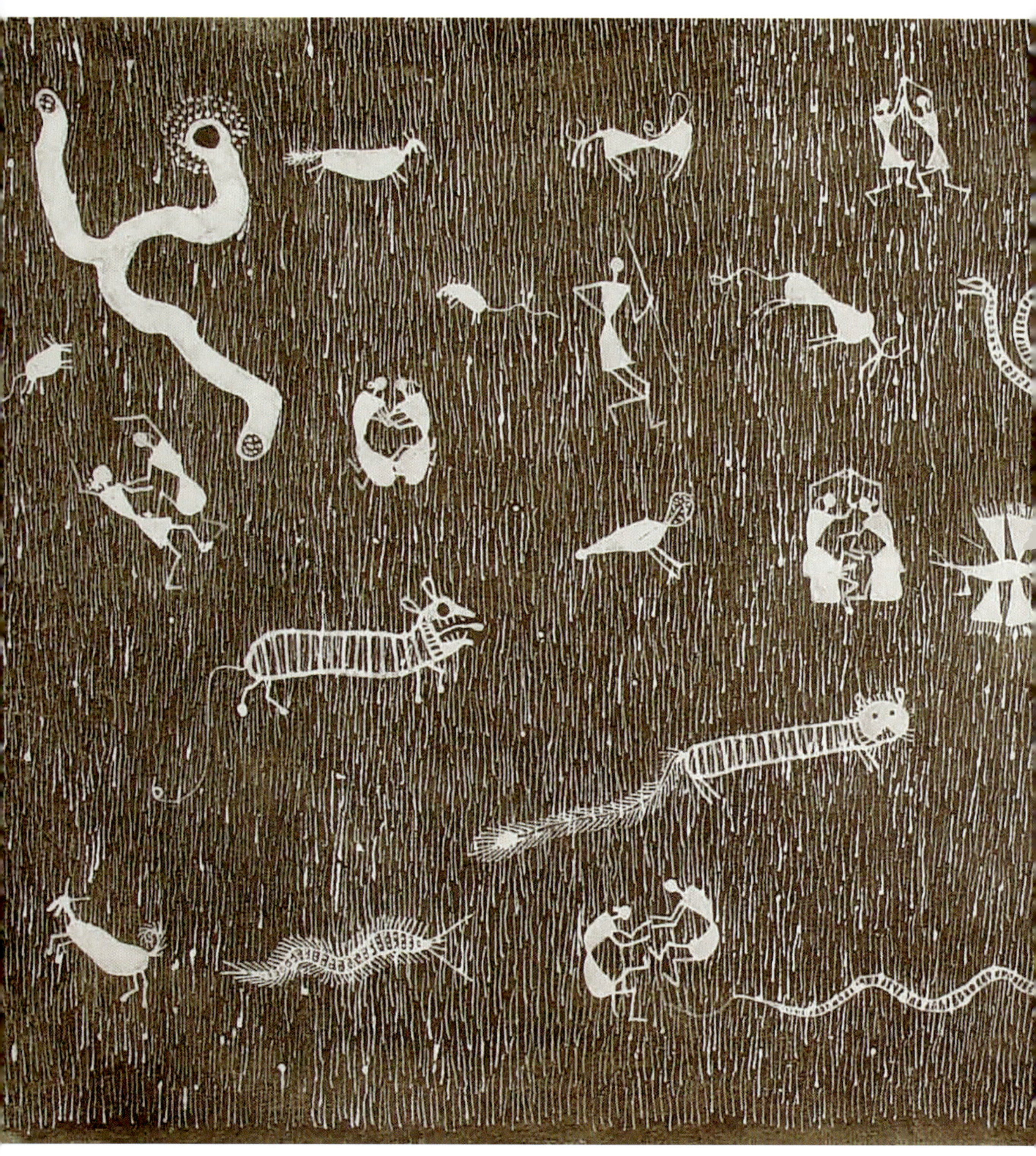

Jivya Soma Mashe, *Untitled*, circa 1990,
acrylic and cow dung on canvas,
46 × 91 cm; 18.11 × 35.82 in.
Zarrina and Antony Kurtz Collection.

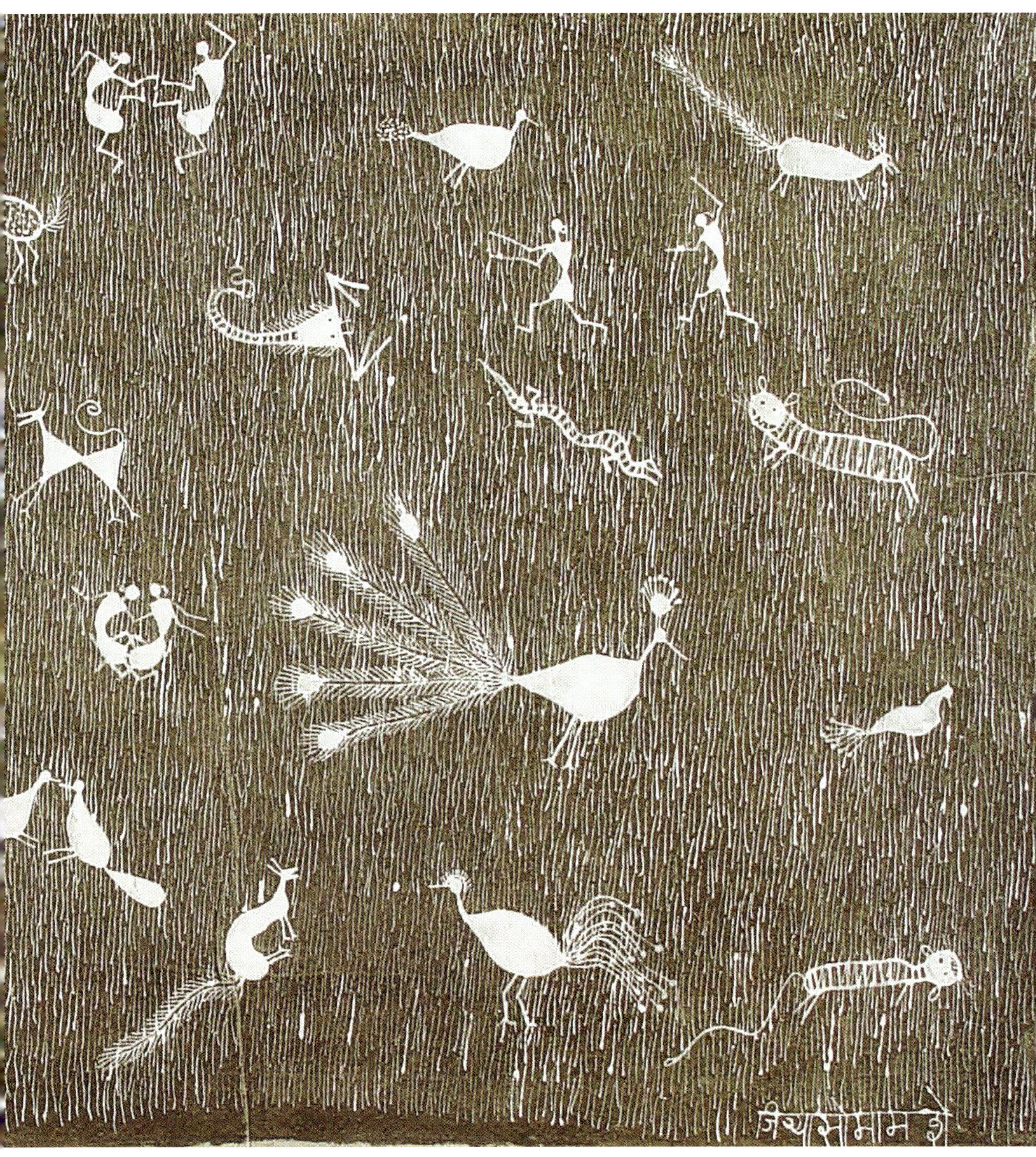

Pages 228–229
Jivya Soma Mashe, *Untitled*, 2003,
acrylic and cow dung on canvas,
138 × 178 cm; 54.33 × 70.07 in. (*detail on pages* 230–231)
Courtesy Galerie Jeanne Bucher Jaeger, Paris-Lisbon.
Photo by Jean-Louis Losi.

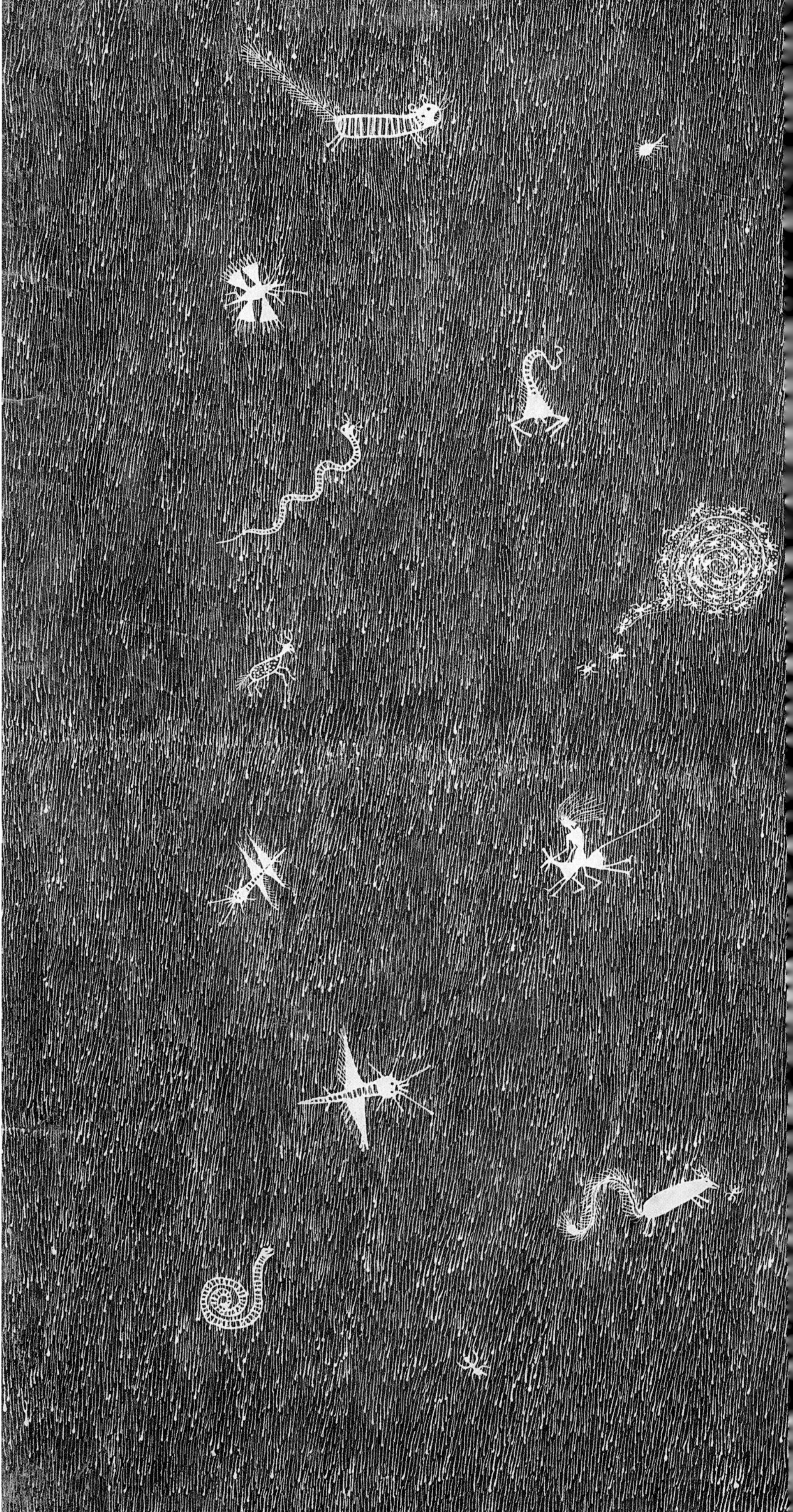

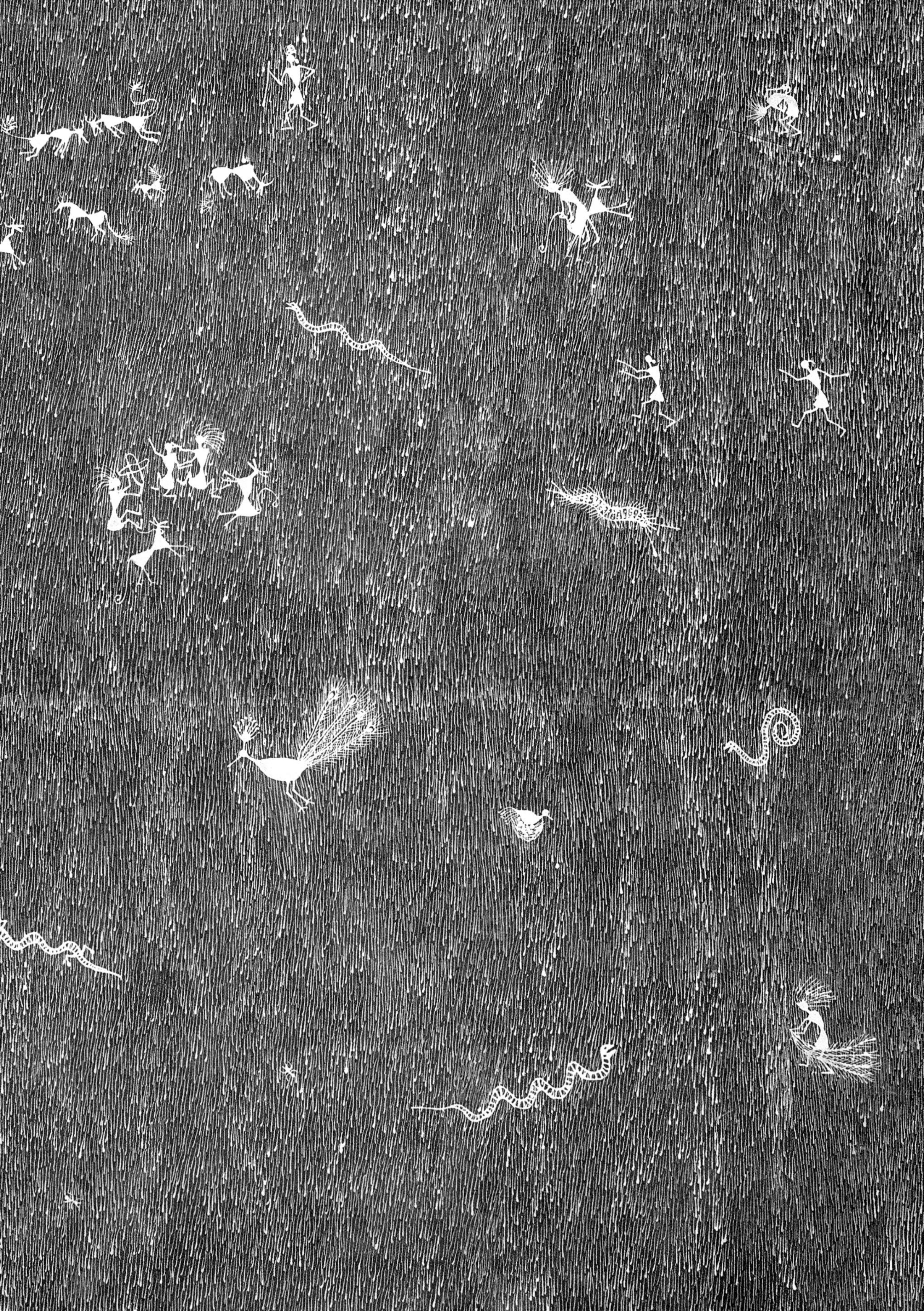

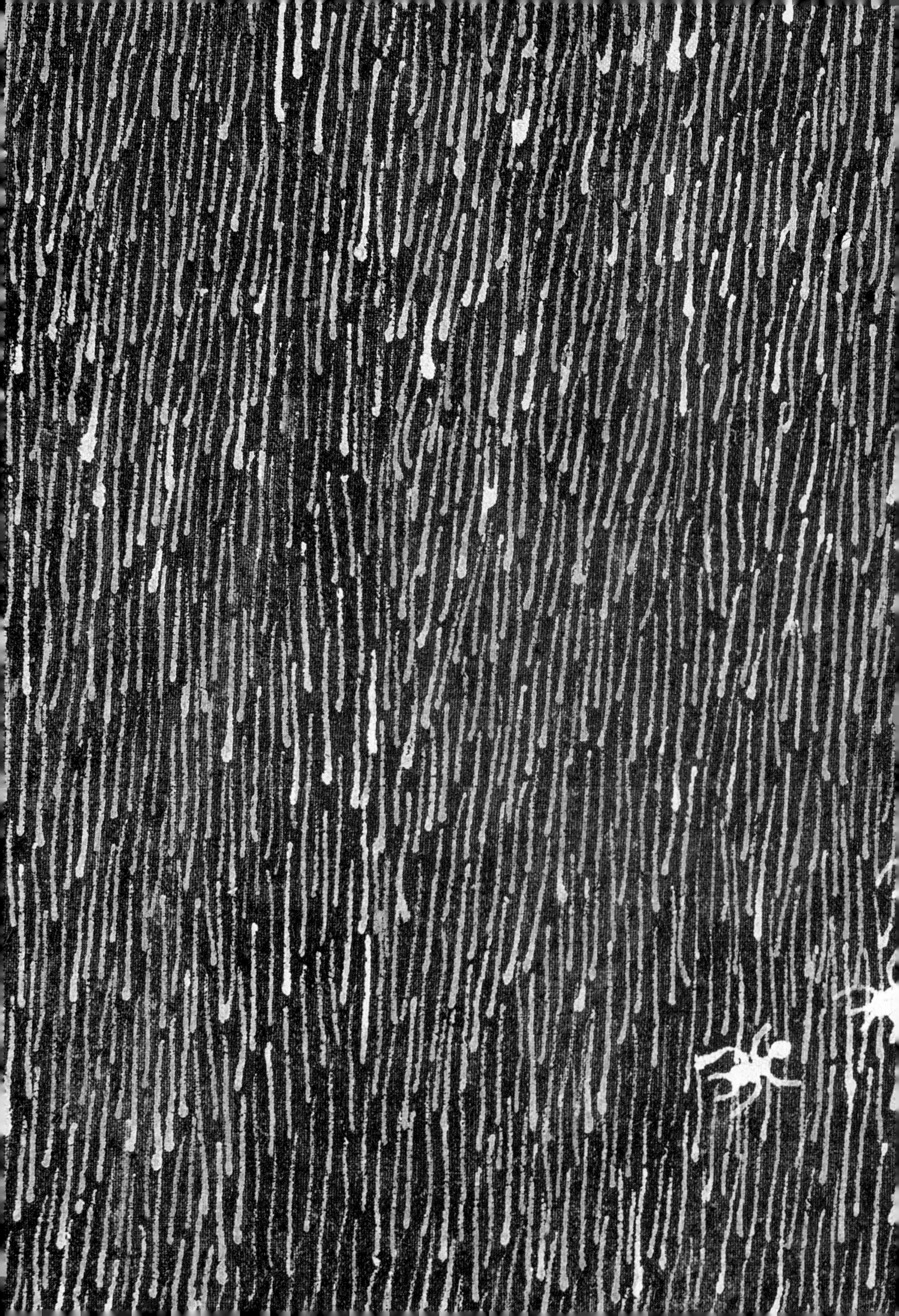

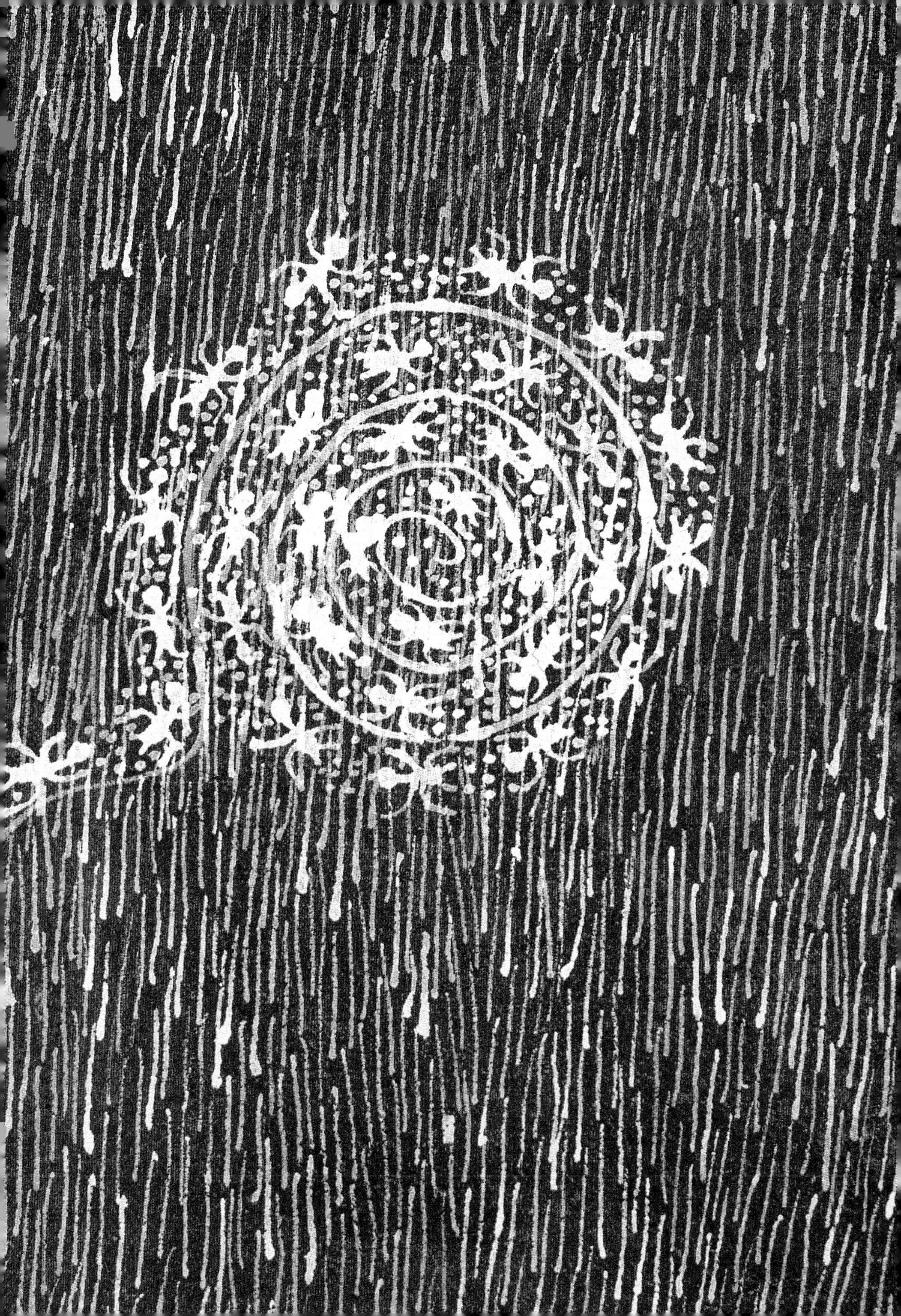

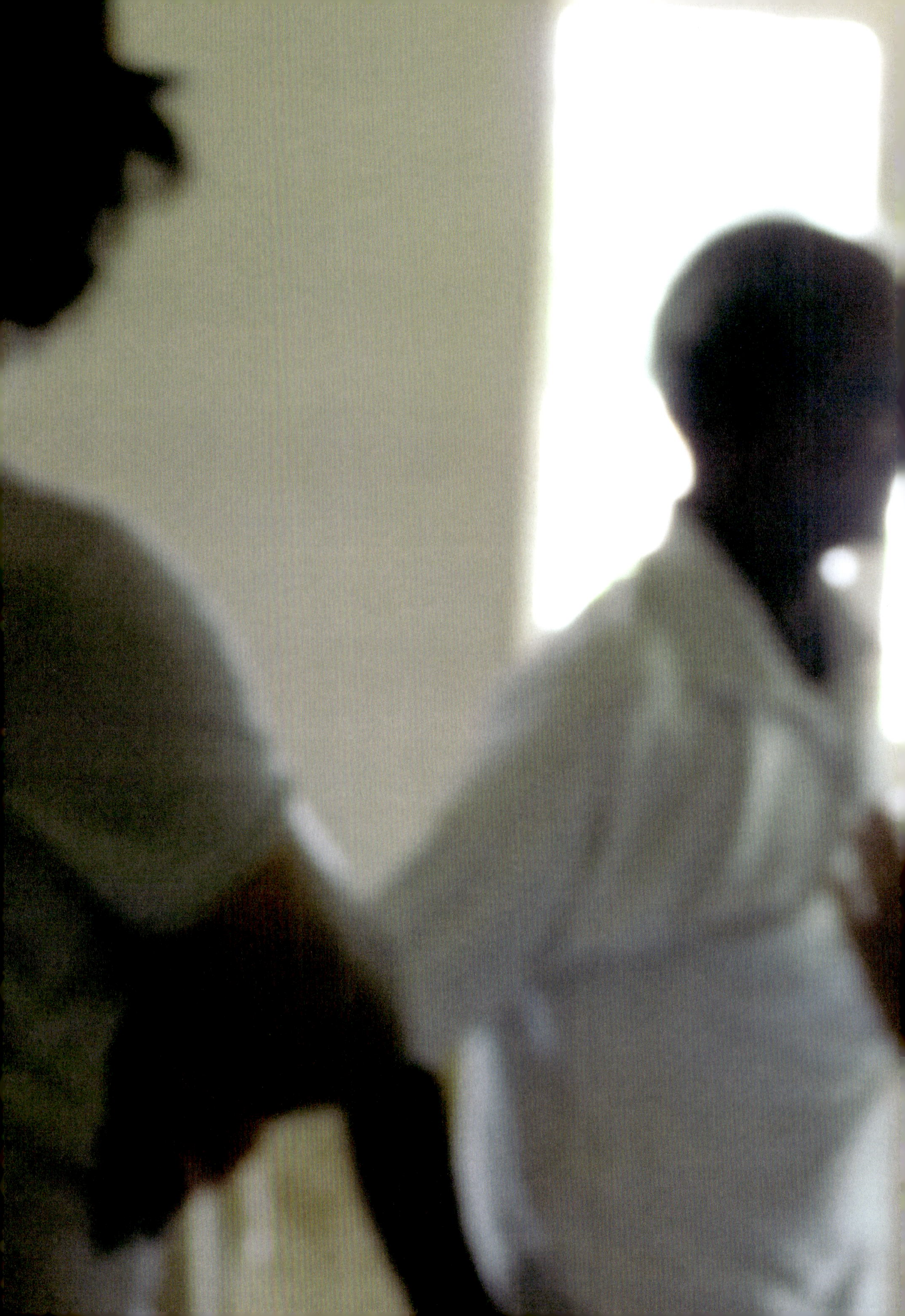

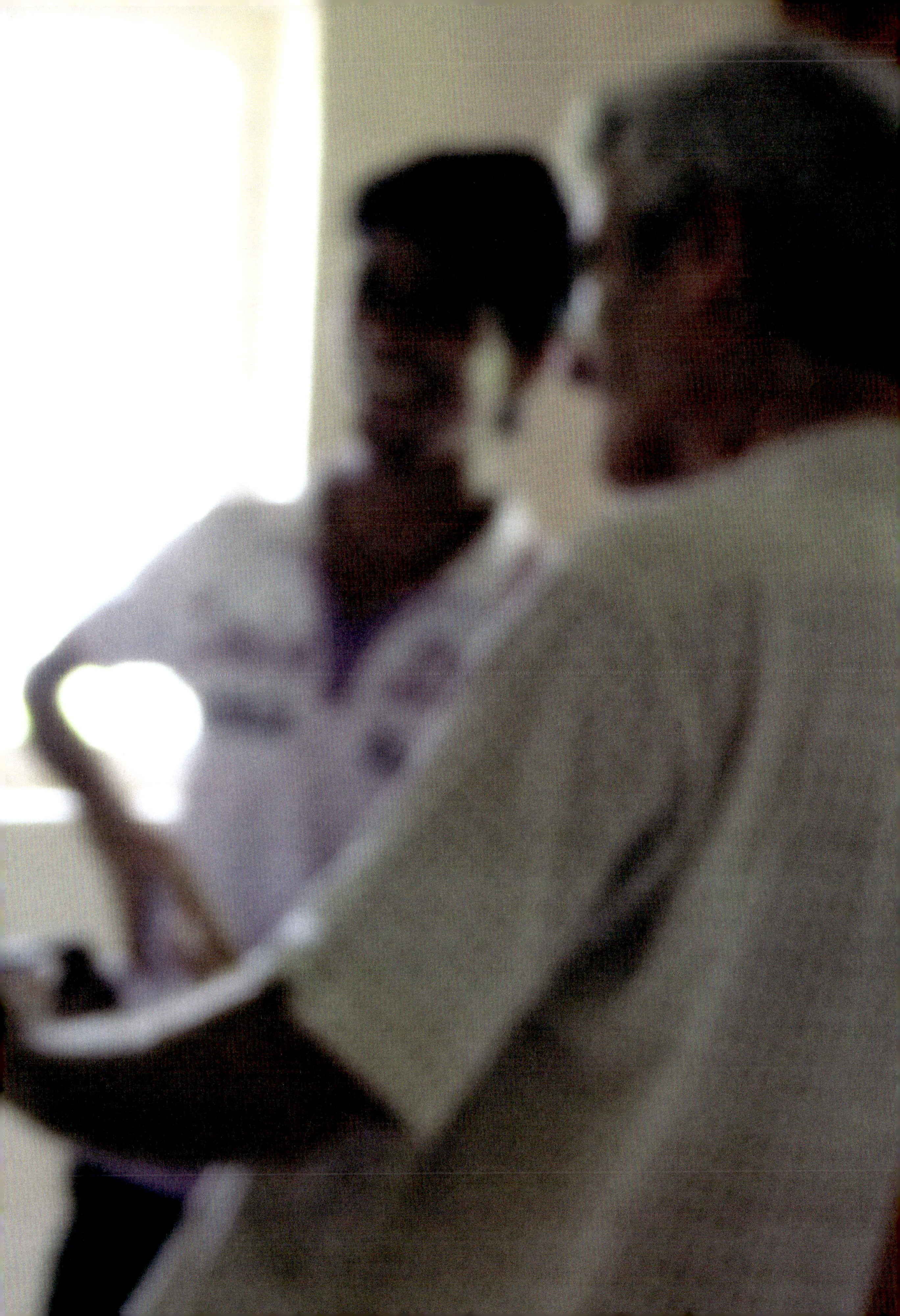

This large painting unites several stories. In it, Vira, the statue of the ancestors and the standing man is shown in the simple silhouette of a head and body near a large tree ringed by snakes. The painting symbolises the powers of fertility and death. Among the Warlis, marriage and burial rituals are not kept at a distance: death does not represent an end but the start of a new life. Thus, death is celebrated in the same way as a wedding, as a union with another state. On the left side of this painting, at the top of the hill, we can see a couple lying in an embrace.

Cette peinture de grand format réunit plusieurs histoires. On peut notamment y apercevoir, près d'un grand arbre entouré de serpents, Vira, la statue des ancêtres, de l'homme debout, simple silhouette évoquant un corps et une tête. Elle symbolise les pouvoirs de la fertilité et de la mort. Chez les Warlis, les rituels propres aux cérémonies nuptiales et funéraires ne sont pas éloignés. Pour eux, la mort n'est pas une fin en soi mais le début d'une autre vie. On célèbre alors la mort comme un mariage, comme l'union avec un autre état. Dans la partie gauche de cette peinture et en haut de la colline on distingue un couple allongé, enlacé.

Pages 232–233
Jivya Soma Mashe, Kishor Mashe, and Hervé Perdriolle,
Ganjad (Maharashtra, India).
Photo by T. Venkanna, 2012.

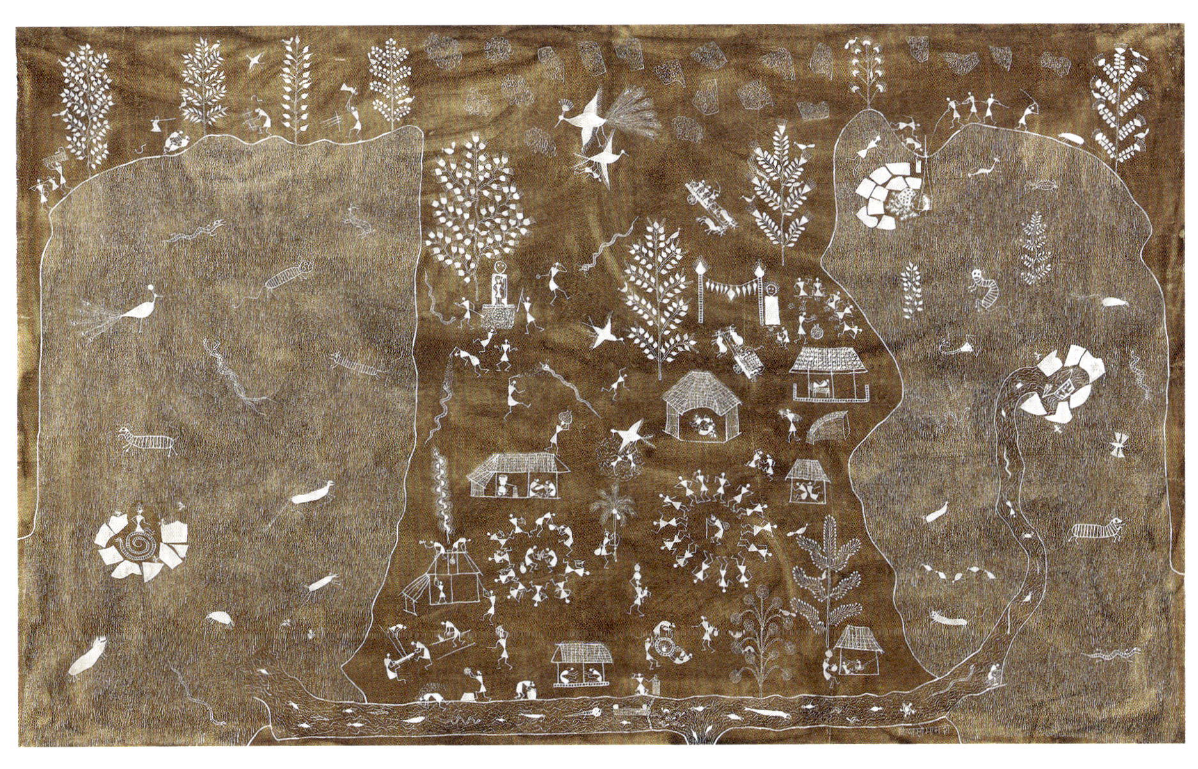

Jivya Soma Mashe, *Untitled*, 1998,
acrylic and cow dung on canvas,
138 × 230 cm; 54.33 × 90.55 in. (*detail on pages* 236–237)
Richard Lepeu Collection.
Photo by Christian Baraja.

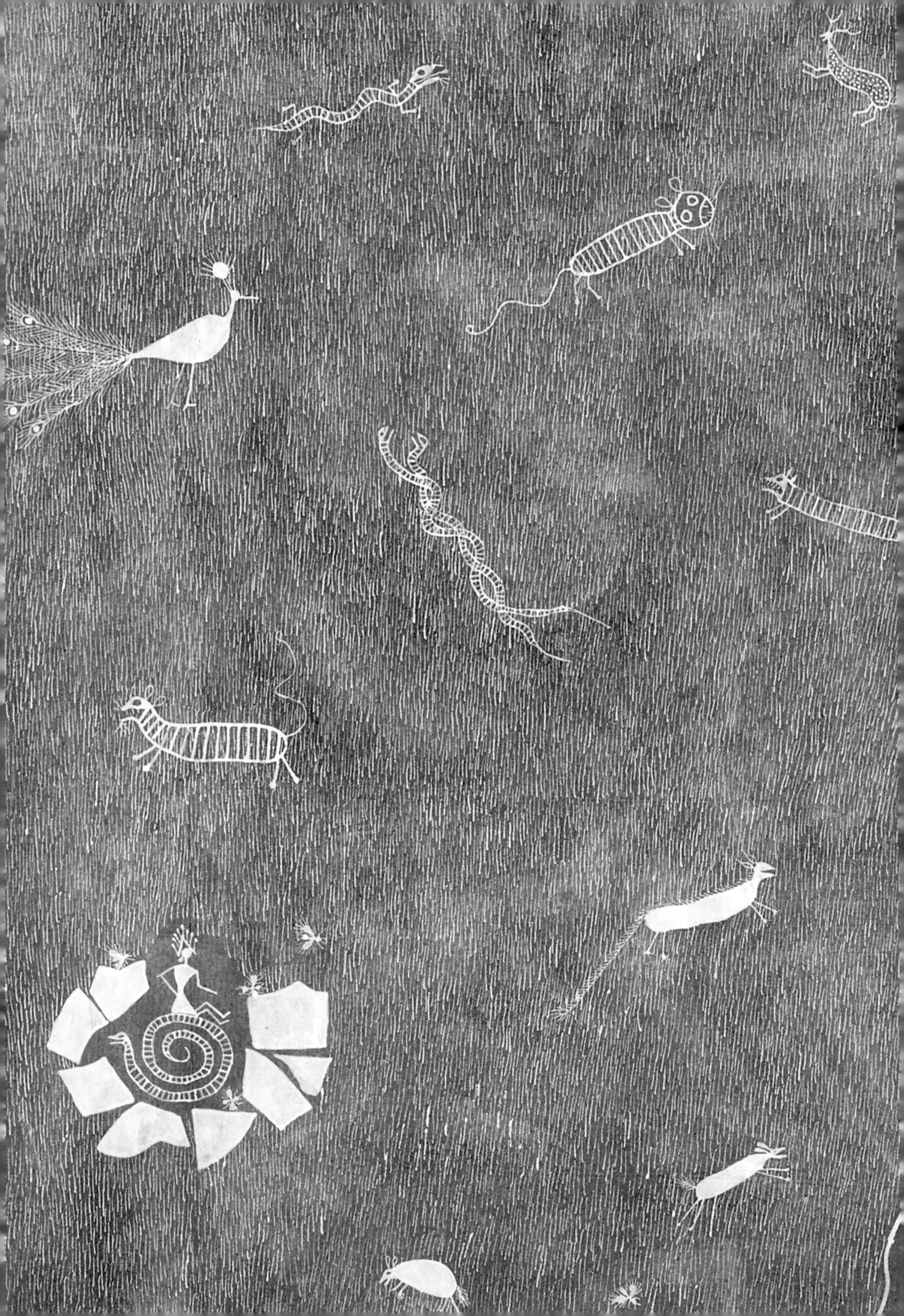

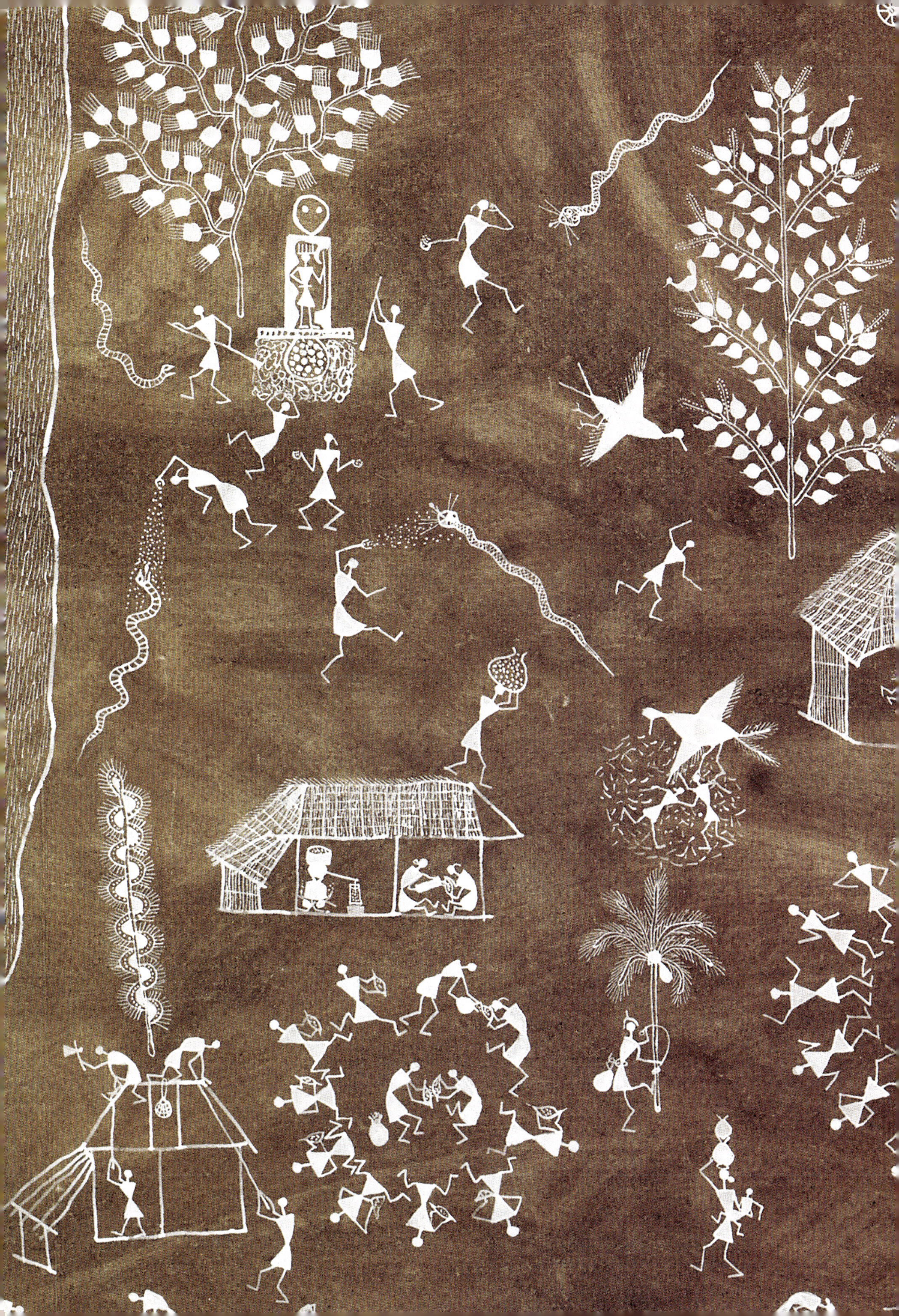

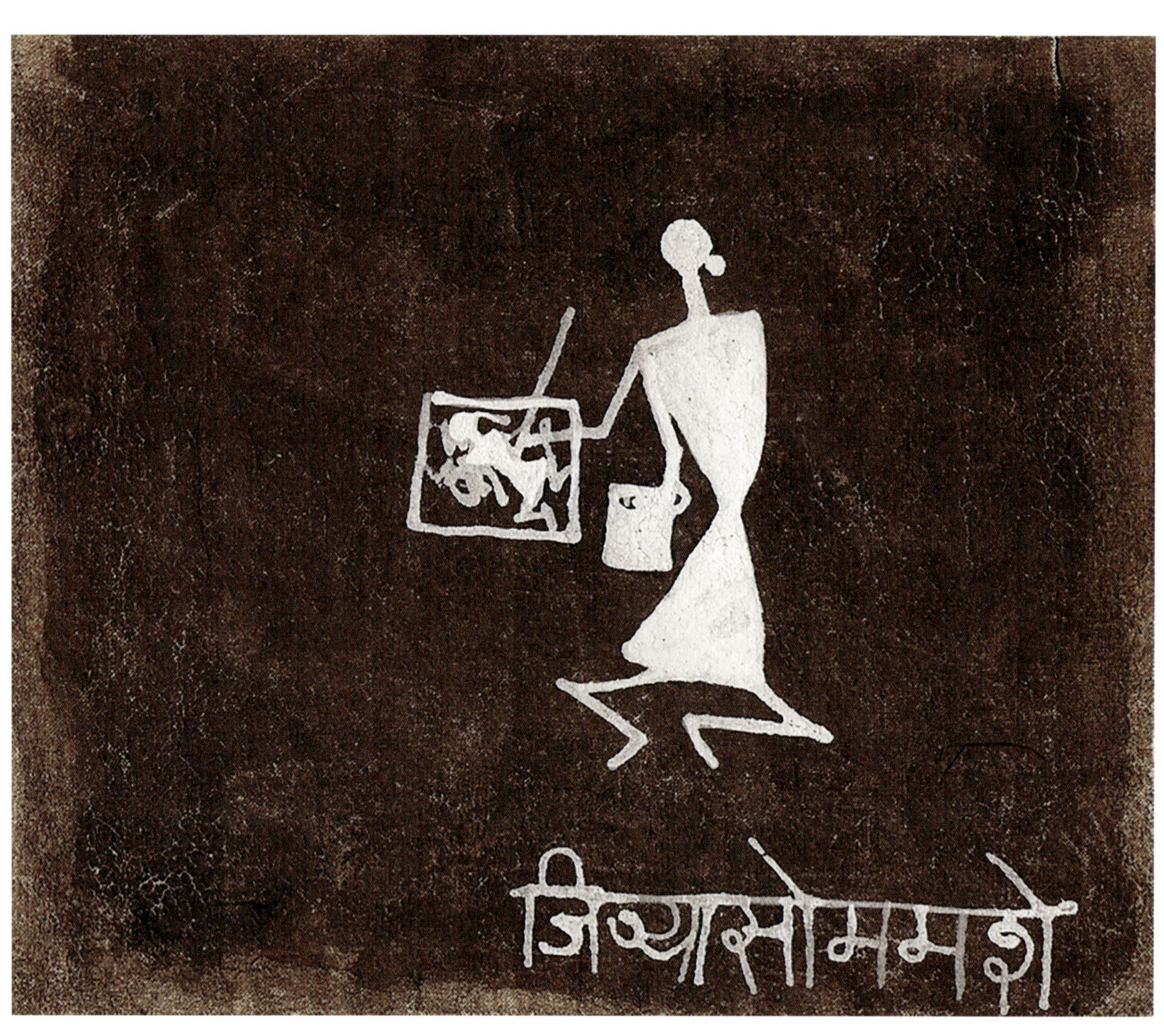

Jivya Soma Mashe, *Warli woman painter at work*, 2003,
acrylic and cow dung on canvas,
20 × 24 cm; 7.87 × 9.44 in.

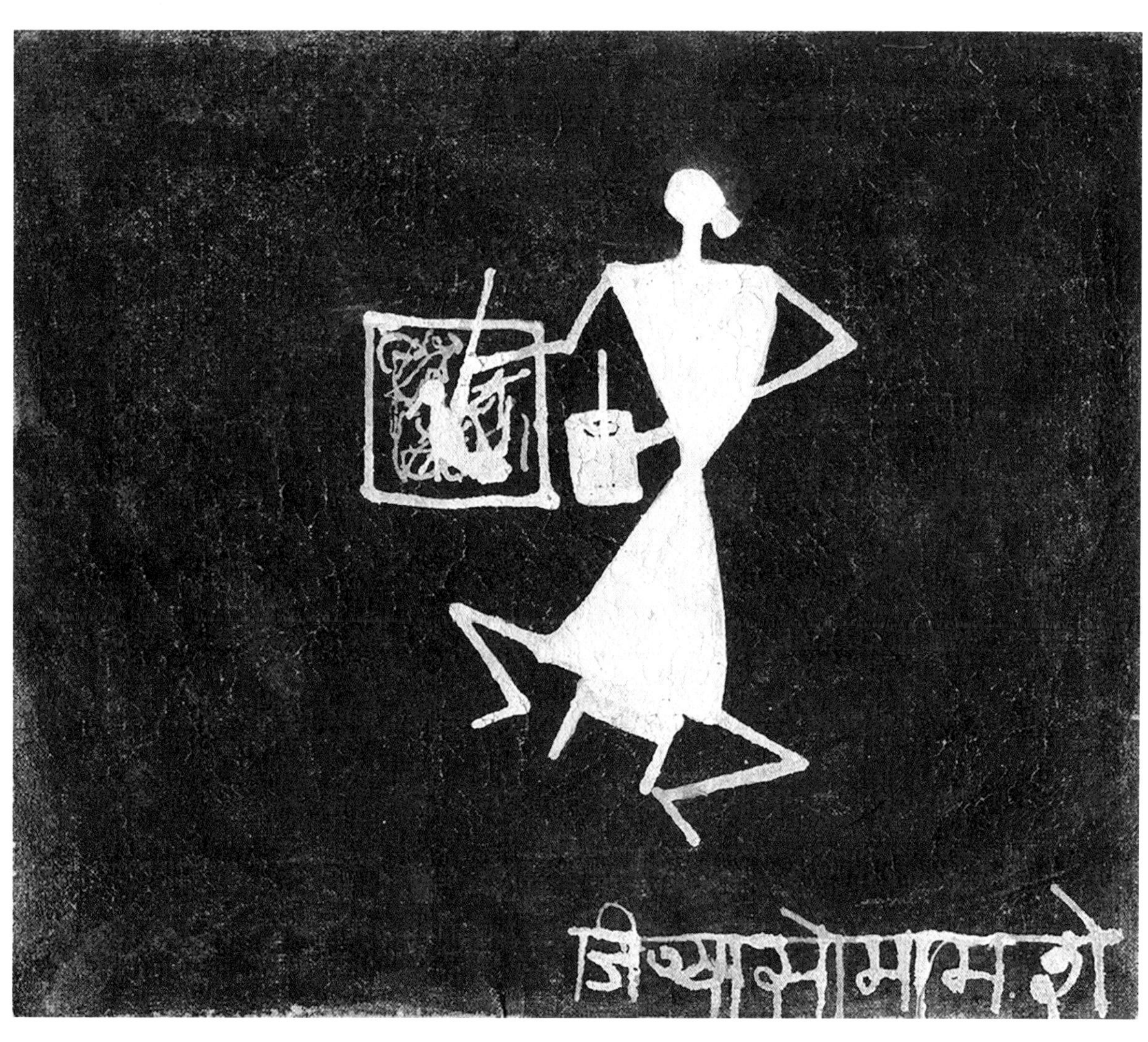

Jivya Soma Mashe, *Warli woman painter at work*, 2003,
acrylic and cow dung on canvas,
20 × 24 cm; 7.87 × 9.44 in.

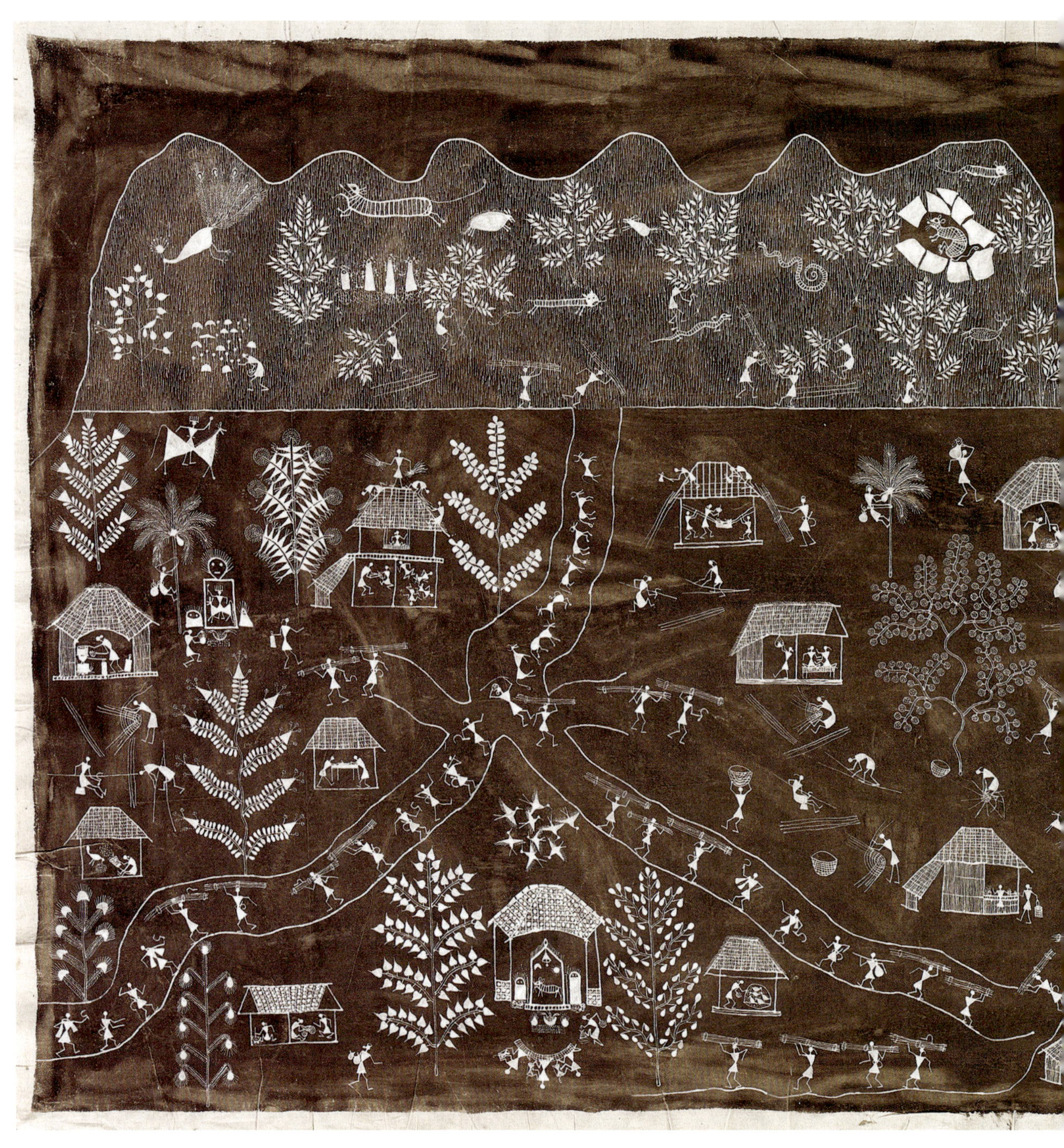

Jivya Soma Mashe, *Warli Life and Death*, 1999,
acrylic and cow dung on canvas,
137 × 282 cm; 53.93 × 111.02 in. *(details on pages 242, 243, 245)*
Alain-Dominique Perrin Collection.
Photo by Christian Baraja.

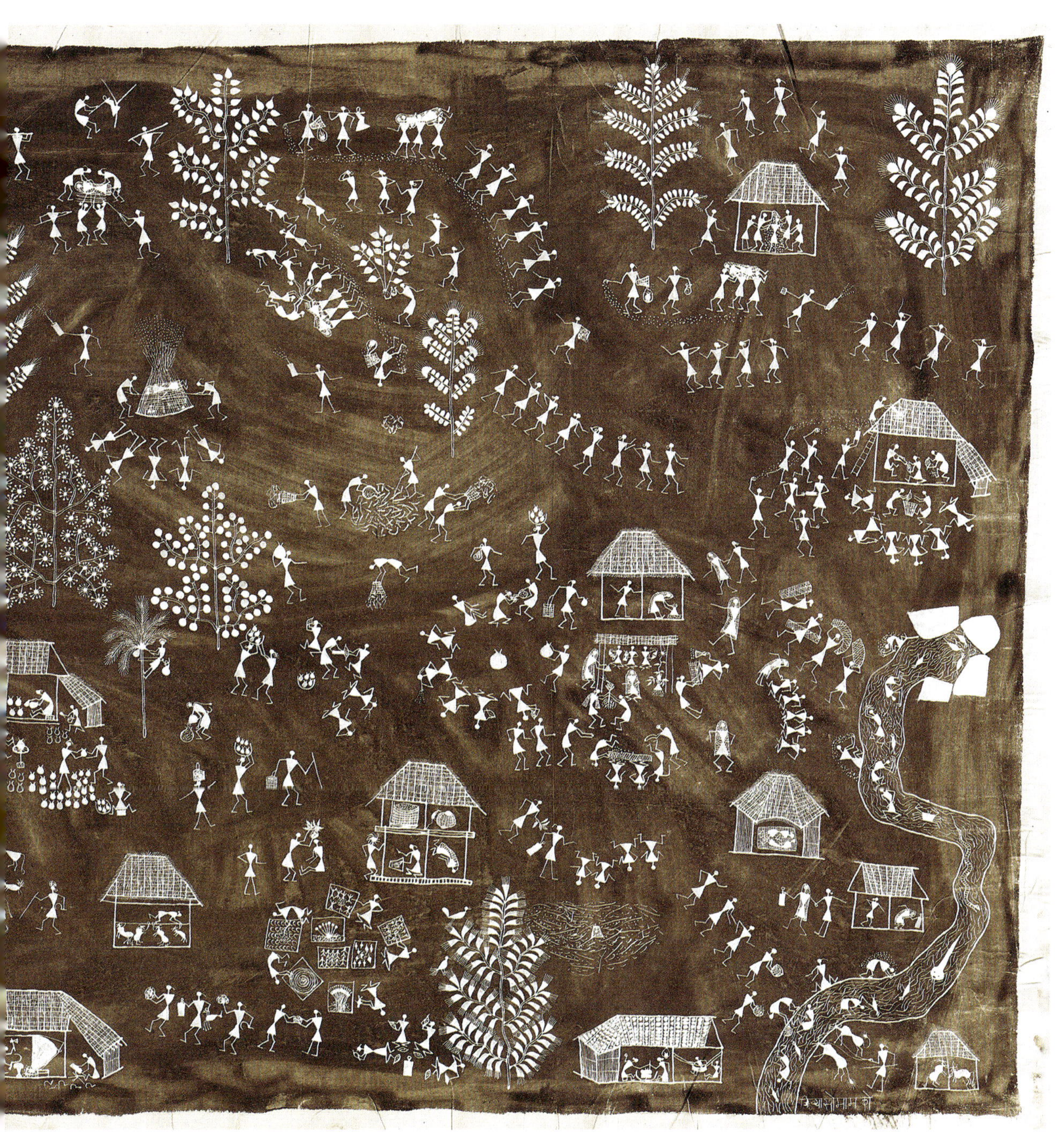

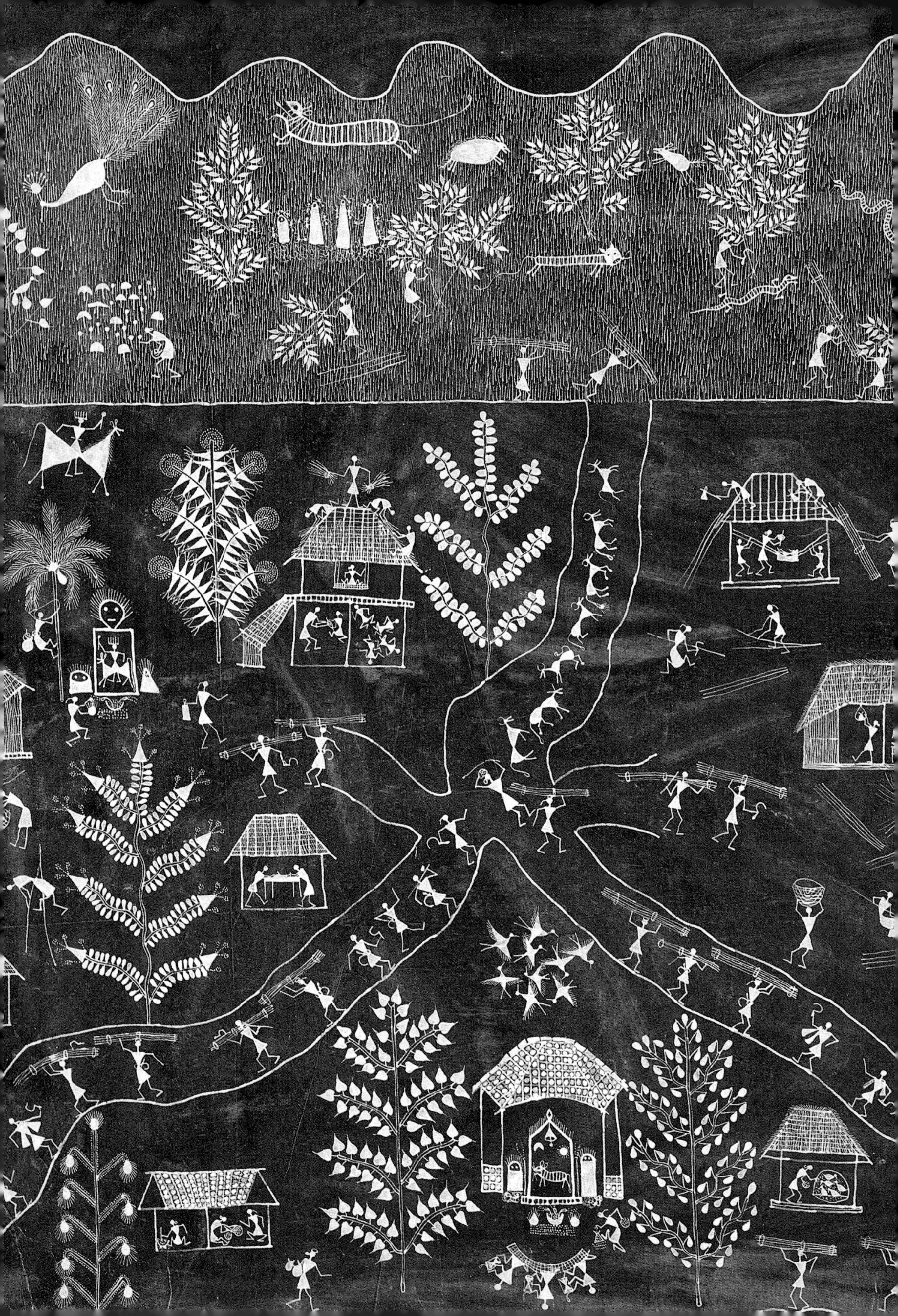

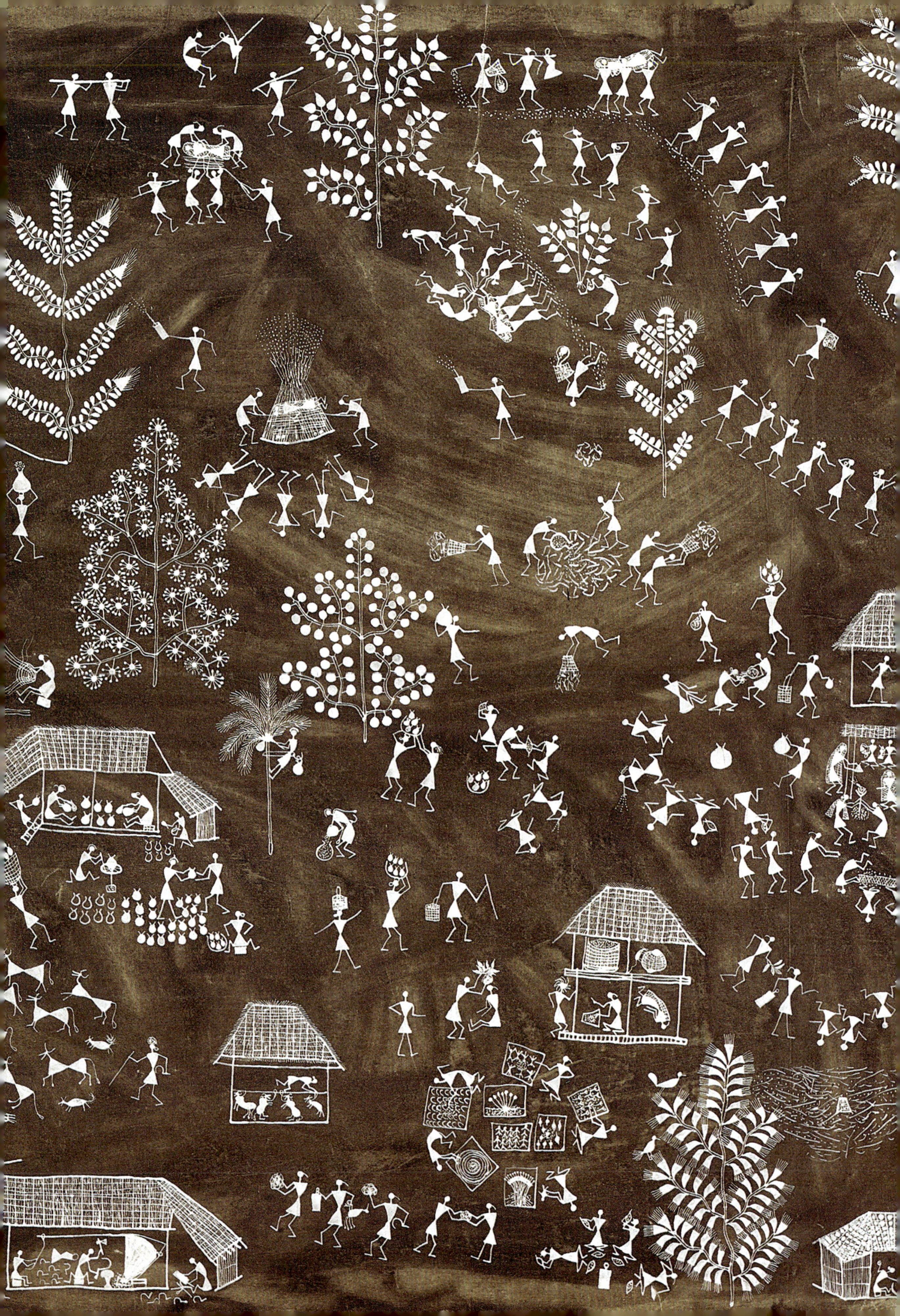

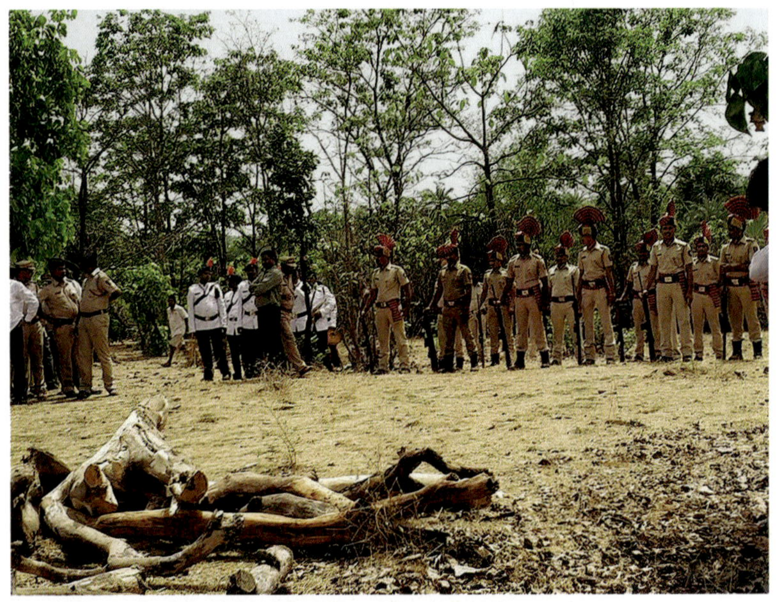

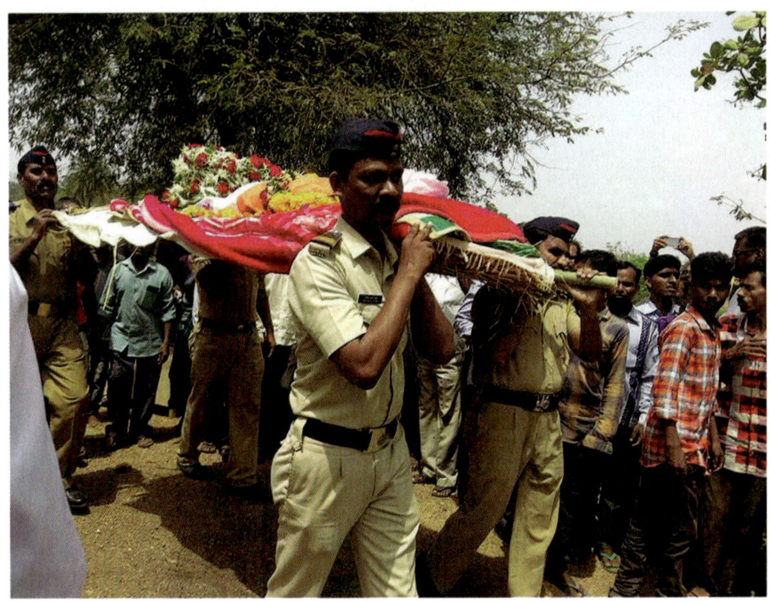

Funeral of Jivya Soma Mashe in Ganjad, 2018. During his life, the Indian government awarded Jivya Soma Mashe the highest distinctions for his contributions to the culture of his community and country. For this reason, his funeral was treated as an official ceremony and held in the presence of regional and national authorities.

Funérailles de Jivya Soma Mashe à Ganjad, 2018. Jivya Soma Mashe a reçu tout au long de sa vie les plus hautes récompenses du gouvernement indien pour sa contribution à la valorisation de la culture de sa communauté et de son pays. À ce titre, une cérémonie officielle est organisée en présence des autorités régionales et nationales.

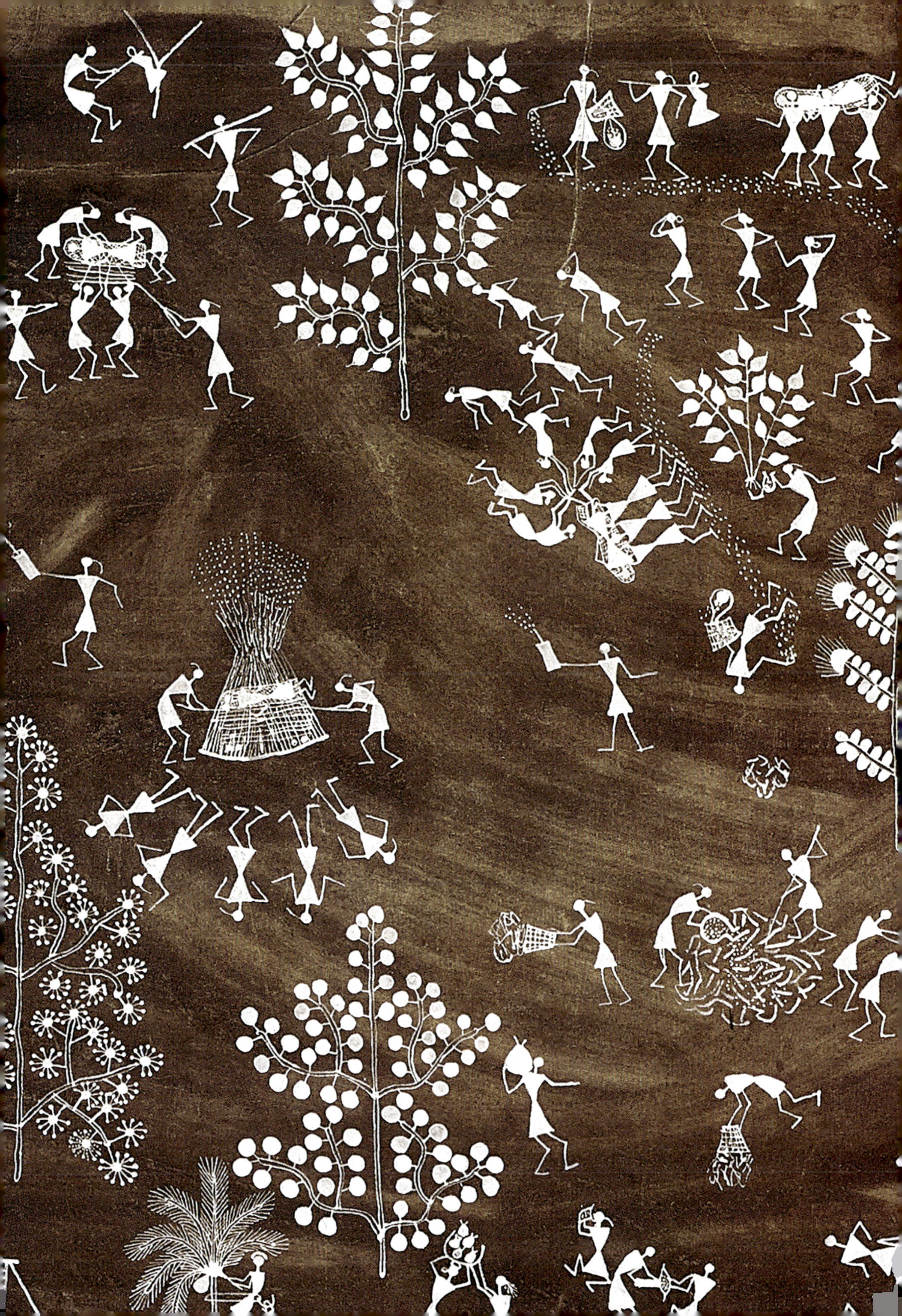

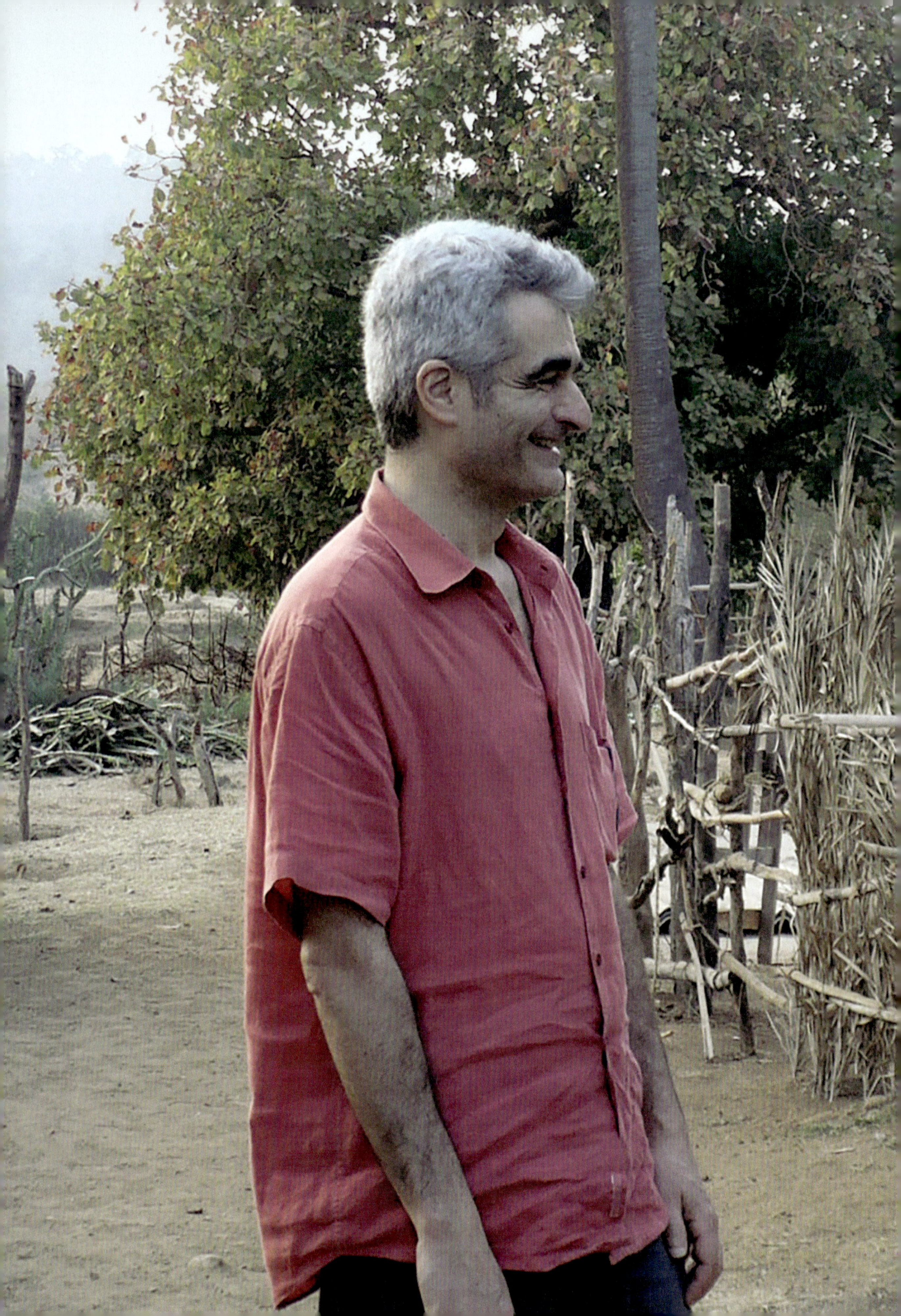

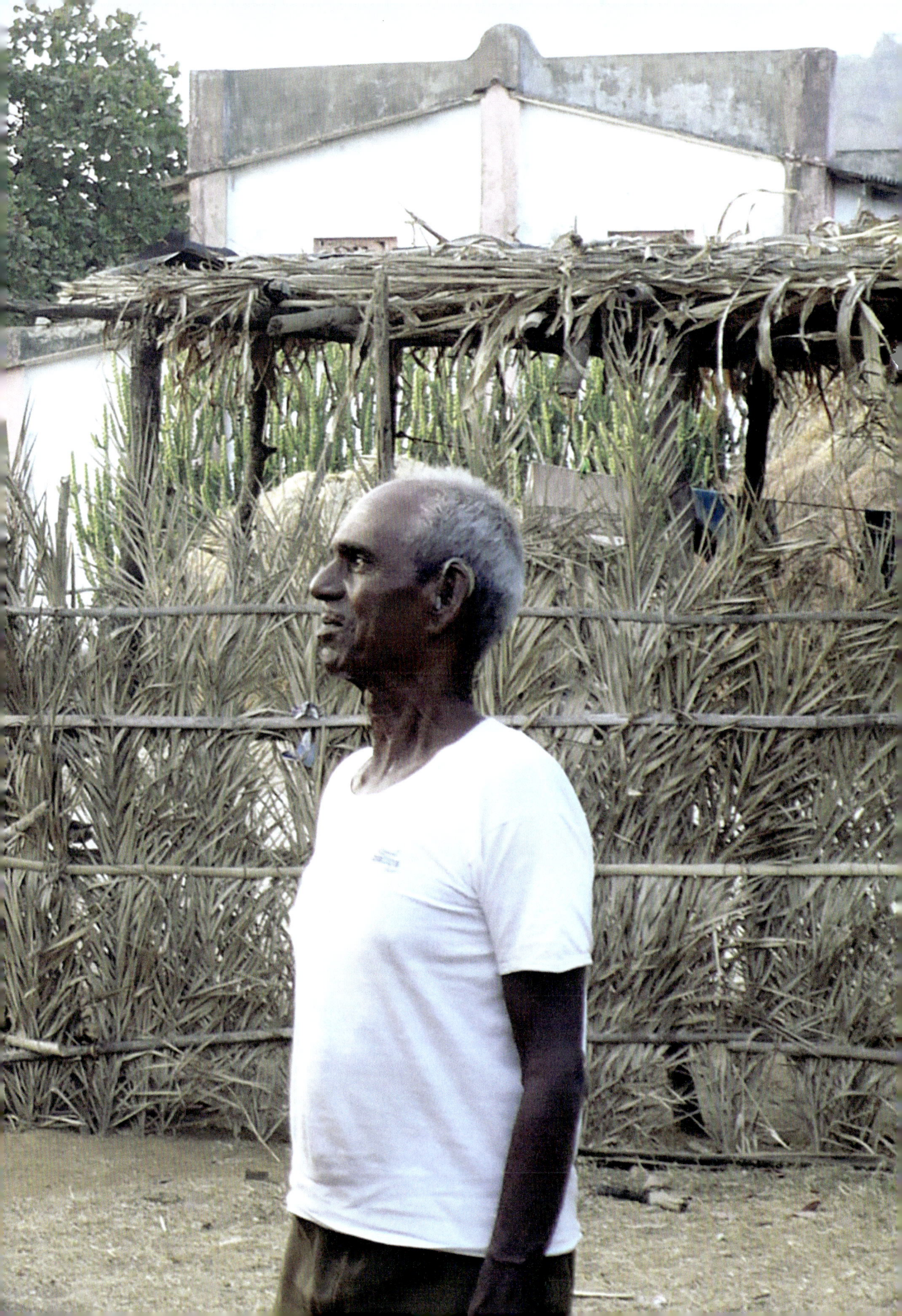

Here are two photos in which we are seen together. The first was taken by Lucile Allanche in 2009, the second by Kishore in 2017.

For me, the second (and last) photo is particularly moving. I had become aware, without any specific reason other than his advanced age and the decline of his vitality (Jivya Soma Mashe had recently begun to have difficulty moving around), that he would soon pass on and that this could well be the last time I would see him. Jivya Soma Mashe spoke to me in his dialect, which his grandsons Kishore, Vijay, and Pravin translated. Jivya talked about us, recalled his memories, and, above all, for the first time in front of me, he told his grandsons how much he valued the moments we had spent together.

How to find the right words to describe our relationship? I had seen his family grow up: his children, grandchildren, and great-grandchildren. In some way, I had begun to become part of his family and community.

I had lost more than a friend: he was a marvellous man and a silent mentor, and our shared silence had become the essence of all my past, present, and future aspirations.

Deux photos où l'on nous voit tous les deux ensemble. La première a été faite par Lucile Allanche en 2009. La seconde, et dernière photo, a été prise par Kishore en 2017.

Dernière photo particulièrement émouvante. Je sais alors, sans raison précise autre que l'âge avancé et la disparition progressive de ses forces vives (Jivya depuis peu peine à se déplacer), qu'il va bientôt partir, que c'est peut-être la dernière fois que je le vois. Jivya me parle dans son dialecte. Kishore, Vijay et Pravin, ses petits-fils, traduisent. Jivya parle de nous, évoque des souvenirs, et surtout, pour la première fois devant moi, dit à ses petits-fils tout le bien qu'il pense de nos nombreux moments passés ensemble.

Trouver les bons mots pour mieux faire comprendre notre relation. J'ai vu grandir la famille, enfants, petits-enfants et arrière-petits-enfants. D'une certaine manière, je commençais à faire partie de la famille, de la communauté.

J'ai perdu plus qu'un ami, un homme merveilleux, un mentor silencieux, ce silence partagé, essence même de toutes mes aspirations passées, présentes et futures.

Jivya Soma Mashe died in 2018 while I was organising the *Inde* exhibition at the Manoir de Martigny in Switzerland. The exhibition and its catalogue were dedicated to him.

Mashe's artistic and commercial success never changed his way of life or being. He always remained humble, and when he showed visitors the photo albums where he could be seen receiving honorary awards or exhibiting around the world, it was simply for the pleasure of sharing a few cherished moments with them. These were simple photo albums, kept as best as possible over time and from the wear and tear of the elements, simply to tell stories.

Curiously, I have always remembered the title of a comic strip I knew as a child, although I didn't read – *Les Belles histoires de l'Oncle Paul*. I no doubt had in me that desire to become a member of the tribe of storytellers. I write little, I speak less. I prefer images.

It is in practising the professions of graphic designer, art critic, exhibition curator, and gallerist that I tell stories, like the one that is the subject of this book.

Jivya est décédé en 2018, alors que j'organisais l'exposition *Inde* au Manoir de Martigny, en Suisse. Cette exposition et son catalogue lui furent dédicacés.

La réussite de Jivya n'a jamais modifié son mode de vie, sa façon d'être. Il est toujours resté humble et, lorsqu'il montre à ses visiteurs les albums photos dans lesquels on le voit recevoir des récompenses honorifiques ou exposer à travers le monde, c'est simplement pour le plaisir de partager avec eux quelques bons moments passés. Il s'agit de simples albums photos-souvenirs conservés tant bien que mal au fil du temps et des intempéries. Simplement pour raconter des histoires.

Curieusement, je me suis toujours rappelé le titre d'une bande dessinée de mon enfance, que pourtant je ne lisais pas, *Les Belles histoires de l'Oncle Paul*. J'avais sans doute en moi déjà cette envie de rejoindre la tribu des conteurs. J'écris peu, je parle peu. Je préfère les images.

C'est en pratiquant les métiers qui furent les miens, graphiste, critique d'art, commissaire d'exposition, galeriste, que je raconte des histoires, comme celle qui fait l'objet de ce livre.

Pages 246–247
Hervé Perdriolle and Jivya Soma Mashe,
Ganjad (Maharashtra, India), 2009.
Photo by Lucile Allanche.

Pages 250–251
Hervé Perdriolle and Jivya Soma Mashe,
Ganjad (Maharashtra, India), 2017.
Photo by Kishor Mashe.

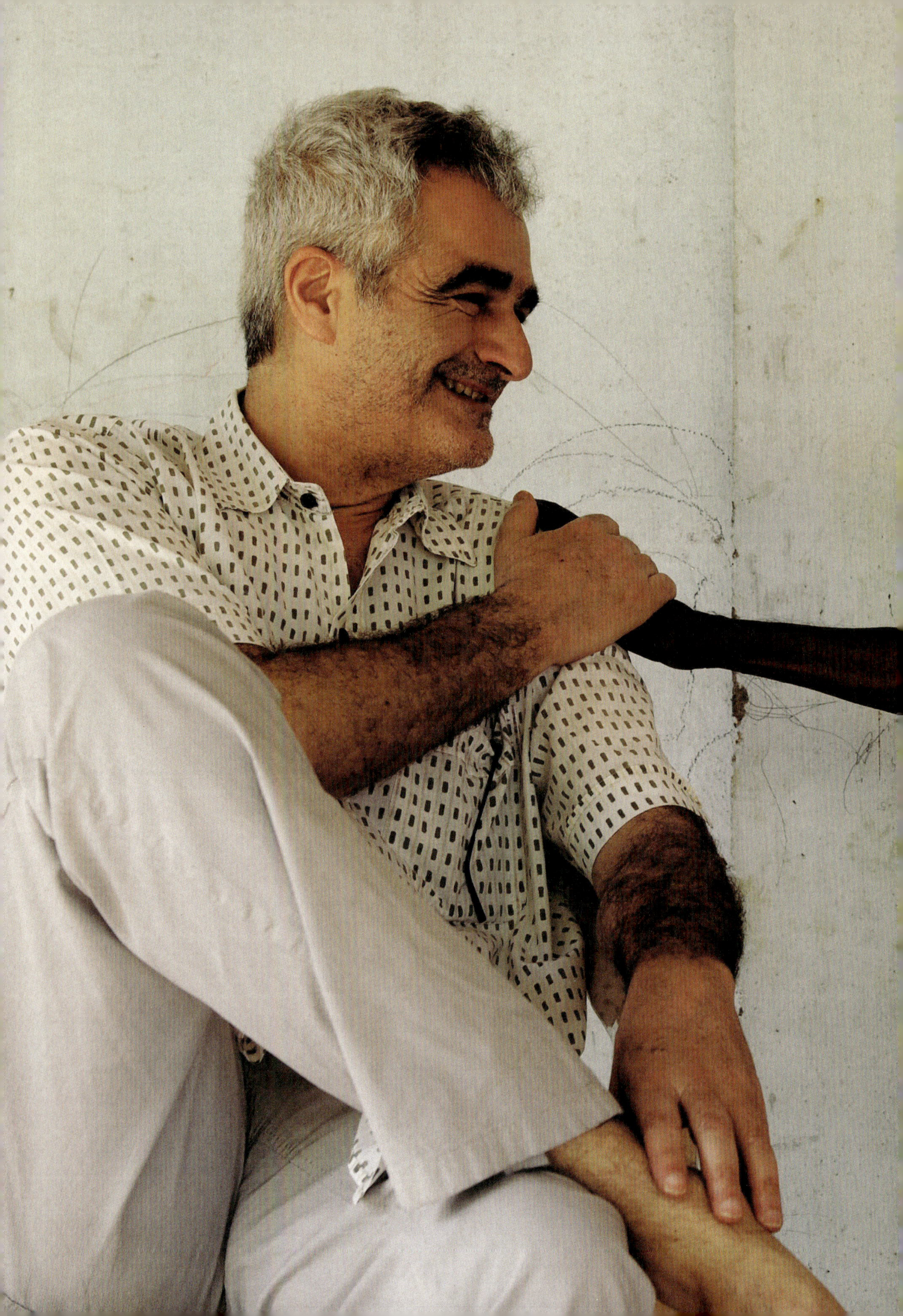

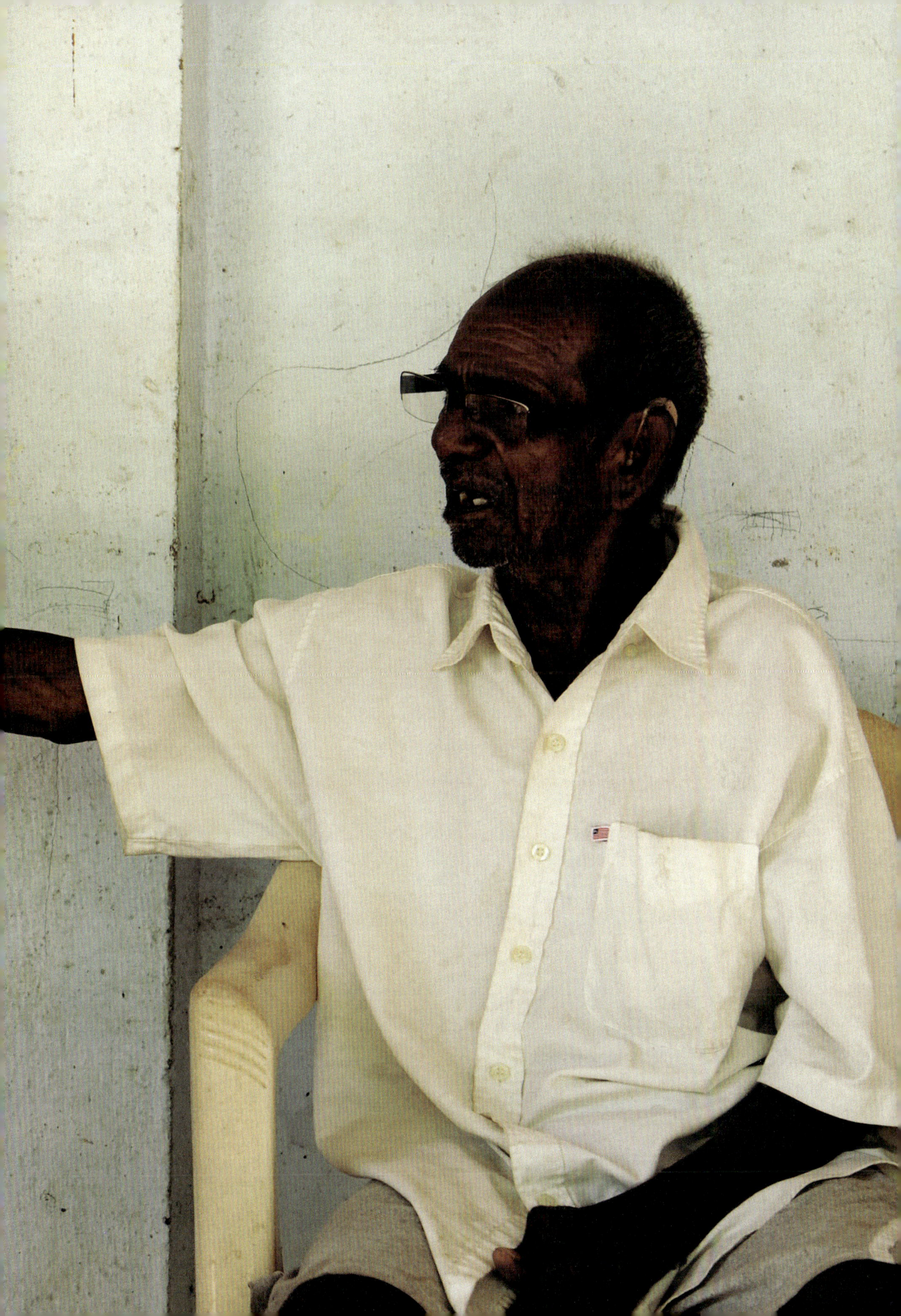

Remembering the 'Other Master', Jivya Soma Mashe

French art critic Hervé Perdriolle on the Warli art legend who died last week and the exhibition he is curating in tribute

Artist and Padma Shri awardee Jivya Soma Mashe, who put Warli art on the global map, died on 15 May, aged 84, at his village, Ganjad, in Maharasthra.

In an email interview, the French art critic Hervé Perdriolle, a friend of his, recounts his memories of meetings with Mashe. Perdriolle, who is also the founder of the Galerie Hervé Perdriolle, has over the last two decades tirelessly promoted the work of contemporary tribal and folk Indians artists, whom he labelled the "Other Masters of India". He spoke to *Lounge* while putting together an exhibition of Mashe's work at the Manoir de Martigny in Martigny, Switzerland, which opens today. Edited excerpts:

You have collected more than 400 works of Vernacular Contemporary Indian art, including the works of Mashe and Jangarh Singh Shyam. Could you explain the term?

Vernacular, In The Contemporary was the title of an exhibition at the Devi Art Foundation in 2010 and it is more appropriate and less restrictive than the word "tribal". It is often thought that contemporary art is an art form that is exclusively an extension of the Western historical avant-gardes. However, more and more cultural actors think that contemporary art should not be reduced to this single vision. Such was the case in India in the 1970s, when the government, under the influence of Pupul Jayakar, made the decision to present major figures from minority cultures with the same National Awards that were awarded to the artists in modern art. Thus, Indira Gandhi presented Jivya Soma Mashe's first National Award in 1976. Jivya Soma Mashe and Jangarh Singh Shyam are the masters of my collection.

Tell us about your first and last meeting with Mashe—how had his global fame impacted his outlook?

My first encounter with Jivya Soma Mashe was not easy. In the middle of the 1990s, there was no internet or mobile phone. It was impossible to inform him of my visit and it took me three trips to finally meet him. I guess my insistence must have pleased him. The last time we met was in March, and it was very moving. I noticed that his health was declining very quickly, and I knew that soon I wouldn't have the chance of seeing him again. As always, we sat side by side and

BERTRAND LANGLOIS/AFP

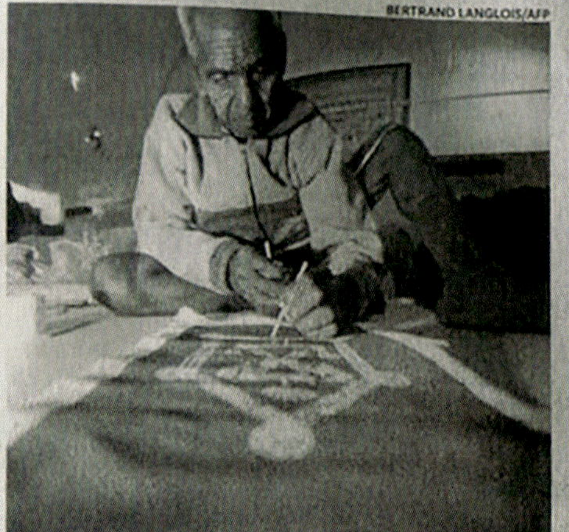

COURTES

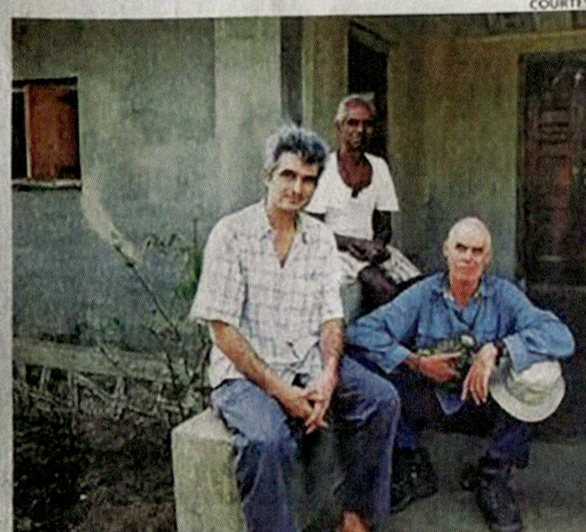

(left) Artist Jivya Soma Mashe; and Hervé Perdriolle, Jivya Soma Mashe and sculptor Sir Richard J. Long, Ganjad, 2003.

COURTESY HERVÉ PERDRIOLLE / FROM FONDATION CARTIER COLLECTION

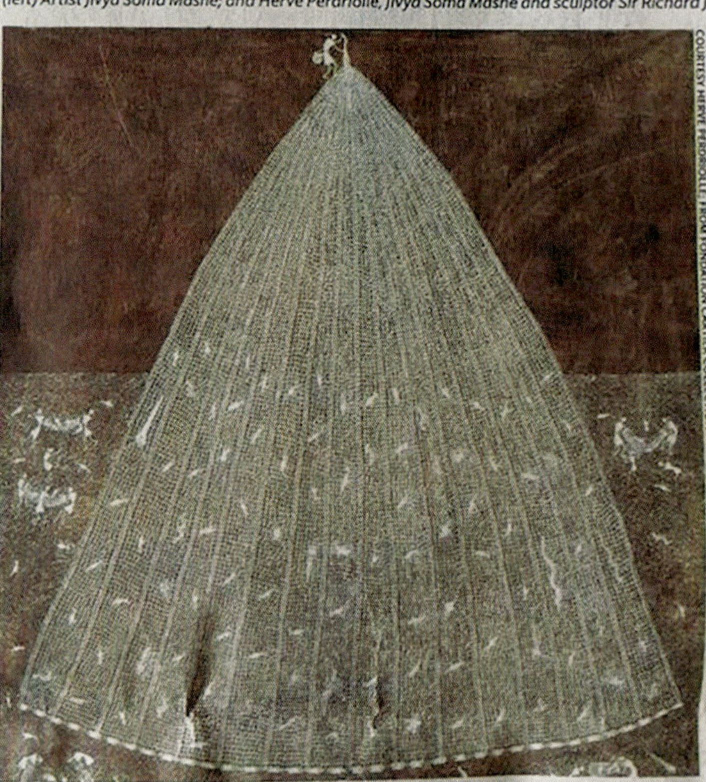

'Fishnet' (2009), acrylic and cow dung on canvas, by Jivya Soma Mashe.

I do not think that his international fame, despite the many travels and honours, had any influence on his work. But it did determine his way of life. After his first success, Jivya decided to stay in his native land, in front of the sacred mountain, and live with his family, as he always had. He liked to say he was a painter and a peasant, and, in fact, he ate only the rice he grew himself.

Warli art has several recurring

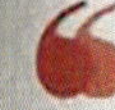

After his first success, Jivya decided to stay in his native land, in front of the sacred mountain, and live with his family

One of the most apprecia collectors is the fishing net. one does not necessarily se some see a representation c world, a sacred mountain. C surprised by the infinite r mesh of the net. Jivya repeat thousands of small circles v lassitude. This repetition, en of nuances, evokes pictoria frame of the ragas.

Do you feel Gond art ec attention Warli art rec

Mithila painting was th Indian folk art in the 1970s a the years 1990-2000, it was art. Since 2010, the art of the present. These are cycles m The need to renew our v knowing that we always revi of our cultures.

What are your thou motifs being used ir other places as decora

In Western contempora mon practice. Many muse products derived from the ists. What is essential is that is not distorted or misunder *important point is respect property. It is necessary th* their rights-holders give the and collect royalties.

What are your curatori exhibition at the Manoi

This exhibition continu show contemporary art reg gins, rural and urban. emblematic figures of Jiv and Jangarh Singh Shyam work of Shine Shivan and T graduates of Indian art scho tion includes some 100 wo collectors.

The exhibition is on till 5 Au

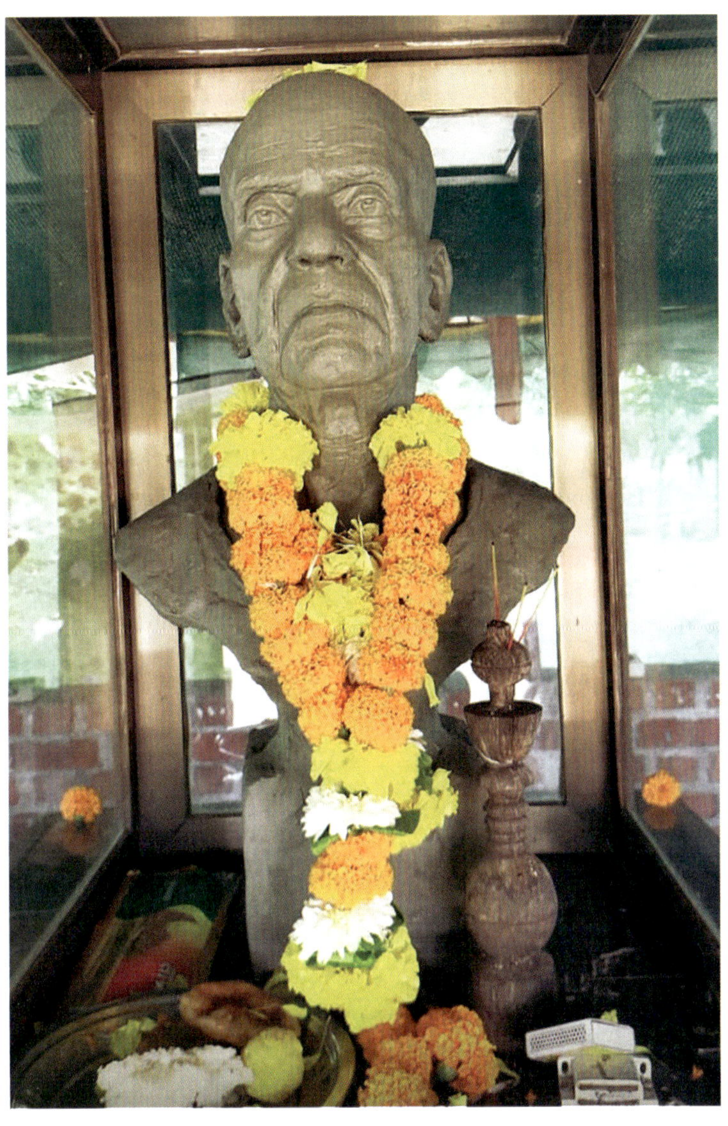

Radhika Lyengar's interview with Hervé Perdriolle following the death of Jivya Soma Mashe, published in *Mint Lounge India*, 31 May 2018.

Devotional space dedicated to Jivya Soma Mashe installed next to the home of Jivya and Sadashiv Mashe, 2021. Photo by Kishore Mashe.

ACKNOWLEDGEMENTS
REMERCIEMENTS

I have fond memories of Jivya Soma Mashe and all the marvellous moments we spent together, as well as of his wife, Pavani, their sons, Sadashiv and Balu, and their grandchildren, Kishore, Vijay, and Pravin. My thoughts also go to their friends Shantaram Gorkhana and Balu Dhumada, both artists and neighbours, who rounded out my initiation into Warli art. And not forgetting Mayur and Tushar Vayeda, with whom I was fortunate enough to continue my adventures in the Warli region.

I wish to thank especially the Fondation Cartier pour l'art contemporain, Pierre-Alexis and Sophie Dumas, Lina and David Lebard, Maximiliano Modesti, Bérengère Primat, and Garance Primat, without whose support this book would never have seen the light of day.

My gratitude goes to Yashodhara Dalmia, who spontaneously allowed me to include an excerpt from his wonderful book *The Painted World of the Warlis*.

My appreciation is also due to all the collectors who placed their trust in me during the times when the art of the Warli tribe and work of Jivya Soma Mashe were still little known.

I am indebted to Shireen Gandhy and the Chemould Gallery for allowing me access to their records; to the Alliances Françaises of Pondicherry and Bangalore, where I first presented my research on contemporary Indian tribal art; to Marie-Claude Beaud and the Musée des Arts Décoratifs in Paris for hosting my first exhibition in France; to Jean-Hubert Martin; the Museum Kunstpalast; the Padiglione d'Arte Contemporanea; to Martine Lusardy and the Halle Saint Pierre; to the Manoir de Martigny; to Hervé Chandès and the Fondation Cartier for their constant support; and to Artcurial in Paris and Brussels.

Lastly, I am grateful to Robin and Antoine Perdriolle, Lucile Allanche, Richard Long, Denise Hooker, Marc Pottier, Abhay Maskara, Shine Shivan, and T. Venkanna for having accompanied me on my Indian adventures.

Mes pensées restent intimement liées à Jivya Soma Mashe et à tous ces moments merveilleux passés ensemble, à sa femme, Pavani, leurs fils Sadashiv et Balu, leurs petits-fils, Kishore, Vijay et Pravin. À leurs amis, artistes et voisins, Shantaram Gorkhana, Balu Dhumada, qui ont complété mon initiation à l'art warli. À Mayur et Tushar Vayeda, avec lesquels j'ai la chance et le bonheur de continuer mes aventures sur les terres warli.

Je tiens à remercier tout spécialement la Fondation Cartier pour l'art contemporain, Pierre-Alexis et Sophie Dumas, Lina et David Lebard, Maximiliano Modesti, Bérengère Primat et Garance Primat, sans le soutien desquels ce livre n'aurait pu voir le jour.

J'exprime toute ma gratitude à Yashodhara Dalmia, qui a spontanément accepté que je reprenne dans ce livre un extrait de son si précieux livre *The Painted World of the Warlis*.

Je remercie chaleureusement tous les collectionneurs qui m'ont apporté leur confiance en des temps où l'art de la tribu warli et l'œuvre de Jivya Soma Mashe étaient méconnus. Mes remerciements vont également à Shireen Gandhy et à la galerie Chemould pour l'accès à leurs archives.

Aux Alliances Françaises de Pondichéry et de Bangalore, où j'ai montré pour la première fois mes recherches sur l'art tribal contemporain indien. À Marie-Claude Beaud et au musée des Arts décoratifs de Paris pour avoir accueilli ma première exposition en France. À Jean-Hubert Martin, au Museum Kunstpalast et au Padiglione d'Arte Contemporanea, à Martine Lussardy et à la Halle Saint-Pierre, au Manoir de Martigny, à Hervé Chandès et à la Fondation Cartier pour leur soutien constant, à Artcurial Paris et Bruxelles.

Et enfin, à Robin et Antoine Perdriolle, Lucile Allanche, Richard Long, Denise Hooker, Marc Pottier, Abhay Maskara, Shine Shivan et T. Venkanna pour m'avoir accompagné dans mes aventures indiennes.

5 CONTINENTS EDITIONS

Editor-in-Chief | Rédacteur en chef
Aldo Carioli

Design and Layout | Projet graphique et mise en page
Fayçal Zaouali

Production department | Direction de production
Oliver Barstow

Editor | Rédactrice
Lucia Moretti

Translations | Traductions
Timothy Stroud, Elisabeth Raffy

Editing | Sécretariat de rédaction
Olivier Godefroy, Charles Gute

Pre-press | Photogravure
Maurizio Brivio, Milan, Italy

Published and distributed in India by Roli Books Pvt. Ltd.

Ce livre a bénéficié du soutien de
This book has been published with the support of

Fondation Cartier
pour l'art contemporain

5 Continents Editions
Piazza Caiazzo, 1
20124 Milan, Italy
www.fivecontinentseditions.com

ISBN 979-12-5460-088-7

Printed on Sappi Magno Volume 150 gr paper and bound in Italy in June 2025 by Tecnostampa – Pigini Group Printing Division Loreto – Trevi, Italy for 5 Continents Editions, Milan
Achevé d'imprimer en Italie en juin 2025 sur papier Sappi Magno Volume 150 gr sur les presses de Tecnostampa – Pigini Group Printing Division Loreto – Trevi, Italie pour le compte de 5 Continents Editions, Milan

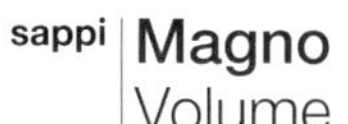

Distributed by ACC Art Books throughout the world, excluding Italy. Distributed in Italy and Switzerland by Messaggerie Libri S.p.A.
Distribution en France et pays francophones BELLES LETTRES / Diffusion L'entreLivres

Cover / Couverture
Jivya Soma Mashe, *Fishnet*, 2009, acrylic and cow dung on canvas, 167 × 148 cm; 65.74 × 58.26 in.
Fondation Cartier pour l'art contemporain Collection.
Photo by André Morin.
Back cover / Quatrième de couverture
Jivya Soma Mashe, *How People Got Their Name*, 1999, acrylic and cow dung on canvas, 138 × 230 cm; 54.33 × 90.55 in. (*detail*)
Fondation Cartier pour l'art contemporain Collection.
Photo by André Morin.